Making Makers

Making Makers

The Past, the Present, and the Study of War

MICHAEL P. M. FINCH

Great Clarendon Street, Oxford, OX2 6DP,
United Kingdom

Oxford University Press is a department of the University of Oxford.
It furthers the University's objective of excellence in research, scholarship,
and education by publishing worldwide. Oxford is a registered trade mark of
Oxford University Press in the UK and in certain other countries

© Michael P. M. Finch 2024

The moral rights of the author have been asserted

All rights reserved. No part of this publication may be reproduced, stored in
a retrieval system, or transmitted, in any form or by any means, without the
prior permission in writing of Oxford University Press, or as expressly permitted
by law, by licence or under terms agreed with the appropriate reprographics
rights organization. Enquiries concerning reproduction outside the scope of the
above should be sent to the Rights Department, Oxford University Press, at the
address above

You must not circulate this work in any other form
and you must impose this same condition on any acquirer

Published in the United States of America by Oxford University Press
198 Madison Avenue, New York, NY 10016, United States of America

British Library Cataloguing in Publication Data
Data available

Library of Congress Control Number: 2023947791

ISBN 9780192867124

DOI: 10.1093/9780191959257.001.0001

Printed and bound in the UK by
Clays Ltd, Elcograf S.p.A.

Links to third party websites are provided by Oxford in good faith and
for information only. Oxford disclaims any responsibility for the materials
contained in any third party website referenced in this work.

Contents

Acknowledgements	vii
List of Figures	ix
Introduction: The Making and Remaking of *Makers*	1
1. War Now Thrusts Itself upon Us All: War, History, and the Context of *Makers*	13
A New Military History for the Twentieth Century	15
The Pioneer	19
'With Special Reference to the Conditions of Modern War'	22
Naval History in the Service of the Nation	27
Frustrations of the First World War	30
Post-War Opportunities	36
Conclusion	43
2. Making *Makers*: Edward Mead Earle, the Institute for Advanced Study, and the Second World War	46
An Oddity in the School of Economics	51
Earle against the Torrent	57
The Seminar and the Book	62
Making *Makers*	71
Succeeding, Revising, Failing	83
Conclusion	95
3. Revisiting *Makers*: Theodore Ropp and the Afterlife of the Book	99
Cold Warriors and Scholars	100
Theodore Ropp: Making a Military Historian	106
Military History and *Makers*	113
Operation Military History Singapore	115
After Singapore	127
Conclusion	130
4. Remaking *Makers*: Peter Paret and the Genesis of a New Edition	134
Peter Paret and the Limits of Military History	135
The Origins of a New *Makers*	142
Sticking Points	146
Scoping the Project	150
Remaking *Makers*	156
Gordon Craig and the Urgency of the Present	162
Final Hurdles	168
Conclusion	173

vi CONTENTS

5. Scholarship from the Arsenal of Democracy: The Reception
of Paret's *Makers* and the Legacy of the Book — 176
The Reception of Paret's *Makers* — 177
Makers in the Shadow of Its Predecessor — 183
Making Modern Strategy? — 186
Curating the Canon — 194
Makers and the Ancients — 204
Conclusion — 209

Conclusion: Historians of War and the Lineage of *Makers* — 213

Appendix: Contributors and Collaborators in the *Makers Project*, 1943–86 — 221

Bibliography — 237
Index — 251

Acknowledgements

Books have their own peculiar evolutions. This one is no exception. Its origins lie in my time at Oxford University, both as a student and as postdoctoral researcher. For those reasons I should start by thanking the fellows and staff at Pembroke College, Oxford, the Changing Character of War Centre, and particularly Adrian Gregory and Rob Johnson, for providing an ideal academic environment in which to begin a process of thinking about war, books, and the people who write them. That process continued at King's College London and the Joint Services Command and Staff College at the Defence Academy of the United Kingdom. Working alongside my colleagues in the Defence Studies Department, as well as our counterparts in uniform, taught me a great deal about war, conflict, and international affairs, far beyond the confines of historical study. I remain grateful to them for the collegiality and the camaraderie. I am especially grateful to Greg Kennedy for the interest he showed in my early research, and for bringing Theodore Ropp and his *Makers Revisited* to my attention. Had he not done so, I doubt this book would exist.

This project became a book in Australia. Like the first book that it chronicles, it was written during a period of global crisis, although one quite distinct from the Second World War. No matter their particular character, crises reveal a lot about the difference that the support of individuals and institutions can make in matters both professional and personal. To that end I would like to thank Jean Bou, John Blaxland, Garth Pratten, Greg Raymond, and especially Andrew Stewart. Since 2018 I have been fortunate to work at the Australian War College, and have benefited greatly from daily interactions with Australian Defence Force staff and course members, as well as the international course members and overseas directing staff who attend the college every year. In 2022 I joined Deakin University, and have been fortunate thereafter to work alongside an engaged, enthusiastic, and supportive academic team as part of the Centre for Future Defence and National Security. I would like to thank all my Deakin colleagues, and in particular Michael Hatherall, Liam Kane, and Bel Corujo.

Garnering materials for this project proved physically challenging at certain points, so I am grateful to Jenny Fichmann and Joshua Tapper for providing crucial research assistance at the Hoover Institution and Stanford University Library respectively. I would like to thank the editors and staff of *The Journal of Military History* for permission to use parts of two articles published in their pages in 2016 and 2018, and particularly the late Bruce Vandervort, who was enthusiastic about those pieces. I would like to thank the trustees of the Liddell Hart Centre for

viii ACKNOWLEDGEMENTS

Military Archives at King's College London for permission to cite material from the Liddell Hart Papers. I would also like to thank the Shelby White and Leon Levy Archives Center at the Institute for Advanced Study, Princeton, for permission to use their archive materials, and give particular thanks to the archivists, who were extremely helpful during my initial research on Edward Mead Earle.

Numerous friends and colleagues have given their time and attention to help me with this project over the years. James Kitchen, Jeff Michaels, Ryan Miller, and Dan Marston read large parts of the manuscript, and I am indebted to them for the insightful comments and improvements they suggested. Sir Hew Strachan supported this project from its inception, read drafts, offered his thoughts, and gave me timely advice on numerous occasions. Cian O'Driscoll made time to read and discuss my work during a crucial period towards the completion of the book. Aimée Fox's insights and assistance were vital in helping me turn plans into reality. David Morgan-Owen deserves particular praise for his willingness not only to read my work, but to discuss and debate ideas on this book and much else besides over a number of years. Both he and Aimée have offered support far beyond professional matters, for which I will be grateful for a long time to come. I would like to thank my editors at Oxford University Press, particularly Cathryn Steele and Stephanie Ireland, for taking on what I am sure seemed—and perhaps still seems—a rather unusual proposition.

My greatest debt is to Soomin, and to our children, Yura and Yoonjae. Your love and support carried me through. Thank you.

List of Figures

2.1	Princeton University Press advertisement for *Makers of Modern Strategy*.	47
2.2	Abraham Flexner, *c*.1943.	51
2.3	Edward Mead Earle being presented with the Presidential Medal for Merit by US Army Air Force General Carl A. Spaatz, 1946.	59
2.4	Members of Earle's seminar, 1939–44.	68
2.5	Felix Gilbert in 1981.	70
2.6	Tentative outline of *Foundations of Modern Military Thought*.	73
2.7	Table of contents for *The Development of Modern Military Thought*, 7 April 1943.	74
2.8	Table of contents for *The Development of Modern Military Thought*.	75
2.9	Earle's ranking of reviews of *Makers of Modern Strategy* in 'English' journals.	86
3.1	Theodore Ropp teaching *c*.1950.	110
3.2	Theodore Ropp, August 1979.	116
3.3	New chapters for *Makers of Modern Strategy Revisited* as of September 1979.	120
3.4	Revised schedule for the National University of Singapore seminars, 1980.	120
3.5	New schedule for the National University of Singapore seminars, 1980.	121
4.1	Peter Paret in his office at Stanford University, 1986.	140
4.2	Paret and Craig's assessment of Earle's *Makers of Modern Strategy*.	152
4.3	Paret's proposed table of contents, June 1982.	153
4.4	Paret's amended table of contents, July 1982.	155
4.5	Gordon Craig at Stanford University.	164
4.6	Jacket design for Paret's *Makers of Modern Strategy*.	173

There are in history no beginnings and no endings. History books begin and end, but the events they describe do not.

—R. G. Collingwood, *An Autobiography*

Introduction: The Making and Remaking of *Makers*

'The historian belongs not to the past but to the present.'

—E. H. Carr[1]

This is a book about books and the people who made them. To be more precise, it is about one particular book concerned with the study of war. That book, *Makers of Modern Strategy*—or *Makers* for short—has exercised such a hold over the imagination of scholars that they sought to revise and remake it on a number of occasions across the decades since it first appeared in print during the Second World War. Not all such attempts were successful: it took more than forty years before a new volume was published in final years of the Cold War. Yet few books have held such allure for so many invested in the study of war, and fewer still have experienced such a peculiar afterlife, stretching far beyond their original conception.

When he turned his attention to the new *Makers* project in the early 1980s Herbert S. Bailey, the director of the Princeton University Press, was firm in his conviction that the original was a 'modern classic'.[2] Indeed, such a consensus began to form almost as soon as *Makers* was published. In the same month that it was released, the political commentator Walter Lippmann confidently asserted that it was a 'monumental work' which would 'exert its influence, long after this war ends, upon those who really take seriously the task of making a long peace. For the book will establish the study of military history and the development of military doctrine as an indispensable subject in higher education and in the intellectual life of the nation.'[3]

As Lippmann predicted, *Makers* continued to influence minds after the Second World War had concluded, but its reach was not confined to American shores. A particularly striking example of this can be found in the person of Sir Michael Howard. In 1953 Howard was presented with an opportunity to revitalize the study of war at King's College London. Appointed Lecturer in Military Studies,

---

[1] E. H. Carr, *What Is History?*, 2nd edition (London: Penguin, 1987), p. 25.

[2] Princeton University Press Archives (hereafter PUP), Seeley G. Mudd Manuscript Library, Princeton University, Princeton, NJ (hereafter MLP), Box 350, Folder 2 (CO728). Bailey to Paret, 11 September 1984.

[3] W. Lippmann, 'The Serious Study of War', *The Washington Post*, 30 October 1943.

Howard brought with him the credentials of a decorated army veteran, and he had also recently co-authored a history of his old regiment.[4] Despite this, he did not consider such achievements sufficient to prepare him for the task at hand. The regimental history, in particular, he viewed 'as a graceful farewell to arms rather than the beginning of a new relationship with them'.[5] Granted a year-long sabbatical by the college, Howard set about deepening his knowledge of the conduct of war and its past. Following advice from the recently retired Chichele Professor of the History of War at the University of Oxford, Cyril Falls, he turned to *Makers*. The result was a revelation. 'By following up its references,' he observed:

> I started to build up a corpus of knowledge. Gradually it became clear what a huge and fertile field I had been set to cultivate and how very little had as yet been tilled—at any rate by British historians. The history of war, I came to realize, was more than the operational history of armed forces. It was the study of entire societies. Only by studying their cultures could one come to understand what it was that they fought about and why they fought in the way that they did. Further, the fact that they did so fight had a reciprocal impact on their social structure. I had to learn not only to think about war in a different way, but also to think about history itself in a different way.[6]

Howard's encounter with *Makers* constituted a turning point in his intellectual development. Having previously thought of military history as a fusty pursuit of limited interest to serious scholars, he now embraced a broad form of inquiry that would be hailed as pioneering the 'war and society' approach in post-Second World War scholarship. Moreover, the inclusive study of war that *Makers* inspired played a role in the foundation of both of the Department of War Studies in 1961 and the academic discipline of the same name.[7]

It was not just those in academe who came to the book at significant points in their careers. Those in uniform did so too. Lieutenant-General Paul Van Riper, for example, reflecting on the importance of history to professional military education, noted having read *Makers* in the late 1970s as part of an ongoing process of historical self-education, following completion of the Command and Staff Course at a US Naval War College reoriented towards an historical curriculum in the aftermath of the Vietnam War. In contrast to earlier reading which often focused on combat motivation and the human experience of war, Van Riper

---

[4] M. Howard and J. Sparrow, *The Coldstream Guards, 1920–1946* (London: Oxford University Press, 1951).

[5] M. Howard, *Captain Professor* (London: Continuum, 2006), p. 141.

[6] Ibid., pp. 144–5. See also M. Howard, *A Professional Autobiography* (unpublished typescript, Eastbury, Berkshire, 2 October 1991).

[7] For the limitations of Howard's conception of war studies as an academic discipline see D. Morgan-Owen and M. Finch, 'The Unrepentant Historian: Sir Michael Howard and the Birth of War Studies', *The British Journal of Military History*, Vol. 8, No. 2 (September 2022), pp. 55–76.

THE MAKING AND REMAKING OF *MAKERS*   3

'probed' *Makers* 'to expand my understanding of strategic thought'.[8] In 1991 Alan Gropman, a retired USAF colonel turned professor, described the book as 'an old friend, entirely read several times, reread in part a dozen times, and mined for highlighted ideas before lectures or seminars 100 times'. He could not think of 'a more used, useful or influential book on the arts of war'.[9]

Not only did *Makers* appeal across the academic and military worlds, the book—along with its editor, Edward Mead Earle—has been credited for its role in establishing new disciplines. According to David Ekbladh, by blazing a trail from the mid-1930s, during which he anticipated concerns more widely held in the post-war era, Earle distinguished himself as a forgotten founder of security studies, with *Makers* the most enduring expression of his agenda.[10] In a similar vein, Andrew J. Bacevich has written that that the origins of strategic studies 'can be traced with some precision to a seminar organized in 1941 by the scholar Edward Mead Earle at the Institute for Advanced Study in Princeton' and that 'the chief product of Professor Earle's initiative was a collection of remarkable essays published two years later under the title *Makers of Modern Strategy*'.[11] Likewise, Eliot Cohen has written that the book 'marks the birth of modern strategic studies' since 'when taken together the essays lead the reader to conceive of a discipline of strategy, distinct from history and political science, although deeply indebted to them'.[12] Sir Hew Strachan contends that it was 'the standard text on the evolution of strategic thought well into the 1970s' and was 'supplanted only' in 1986 when Peter Paret published a new and updated version'.[13]

For scholars of strategic studies, as well as historians whose research encompasses strategic affairs, much of the significance of Earle's book lies in its editor's contribution to the articulation of grand strategy. Indeed, Earle's stock as a key figure in broadening the scope of strategy has risen in step with the resurgence of interest in the concept and history of grand strategy in the first decades of the twenty-first century.[14] Williamson Murray, for example, contends that

---

[8] P. K. Van Riper, 'The Relevance of History to the Military Profession: An American Marine's View', in W. Murray and R. H. Sinnreich (eds.), *The Past as Prologue: The Importance of History to the Military Profession* (Cambridge: Cambridge University Press, 2006), pp. 40–7.

[9] A. Gropman, 'Landmarks in Defense Literature', *Defense Analysis*, Vol. 7, No. 1 (1991), p. 111.

[10] D. Ekbladh, 'Present at the Creation: Edward Mead Earle and the Depression-Era Origins of Security Studies', *International Security*, Vol. 36, No. 3 (Winter 2011/12), pp. 107–41. See also D. Ekbladh 'The Interwar Foundations of Security Studies: Edward Mead Earle, the Carnegie Corporation and the Depression-Era Origins of a Field', *Global Society*, Vol. 28, No. 1 (2014), pp. 40–53.

[11] A. J. Bacevich, 'Strategic Studies: In from the Cold', *SAIS Review*, Vol. 13, No. 2 (Summer–Fall 1993), p. 11.

[12] E. Cohen, review of *Makers of Modern Strategy* in *Foreign Affairs*, Vol. 76, No. 5 (September–October 1997), p. 220.

[13] H. Strachan, 'The Future of Strategic Studies: Lessons from the Last "Golden Age"', in R. Glenn (ed.), *New Directions in Strategic Thinking 2.0* (Canberra: ANU Press, 2018), p. 150.

[14] On this issue, see D. Morgan-Owen, 'History and the Perils of Grand Strategy', *The Journal of Modern History*, Vol. 92, No. 2 (June 2020), pp. 351–61, and H. Brands, 'The Promise and Pitfalls of Grand Strategy', US Army War College, Strategic Studies Institute Monograph (August 2012), pp. 1–10.

'the subject of grand strategy as a topic for rigorous historical examination first appears in serious form in Edward Mead Earle's classic *Makers of Modern Strategy*.[15] Hal Brands, meanwhile, identifies Earle alongside Liddell Hart as a significant actor responsible not only for broadening the definition of strategy to reach its grand state, but also for bringing that concept to a greater audience during the 1940s and 50s.[16] Earle was far from the first amongst scholars, soldiers, and statesmen to make reference to 'grand strategy'.[17] It is certainly the case, however, that by insisting on the need for strategy to incorporate all the elements of national power, by emphasizing its critical position as a tool of statecraft, and in using *Makers* as a vehicle to articulate this concept for mass consumption, he made great strides towards its popularization.

Yet *Makers* was significant not only for the conceptual framework that it purported to advance. It was also noteworthy for its role in bringing a certain set of 'makers' of strategy into contemporary focus. As Strachan has noted, as 'the founding text of strategic studies' *Makers* can be ascribed a leading role in devising the canon of strategic thought in the English-speaking world, since 'Earle's contributors established who was in the canon and who, by implication, was out of the canon'.[18] It was this canon, more than the concept of strategy, that provided the allure for Earle's successor as chief editor of the next *Makers*, Peter Paret. For Paret, who was not a scholar of strategic studies, the canon offered a lens for examination of the history of military thought and of war itself.

Paret's *Makers*, like its predecessor, enjoyed scholarly and commercial success. Herbert Bailey's confidence that 'the new volume will be, indeed, another "modern classic"' was largely borne out by the reception it received from those who held the original in some affection but recognized the necessity for updated scholarship after forty years.[19] As Paret himself put it, the new book was needed 'to return <u>Makers of Modern Strategy</u> to its original vitality'.[20] Reviewers tended to agree. Thus Brian Holden Reid wrote that 'Professor Paret's volume has equalled—if not surpassed—the standards set by the first edition', comparing the experience of reading it to a walk in the Scottish Highlands, during which 'we recognize old and familiar features at once, but each time we return there is something fresh to admire'.[21] Dennis Showalter thought it 'a distinguished

---

[15] W. Murray, 'Thoughts on Grand Strategy', in W. Murray, R. H. Sinnreich, and J. Lacey (eds.), *The Shaping of Grand Strategy* (Cambridge: Cambridge University Press, 2011), p. 7.

[16] H. Brands, *What Good Is Grand Strategy? Power and Purpose in American Statecraft from Harry S. Truman to George W. Bush* (Ithaca, NY: Cornell University Press, 2014), pp. 2–3.

[17] For an account of the emergence of grand strategy in the modern period see L. Milevski, *The Evolution of Modern Grand Strategic Thought* (Oxford: Oxford University Press, 2016).

[18] H. Strachan, 'How Is War Directed? The Problem of Strategy', Humanitas lecture for CRASSH, University of Cambridge, delivered 3 February 2011. A recording of the lecture can be found here: https://www.youtube.com/watch?v=FHWyffZn5-c.

[19] MLP, PUP, Box 350, Folder 2 (CO728). Bailey to Paret, 11 September 1984.

[20] MLP, PUP, Box 344, Folder 3 (CO728). Paret to Bailey, 11 May 1982.

[21] B. Holden Reid, review of *Makers of Modern Strategy* in *History*, Vol. 73, No. 237 (February 1988), p. 90.

manifestation of both the revival of academic interest in military history and the renaissance of concern for the historic element of strategic thought'.[22] Strachan, meanwhile, judged that 'Makers of Modern Strategy from Machiavelli to the Nuclear Age is a book which no student of the subject will be able to ignore'.[23] Such sentiments were echoed by others, who contended that the book 'will become the standard work' and that it 'deserves and will doubtless find a large audience'.[24] Paret's volume remains in print today.

The significance of Makers crossed disciplinary boundaries, from history to security studies and strategic studies. The longevity of the original volume, and the appearance of Paret's successor, ensured that the work transcended the context of its wartime creation. Makers meant—and continues to mean—a great deal to a great many scholars of war. And yet it is clear that, for those interested in it, the resonances of the book have never wholly overlapped. Different constituencies have taken different things from it. In this sense, the success of the work in bringing together a corpus of strategic thought belies deeper fissures.

Ostensibly, the essence of the work is clear. The first book was an edited collection of essays, predominantly organized around prominent theoretical approaches to, and the practical conduct of, armed conflict, spanning the early modern era through to the mid-twentieth century, incorporating scholarship on the war then in progress and far from resolved at the point of publication in 1943. The second volume, published in 1986, though retaining much of the organization of the original as its guide, constituted an expanded offering. Most of the chapters were new, even where the titles remain the same, and only a few of the original chapters were carried over unchanged. The volume introduced new reflections encompassing transformations in the character of war since 1945, placed a heavier emphasis on strategist practitioners where the original erred towards theorists, and moved further towards consideration of national approaches to strategy over individual ones.

When subjected to closer scrutiny, however, it is less easy to discern just what kind of books Earle's Makers and its successor really are. As Paret once observed of Earle's volume, Makers 'was never intended to be a textbook, and was not written as a textbook. It welcomed originality, and yet it has been assigned as a basic text in many classes over the decades'.[25] Similarly, Showalter observed of Paret's book that whilst it was 'a superb guide to where we have been and what we have

---

[22] D. Showalter, review of Makers of Modern Strategy in Military Affairs, Vol. 51, No. 2 (April 1987), p. 100.

[23] H. Strachan, review of Makers of Modern Strategy in The English Historical Review, Vol. 103, No. 406 (January 1988), p. 158.

[24] G. Wiseman, review of Makers of Modern Strategy in International Affairs, Vol. 63, No. 3 (Summer 1987), p. 502. W. J. Fuller, review of Makers of Modern Strategy in The Journal of Modern History, Vol. 61, No. 1 (March 1989), p. 135.

[25] MLP, PUP, Box 344, Folder 3 (CO728). Bailey to Paret, 24 May 1983. Guidance to authors appended to letter.

6 MAKING MAKERS

done. It is not a handbook on waging, winning, or preventing wars.'[26] The book has a legacy in military history, attested to by the transformative experience in Howard's thinking and reflected in the experience of many others, Paret included. Yet despite Lippmann's claim that the book would establish military history in the mainstream of higher education, the book's first editor never intended that it should be a vehicle to promote military history. Nor, by the time he came to it, did Paret conceive of his *Makers* in such terms. That volume, he wrote, tried to 'suggest the usefulness of integrating the history of military thought and policy with general history'.[27] Neither man approached their project with the discipline of strategic studies in mind. Earle, because that discipline had yet to emerge, and Paret because it was not of interest to him.

The legend that emerged around the first *Makers* simplified rather than clarified its origins, and thus the purpose of the book. In the years after Earle's book was published the account of its genesis coalesced and reduced around the notion that it was the product of a seminar on American foreign policy and security that Earle organized at the Institute for Advanced Study (IAS) during the war years. As this story was retold over time, the memories of those who were present in Princeton during the early 1940s dimmed. By the beginning of the 1980s the recollections of Earle's editorial assistants, Felix Gilbert and Gordon Craig, had faded to the extent that when asked for information about that time by Theodore Ropp—himself an author for the Earle volume and then engrossed in his own *Makers* project—they claimed that they could no longer remember much about the circumstances surrounding its creation.[28] Although they both offered Ropp more substance in spite of their protestations, some of what Gilbert recalled was wrong.[29] Years earlier, Herbert Bailey, privy to the Princeton University's Press's records of the original work, wrote that 'the book grew out of a conference held at the institute'.[30] Again, this was not correct.

The absence of the book's chief protagonist from all but a short period of the post-Second World War era compounded this state of affairs. Earle's death in 1954, at the age of sixty, robbed him of the chance to better mould and shape the

---

[26] Showalter, review of *Makers*, p. 100.

[27] Paret, 'Introduction', in P. Paret (ed.), *Makers of Modern Strategy: From Machiavelli to the Nuclear Age* (Princeton, NJ: Princeton University Press, 1986), p. 8.

[28] Papers of Donald Mackenzie Schurman, in the care of Prof. Greg Kennedy, Defence Studies Department, King's College London (hereafter DSP). Ropp to Craig and Gilbert, 20 December 1979. MLP, PUP, Box 344, Folder 3 (CO728). Gilbert to Ropp, 8 January 1980. Craig to Ropp, 28 January 1980.

[29] Gilbert claimed that the chapter on Clausewitz was originally meant to be written by Herbert Rosinski rather than Hans Rothfels. He also wrote that Craig and Earle were good friends, although Craig wrote at the same time that he did not know Earle prior to working on the book. MLP, PUP, Box 344, Folder 3 (CO728). Gilbert to Ropp, 8 January 1980.

[30] Shelby White and Leon Levy Archives Centre, Institute for Advanced Study Princeton (hereafter IAS), Institute for Advanced Study Princeton (N.J.). Director's Office. Faculty records, Box 7/Earle, Edward Mead, 1950–1970. Bailey to Oppenheimer, 13 January 1960.

THE MAKING AND REMAKING OF *MAKERS* 7

legacy of his volume. Despite having been an early hire for the IAS, appointed even before the institute had acquired permanent buildings, after he died Earle's role and activities became obscured to institutional memory with the turnover of members and changes in the institute's leadership. By 1980 it was left to Felix Gilbert to emphasize to then IAS Director Harry S. Woolf not only Earle's role in bringing other historians to the institute, but also that he 'was really a historian and not a political scientist'.[31] The following year he requested that Earle's listing in the IAS's *A Community of Scholars* publication be amended so that 'behind his name, and before "military historian," it would be desirable to insert either "modern history" or "international relations"', since his published work in military history was small, and his interests ranged 'far beyond the field of military history'.[32]

Yet *Makers* has a history, and that history illuminates the origins, purpose, and reworking of the book. It is the aim of this book to explore the allure that *Makers* held for those scholars—predominantly historians—working over a fifty-year period from the mid-1930s to the mid-1980s. It focuses on the attempts made by these scholars across the decades to create and to remake the book, some of which were successful and others which were not. In all cases, the interactions between the scholarly editors and their versions of *Makers* are understood not simply as exercises in how to compile and collate an edited volume—or indeed in how to fail in the attempt—but also for what they reveal about how the scholars in question conceptualized and delineated the study of war and expressed this through their visions for the book. In this sense, this study encompasses both a series of formal *Makers* projects undertaken with specific goals in mind, and a larger informal project, bound over time after 1943 by the links each subsequent actor held to the original tome.

The book follows a chronological structure. Chapter 1 analyses academic engagement with war and strategy during the first decades of the twentieth century, with a particular emphasis on historical study, to provide deeper context for the emergence of the first *Makers of Modern Strategy*. When Edward Mead Earle wrote in the introduction to that book that 'war now thrusts itself upon the attention of us all' he was reflecting on the all-encompassing character of the world war that the USA had joined. Yet his words also spoke to the growth of civilian engagement with the problems and challenges of war in the years leading up to that point. If the First World War had underlined that war was 'too important to be left to the generals', this applied to those who thought about war as well as to those who practised it. Thus, this chapter explores that engagement in order to demonstrate that, however fitful, the notion of the civilian understanding of war

---

[31] IAS, Institute for Advanced Study Princeton (N.J.). Director's Office. Faculty records, Box 12/ Gilbert, Felix. Gilbert to Woolf, 19 September 1980.
[32] IAS, Institute for Advanced Study Princeton (N.J.). Director's Office. Faculty records, Box 12/ Gilbert, Felix. Gilbert to Woolf, 28 August 1981.

was a growing feature in the study of war in the early twentieth century, and that when viewed in some of its international dimensions—which would themselves feed into the *Makers* project—this becomes clearer still. In so doing, it places Earle's endeavours and his achievements into sharper perspective.

Chapter 2 situates the production of Earle's *Makers of Modern Strategy: Military Thought from Machiavelli to Hitler* within the intellectual atmosphere of the Institute for Advanced Study, Princeton. It does so by paying close attention to the founding years of the institute, to Earle's arrival there in the mid-1930s, and to the opportunities afforded him to shape and contextualize his understanding of the study of war. Fuelled by a prescient sense of the urgency of the moment, the expansive approach he adopted placed him in an ideal position to capitalize on academic opportunities once the United States entered the Second World War. Nevertheless this chapter also shows that whilst the book that would become *Makers* was a product of Earle's seminar on military studies in a certain sense, the particulars of its creation were driven by a narrower group of key individuals, amongst whom not only Earle but also Felix Gilbert and Gordon Craig figured highly. The book that they fashioned was written and collated in remarkably short order, at a time when the membership of Earle's seminar had for the most part moved away from Princeton and into government service, and by the time it was published it had partially transformed from its origins in understanding the foundations of military thought towards encompassing analysis of the war in progress. In part, this was a consequence of the emphasis Earle placed on linking past to present. Yet it was the same desire to balance past and present in light of contemporary developments that led Earle to begin the ill-fated pursuit of a revised edition of *Makers* even before the Second World War had concluded.

Chapter 3 shows that whilst no revised *Makers* was published during the decades from the late 1940s to the 1980s this did not mean that activities associated with the volume ceased altogether. In the late 1970s, moreover, a sustained and ultimately unsuccessful attempt to revise the book was undertaken by Theodore Ropp, a long-serving professor at Duke University, who co-opted a nascent exchange programme between his employer, the University of Singapore, and the Singapore Armed Forces, to work on a new *Makers* project. Ropp's experience of writing for the 1943 volume as a young scholar had been a key staging post in his transformation into a military historian. The project that he undertook towards the end of his career would constitute an appropriate bookend to a professional life heavily invested in the teaching of military history and its development as a sub-field in the post-Second World War era. Profoundly influenced by the deference that he felt towards the Earle volume, Ropp would come to propose a 'revisit' rather than a revision: a companion publication of complementary essays intended to account for things that Earle and his contributors had missed, and for subsequent developments that they could not reasonably have foreseen. Unable to overcome the impediments to the realization of his project, Ropp's

THE MAKING AND REMAKING OF *MAKERS*   9

Makers Revisited unravelled in the early 1980s. Despite this, his efforts are instructive in understanding the parameters of academic military history and his proposed volume offers an alternative vision to the new *Makers* that was to appear just half a decade later.

That volume is the subject of Chapter 4. The project that began in 1982 and which would eventually lead to the publication of *Makers of Modern Strategy: From Machiavelli to the Nuclear Age* took a different path to its wartime predecessor. Where Earle's book had been presented to the Princeton University Press as a complete manuscript, with the major decisions on form and content decided prior to submission, in the 1980s key figures at the press provided the impetus towards the new edition and played a greater consulting role on the form it would take. This chapter explores the genesis of the project, demonstrating the manner in which Peter Paret, Gordon Craig, and Felix Gilbert coalesced as an editorial team, whilst also underlining the influence of Michael Howard in shaping the volume. It charts the progress of the book towards production over a four-year period—more than twice as long the 1943 edition—as the editorial team encountered hindrances and complications that often echoed the experiences of forty years earlier. The book that they eventually produced followed a pragmatic approach in scaffolding to the original structure whilst adding a large amount of new content, much of which reflected a greater emphasis on the USA. As this chapter also shows, the project was moulded by its two most enthusiastic editors, Paret and Craig, who between them placed differing emphasis on past and present. Craig's editorial involvement with the second *Makers* was more substantial than his first experience had been, and of its editors he was consistently the most inclined to view the project in its alignment with the needs of the present, even if his efforts to establish such links in writing were tempered in collaboration with Gilbert. Paret, meanwhile, approached the present with reservations borne of much earlier professional experiences. He was, however, far more intellectually invested in the relation of *Makers* to the historical study of war, positioning the work in terms of the history of war, or even general history, and tending to reject the idea that it was a work of military history. In so doing he again cleaved to distinctions he had established some years prior.

Having examined the successful and failed attempts to create versions of *Makers* by Earle, Ropp, and Paret, the final chapter adopts a comparative approach to illuminate the legacy of the book. In his introduction to the 1986 edition, Paret described Earle's book as a 'scholarly contribution from the arsenal of democracy, in the best sense of that contemporary term'. This chapter explores the parameters of that contribution. It considers the reception of Paret's *Makers*, both in its own right and as a crucial moment in reinforcing the significance of Earle's *Makers*. It examines the differences in the conceptualization of strategy between the books and their editors, explores the manner in which *Makers* affected the canonization of particular strategic thinkers, and explains the omission of others. In so doing it

10 MAKING MAKERS

also considers the continuation of the legacy of *Makers* into the twenty-first century, in particular through the appearance of Williamson Murray, MacGregor Knox, and Alvin Bernstein's *The Making of Strategy* and, later, Victor Davis Hanson's *Makers of Ancient Strategy*.

Reflecting on what can be learned from studying acknowledgements, Emily Calacci writes that they:

> expose the messy interplay of institutional support, finances, intellectual genealogies, and interpersonal chaos that shape how an idea is brought into the world. In aggregate, they offer a glimpse into the political economy of academic life, revealing truths that we intend to share, as well as many that we do not.

In so doing they underline that 'books are the products not just of minds, but also of lives'.[33] If this last point is true of a single-authored work, it is surely even more emphatic in the case of collaborative edited volumes. Charting the development of the various incarnations of *Makers* amounts to scrutinizing acknowledgements on a large scale. In this manner, this book forms something of a collective intellectual biography. It is the history of a book and the efforts—fruitful and barren—to create a successor volume. It is equally a history of the people involved in its creation. Following these individuals—editors, authors, commentators, publishers—through their interactions with *Makers* tells us about how they lived and worked; how they were hired and advanced; their networks and lines of patronage. Since this book is as concerned with contingency and unfinished business as it is with work completed and scholarship produced, all of this matters when considering the contexts and circumstances in which *Makers* was conceived, revised, and remade. In the words of Quentin Skinner, 'an understanding of the past can help us to appreciate how far the values embodied in our present way of life, and our ways of thinking about those values, reflect a series of choices made at different times between different possible worlds'.[34]

Taken as a whole, the episodes considered in this book attest to the longevity of the *Makers* project in the minds of those who shaped it and were shaped by it, and who came to interact with it at various points in their careers. Indeed, it is a remarkable feature of the book that those who were touched by it often came back to it. This is evidently the case with regard to its first editor, Earle, who was drawn to thoughts of revising *Makers* very soon after it was published. It is equally true of Earle's editorial assistants, Gilbert and Craig, who came to the first book as young academics keen to make their mark, and to the second as respected senior scholars. *Makers*'s would-be editor Ropp found the book for which he had written both a key reference point for historical study and an enduring source of

---

[33] E. Callaci, 'On Acknowledgments', *American Historical Review* (February 2020), pp. 126–7, 131.
[34] Q. Skinner, *Visions of Politics, Vol. 1: Regarding Method* (Cambridge: Cambridge University Press, 2002), p. 6.

fascination, one which he returned to at intervals throughout his professional life. Even Paret, although not a participant in the first book project, had an indirect link to the influence of *Makers*. As a student in the 1950s he chose to study at King's College London, working under the supervision of Michael Howard in the aftermath of his *Makers*-induced revelation about the parameters of the history of war. For his part, Howard, though never an editor, would come to play an unofficial role in shaping the book that would become Paret's successor volume.

Above all, however, this is a book about historians and their contribution to the scholarship of war. It seems all the more important to insist on this given that the legacy of *Makers* in security and strategic studies is perhaps more straightforward to those fields than its relationship to the discipline of history. The editors of *Makers*—both those who succeeded and those who failed—were historians, as were the editorial assistants, as were the majority of the contributors, and they brought the considerations of the historian to their work. Nevertheless, the history of the project shows that the draw of *Makers* was not limited to a particular type of historian. The roster included those such as Paret, Craig, and Gilbert, best known for their individual contributions to scholarship; others such Ropp, known rather as a teacher and supervisor of doctoral students; and Earle, a scholar whose contribution to research became increasingly collaborative as his career progressed. Each of these brought to their own project differing perspectives on the role that history should play in the study of war. For Earle, this meant emphasizing history in relation to the need to address contemporary questions in alliance with the social sciences. For Ropp, it meant asserting the scope and breadth of military history as an appropriate vehicle for understanding war against the challenge of competitor disciplines. For Paret, meanwhile, it became a question of emphasizing a more intellectually useful broader history of war in contradistinction to a narrower, less insightful military history. In this sense, and in conformity with its quasi-biographical approach to the principal actors, this book is concerned with how historians thought of themselves, and with the intellectual developments that brought them to identify with certain positions on the past and the present, on war and history.

Despite the differences in understanding that can be observed both between these individuals and across time, however, all these actors held in common the desire to approach the historical study of war in broad rather than narrow terms, and to understand war not simply in the application of battlefield violence, but also in its wider dimensions. This does not mean that the history they practised would be accepted as sufficiently broad when judged against the most contemporary standards.[35] It does speak to their ambition. As such, this book also offers a

---

[35] For the contemporary parameters of military history see R. Citino, 'Military Histories Old and New: A Reintroduction', *The American Historical Review*, Vol. 112, No. 4 (October 2007), pp. 1070–1. Also T. Davis Biddle and R. Citino, 'The Role of Military History in the Contemporary Academy', Society for Military History White Paper (November 2014).

more constructive portrayal of historians and the study of war than oft-repeated tropes on the fortunes of military history. As far as military history is concerned, both its defenders and its critics tend to hang their case on a narrative of decline, the former to lament the progressive loss of posts for military historians— particularly those with an operational emphasis—and the latter to suggest that such losses are an appropriate consequence of the diversification of historical scholarship which has progressively loosened military history's once dominant grip.[36] Rather than chart decline from a supposed 'golden age' prior to the Second World War—the idea of which, in any case, is mythical—the history of the *Makers* project reflects on some of the ways in which the historical study of war developed across the twentieth century, which includes consideration of the growth of military history as a specialization in historical inquiry amongst competitor sub-fields.

Finally, this book is itself a reflection on the progress of history amongst competitor disciplines in the study of war. Here too, the longer-term perspective offers a more positive impression. Despite historians' frequent anxieties—manifest most obviously in this work in the person of Theodore Ropp—that the historical mode of study would be displaced by forms of inquiry which seemed to propose quicker fixes and more definite answers than historical scholarship could provide, this doomsday did not come to pass. It has not yet come to pass. The *Makers* project, conceived of and driven by historians in all its forms, attests to the enduring value of history in the study war.

Making Makers: The Past, the Present, and the Study of War. Michael P. M. Finch, Oxford University Press.
© Michael P. M. Finch 2024. DOI: 10.1093/9780191959257.003.0001

---

[36] Arguments such as these tend to break out periodically via social media, especially the twitter-sphere. For an example of the opposing positions, see R. Neer, 'The U.S. Military is everywhere, except in history books', Aeon, 16 March 2016, https://web.archive.org/web/20160711223312/https://aeon.co/ideas/the-us-military-is-everywhere-except-history-books and the response from A. M. Little, 'Here we go again: military historian complains that no one teaches or writes about military any more, part eleventybillion', *Histoirann*, 19 March 2016, https://web.archive.org/web/20160805212953/https://historiann.com/2016/03/19/here-we-go-again-military-historian-complains-that-no-one-teaches-or-writes-about-military-history-any-more-part-eleventybillion/. Also, P. Huard, 'The Battle over U.S. Military History', *War is Boring*, 28 April 2016, https://medium.com/war-is-boring/the-battle-over-u-s-military-history-94dc2c82c3d6. Huard writes that 'from the late 19th century through the 1950s, military history *was* history—along with diplomatic and political history, it dominated the scholarly study of the past', while Little writes that 'history departments used to be *only* focused on political and military history—at least, up until the 1920s'.

1

War Now Thrusts Itself upon Us All

War, History, and the Context of *Makers*

War now thrusts itself upon the attention of us all. And since it is the concern of all the people, all the people must realize that it *is* their concern. In wartime this involves a total effort; in time of peace, as in time of war, it demands wide understanding.

—Edward Mead Earle, 1943[1]

When *Makers of Modern Strategy* was first published in October 1943 it proved to be an instant success. Before the year was over the initial print run was almost exhausted, and it was apparent that the appeal of the book extended beyond those directly involved in the conduct of the Second World War. Those in uniform bought the book, so too did those in universities. More surprisingly perhaps, the book also appealed to the general public. In December 1943 *Makers* even appeared in *The New Yorker* as one of that year's 'Books for Christmas'.[2] The book responded to the needs of the moment, offering its readers an account of the development of thinking and practice on war from the fifteenth century to the twentieth century, which included consideration of the war still raging across the globe, and which was conveyed concisely across little more than five hundred pages of a single volume.

This response was a vindication for the book's editor, Edward Mead Earle. As he explained in his introduction, since war 'is the concern of all the people, all the people must realise that it *is* their concern'.[3] With *Makers* he had found a collaborative outlet for such a view which connected across a broad swathe of American society. When Earle wrote that 'war now thrusts itself upon the attention of us all', his specific reference was to the pervasiveness of the Second World War experience, which meant that international conflict could not be seen as remote from the life of the average citizen.[4] At the same time, his words spoke to the need for civilian understanding of war, both in practical and academic terms. Indeed, the appearance of his book has been seen as a marker helping to usher in the

---

[1] E. M. Earle, 'Introduction', in Earle, *Makers of Modern Strategy: From Machiavelli to Hitler* (Princeton, NJ: Princeton University Press, 1943), p. xi.

[2] Earle Papers, Seeley G. Mudd Manuscript Library, Princeton University, Princeton, NJ (hereafter MLP), MC020/Box 36/Makers of Modern Strategy 1943–1945 [3 of 5] 'Books for Christmas', *The New Yorker*, 11 December 1943.

[3] Earle, 'Introduction', p. xi.   [4] Ibid., p. xi.

14 MAKING MAKERS

'golden age' of strategic studies that began with the end of the war, 'the moment when civilians began to take over the study of strategy and when its purpose became the avoidance of war through deterrence, not its conduct through fighting.'[5]

Yet if Earle's exhortation stood at the threshold of the civilian capture of strategy, it can also be understood as the culmination of another process. Part of this was personal. Earle's commitment to the need for public and academic understanding of war stretched back into the 1930s. These concerns will be considered in the next chapter in relation to his career and the development of the first incarnation of *Makers*. This chapter focuses instead on the broader part of that process: academic engagement with the study of war during the first decades of the twentieth century, particularly through the lens of historians. In so doing it demonstrates a longer-standing commitment to this goal that helps to contextualize the appearance of *Makers* as a historical project.

To be sure, this was a fitful engagement, characterized by the failure of individuals to translate aspirations into more sustained programmes and enduring disciplinary or institutional legacies such as were achieved after 1945. In this sense, it cannot be denied that an interest in war, especially prior to the 1930s, was something of a minority academic preserve, or that the scholarly environment in the second half of the century was not radically different to that of the first. In the realm of ideas, however, there is rather more continuity. By focusing on what certain individuals thought and did—such as Hans Delbrück, Spenser Wilkinson, John Knox Laughton, and Frederick Maurice—as well as the institutional contexts in which they operated, it becomes clearer that much of Earle's argument for the importance of the study of war was an extension of claims that had been made in the preceding decades, in whole or in part, at various times, and by individuals with distinct backgrounds.

Equally, such recognition is illuminated in an international context. Just as the history of *Makers* was not a uniquely American story, so growing scholarly recognition of the importance of the study of war can be better understood by looking across national boundaries. In the early part of the twentieth century the United States was not the leader in the study of war that it would later become, and those who inclined towards the view that the American university should do more to establish it within their walls tended to look with envy towards Europe, considering that they were lagging behind developments there. That such efforts as took place, particularly in the United Kingdom, were not ultimately enduring played a role in 'the transfer of intellectual leadership in this field to the United States', and so helped create the opportunity for Earle to become 'the pioneer in American military studies'.[6] Thus, the European dimensions of the academic study of war in

---

[5] H. Strachan, 'The Future of Strategic Studies: Lessons from the Last "Golden Age"', in R. Glenn (ed.), *New Directions in Strategic Thinking 2.0* (Canberra: ANU Press, 2018), p. 151.

[6] T. Ropp, 'Duke University—University of North Carolina National Security Policy Seminar', *Military Affairs*, Vol. 27, No. 1 (Spring 1963), p. 12.

the early part of the twentieth century are important in understanding later American developments, and in particular the transnational aspects of the *Makers* project. In sum, intellectual recognition that 'war thrusts itself upon us all' began much earlier than 1943. As Earle himself later wrote, 'we learned in the period between two wars that historical interpretation is no mere academic exercise conducted in an ivory tower'.[7]

A New Military History for the Twentieth Century

In fact, the rumblings of such a realization began before the inter-war period, and were as apparent to some in the USA as they were to their counterparts in Europe. In 1912 the American Historical Association devoted a session of its annual meeting to a conference on military history. This was not a regular occurrence. Rather, as the session chair noted, it had been scheduled in response to a request from a number of participants who thought that 'the science of military history has entered upon a new aspect' such that it was 'to the advantage of the American people that there should be a more intelligent understanding of military history, with a view to the protection of the Nation in the future'.[8] Chief amongst those participants was Robert Matteson Johnston, an assistant professor at Harvard University. A few months earlier Johnston had published an article in the *Infantry Journal* asking 'what can be done for our military history?'[9] At the conference, which came about largely as a consequence of this piece, he expounded on similar themes.[10] Military history, he contended, was:

> at the present moment under a cloud. There is more than a disposition to frown it down, to taboo it as being in some way antagonistic to the call of pacifism which holds the public ear. The study of war in the minds of many would make us accessories to putting back the clock of civilization.[11]

If military history found itself under a cloud, however, it was not due to a lack of published work. The *American Historical Review*, for example, devoted a healthy proportion of its pages to articles on military subjects from its foundation in 1895

---

[7] E. M. Earle, 'A Half-Century of American Foreign Policy: Our Stake in Europe, 1898–1948', *Political Science Quarterly*, Vol. 64, No. 2 (June 1949), p. 184.

[8] 'X. Proceedings of the Conference on Military History', *Annual Report of the American Historical Association for the year 1912* (Washington, DC, 1914), p. 159. The session chair was Professor Albert Bushnell Hart, an eminent Harvard historian and president of the American Historical Association in 1909.

[9] R. M. Johnston, 'What Can Be Done for Our Military History', *Infantry Journal*, Vol. 9 (September–October 1912), pp. 236–9.

[10] 'Our Military History', *Infantry Journal*, Vol. 9, No. 3 (November–December 1912), p. 380.

[11] 'Proceedings of the Conference on Military History', p. 159.

16 MAKING MAKERS

to the start of the First World War and there were many popular titles that a reader might choose from.[12] Nor was military history without its proponents. As recently as 1902 the eminent naval historian Alfred Thayer Mahan had served as president of the American Historical Association, and had made consideration of military history an explicit part of his presidential address.[13] Rather the problem, as the editors of the *Infantry Journal* put it, was that 'most of our military history, if not our general history, is deplorably bad', deficient in both accuracy and quality.[14] At the conference Captain Arthur Conger pushed the charge still further, arguing that 'those in exclusive control of the main sources', that is to say the military, 'either do not know how to use, or for some reason will not use them intelligently, to write military history'.[15] Johnston took a more nuanced view, arguing that the relative absence of good histories was a measure of the difficulty of the task at hand. In the not-too-distant past, he alleged, the military historian had 'concentrated on the flags and the drums, on the roar of the guns, and the awful carnage; and he made extremely vivid and completely false pictures out of it all'. The military historian of the twentieth century, however, had 'abandoned the drum and trumpet and begun to analyse the psychology of generals, on the documents critically examined, and their tactical and strategical methods as seen from a technical point of view'.[16]

Johnston's reference to 'drums and trumpets' is striking. Later in the century, the same allusion would serve to distinguish between the purportedly innovative 'war and society' approach to military history and the ostensibly old-fashioned focus on military operations.[17] Johnston's remarks, however, related to a more fundamental transformation in the study of history itself. In the second half of the nineteenth century the modern discipline of academic history developed its professional form, encompassing—according to Robert Townsend—four principal elements: 'an idealized site for employment in academia, an ideology centered on the "scientific" study of history, a system of training and certification, and an institutional apparatus for disseminating the fruits of the new scholarship'.[18] If the university provided the site, the doctorate the principal means of training and certification, and the monograph the ideal vehicle for the published dissemination of research, the 'scientific' means of study undergirded the entire enterprise.

---

[12] J.-P. Herubel and E. Goedeken, 'Trends in Historical Scholarship as Evidenced in *The American Historical Review*: 1896–1990', *Serials Review*, Vol. 19, No. 2 (Summer 1993), pp. 79–83. In the period 1896–1915 'diplomatic/military' history, considered by the authors as a single category, accounted for 19 per cent of articles published, second only to the 43 per cent of articles on political history.

[13] For Mahan's address see A. T. Mahan, 'Subordination in Historical Treatment', in *Annual Report of the American Historical Association for the year 1902* (Washington, DC, 1903), pp. 49–63.

[14] 'Our Military History', p. 376.

[15] 'Proceedings of the Conference on Military History', p. 169.   [16] Ibid., p. 160.

[17] See, for example, D. Showalter, 'A Modest Plea for Drums and Trumpets', *Military Affairs*, Vol. 39, No. 2 (April 1975), pp. 71–4.

[18] R. B. Townsend, *History's Babel: Scholarship, Professionalization, and the Historical Enterprise in the United States, 1880–1940* (Chicago, IL: University of Chicago Press, 2012), p. 14.

The idea of a 'scientific' approach to historical study may have been 'vaguely defined and loosely used', but with its adhesion to the pursuit of objective study through the scrutiny of primary sources it could boast sufficient cohesion to distinguish it from an older, increasingly disparaged, 'literary' tradition of history writing, that held to the importance of the story over critical analysis.[19]

It was to this new mode of historical study that Johnston wished to tether the study of military history. In so doing, he—and his conference colleagues—were seeking to contribute to the specialization of historical study, capitalizing on the possibilities offered by the American Historical Association. The AHA, which had been founded only in 1884, had over the previous quarter century played its own role in shaping the professionalization of the historical discipline, delineating the boundaries of the discipline and emphasizing standards of scholarship. By 1912 that process was unfinished, such that it was not uncommon for scholars to identify as belonging to more than one discipline.[20] Despite this, it was already apparent that burgeoning trends in historical scholarship below the disciplinary level, which saw scholars move into social and economic domains, for example, challenged the monopoly of political subjects and called for specific attention. Consequently, in 1910 the AHA formalized the organization of its meetings to comprise of sessions dedicated to research specializations.[21] The conference on military history at the 1912 meeting followed on from this development. The attention devoted to a 'scientific' military history at such an early stage in the diversification of academic scholarship placed it amongst the pioneers of historical sub-fields.

Nevertheless this 'new' military history was without solid foundations. What was needed, and what the conference sought to identify, were the bases for a modern field which might speak to soldiers, civilians, and the nation. In response, Johnston, both at the conference and in his article, put forth several ideas. He advocated the establishment of a historical section within the US Army General Staff to mirror developments in Europe—and Germany in particular—to put history in the service of future military effectiveness. He proposed that university seminars, a dedicated journal, and a national society be founded to encourage study of the subject. Although a number of military history societies already existed, Johnston charged that these had 'never shown any ability or inclination to undertake the cool, scientific, absolutely detached investigation of war as war', preferring instead to 'always to turn toward the local and personal interest rather than to the impersonal and the national', which rendered them unfit to form a

---

[19] Ibid., pp. 17–18.

[20] Ibid., p. 15. Townsend notes that 'As late as 1911, almost a quarter of the membership of the AHA still listed at least partial affiliation with another discipline, reflecting considerable ambiguity at the disciplinary boundaries that we now see as fairly solid.'

[21] Ibid., pp. 78–81.

basis for action.[22] As for seminars, there were next to none. Johnston considered that his survey of European and American warfare across the nineteenth century, incorporating military thinkers as well as practitioners and campaigns, was the sole course in existence in the United States, and even this he described as a 'half-course', delivered only intermittently.[23]

Johnston's proposals found a broadly receptive audience, and the conference ended on a positive note with a resolution that 'military history should be pursued in a more systematic way'. A five-man committee was created, with Johnston as its chair, 'to consider the best method of furthering the study and presentation of military history and of bringing into common action professional and civilian students'.[24] The following year the AHA again held a session on military history as part of its annual meeting and also established funding for a prize in military history. Yet these developments did not presage sustained progress towards the establishment of academic military history in the USA. In 1913 the military history committee failed to submit the report it had promised the previous year, although Johnston offered a report on the current state of military history in the USA in its stead.[25] Likewise in 1915, the first year that the military history prize was due to be awarded, its committee reported that none of the entries had achieved the requisite standard. Consequently, an award was not made.[26]

Much of the impetus for these developments stemmed from Johnston. As well as offering the only extant university course on military history at the beginning of the twentieth century, he was an active writer on historical and contemporary military affairs whose published works encompassed such subjects as the life of Napoleon, the French Revolution, Ferdinand Foch, and US Army reform.[27] He also attempted to follow through on one of his stated goals with the foundation of a journal, *The Military Historian and Economist*, which he edited with Captain Arthur Conger. The publication only ran from 1916 to 1918, however, spanning three volumes. It was discontinued when Johnston left for France to serve in the US Army as Chief of the Historical Section of the General Staff. Poor health saw him invalided back to the USA in 1919, and when he died at the beginning of

---

[22] Johnston, 'What Can Be Done for Our Military History', p. 238. The editors of *Infantry Journal* noted that 'it should be a matter of regret that Harvard is perhaps the only institution of similar character in the United States that has a course of this nature': 'Our Military History', p. 378.

[23] 'Proceedings of the Conference on Military History', p. 161.   [24] Ibid., p. 197.

[25] *Annual Report of the American Historical Association for the Year 1913* (Washington, DC, 1915), pp. 42–3, 61.

[26] *Annual Report of the American Historical Association for the Year 1915* (Washington, DC, 1917), p. 51.

[27] R. M. Johnston, *Napoleon: A Short Biography* (New York: Henry Holt & Co., 1904), R. M. Johnston, *Leading American Soldiers* (New York: Henry Holt & Co., 1907), R. M. Johnston, *The French Revolution: A Short History* ((New York: Henry Holt & Co., 1909), R. M. Johnston, *Arms and the Race: The Foundations of Army Reform* (New York: The Century Co., 1915), R. M. Johnston, *General Foch, the Man of the Hour* (New York: A. L. Burt Co., 1918).

1920 the momentum he had created was lost.[28] By the 1930s there were seemingly as few opportunities for military historians as there had been thirty years earlier. 'American military historians were as numerous then as lion tamers,' quipped the Duke University historian Theodore Ropp late in his life, noting that there were no graduate courses in military history available when he became eligible for one in 1934.[29] Similarly, in 1975 Maurice Matloff noted that prior to the Second World War there was only one course in military history available throughout the USA, which could be found at the University of Chicago.[30]

The Pioneer

Despite its failure, the Johnston-led attempt to grow a scientific military history in the United States attested to an ambition to bring a more substantial approach to the study of war than a literary account of leaders and battles. Moreover, the inspiration for the initiative stemmed from the notion that in other countries such a transformation was already underway. In Germany and France, Johnston noted, the demise of the 'drums and trumpet' approach was 'generally known', whilst in Britain it was 'rapidly becoming known'.[31] This issue was partly bounded to the use of history by military institutions. Johnston and his colleagues looked to Germany and France primarily because of the progress they had made in bringing technically grounded historical study into military planning. What had begun in Prussia, and found vindication during the wars of German unification, had been subsequently incorporated into French military planning after the defeat of 1870–1, so that by the turn of the twentieth century both nations—and others besides—had established historical sections within their general staff.[32] In this manner, Johnston explained, 'a present necessity, an actual military problem, has inspired much of the best work that has been done' through 'making the historical study of war the basis for the efficient organization of their national armies'.[33] The United States Army, by contrast, lacked a historical section within its General Staff, an absence that many of the conference participants felt warranted swift rectification. Yet developments within the academic sphere also drew comment.

---

[28] For Johnston's biography see A. Baltzly, 'Robert Matteson Johnston and the Study of Military History', *Military Affairs*, Vol. 21 No. 1 (Spring 1957), pp. 26–30. *The Harvard Crimson*, 29 January 1920, https://www.thecrimson.com/article/1920/1/29/robert-matteson-johnston-pthe-death-yesterday/.

[29] DSP, T. Ropp, 'Military Historians. History 352.1', 12 February 1981. T. Ropp. 'Military Historians: My Brilliant Career. Marcus's "What's My Line?"' Durham Rotarians, 16 March 1981.

[30] M. Matloff, 'The Nature and Scope of Military History', in R. Weigley (ed.), *New Dimensions in Military History* (San Rafael, CA: Presidio Press, 1975), p. 406.

[31] Johnston, 'What Can Be Done for Our Military History', p. 236. In the USA, by contrast, he considered the matter 'as yet unrealised'.

[32] H. Strachan, *European Armies and the Conduct of War* (London: Allen & Unwin, 1983), p. 2.

[33] 'Proceedings of the Conference on Military History', p. 160.

20 MAKING MAKERS

Johnston made particular reference to 'a famous seminar in military history, that of Prof. Delbrück at Berlin', as an indication of how far his own country had to go.[34] Hans Delbrück, however, was more a pioneering outlier than an indication that the study of war had taken deep root within the German university.

Delbrück's academic reputation was made with the publication of his *History of the Art of War in the Framework of Political History*, the first volume of which appeared in 1900.[35] With this work, Delbrück brought the scientific study of history to the subject of war in an innovative fashion which enabled him to cast judgement on the veracity of historical claims stretching back into antiquity. His methodology, which he dubbed *Sachkritik*, applied critical perspectives to written sources through contemporary means, using modern knowledge of geography, weapons, equipment, logistical, and technical understanding to test for feasibility.[36] This method allowed him to demonstrate convincingly, for example, that Xerxes the Great could not possibly have led a force of millions into Greece in his second invasion of 480 BC.[37] Yet Delbrück's interest did not solely lie in the recreation of battle. He combined it with a commitment to integrate military history into general history, which meant considering politics, economics, and society, alongside the clash of arms. As a result, he was able to produce what he called a 'longitudinal history' of the development of warfare from antiquity, through the medieval, and into the modern age, in a manner which bore similarities to the *Annales* school of the 'long durée'.[38] It also drove him to develop substantial themes in his work: a focus on the evolution of tactics, an insistence on the relationship between war and politics across historical periods, and the idea that all strategies could be divided into two camps—strategies of annihilation and strategies of exhaustion.[39]

Arden Bucholz has argued that Delbrück was 'not only the pioneer of the modern scientific and universal approach' to military history, 'but the prototypical twentieth-century academic strategist'.[40] As Johnston's reference attests, he certainly enjoyed contemporary international renown in the early twentieth century. Johnston's partner in his endeavours, Arthur Conger, had attended Delbrück's lectures at Berlin University prior to the outbreak of the war.[41] In the United

---

[34] Ibid., p. 161.   [35] The final volume of four was published in 1920.

[36] G. Craig, 'Delbrück: The Military Historian', in E. M. Earle (ed.), *Makers of Modern Strategy: Military Thought from Machiavelli to Hitler* (Princeton, NJ: Princeton University Press, 1943), p. 265. C. Bassford, *Clausewitz in English: The Reception of Clausewitz in Britain and America 1815–1945* (Oxford: Oxford University Press, 1994), p. 180.

[37] Delbrück gave a summary of his approach in lectures at the University of London in 1913, which were subsequently published as *Numbers in History* (London: University of London Press, 1913), see especially pp. 22–32.

[38] A. Bucholz, 'Hans Delbrück and Modern Military History', *The Historian*, Vol. 55, No. 3 (Spring 1993), pp. 520–1, 525.

[39] Craig, 'Delbrück', p. 268.

[40] Bucholz, 'Hans Delbrück and Modern Military History', p. 526.

[41] H. Delbrück (ed. and trans. A. Bucholz), *Delbrück's Modern Military History* (Lincoln, NE: University of Nebraska Press, 1997), p. 34.

WAR, HISTORY, AND THE CONTEXT OF *MAKERS*   21

Kingdom, Spenser Wilkinson, the Chichele Professor of Military History, was aware of his work, and he was invited to lecture at the University of London in 1913.[42] By the time that Earle's *Makers* was compiled his reputation and qualities as an academic progenitor, carried by the German contingent involved in the project, was such that he was put forward as the exemplar of 'the military historian'.

During his lifetime, however, he was not held in such esteem by his peers. His fellow scholars tended to look upon his choice of study with some disdain. This was apparent early on in his career, when the dean of the University of Berlin objected to his young colleague's decision to lecture on the Austro-Prussian War, not only because he had not received permission to do so but because the subject was so recent.[43] The intellectual opposition to Delbrück's *metier* stemmed from the conviction that military history was a *Fachwissenschaft*, 'a technical science not legitimate for university teaching or scholarship', which contrasted with the *Geisteswissenschaft*, the ' "pure" history, concentrating on politics or the development of ideas' that constituted an acceptable 'humanistic discipline'. As Bucholz writes, 'War and military history were not viewed as important elements of culture or the proper concern of a university faculty'.[44] Rather than back down or change course, Delbrück decided to fight his corner. The result was that 'throughout his life, he was constantly arguing the legitimacy of his historical field'.[45] It was a decision that brought a professional cost, as demonstrated by his slow advancement. Delbrück did not become a professor until 1895, and even when he was appointed to a chair in 1897 it was in world history, not military history.[46]

Delbrück's relationship with the military was equally fraught. Here, too, opposition began early in his career, when some in the army pushed for the cancellation of all courses in military history at the University of Berlin, and continued into the twentieth century.[47] In venturing into scrutiny of the military conduct of war, Delbrück thrust himself into territory that both professors and generals agreed was best left to the professionals. The German army was a powerful institution

---

[42] Bassford, *Clausewitz in English*, p. 178.

[43] G. Craig, 'Delbrück: The Military Historian', in P. Paret (ed.), *Makers of Modern Strategy: From Machiavelli to the Nuclear Age* (Princeton, NJ: Princeton University Press, 1986), p. 329. It hardly helped matters that Delbrück, having served as tutor to Prince Waldemar, youngest son of the future Emperor Frederick III during the 1870s, had attempted to use royal connections to secure an academic position and to enter at the higher, associate professor, level. Although the latter part of this attempt failed, it did not lessen the resentment that his colleagues felt towards him. A. Bucholz, *Hans Delbrück and the German Military Establishment: War Images in Conflict* (Iowa City, IA: University of Iowa Press, 1985), pp. 26–7.

[44] Bucholz, *Hans Delbrück and the German Military Establishment*, p. 27.

[45] Craig, 'Delbrück', p. 283. Christopher Bassford writes that Delbrück's 'writings reflect a great bitterness at the superciliousness of colleagues who felt that this was not a proper topic for a serious scholar'. Bassford, *Clausewitz in English*, p. 178.

[46] Craig, 'Delbrück', p. 330. Bucholz, 'Hans Delbrück and Modern Military History', p. 519.

[47] R. Bauer, 'Hans Delbrück', in B. Schmitt (ed.), *Some Historians of Modern Europe: Essays in Historiography by Former Students of the Department of History of the University of Chicago* (Chicago, IL: University of Chicago Press, 1942), p. 104.

22 MAKING MAKERS

in a nation forged by war, 'a subculture unto itself, isolated and set apart from civil society', which jealously guarded its history and heritage. As a consequence of this 'war history was considered sacrosanct. Armies were unique institutions and their image was also unique. Military history was special because of the institutions and activity it represented and could not be properly treated as a normal part of political and cultural affairs.'[48] Delbrück, then, was bound to be seen as a meddler and could hardly avoid controversy where his work impinged on the German army's perception of its martial prowess, suggesting as it did that Frederick the Great should be considered an exponent of the strategy of exhaustion, rather than of the strategy of annihilation, which appealed more to their contemporary sensibilities.[49] As Azar Gat notes, Delbrück 'undermined the all-powerful conception of war and its conduct which postulated as the sole legitimate form of war out-and-out effort to achieve the total overthrow of the enemy by means of a gigantic clash of forces.'[50] There was an irony here, since the Historical Section of the German General Staff did in fact recognize the utility of his *Sachkritik* for their purposes.[51] No less a figure than Field Marshal von Schlieffen was taken with Delbrück's analysis of the Battle of Cannae for what it suggested on the issue of envelopment.[52] Yet just as with his academic colleagues, Delbrück did not seek intellectual conciliation. Rather he aggravated those in uniform by contending that not only was it legitimate for the historian to study military history, but that the historian had a more legitimate claim to do so than the military professional.[53] As a result, while Delbrück succeeded in developing a scientific approach to war as a historical phenomenon by the beginning of the twentieth century, from which he was able to make broader claims about strategy, he struggled to convince many of his academic colleagues and his military counterparts that they should pay more attention to it.

'With Special Reference to the Conditions of Modern War'

Delbrück's travails demonstrated that in Germany pioneering scholarship lacked institutional support. In Britain the situation at the beginning of the twentieth century was somewhat different, offering an early indication of the way that the experience of war might generate scholarly engagement and university provision. The Second Boer War of 1899–1902 exposed deficiencies in British military

---

[48] Bucholz, 'Hans Delbrück and Modern Military History', p. 521.

[49] A. Gat, *A History of Military Thought: From the Enlightenment to the Cold War* (Oxford: Oxford University Press, 2001), pp. 373–6. Bauer, 'Hans Delbrück', p. 119. Bucholz, *Hans Delbrück and the German Military Establishment*, pp. 10–15.

[50] Gat, *A History of Military Thought*, p. 376.   [51] Craig, 'Delbrück', p. 267.

[52] Bassford, *Clausewitz in English*, p. 178.

[53] Bucholz, *Hans Delbrück and the German Military Establishment*, pp. 10–12.

performance, ushering in a period of reform which continued through much of the rest of the decade.[54] As Adam Dighton has shown, this process also encompassed military education, resulting in a War Office-led attempt to promote officer education under a 1903 scheme which allowed for the universities of Oxford, Cambridge, Manchester, Dublin, and London to award of a number of commissions to students undertaking exams in military subjects, including military history, so encouraging growth in these areas.[55] In practice the success of the scheme was limited. The University of Manchester, for example, failed to graduate any students through the scheme. Efforts at the University of London were only slightly more successful. Although just one student had graduated through the scheme by 1909, the university persisted with the development in 1910 of a new curriculum in 'military science' for Officer Training Corps students studying for bachelor's degrees, including a final year course on military history and strategy, which came into effect in 1913. Those appointed to teach such courses were given short-term contracts, thus ensuring that they left no enduring footprint within their respective universities.[56]

In Oxford, however, the scheme provided the impetus for a more consequential development. Here the presence of military history was already somewhat better established. In 1899 military history became part of the undergraduate syllabus with the approval of an option in the final of the year of the honour school.[57] Amongst academics, too, were some whose research incorporated aspects of war. Montagu Burrows, for instance, the Chichele Professor of Modern History from 1862, was a retired officer of the Royal Navy, who brought his experience at sea to bear on his scholarly output, publishing a number of works on naval history.[58] He was followed by others who incorporated war into their published research, such as J. A. Froude, Samuel Rawlinson Gardiner, Charles Firth, and Charles

---

[54] On the transformation of the British Army as a consequence of the Boer War see B. Poe II, 'British Army Reforms, 1902–1914', *Military Affairs*, Vol. 31, No. 3 (Autumn 1967), pp. 131–8. S. Jones, *From Boer War to World War: Tactical Reform of the British Army, 1902–1914* (Norman, OK: University of Oklahoma Press, 2012).

[55] A. Dighton, 'Army Officers, Historians and Journalists: The Emergence, Expansion and Diversification of British Military History, 1854–1914', PhD thesis, University of Salford, 2016, pp. 294–5.

[56] Ibid., pp. 299–302, 305–7. The University of London appointed Colonels F. N. Maude and H. A. Sawyer as lecturers in 1904. The University of Manchester also appointed Maude to a two-year lectureship on 'Military Subjects' in 1905–7, and then Henry Spenser Wilkinson in 1907–8. Despite its inclusion in the scheme, the University of Cambridge did not appoint an equivalent lecturer in military matters during the same period, although it did establish two papers on military history in 1909.

[57] Having existed for the previous two decades in amalgamated form as part of the School of Law and Modern History, Modern History itself was established as an independent school within the university in 1872. Charles Oman and Charles Firth were the figures in proposing that military history be added to the syllabus. R. Soffer, 'Duty, Character and Confidence: History at Oxford, 1850–1914', *The Historical Journal*, Vol. 30, No. 1 (March 1987), p. 77. J. Hattendorf, 'The Study of War History at Oxford, 1862–1990', in J. Hattendorf and M. Murfett, *The Limitations of Military Power: Essays Presented to Professor Norman Gibbs on his Eightieth Birthday* (Basingstoke: Macmillan, 1990), p. 5. Dighton, 'Army Officers, Historians and Journalists', pp. 293–4.

[58] Ibid., pp. 5–7.

24 MAKING MAKERS

Oman.[59] Oman, appointed Chichele Professor of Modern History at All Souls College in 1905, was particularly notable as one of the pre-eminent military historians of the first half of the twentieth century, a reputation cemented by his history of the Peninsular War, which appeared in seven volumes between 1902 and 1930.[60]

In 1905 the university created a three-year lectureship in military history, with the intention that the holder would deliver a new 'military special subject' suitable for all undergraduates, whether engaged in the War Office scheme or not. The position was created at All Souls College, thanks to funding from its warden, Sir William Anson, and given to another fellow of the college, Sir Foster Cunliffe.[61] Cunliffe had credentials that rendered him suitable for the job, having recently completed a two-volume history of the Boer War.[62] He quickly discovered, however, that the requirement to lecture 'on military history, not confined to any special period of history, but in all cases bearing upon the conditions of modern warfare' would be especially challenging given the War Office's desire to change the focus of the military special subject on an annual basis.[63] In 1908 Cunliffe recommended that the faculty take control over the choice of campaign, and fix it for a number of years, a proposal to which the university agreed and the War Office conceded the following year.[64] Despite these challenges, the experience at Oxford was sufficiently encouraging that in 1909 the fellows of All Souls proposed to the university the establishment of a chair in military history. Anson explained

---

[59] Firth, who became Regius Professor of Modern History in 1904, extended his research on the English Civil War to encompass multiple facets including the social dimensions and military conduct of the war. Dighton, 'Army Officers, Historians and Journalists', pp. 281–2.

[60] Oman established his credentials as a military historian at a young age with a prizewinning essay on the 'Art of War in the Middle Ages' in 1884. The essay, which was published in its own right the following year, marked the first step towards a large corpus of published work on the development of warfare from the Middle Ages to the early nineteenth century. He was appointed Chichele Professor of Modern History in 1905. Dighton, 'Army Officers, Historians and Journalists', pp. 282–7.

[61] Anson, warden of All Souls since 1881, was lobbied by Leo Amery, military correspondent of The Times and editor of the Times History of the War in South Africa, who wanted to see the growth of military history at Oxford. Having long shown himself favourably disposed towards military education at the university, he doubtless took little persuading. Hattendorf, 'The Study of War History at Oxford', pp. 9–12. Dighton, 'Army Officers, Historians and Journalists', pp. 296–7.

[62] Dighton, 'Army Officers, Historians and Journalists', p. 297. Conveniently, he was also a close personal friend of Amery.

[63] Under the arrangement made with the university, the War Office retained the final say over the choice of campaign from a period running from 1792 to 1878, and was keen to ensure that the paper retained what it thought to be contemporary relevance. In the first year the Franco-Prussian War was selected, but the following year the War Office opted instead for a study of the Peninsular War, limited to a period between March 1811 and October 1813. Cunliffe, along with Oman—who also taught on the special subject—thought that it was a bad choice, which entailed overhauling lectures and brought with it challenges of selecting and sourcing new reading material at short notice, a task made more difficult by the inability of many students to master the foreign-language works necessary to study continental campaigns. Hattendorf, 'The Study of War History at Oxford', pp. 11–14. Dighton, 'Army Officers, Historians and Journalists', pp. 295–6.

[64] Hattendorf, 'The Study of War History at Oxford', pp. 13–14. Dighton, 'Army Officers, Historians and Journalists', p. 304.

to the vice-chancellor of the university that: 'We think that this subject is too important in itself, and to the University in its relation to the War Office to be dealt with either by a College tutor engaged in other historical work or by a non-resident who would come to Oxford for a time limited by the bare requirements of his lectures.'[65] The university agreed, and in the same year Henry Spenser Wilkinson was elected the inaugural Chichele Professor of Military History.[66]

Wilkinson's selection was significant. In part, this was because he was a civilian appointed at a time when such posts often went to military men. Indeed, Wilkinson was not the universally favoured applicant for the Chichele professorship. The War Office preferred Colonel Charles Callwell, author of the well-known guide to irregular warfare *Small Wars*, who had recently, and unhappily, retired from active service.[67] Wilkinson could not underline his credentials with a similar record of military service. Nor could he offer a deep record of academic experience. His previous role as Lecturer on Military Subjects at the University of Manchester, in 1907–8, was his only other university post. Rather, most of his experience lay in the field of journalism. Nevertheless, he had cultivated an interest in war across the course of that career. Whilst still a student at Oxford in the 1870s he had joined the university volunteer corps and founded the Oxford Kriegspiel Club. Returning subsequently to his native Manchester to practise law he joined the 2nd Manchester Volunteers and was a founder of the Manchester Tactical Society in 1881. Wilkinson's work with the Tactical Society, for which he wrote numerous pamphlets, essays, and commentaries, opened a door to journalism. In 1882 he wrote commentary on the Egyptian campaign for the Manchester *Guardian* and shortly afterwards joined its staff as a special correspondent. In 1892 he published *Imperial Defence*, co-authored with the MP Sir Charles Dilke, which brought him to the attention of Lord Roberts. After losing his post at the *Guardian*, Roberts helped Wilkinson secure a new appointment at the *Morning Post* in 1895. Ostensibly the paper's drama critic, Wilkinson used his position to continue writing on military affairs. He travelled with Roberts to India, visiting the north-west frontier, and later reported on the conduct of the Second Boer War, all the while continuing to write significant books such as *The Brain of an Army* (1890) and *The Brain of the Navy* (1895).[68]

---

[65] Anson quoted in Hattendorf, 'The Study of War History at Oxford', pp. 14–15.

[66] Ibid., pp. 14–15. Dighton, 'Army Officers, Historians and Journalists', p. 303.

[67] Dighton, 'Army Officers, Historians and Journalists', p. 304. For Callwell's pre-1914 period of retirement see D. Whittingham, *Charles E. Callwell and the British Way in Warfare* (Cambridge: Cambridge University Press, 2020), pp. 148–57.

[68] For Wilkinson's biography and career, see J. Luvaas, *The Education of an Army: British Military Thought, 1815–1940* (Chicago, IL: University of Chicago Press, 1964), pp. 253–90. Hattendorf, 'The Study of War History at Oxford', pp. 15–21. Strachan, 'The Study of War at Oxford', pp. 204–10, P. M. Ramsey, 'Professor Spenser Wilkinson, Admiral William Sims and the Teaching of Strategy and Sea Power at the University of Oxford and the United States Naval War College, 1909–1927', in N. Rodger, J. Dancy, B. Darnell, and E. Wilson (eds.), *Strategy and the Sea: Essays in Honour of John B. Hattendorf* (Rochester, NY: Boydell Press, 2016), pp. 213–25.

26   MAKING MAKERS

As a journalist and contemporary commentator whose interest in historical campaigns developed with the passage of time, elevated to a professorship on the strength of a record of writing on war outside academe, Wilkinson cut something of an unorthodox figure.[69] At the same time, his background seemed to put him good stead to fulfil a role which maintained the requirement that had pertained to the lecturer in military history, that the holder 'give instruction in Military History with special reference to the conditions of modern warfare'.[70] As Hew Strachan has noted, the condition that the professor devote himself to 'contemporary and even future war' in addition to historical study was not simply a consequence of the needs of military education. It was in keeping with the purpose of historical study at the University of Oxford at that time, where 'history was not only a professional discipline, but also an education for public life'.[71] Wilkinson, for his part, accepted the relevance of the study of the past for the purpose of the present, and embraced scrutiny of contemporary developments, not because of his understanding of academic history but due to a professional background in journalism and commentary that had long since oriented him in such a direction.

One month after his election to the Chichele professorship in October 1909, Wilkinson delivered an inaugural lecture which offered a clear-eyed assessment of the purpose and scope of military history within the university. In creating his position, Wilkinson contended, the university had 'bestowed its full franchise upon the study of war' as the culmination of 'that close contact which has long existed, and which from year to year becomes more intimate, between Oxford and the national life of England'.[72] It was no longer possible to 'think of the University as capable of doing its duty without having in its scheme of work a place for the study of war', because of its necessity 'to cultivate true ideas or to advance a healthy learning' that would produce 'citizens or statesmen equipped for their functions in the actual State'.[73] Having cast the mission in terms which encompassed nation, statesmen, and citizens, and not just soldiers, Wilkinson then articulated a conception of military history that went beyond an operational framework. 'Military History', he argued, 'is the effort to understand war, to get to know what war is and what it means.' Understanding war, in turn, could only be achieved by studying 'as many wars as possible, in order by comparison between them to learn what features and characteristics they have in common, whether

---

[69] Luvaas, *The Education of an Army*, p. 279. As Luvaas notes, Wilkinson's interest and activities in the realm of military history developed shortly in advance of his appointment: 'he was interested in education [...] and had long maintained that military history might be a fruitful field to develop in the universities. He had moreover recently completed a series of thirty lectures on the early campaigns of Napoleon at the University of Manchester, which suggests that already his interests had turned in the direction of military history.'

[70] Dighton, 'Army Officers, Historians and Journalists', p. 303.

[71] Strachan, 'The Study of War at Oxford', p. 208.

[72] H. Spenser Wilkinson, *The University and the Study of War* (Oxford: Clarendon Press, 1909), p. 9.

[73] Ibid., pp. 9, 10.

the events which composed them happened at random, or whether they happened as they did by reason of some inherent necessity'.[74] This study encompassed an understanding that 'the developments of war are the developments of the organization of society, and its increasing intensity, rapidity, and decisiveness are the results of progressive organization which more and more identifies the whole people with the State'.[75] Its final purpose was to achieve insight into the 'nature of war' that the historian would 'attempt to express in a view or theory of its nature and of its several parts or manifestations'.[76]

Over the next fourteen years, Wilkinson would attempt to bring this commitment to developing the theory of war, drawn from its history, to his work. Although he published a number of works on historical campaigns and correspondence, he was increasingly drawn towards 'exploring and understanding intangible factors such as the currents of national energy, the interrelationship of war and society, the nature of duty within the framework of total war and the conditions of national existence'.[77] This led him to underscore—in a manner that presaged later developments—the importance of military understanding of principles of national policy, of statesmen's understanding of the military and naval means at their disposal and the consequences of decisions made, and of the fundamental need for the study of the relationship between strategy and policy that the university could facilitate. In the words of Hew Strachan, 'Wilkinson set the agenda for the academic pursuit of what in the Cold War came to be called strategic studies, but he—and as a result Oxford—saw its principal constituent discipline not as game theory or mathematical probability, but as history'.[78]

Naval History in the Service of the Nation

In the early twentieth century, Delbrück and Wilkinson were not the only scholars engaged in an attempt to understand war in a broad context and to develop theory from it. Several of the era's naval historians worked in a similar direction. The most renowned of them was Captain Alfred Thayer Mahan. Mahan came to a life of writing only in middle age, when he was appointed as lecturer and president of the newly established US Naval War College in 1886. This proved to be the turning point in a career that had hitherto been undistinguished.[79] At the war college he crafted the lecture series that would form the basis of his first and most famous

---

[74] Ibid., pp. 12–13.   [75] Ibid., p. 16.   [76] Ibid., p. 25.

[77] Luvaas, *The Education of an Army*, pp. 280, 285. The works he published during this time included *Hannibal's March through the Alps* (1911), *The Early Life of Moltke* (1913), *The French Army before Napoleon* (1915), *Moltke's Correspondence during the Campaign of 1866* (1915), *Moltke's Military Correspondence 1870–71* (1922), *The Defence of Piedmont* (1927).

[78] Strachan, 'The Study of War at Oxford', pp. 208–9.

[79] P. Crowl, 'Alfred Thayer Mahan: The Naval Historian', in Paret (ed.), *Makers of Modern Strategy*, p. 446.

28 MAKING MAKERS

book, *The Influence of Sea Power upon History* (1890), and which would eventually result in a series of 'influence' books encompassing *The Influence of Sea Power upon the French Revolution and Empire* (1892), *Sea Power in Its Relations to the War of 1812* (1905), and his biography of Nelson, *Life of Nelson: The Embodiment of the Sea Power of Great Britain* (1897). The success of his works enabled him to live primarily as a writer and the US 'national naval schoolmaster' until his death in 1914.[80] They also afforded him international prestige, appealing to readers both in the pre-eminent naval power of the United Kingdom and the rising naval power of Germany for the way in which they connected mastery of the sea to national power.[81] By forging such a link Mahan made a major contribution towards broadening the study of naval history, even if he tended to use the historical record to justify his principles more than to derive his principles from interrogation of the past.[82] As Don Schurman wrote, 'he found it [naval history] a record of battles, and left it as a subject that was intimately connected with foreign policy and the general history of the nation state'.[83] Jon Sumida goes further still, contending that Mahan 'invented historically based and broadly focused international security studies, which differed from earlier writing about military affairs through its relationship of policy and operations to political, political-economic, and governmental questions on a global scale'.[84]

Whilst Mahan may have been the most famous naval historian of his age, the most pivotal figure in bridging the divide between the naval institution, the university, and the scholarship of war was John Knox Laughton. Laughton joined the Royal Navy as an instructor in 1853, teaching at the Royal Naval College from 1866, first in Portsmouth and then, from 1873, at its new site in Greenwich. Educated as a mathematician at Cambridge University, his initial teaching concerns were scientific.[85] At Greenwich he first served as head of the Department of Meteorology and Marine Surveying. He began publishing on naval history as early as 1866, however, and in 1876 gave the first lectures on naval history at the Royal Naval College.[86] Thereafter, he amassed an impressive body of historical works, spanning multiple books, articles, and hundreds of entries for the *Dictionary of National Biography*.[87] Such was the strength of his scholarly record

---

[80] D. Schurman, *The Education of a Navy: The Development of British Naval Strategic Thought, 1867–1914* (London: Cassell, 1965), p. 67.

[81] Crowl, 'Alfred Thayer Mahan', pp. 447–8, 473–4.   [82] Ibid., pp. 449–55.

[83] Schurman, *The Education of a Navy*, p. 82.

[84] J. T. Sumida, *Inventing Grand Strategy and Teaching Command: The Classic Works of Alfred Thayer Mahan Reconsidered* (Baltimore, MD: The Johns Hopkins University Press, 1997), pp. 99–100. See also J. T. Sumida, 'Alfred Thayer Mahan, Geopolitician', *The Journal of Strategic Studies*, Vol. 22, Nos. 2–3 (1999), pp. 39–62.

[85] He graduated with a first-class degree in the Mathematical Tripos in 1852. A. Lambert, *The Foundations of Naval History: John Knox Laughton, the Royal Navy and the Historical Profession* (London: Chatham Publishing, 1998), pp. 14–30.

[86] Ibid., pp. 28–9, 49–51. Schurman, *The Education of a Navy*, pp. 83–4.

[87] Schurman, *The Education of a Navy*, p. 84.

by the time he retired from the service in 1885 that he was able to make the transition to university education, joining King's College London as Professor of Modern History.

The broadness of Laughton's title did not prevent him from continuing work on the development of naval history until his retirement in 1914. Nor was he solely absorbed in his own scholarship. Much of his energy was directed towards activities which promoted the professionalization of his field. In the late 1870s, for example, he successfully gained access to Admiralty Records for the purpose of study, leading the way to the opening of the records to scholars by the late 1880s.[88] More significant still was his work as a founder of the Navy Records Society (NRS), which he served as Secretary and Editorial Director from its establishment in 1893 until 1912.[89] Through the production of numerous volumes, many of which were edited by Laughton himself, the NRS offered a crucial means for the dissemination of the published primary source material which provided the 'scientific' basis for modern scholarship. As Andrew Lambert writes:

> Laughton's object in founding the Navy Records Society, and in taking on a large amount of unpaid work, was the promotion of naval history as the basis of service education, and the naval case in national defence. By publishing archival material he hoped to build a durable foundation for the subject, so that it could bear the weight of scholarship and service polemic without compromise.[90]

Despite transitioning from the service to the civilian world, Laughton never came to view the pursuit of naval history as an end in itself. His aim was unashamedly 'to maintain and improve the Royal Navy as an efficient national instrument of war'.[91] The 'naval scares' of the pre-First World War era led him to recognize that naval history had a role to play in public education, since civilian understanding of the naval contribution to British national power was just as important as naval understanding of how the instrument might continue to serve the maintenance of that power.[92] Ultimately, however, it was the utility of history in the development of a 'modern doctrine', 'that covered every aspect of naval service, including strategy, tactics, leadership, personnel, administration and morale', which mattered most.[93]

If one consequence of this approach, combined with 'temperament, the pressure of other commitments, or the need to write swiftly for money', was that Laughton never developed 'a sustained philosophy of history', this was not the case for some of those who benefited from his encouragement.[94] Laughton's work,

---

[88] Ibid., pp. 87–8.
[89] For Laughton's work with the NRS see Lambert, *The Foundations of Naval History*, pp. 142–72.
[90] Ibid., p. 151.   [91] Schurman, *The Education of a Navy*, p. 98.
[92] Ibid., p. 103.   [93] Lambert, *The Foundations of Naval* History, p. 232.
[94] Schurman, *The Education of a Navy*, p. 97.

30   MAKING MAKERS

for example, provided a direct inspiration to Admiral Stephen B. Luce in setting up the US Naval War College and in Luce's instructions to Mahan in the early years of that institution. Mahan, in turn, developed close relations with Laughton in the two decades prior to his death, with both men recognizing 'the cause they shared, the importance of history in demonstrating the central role of naval power in national policy'.[95]

More significant still was Laughton's role in the intellectual development of Julian Corbett. An entirely civilian scholar of naval history, Corbett studied law at Cambridge, was called to the Bar at the Middle Temple, and then led an exceedingly short legal career.[96] Freed from the obligations of following a set path thanks to family wealth, he spent time travelling, wrote several works of historical fiction, then made his first forays into history with short biographies of George Monck (1889) and Francis Drake (1890). In 1893 Laughton persuaded Corbett to join the NRS, coaxing him towards the study of history through primary sources and broadening his access to contemporary naval figures, thereby encouraging his development 'from a romantic novelist into a historian for the navy'.[97] Over the next twenty years, Corbett published a series of books charting the development of British strategy from the Tudor era to the age of Nelson, which were marked by the rigour of their historical analysis.[98] Moreover, he used historical research as a foundation for the development of theory, which found its most concise expression in his book *Some Principles of Maritime Strategy* published in 1911. As Schurman notes, Corbett's 'great aim [...] was to attempt a marriage between principles and history while not ignoring the canons of historical accuracy nor the requirements of research in depth'.[99] In this respect, his civilian status became a 'critical asset' which enabled him to see beyond the clash of fleets, to develop a broader purview on war and strategy—albeit in a British context—and to forge a theory that linked the land and maritime domains.[100]

Frustrations of the First World War

Although developments in military and naval history in the United Kingdom prior to 1914 appeared to hold much promise for the future, the coming of the First World War brought serious setbacks to further growth. The war disrupted pre-existing transatlantic and European academic networks, reorienting international

[95] For Laughton's relationship with Luce and Mahan see Lambert, *The Foundations of Naval History*, pp. 30, 121–35.
[96] For Corbett's life and work see D. Schurman, *The Education of a Navy*, pp. 147–84 and A. Lambert, *The British Way of War: Julian Corbett and the Battle for a National Strategy* (New Haven, CT: Yale University Press, 2021).
[97] Lambert, *The British Way of War*, p. 54.   [98] Schurman, *The Education of a Navy*, p. 149.
[99] Ibid., p. 184.   [100] Lambert, *The British Way of War*, pp. 7–8.

linkages between universities and progressively excluding once pre-eminent German institutions.[101] At the same time, it promoted national processes in which 'scholars were definitively cast as national actors, working in the national interest, on initiatives organized by national governments and armies', incorporating not only the lethal and technical application of the sciences but also the propagandizing and justificatory potential of the humanities.[102] This left little opportunity to expand the study of war in a more enduring way.

Such was the experience of Spenser Wilkinson. Before the war, Wilkinson had looked to the future with optimism. In his inaugural address he mused on the possibilities, noting that:

> To-day, I cannot but dream of an Oxford School of War developing that which time has confirmed of the ideas of the older writers into a fresh yet true idea adequate to the needs of the present day and of our own people. It would attempt to be a vision and not a dream, and would base itself upon such knowledge as Oxford can supply of the nature of society and of the State.[103]

As the war began, Wilkinson initially found himself in demand. During 1914 and 1915, as large numbers of students sought commissions through the Officer Training Corps, to be joined in uniform by staff, servants, and some fellows, Wilkinson lectured to packed theatres and published on war issues as part of the 'Oxford Pamphlets'.[104] Yet this level of activity did not persist beyond the initial period of mass mobilization, as the numbers of students registered at the university fell dramatically across the course of the war.[105] Wilkinson soon found that his services were no longer needed.[106] It was his misfortune that the most significant conflict of his lifetime arrived after the peak of his influence had passed.

---

[101] T. Irish, 'From International to Inter-Allied: Transatlantic University Relations in the Era of the First World War, 1905–1920', *Journal of Transatlantic Studies*, Vol. 13, No. 4 (November 2015), pp. 311–25. See also T. Irish, *The University at War, 1914–25* (Basingstoke: Palgrave Macmillan, 2015).

[102] T. Irish, 'Scholarly Identities in War and Peace: The Paris Peace Conference and the Mobilization of Intellect', *Journal of Global History*, Vol. 11, No. 3 (November 2016), p. 373. Irish, *The University at War*, pp. 15–38.

[103] Spenser Wilkinson, *The University and the Study of War*, p. 26.

[104] Hattendorf, 'The Study of War History at Oxford', p. 19. For the 'Oxford Pamphlets' published by the Clarendon Press in the early part of the war see H. Pogge von Strandmann, 'The Role of British and German Historians in Mobilizing Public Opinion in 1914', in B. Stuchtey and P. Wende (eds.), *British and German Historiography, 1750–1950: Traditions, Perceptions, and Transfers* (Oxford: Oxford University Press, 2000), pp. 352–63.

[105] At the start of the 1915–16 academic year around half the student body of most colleges were recorded as away on military service. By 1918, only 12 per cent of the university's pre-war population was in residence in the city. J. M. Winter 'Oxford and the First World War', in B. Harrison (ed.), *The History of the University of Oxford*, Vol. 8: *The Twentieth Century* (Oxford: Oxford University Press, 1994), p. 9.

[106] Along with the decline in numbers, students seeking a commission were no longer required to study military history, and external bodies stopped requesting his support. Hattendorf, 'The Study of War History at Oxford', pp. 19–20.

32   MAKING MAKERS

As Luvaas writes: 'No longer was he the foremost military commentator in the press, as he had been during the Boer War. No longer did he have much influence in the War Office. Time after time he volunteered his services only to be informed that "after careful enquiry at the Admiralty and War Office [...] there is at present no opportunity." '[107]

Yet if no 'school of war' developed at Oxford, either during or after the First World War, part of the blame lay with Wilkinson himself. Rather than seizing any opportunity presented by the war, Wilkinson compounded his position by turning away from the war in progress and towards historical studies. Although this may have been driven by his conviction that 'a war that is taking place cannot be fully known', it nonetheless offered 'a bizarre contrast with the realities of the Great War as it reached its climax in 1917–18'.[108] By the war's end he had become a paradoxical figure, so frustrated by the stipulation that he lecture 'with special reference to the conditions of modern warfare' that in 1919 he requested that it be removed, on the grounds that the focus on modern warfare suggested 'a technical study of contemporary methods, such as is inappropriate except in a professional institution'.[109] The appeal coincided with his attempt to secure a third term in post, giving fuel to those who believed that a military figure would do a better job.[110] Although Wilkinson was given a final four-year term in 1919, after he retired in 1923 the electors chose as his successor Major General Sir Ernest Swinton.[111] Swinton's record in the role was so lacklustre that Basil Liddell Hart later alleged that it led to 'a proposal to abolish the chair and transfer its endowment to another subject'.[112] Whether this was true or not, when Swinton retired in 1939 the electors decided not to fill the vacant chair until after the Second World War reached a conclusion.[113]

Thus, personal shortcomings played a significant role in preventing the realization of an 'Oxford school of war' with history as its foundation. It is important to note, however, that the impediments to achieving such a goal also lay with the

---

[107]   Luvaas, *The Education of an Army*, p. 282.

[108]   Spenser Wilkinson, *The University and the Study of War*, pp. 11–12. Strachan, 'The Study of War at Oxford', p. 209.

[109]   Hattendorf, 'The Study of War History at Oxford', p. 18. Wilkinson quoted in Strachan, 'The Study of War at Oxford', p. 210.

[110]   Opponents wanted to appoint Major General Guy Dawnay instead of Wilkinson. Strachan, 'The Study of War at Oxford', p. 210.

[111]   Best known today as an advocate of the tank during the First World War, Swinton had served as head of the Historical Section of the Committee of Imperial Defence for three years prior to the First World War, during which time he had overseen the compilation of the official history of the Russo-Japanese War.

[112]   Liddell Hart Papers, Liddell Hart Centre for Military Archives, King's College London (hereafter LHCMA) LH 1/608/115, Liddell Hart to Ropp, 24 February 1964.

[113]   Strachan, 'The Study of War at Oxford', p. 213. Certainly, the account of his time at All Souls offered in his autobiography, published shortly after his death in 1951, gives evidence of a man with relatively little concern for scholarship, and rather more interest in personalities and the peculiarities and rituals of university and college life. See E. Swinton, *Over My Shoulder* (Oxford: George Ronald, 1951), pp. 255–82.

institution. As Hew Strachan has stressed, in the inter-war period modern history ceased to be the school of choice for those seeking an education as preparation for public life. Instead, the School of Philosophy, Politics, and Economics, established in 1920, took its place: 'History refused to compete with PPE, and the two subjects—history and politics—pursued increasingly divergent courses.' For the Chichele Professor of Military History—renamed as History of War with the appointment of Cyril Falls in 1946—the challenges to maintaining a link between the history of war and modern war thereby increased. The result was that 'as history qua history grew as a discipline it would elbow out the study of war as many theorists [...] understood it'.[114]

For the naval historians the story was also one of frustration and disappointment. In the final years of his life, John Knox Laughton was deeply convinced of the need to grow civilian focus on naval history within the university. To that end he attempted to leverage the prestige he had built for himself within the recently federated University of London to lobby for the creation of a Department of Naval History at King's College London.[115] By the time of his death in 1915, however, neither a department nor a dedicated chair to match the Chichele professorship had been established.[116] The college did buy some of his books and open a memorial library. Reflecting on this development and the significance of the work of his late colleague, Julian Corbett observed how Laughton had spent his career 'quietly, devotedly, without ostentation and for long without recognition [...] opening up the foundations and preparing the material for a greater and more enduring structure. The completion of that work is one of the tasks that lie before the Department of Naval History, of which it is hoped that the new Laughton Library is but the first stone'.[117]

No further stones were laid in the following decade. Lambert attributes this inaction to 'post-war pressure on space at King's College and, more fundamentally, a complete lack of interest on the part of the college', exacerbated by the lack of 'a powerful advocate within or outside the college'.[118] Corbett, the individual best suited to fulfil such a role, had begun the century believing 'that only the Admiralty could support the spirit of the subject'.[119] After Laughton's death he revised his position. Yet despite his assertion that 'a great war does not kill the past, it gives it new life' such that 'no moment, then, could be more opportune than the present for a Department of Naval History to start its career', he proved no more successful in the task than his mentor.[120] He raised

---

[114] Strachan, 'The Study of War at Oxford', pp. 212–13.

[115] Such was Laughton's status in the university that he was selected as the first chair of its History Board. See A. Lambert, 'Laughton's Legacy: Naval History at King's College London', *Historical Research*, Vol. 77, No. 196 (May 2004), pp. 277–9.

[116] Lambert, *The Foundations of Naval History*, pp. 212–17.

[117] J. Corbett, 'The Revival of Naval History', *The Contemporary Review* (1 July 1916), p. 735.

[118] Lambert, *The Foundations of Naval History*, pp. 216–17, 226.   [119] Ibid., p. 220.

[120] Corbett, 'The Revival of Naval History', p. 740. Lambert, *The British Way of War*, p. 414.

34 MAKING MAKERS

the issue again in his Creighton Lecture at King's in 1921, but died the following year with nothing achieved.[121]

Although London was not listening, in Cambridge there was a more encouraging development. In 1919 the university established a dedicated chair in naval history, funded by an endowment from the press baron Lord Rothermere.[122] As a condition of his benefaction, Rothermere stipulated that John Holland Rose, a fellow of Christ's College, be made the first Vere Harmsworth Professor of Naval History.[123] Since Rose had little background in naval history, and was best known for his *Life of Napoleon* (1901), he was a curious choice.[124] Even Rose seemed to recognize this, since he engaged in an unsuccessful attempt to persuade Corbett to apply for the position before finally accepting the role.[125] Although he recognized the significance and potential of the Harmsworth professorship, going so far as to advocate the creation of a 'school of naval studies' at Cambridge prior to his appointment, Rose's achievements in post were meagre. It hardly helped matters that strong voices within the university, such as the ancient historian James Smith Reid, found the notion of a 'school of naval studies' flowing from the establishment of a naval chair abhorrent.[126] Towards the end of his tenure Rose compounded matters by suggesting that the post should be renamed Professor of Imperial and Naval History for his successor. The History Faculty Board and Lord Rothermere concurred.

With this change 'the intention', writes Ronald Hyam, 'was that the chair would in future be open to one who professed solely (or chiefly) the history of the British empire *or* naval history: in other words that the chair might remain afloat, or be firmly planted on dry land, or become daringly amphibious'.[127] In the event, the chair was kept briefly afloat. Rose's successor was Sir Herbert Richmond, another pre-eminent naval historian, who had benefited from his connections to both Laughton and Corbett. In 1934, Richmond joined Cambridge following a lifetime of service in the Royal Navy.[128] After just two years in the role, he chose to take up

---

[121] Lambert, *The Foundations of Naval History*, pp. 216–17.

[122] The chair was established to commemorate his son Vere Harmsworth, who died in 1916 whilst serving with the Royal Naval Division in France.

[123] Lambert, *The Foundations of Naval History*, p. 415. Lambert, *The Foundations of Naval History*, pp. 226–7. R. Hyam, *Understanding the British Empire* (Cambridge: Cambridge University Press, 2010), p. 513.

[124] For a summary of Holland Rose's work see E. Wilson Lyon, 'John Holland Rose', in Schmitt (ed.), *Some Historians of Modern Europe*, pp. 367–91.

[125] Corbett, in ill health and consumed by his work on the official history of naval operations in the Great War, turned down the opportunity.

[126] Lambert, *The British Way of War*, pp. 416–19.

[127] Hyam, *Understanding the British Empire*, pp. 513–14.

[128] He had joined the Royal Navy as a thirteen-year-old midshipman and risen to the rank of admiral, becoming the first Commandant of the Imperial Defence College in 1927. See A. Stewart, *Royal College of Defence Studies 1927–2017: Ninety Years of Preparing Strategic Leaders* (London: Royal College of Defence Studies, 2017), pp. 22, 25–7, 32–3.

WAR, HISTORY, AND THE CONTEXT OF *MAKERS*   35

a new position as master of Downing College. His successor as Harmsworth Professor was a dedicated imperial historian, as have been all appointees since.[129]

In Germany, Hans Delbrück fared no better in his attempt to build a legacy. The war exacerbated the pre-existing rift between him and the leading elements of the German armed forces. Prior to 1914, Delbrück had held to a distinction between the role of the military historian and that of the military critic, where the former was concerned with clarifying the record of events and left interventions in the conduct of war to the latter. Once it became clear that Germany would not achieve the decisive results in short order, however, he found that he could no longer maintain the separation. This was not simply a consequence of patriotic sentiment, but a result of the theory which had developed from his historical study. After the failure of German offensive plans in 1914 he concluded that the nation could not afford to adopt a strategy of annihilation, and that her best hope lay in pursuing a strategy of attrition as a means to seek a negotiated peace.[130] Thus, in 1915 he organized a counter-petition of several hundred signatories in opposition to the 'petition of the intellectuals', and the following year he spoke out on the deleterious strategic consequences of unlimited submarine warfare.[131] In addition, he made clear his opposition to territorial annexations in Western Europe as an impediment to peace negotiations, thereby becoming 'the principal public opponent of the grandiose schemes of territorial expansion in Europe which grew to dominate both German policy and public opinion during the war'.[132]

Germany's defeat did not persuade him to desist. Instead, he carried his critique of the high command into the post-war period, taking aim at their failure to subordinate military strategy to political aims and engaging in feuds with Alfred von Tirpitz and, particularly, Erich von Ludendorff, who he charged 'did not understand the strategic requirements of the war and, by his resistance to the king and government, brought on the revolution that finally buried the German Empire'.[133] However principled this stance, it did little to enhance Delbrück's case for the expansion of provisions for military history, to stem attacks on his professional standing, or persuade military professionals or his academic colleagues. As he approached retirement in 1921, he appealed to the University of Berlin to create a chair in military history. The professoriate were as clear in their opposition

---

[129] Hyam, *Understanding the British Empire*, pp. 514–17. Lambert dubs the appointment of Eric Walker as Richmond's successor in 1936 'a brutal annexation of the chair by other historical interests'. Lambert, *The British Way of War*, p. 419.

[130] F. Gilbert, 'From Clausewitz to Delbruck and Hintze: Achievements and Failures of Military History', *Journal of Strategic Studies*, Vol. 3, No. 3 (1980), pp. 13, 17–18. See also Bucholz, *Hans Delbrück and the German Military Establishment*, pp. 86–110.

[131] Bucholz, 'Hans Delbrück and Modern Military History', p. 524. One thousand professors in German universities signed the 'petition of the intellectuals' in support of the government's bid for total victory.

[132] Gat, *A History of Military Thought*, pp. 376–7.

[133] Delbrück, *Delbrück's Modern Military History*, p. 192.

36   MAKING MAKERS

as they had been in the 1880s: the proposal was rejected.[134] Delbrück, who died in 1929, 'had failed to create a new school of military history research: he had no followers'.[135]

Post-War Opportunities

The disappointments experienced by figures such as Wilkinson, Laughton, and Delbrück underlined the manner in which the First World War appeared as a point of rupture, eroding or destroying pre-war lines of effort. Yet for others the war proved to be a starting point. Just as had been the case in Britain after the Boer War, the experience of the First World War prompted reflection in its aftermath on the need for better understanding of war as a phenomenon. As the former Chief of the British Imperial General Staff Sir William Robertson observed in the 1920s:

> The activities of war embrace every element of the national life, and upon the Cabinet devolves the responsibility for combining the whole military, naval, diplomatic, financial, and economic forces of the nation for the defeat of the enemy. This is a formidable duty, and cannot be properly discharged unless those holding ministerial office have, by previous study, made themselves acquainted with the principles upon which the business of war should be conducted.[136]

Such consideration naturally extended into the domain of scholarship and the organization of academic institutions. Whilst it would be an exaggeration to suggest that this represented a widespread change—there remained plenty of opposition to war as a valid field of study—it is equally possible to discern new currents of thought and activity, some of which would take better root once world war returned.

Some individuals were inspired by their forebears. Such was the case for Albert Frederick Pollard, who had become acquainted with Laughton whilst working at the *Dictionary of National Biography* in the late 1890s and subsequently came under his influence. When Pollard became head of the Board of Studies in History at the University of London in 1910, Laughton hoped that he might take on his quest to create a Department of Naval History and see it through to completion.[137] Although he did not do so, he served the field in another respect. As his tenure as chairman of the University of London Board of Studies in History drew to a close, he became the instrumental figure in the creation of the Institute of Historical

---

[134] Bucholz, *Hans Delbrück and the German Military Establishment*, pp. 132–4, 139–42.
[135] Ibid., p. xi.
[136] W. Robertson, *Soldiers and Statesmen, 1914–1918*, 2 vols. (London: Cassell, 1926), ii, p. 301.
[137] Lambert, *The Foundations of Naval History*, pp. 212–14.

Research, serving as director from its establishment in 1921 and then as honorary director from 1931 to 1939.[138] Under Pollard's leadership, the institute made the study of war one of its areas of specialization. A report of 1934 noted that since its foundation 'special provision' had been made 'for the study and teaching of war history'. This included allocating two seminar rooms, one for military studies and the other for naval studies, and the acquisition of a library, which incorporated part of Corbett's collection amongst others. Although no seminars had been established by that point, the report stressed that 'a certain amount of work has been done, especially upon those aspects of naval history which touch the fields of administration, merchant marine, and colonial development' and that a 'Julian Corbett Prize' in naval history had been created. These activities were seen as a useful preliminary to 'the ultimate establishment of seminars for the scientific study of war history in all its branches', which was 'among the objects to which the Institute Committee attaches great importance'.[139]

There was further activity at King's College London too. In 1927 the college established a Department of Military Studies, and hired Major General Sir Frederick Maurice to lead it.[140] Maurice had gained renown during the First World War as Director of Military Operations at the War Office, although his career had ended in controversy after he accused Prime Minister David Lloyd George of misleading parliament in 1918.[141] In 1925 Maurice Hankey, Cabinet Secretary during Lloyd George's ministry, used his influence on the board of electors to ensure that Maurice would not succeed Wilkinson as Chichele Professor at All Souls.[142] Rebuffed by Oxford, he joined King's two years later.

Maurice used his inaugural address, 'On the use of the study of war', to reflect on the relationship between past and present and on the significance of both military and civilian understanding of war as a historical phenomenon.

---

[138] J. E. Neale, 'Albert Frederick Pollard', *The English Historical Review*, Vol. 64, No. 251 (April 1949), pp. 201–2, 204.

[139] Archives of the Institute for Historical Research, London, IHR 9/3/5. Memoranda concerning the development of the range of IHR Library Collections and Seminars as part of the IHR Building Fund Appeal Committee, *c.* May 1934, 'War History at the Institute of Historical Research'. It is noteworthy that in the same report, of the fourteen fields of study addressed, just two concerned historical phenomena—war and imperial history. The other twelve fields were all either national or local areas of study.

[140] This move was not entirely without precedent. As far back as 1848 the college had established a department of 'military science' to deliver a course for officer cadets. That department, however, met with disapproval from 'the army authorities' who 'were not enthusiastic for a military training conducted, independently of themselves, by clergymen'. Student numbers quickly dwindled, and the department began a slow decline that ended with its final abolition in 1864. See, F. J. C. Hearnshaw, *The Centenary History of King's College London, 1828–1928* (London: G. G. Harrap & Co., 1929), pp. 176–8, 260.

[141] J. Gooch, 'The Maurice Debate 1918', *Journal of Contemporary History*, Vol. 3, No. 4 (October 1968), pp. 211–28. Maurice believed that Lloyd-George had misled parliament over the strength of the British army on the Western Front during the opening phase of the German spring offensive.

[142] Hattendorf, 'The Study of War History at Oxford', pp. 23–4. Strachan, 'The Study of War at Oxford', p. 211.

38   MAKING MAKERS

He contended that the Great War had imparted to his generation a visceral understanding that had escaped the older generation: 'that a struggle between nations in which vital interests are involved is not merely the concern of professional soldiers, sailors, and airmen, but affects every citizen, and calls for the whole resources of the nation'. Despite this realization, cogent arguments for the civilian study of war were still vital due to the reluctance of some to engage with the subject in the immediate aftermath of the conflict and the persistent sentiment that the establishment of a position such as Maurice's would be construed as 'promoting militarism, and as tending to mislead youth'.[143] Maurice believed, however, that it was civilian repudiation of the study of war, not military fervour, that posed the greater danger. 'Democracy ignorant of war is as apt to be a danger to peace as are the ambitions of autocratic rulers,' he argued:

> If war is the concern of the whole people, those who can guide public opinion must know war, for the valour of ignorance is not only as dangerous as is militarism, it is an even less certain foundation upon which to build those moral quantities which we know are of cardinal importance, if war comes.

Bitter memories would not be enough to safeguard future peace, so experience had to be backed 'by systematic study'.[144] These observations led Maurice to conclude that the utility of the study of war was twofold. First, it allowed for the promotion of peace through 'an understanding of the realities of war and of the problems which may lead to war'. Second, it ensured that 'war, if it comes, is waged in the best possible way'. Whilst he identified the first point predominantly with the citizen and the second point with the professional, neither could afford to be ignorant of the other. By establishing military studies in London it would be possible to encourage productive interaction between the two groups, since the capital offered 'both a great university and a great military centre, though the mass of the metropolis tends to conceal both from the view of the citizen'.[145]

Maurice's entreaty was in keeping with the ethos of the larger university of which King's formed a part. In the words of Elizabeth Fordham, the University of London 'had from its inception taken pride in its capacity to provide "useful" education, and seen its academic role as one of expanding higher education to meet contemporary needs'. The war had served to enhance its intellectual prestige in this regard, confirming 'its leadership in several fields of modern education including modern languages, the social sciences, engineering, and many areas of the natural sciences'.[146] The study of war itself formed part of this legacy.

---

[143] LHCMA, LH 3/6/19, Prof. Sir Frederick Maurice, KCMG, LL.D (Camb.), 'On the use of the study of war', inaugural lecture to the Department of Military Studies, delivered Friday 14 January 1927.
[144] Ibid.   [145] Ibid.
[146] E. Fordham, 'Universities', in J. M. Winter and J.-L. Robert (eds.), *Capital Cities at War: Paris, London, Berlin 1914–1919*, Vol 2: *A Cultural History* (Cambridge: Cambridge University Press, 2007), p. 275.

WAR, HISTORY, AND THE CONTEXT OF *MAKERS*   39

Besides King's, University College also made an appointment in military history in the same period, hiring Major General Sir George Aston as 'Lecturer on Military History'.[147] Aston served as the driving force in arranging a series of lectures through the Military Education Committee of the University of London for the 1925–6 academic year, which focused variously on sea, land, air, economic, and chemical warfare, and were delivered by practitioner-scholars such as Sir Herbert Richmond, Sir Edmund Ironside, and Robert Brooke-Popham.[148] In his own lecture, on 'The Study of War', Aston admitted that the subjects addressed reflected only a fraction of what they might, since 'the subject of war is too vast, and too full of complications'. Nevertheless, they responded to the need to speak to war for 'statesmen and citizens' so that 'with greater knowledge will come greater sympathy between the British people and the members of their fighting services, whose business it is to carry out behests, and if need be to sacrifice life or health in the cause of the nation'.[149] Like Maurice, he emphasized the peaceful potential of such developments, noting that 'the strongest anti-militarists are to be found amongst those who are best acquainted with the reality of war, and the abolition of war between nations is more likely to be furthered by knowledge than by ignorance of its realities'.[150] He spoke with enthusiasm about the creation of a 'School of War Studies' within the University of London and the establishment of war studies as an examinable subject for the pass degree.[151]

In the event Aston's and Maurice's rhetoric did not quite translate into reality. Although Maurice continued a course for undergraduates into the 1930s, in 1938 he left to become the Principal of Queen Mary College, and by the Second World War the department appeared to have reverted to military instruction.[152] Efforts elsewhere in the university appeared to falter sooner. Nevertheless, Maurice in particular planted the seeds that Michael Howard would cultivate to establish the Department of War Studies, in what was more an evolution than a revolution in the field, while Aston's advocacy of 'War Studies' presaged even the terminology that Howard would adopt.[153] If the results of that process were felt most keenly after 1945, even in the short term the establishment of such an entity as a military studies department suggested a degree of departure from pre-1914 approaches. Although Maurice was clear that history should form the bedrock, 'military studies'

---

[147] Aston was a Royal Marine. Prior to the First World War he taught at both the Royal Naval College and the Staff College, Camberley. See J. Beach, 'The British Army, the Royal Navy, and the "Big Work" of Sir George Aston, 1904–1914', *The Journal of Strategic Studies*, Vol. 29, No. 1 (February 2006), pp. 145–68.

[148] The lectures were brought together in a volume published in the following decade, G. Aston (ed.), *The Study of War for Statesmen and Citizens* (London: Longmans, Green & Co, 1933). The collection omitted the lecture on economic warfare and added two more essays.

[149] G. Aston, 'The Study of War', in Aston (ed.), *The Study of War*, pp. 6–7.

[150] Ibid., pp. 7–8.   [151] Ibid., pp. viii, 10.

[152] Strachan, 'The Study of War at Oxford', p. 211.

[153] See D. Morgan-Owen and M. Finch, 'The Unrepentant Historian: Sir Michael Howard and the Birth of War Studies', *The British Journal of Military History*, Vol. 8, No. 2 (September 2022), pp. 55–76.

40 MAKING MAKERS

presented a more expansive rubric under which war could be scrutinized, one which was better positioned to encompass multiple disciplines than military or naval history, even when the latter were pitched in terms of broad historical scrutiny.[154] It was not surprising, then, that when Earle came to describe the activities of his group at the Institute for Advanced Studies in the 1930s and early 1940s he frequently deployed 'military studies' as a heading.

The emergence of 'military studies' was thus indicative of the broader, and often collective, scholarly engagement with war which had been made unavoidable by the experience of the First World War.[155] Much of that engagement, it should be noted, did not constitute an embrace of war itself so much as investigation of the 'problem' of war and the pressing need to avoid a future cataclysm. Organizations such as the Royal Institute of International Affairs (1920), and endowed chairs such as the Stevenson Professorship in International History at the London School of Economics (1926) and the Woodrow Wilson Professorship in International Politics at the University of Aberystwyth (1919), looked explicitly towards the preservation of peace.[156] This could not be achieved, however, without acknowledging either the spectre of a new war or the profound effects of the last one. As E. H. Carr recognized in *The Twenty Years' Crisis*, written during his tenure as Woodrow Wilson Professor, 'the war of 1914–18 made an end of the view that war is a matter which affects only professional soldiers and, in so doing, dissipated the corresponding impression that international politics could safely be left in the hands of professional diplomats'.[157]

The most ambitious and sustained scholarly engagement with the problem of war itself, however, was carried out in the United States. In 1926, Quincy Wright, a Professor of Political Science at the University of Chicago, began a seven-year interdisciplinary project on war which saw him co-ordinate twenty-five research assistants working on sixty-six studies, forty-five of which became masters or doctoral dissertations, with a further ten becoming published books.[158] As Fred

---

[154] In its earliest guise, at least, post-war 'war studies' put the same agenda under a more appropriate title.

[155] On the significance of such collective efforts in the birth of strategic studies see J. Michaels and M. Ford, 'Grand Strategy or Grant Strategy? Philanthropic Foundations, Strategic Studies and the American Academy', *Journal of Strategic Studies*, Vol. 46, No. 4 (2023), pp. 769–70.

[156] On the Stevenson chair see D. Stevenson, 'Learning from the Past: The Relevance of International History', *International Affairs*, Vol. 90, No. 1 (2014), pp. 5–22.

[157] E. H. Carr, *The Twenty Years' Crisis, 1919–1939*, reissued with a new preface from Michael Cox (London: Palgrave Macmillan, 2016), p. 3. For an assessment of Carr's thought within the tradition of realist thought in international relations see S. Molloy, *The Hidden History of Realism: A Genealogy of Power Politics* (London: Palgrave Macmillan, 2006), pp. 51–74.

[158] F. Blazich, Jr., *Fifty Years of Interdisciplinary Scholarship: A Brief History of the Triangle Institute for Security Studies* (February 2009), http://tiss-nc.org/wp-content/uploads/2014/08/Final-TISS-Complete-History-24-February-2009.pdf, pp. 39–41. In the 1990s the Triangle Universities Security Seminar—of which Theodore Ropp was a founder (see Chapter 3), undertook an ambitious new attempt to produce an updated 'study of war', hosting ten workshops (covering anthropology, biological sciences, economics, sociology, law, history, psychology, literature, philosophy, religion,

Kaplan notes, 'the very existence of such a project at a major American university was astonishing. Even at Chicago, there were, as late as the mid-1930s, professors of international relations who would not allow war to be discussed in class because its very mention as a serious topic [...] implied that war might not be illegal'.[159] Yet whilst Wright's project was exceptional in its scale and scope, it demonstrated that there existed sufficient interest for it to be undertaken, and backing enough for it to succeed.

Moreover, Wright's project not only gave rise to a plethora of published and unpublished scholarship across a range of disciplines, it also laid the groundwork for his own two-volume work *A Study of War*, which summarized the findings of the project in a coherent form. For Wright, *A Study of War* was undertaken in the service of war's prevention, motivated by the belief that 'continuous thought and study, closely integrated with practical effort by our own and successive generations, is the price that must be paid for a less violent world'.[160] It was a sad irony that by the time the volumes were published in 1942, another global war had broken out and recently ensnarled the United States. This did not dissuade Wright from the pursuit of his goal, however; rather he became more convinced 'that the problem of preventing war is one of increasing importance in our civilization and that the problem is essentially one of maintaining adaptive stability within the world-community, only possible if larger sections of the public persistently view that community as a whole'.[161]

Wright's book, and by extension his broader project, did not entirely exclude the conduct of war.[162] Nevertheless, its legacy was allied to the rejection of the institution. Indeed, Wright's stature as the 'father of peace studies' was such that after his death in 1970 former students and colleagues nominated him for a Nobel Peace Prize.[163] In his preface to the second edition of 1965, Karl Deutsch compared *A Study of War* to Grotius's *On the Law of War and Peace* (1625) to suggest that 'as Grotius' book became a basis for the study of what later became known as "international law," so Quincy Wright's book marks the beginning of much that nowadays has become known as "peace research".'[164] Similarly, William T. R. Fox, who worked as a research assistant to Wright, reflected that the book was 'not a work on strategy, not a handbook on the efficient use of violence for any national

---

linguistics, conflict resolution, and political science) followed by a plenary conference, as a preliminary for a possible ten-year project. The larger project was not pursued, however.

[159] F. Kaplan, *The Wizards of Armageddon* (Stanford, CA: Stanford University Press, 1991), p. 13.

[160] Q. Wright, *A Study of War*, 2 vols. (Chicago, IL: University of Chicago Press, 1942), i, p. ix.

[161] Ibid., i, p. viii.

[162] Chapter 12, for example, dealt with the 'Technique of Modern War' in some detail. Ibid., i, pp. 291–328.

[163] A. Whiting, 'In Memoriam: Quincy Wright, 1890–1970—A Symposium', *Journal of Conflict Resolution*, Vol. 14, No. 4 (December 1970), pp. 445–6. He was not awarded a prize.

[164] K. Deutsch, 'Quincy Wright's Contribution to the Study of War: A Preface to the Second Edition', *Journal of Conflict Resolution*, Vol. 14, No. 4 (December 1970), p. 474.

purpose, not even a purely defensive purpose. [...] *A Study of War* is the benchmark by which international progress in research on peace and international order, whether or not carried on under the banner of "peace research," is to be measured in the second half of the twentieth century.[165]

Yet whilst Fox was keen to assert that 'the precursor of the multitudinous post-World War II strategic studies must be found elsewhere'—indeed, with *Makers of Modern Strategy*—both studies grew from a basic commitment to the importance of understanding war.[166] Nor were the personnel involved in Wright's and Earle's activities entirely distinct from one another. Fox, for one, became a member of Earle's IAS seminar in 1941–2, shortly after working for Wright. Even more significantly, Bernard Brodie, who joined Earle's seminar in 1940 and would go on to play an important role in Earle's considerations for possible revisions to *Makers*, had not only worked as an assistant to Wright, but was his 'star student'. According to Kaplan, when Brodie entered the job market in 1940, 'Wright sent well over a dozen letters to acquaintances in top-notch colleges across the country advertising "an A-number-one man, Bernard Brodie"'.[167] That the father of peace studies could heartily endorse a figure so central to strategic studies underlines how far the roots of such endeavours were intertwined.

Nor was it the case that Earle was alone in drawing an expansive understanding of strategy from contemporary international affairs and the position of the USA in world geopolitics.[168] Perhaps his nearest contemporary in this respect was Nicholas Spykman. Spykman, Sterling Professor of International Relations at Yale University, was born in Amsterdam in 1893, and studied at the University of California, Berkeley, where he gained a PhD in 1923. He became a US citizen five years later. In 1942, a year before his death from cancer at the age of forty-nine, he published *America's Strategy in World Politics*, the fruits of scholarship begun in the late 1930s, which made a case for the centrality of power politics, allied to geographical considerations, in governing American strategic action.[169] 'If the foreign policy of a state is to be practical', he explained:

> it should be designed not in terms of some dream world but in terms of the realities of international relations, in terms of power politics. [...] States exist [...] primarily in terms of their own strength or that of their protector states and, if they wish to maintain their independence, they must make the preservation or improvement of their power position the principal object of foreign policy. Nations which renounce the power struggle and deliberately choose

---

[165] W. Fox, '"The Truth Shall Make You Free": One Student's Appreciation of Quincy Wright', *Journal of Conflict Resolution*, Vol. 14, No. 4 (December 1970), pp. 450–1.

[166] Ibid., p. 451.   [167] Kaplan, *Wizards*, p. 14.

[168] For a detailed assessment of Earle's conception of strategy, see Chapter 5.

[169] On Spykman see C. Gray, 'Nicholas John Spykman, the Balance of Power, and International Order', *The Journal of Strategic Studies*, Vol. 38, No. 6 (2015), pp. 873–97.

WAR, HISTORY, AND THE CONTEXT OF *MAKERS* 43

impotence will cease to influence international relations either for evil or for good and risk eventual absorption by more powerful neighbors.[170]

Spykman's vision was thus far removed from Quincy Wright's hope that war might be understood to be eradicated: power politics led to a zero-sum path. It also bred a degree of scepticism in Earle, who contended that 'the strategy which Mr Spykman recommends [...] would cause us to lose both our shirts and our souls'.[171] If Earle and Spykman disagreed over the guiding tenets, however, a certain concordance existed with regard to their understanding of strategy. Just as Earle would push strategy beyond the realm of war, so Spykman elucidated that 'it is the geographic location of a country and its relation to centers of military power that define its problem of security. [...] In terms of that location, it must conduct its military strategy in war time, and in terms of that location, it should conduct its political strategy in peace time.'[172] If war thrust itself upon all, so too—for men like Earle and Spykman at least—did strategy.

Conclusion

In 1939 Sir Charles Oman published *On the Writing of History*, in which he included 'A Plea for Military History'. Reflecting on the argument that war should not form a part of historical study, he insisted that:

'What touches all is the business of all', and it is no more right to hand over the study of military history to professional soldiers alone, than it would be to permit no one but lawyers to touch constitutional history, or no one but business men [sic] and manufacturers and trade union leaders to study economic history.[173]

That he was moved to put the matter in such terms on the cusp of the Second World War spoke to the persistence of the detractors. It is hard to deny that a liberal aversion to the study of war did exist within the university, which was at times fostered in opposition to those who sought to further it. Nor is surprising to

---

[170] N. Spykman, *America's Strategy in World Politics: The United States and the Balance of Power* (New Haven, CT: Yale University, Institute of International Studies, 1942), p. 446.

[171] E. M. Earle, 'Power Politics and American World Policy', *Political Science Quarterly*, Vol. 58, No. 1 (March 1943), p. 102. Spykman's work was met with a fair degree of criticism from his peers. Colin Gray accredits this, along with his untimely death, with ensuring that Spykman's reputation declined after 1943, and he charges that Earle was the 'the most obvious scholarly villain' amongst the 'big names with relatively closed minds' who 'sought to murder his fame in 1942 and 1943' by way of critical reviews. Gray, 'Nicholas John Spykman', pp. 879–80, 892. In fact, Earle's review of Spykman's work is more balanced, and cautiously complimentary, than Gray suggests.

[172] Spykman, *America's Strategy in World Politics*, p. 447. Spykman also distinguished 'peace strategy' and 'war strategy', p. 6.

[173] C. Oman, *On the Writing of History* (London: Routledge, 1939), p. 172.

44   MAKING MAKERS

note that by the mid-twentieth century those in favour of the study of war appeared pre-emptively defensive on the matter. Thus in 1955 Norman Gibbs, another of Wilkinson's successors as Chichele Professor of the History of War, remarked that 'in our universities the tradition is well established that history stops on the day that wars break out and begins again with the signing of peace. What happens in between is a no-man's-land, fit for exploration by teachers and students at staff colleges, but not by respectable historians.'[174] It is equally apparent, however, that in the first decades of the twentieth century military opposition to such study could be just as pernicious, promoting the idea that only those who had served in arms possessed the requisite technical knowledge to truly understand it, especially in its most contemporary guises.

Yet Oman's words also underlined the persistence of the riposte. As this chapter has shown, even at the outset of the century the study of war aroused interest amongst professional historians, and such interest only grew with the passage of time and the development of modern 'scientific' scholarship which opened up multiple avenues for historical investigation beyond the political and constitutional. Indeed, it is possible to glimpse in the first decades of the twentieth century the initial, albeit halting, steps in a process of civilianization, whereby academics from outside the military sought to understand war and advocate for civilian understanding in turn, contributing towards a gradual legitimization which would become harder for scholar-opponents or military professionals to deny. And it was a process undergirded by the experience of war. Before the Second World War lent power and urgency to Earle's argument, perceptive observers linked the development of the character of war to the necessity of civilian understanding, arguing that the growth in the scale and scope of war gave rise to an increasing civilian stake in it, and a responsibility in its conduct. This was markedly so after the First World War. If that war had given currency to Clemenceau's aphorism that 'war is too important to be left to the generals', the consequences were not only practical. They were also intellectual.

Edward Mead Earle was acquainted with Charles Oman. The two had met when he visited All Souls College in 1938 as part of a professional tour of Europe. He would also come to know Sir Herbert Richmond shortly before the latter's death in 1946. A number of Earle's German collaborators, meanwhile, had indirect links to Hans Delbrück. If Delbrück left no followers in Germany after his death, his influence certainly found its way to *Makers* through the connection. As will be seen in the next chapter, Earle followed his own particular trajectory. This led him towards arguments which bore many similarities to those made by such

---

[174] LHCMA LH 1/312/19, N. Gibbs, 'War & Society', a lecture to the King's College London, Department of History, 4 February 1955. Appended to Gibbs to Liddell-Hart, 3 March 1955. Ironically, Gibbs's critical observations masked a positive development, since his lecture was intended to mark the creation of the War Studies department.

predecessors, whether this was his concern for the risks of public ignorance of war, his conviction that the scholar rather than the officer was best placed to reflect on the past conduct of war, or his advocacy of thinking about the past for the purpose of the present. Although it should not be inferred from this chapter that Earle, or the project that he led, offered an inevitable progression of earlier arguments, it is equally important to stress that he was part of a transatlantic academic community, that he was aware of the work of many of his contemporaries and forebears, and that in some cases—such as with Oman—he had direct links to them.[175] Indeed, it is worth emphasizing the important place that Oxford University, and All Souls College in particular, held for Earle. Despite the fact that he described his group at the IAS as functioning as something like a *centre d'études militaires*, and the importance of French and, especially, German influences in giving form and content to *Makers*, it was the Oxford college to which he was a pre- and post-war visitor which provided much of his mental model. It should not be surprising, then, that Earle appears less of a revolutionary figure when his work is set in the context of earlier efforts to engage with the scholarly study of war. In scrutinizing what came before *Makers* it becomes clearer that bringing the study of war closer to the mainstream of academic work relied on a constellation of individuals, institutions, ideas, and events. For those considered in this chapter, shortcomings in at least one area proved sufficient to stymie plans or inhibit growth. It was Earle's good fortune to bring the first three aspects together in light of the exigencies of the fourth, although even his project had very finite limitations.

Making Makers: The Past, the Present, and the Study of War. Michael P. M. Finch, Oxford University Press.
© Michael P. M. Finch 2024. DOI: 10.1093/9780191959257.003.0002

---

[175] For the pitfalls of the former position see Q. Skinner, 'Meaning and Understanding in the History of Ideas', *History and Theory*, Vol. 8, No. 1 (January 1969), pp. 3–53.

2

Making *Makers*

Edward Mead Earle, the Institute for Advanced Study, and the Second World War

The middle of a great war is not the best time for an accurate assessment of currents of thought—especially the later currents.
—Basil Liddell Hart, 1946[1]

Nestled at the bottom of the second page of Peter Paret's *Makers of Modern Strategy from Machiavelli to the Nuclear Age*—before the title page, copyright information, and the table of contents—there is a sentence acknowledging the co-operation of the Institute for Advanced Study in bringing the new edition through to publication. The older edition, it explains, 'originated in a seminar in American foreign policy and security issues at the Institute and Princeton University in 1941'.[2] The inclusion of this statement—itself the product of a negotiation between the editors, publishers, and the institute, rather than a spontaneous act of acknowledgement—compounded a narrative established shortly after the publication of Edward Mead Earle's *Makers of Modern Strategy*, and held to in subsequent decades. In his editor's note to the 1943 edition, Earle wrote that the volume 'originated in the discussions of the seminar in military affairs of the Institute for Advanced Study and Princeton University about eighteen months ago'.[3] The Princeton University Press further reinforced this impression, marketing *Makers* as a 'distinguished symposium by twenty leading historians and analysts [...] an outgrowth of the famous seminar on military affairs conducted at the Institute for Advanced Studies in Princeton' (see Figure 2.1).[4] Early reviewers, meanwhile, tended to pick up on this in framing their critiques. A review in *The Oxford Magazine* described the book as 'a product of the activity of the seminar on military affairs which the editor has for some time past been conducting at the

---

[1] LHCMA, LH 1/255/6, Liddell Hart to Earle, 24 April 1946.

[2] P. Paret, *Makers of Modern Strategy: From Machiavelli to the Nuclear Age* (Princeton, NJ: Princeton University Press, 1986), p. ii.

[3] E. M. Earle, *Makers of Modern Strategy: From Machiavelli to Hitler* (Princeton, NJ: Princeton University Press, 1943), p. 519.

[4] MLP, Earle Papers MC020/Box 36/Makers of Modern Strategy 1943–5 [3 of 5]. Advertisement for *Makers of Modern Strategy*, 21 October 1943.

Figure 2.1 Princeton University Press advertisement for *Makers of Modern Strategy*.
Source: Mudd Manuscript Library, Edward Mead Earle Papers, MC020 Box 36 Writings: Correspondence and Related Materials, Folder: Books—Makers of Modern Strategy1943–1945 [3 of 5]. Advertisement for *Makers of Modern Strategy*, 21 October 1943.

institute for Advanced Study at Princeton'.[5] In the *VA. Quarterly Review* it was noted as 'one of the by-products of the seminar on military affairs which Edwin [sic] Mead Earle has been conducting at the Institute for Advanced Study these

---

[5] MLP, Earle Papers, MC020/Box 36/Makers of Modern Strategy 1943–5 [3 of 5]. Review in *The Oxford Magazine*, 15 November 1943.

48 MAKING MAKERS

past few years'.[6] In this manner, the idea of the volume as a direct product of the seminar quickly acquired orthodoxy.

This notion, which succinctly conveys the image of a group of academics working to singular purpose, does not offer a wholly accurate representation of the circumstances and the manner in which *Makers of Modern Strategy* was created. As this chapter shows, the reality was more convoluted. Earle's *Makers* was the product of a hybrid process, involving a core set of individuals working across the IAS and Princeton University, and a secondary group of invited contributors working further afield. Those in the latter category had little or no connection to the work of Earle's group at the institute, and were charged with the production of specific contributions. Those in the former group, meanwhile, were more central to Earle's IAS projects, but they brought their own qualities to bear on the *Makers* volume in specific ways: their relative youth, and the non-American perspectives of immigrant academics, French and German in particular. These influences, coupled with the impact of writing, compiling, and editing in the midst of the growing US commitment to the Second World War, combined to produce a volume which spoke to important needs of the moment, whilst also seeking to investigate war in broader terms. In this manner, the idea that *Makers* 'was very much an expression of the seminar' needs to be qualified.[7]

This is important not only for understanding *Makers* as a volume, and as part of the broader chronology by which it was made and remade, but also for understanding its editor, Edward Mead Earle. Until recently, Earle cut a rather obscure figure: significant enough to have a lane named for him in the environs of the IAS, adjacent to Einstein Drive and close by streets honouring Robert Oppenheimer and the institute founder, Abraham Flexner, but not so much that his broader projects and intellectual contributions were well remembered or documented. Recent work by David Ekbladh and Dexter Fergie has done much to rectify this, emphasizing the role of Earle's projects before and during the Second World War in providing the foundation of post-war security studies and transforming the American national security imagination respectively.[8] Ekbladh, in particular, has advanced Earle as a forgotten founder of security studies in the

---

[6] MLP, Earle Papers, MC020/Box 36/Makers of Modern Strategy 1943–5 [3 of 5]. Review in *VA. Quarterly Review*, spring 1944. Stuart Portner's review in *Military Affairs* was a lone voice in offering more clarity: 'For the most part these students are men and women who attended Dr. Earle's seminar courses at the Institute of Advanced Studies at Princeton, but the volume is not exclusively their product.' Review in *Military Affairs*, spring 1944.

[7] D. Ekbladh, 'Present at the Creation: Edward Mead Earle and the Depression-Era Origins of Security Studies', *International Security*, Vol. 36, No. 3 (winter 2011–12), p. 130.

[8] Ekbladh, 'Present at the Creation', D. Fergie, 'Geopolitics Turned Inwards: The Princeton Military Studies Group and the National Security Imagination', *Diplomatic History*, Vol. 43, No. 4 (September 2019), pp. 644–70. See also A. Rabinbach, 'The Making of Makers of Modern Strategy: German Refugee Historians Go to War', *The Princeton University Library Chronicle*, Vol. 75, No. 1 (autumn 2013), pp. 97–108.

mid-twentieth-century United States of America. Challenging an established narrative which considered the emergence of security studies as a response to the dawn of the Cold War and the nuclear age, he relocates the birth of the field as a product of the international tumult of the 1930s, casting Earle as the key figurehead and visionary. Following Earle's career path through the 1930s and into the Second World War, the IAS professor emerges as an early and ardent advocate for the end of US isolationism and of the need for a proactive approach to global security, spurred on in his foresight by his twin preoccupations: the effects of the Great Depression and the rise of totalitarian states. Since the latter saw little distinction between states of war and peace, liberal democracies such as the United States could ill afford to ignore questions of strategy and security or leave them to the military establishment. Rather, an opportunity presented itself to bring scholarship on war and strategy into the academic mainstream, and for such scholarship to exert influence over policy makers and public opinion.[9]

In this manner, recent scholarship has helped ensure that Earle no longer remains simply the unknown editor of a well-known volume. At the same time, it configures Earle's efforts and the work of those drawn into the informal nexus he created around his seminar as a form of proto-security studies, the assemblage of a field in all but name. Although Ekbladh is sensitive to Earle's intellectual development, noting that he 'was no Zeus with the Athena of security studies springing fully formed from his head', his analysis is predicated on Earle's seemingly inexorable march towards security studies, since the 'chronic instability of the 1930s exposed the pathologies of the modern world and demanded that a new field of security studies be made a permanent innovation to allow the United States to contend with perpetual threats'.[10] Yet just as scholars seeking to historicize the origins of international relations as a discipline have debated whether or not the First Great Debate ever actually occurred, so we must consider whether Earle the historian ever really departed from his identity as a historian.[11] It is the contention of this chapter that he did not.

Michael Cox's observation that the existence of a great debate depends 'in part [on] whether different writers at the time were ever quite as conscious of their defined positions as later interpreters have suggested' finds an echo in Earle's

---

[9] Ekbladh, 'Present at the Creation', pp. 107–41. For the established narrative of the birth of security studies see, for example, S. Walt, 'The Renaissance of Security Studies', *International Studies Quarterly*, Vol. 35, No. 2 (June 1991), pp. 213–14. B. Buzan and L. Hansen, *The Evolution of International Security Studies* (Cambridge: Cambridge University Press, 2009), pp. 66–8.

[10] Ekbladh, 'Present at the Creation', p. 108.

[11] The First Great Debate was supposed to have pitted realists against idealists over the publication of E. H. Carr's *The Twenty Years' Crisis*. See B. Schmidt (ed.), *International Relations and the First Great Debate* (London and New York: Routledge, 2012), P. Wilson, 'The Myth of the "First Great Debate"', *Review of International Studies*, Vol. 24, No. 5 (December 1998), pp. 1–16. L. Ashworth, 'Did the Realist-Idealist Great Debate Really Happen? A Revisionist History of International Relations', *International Relations*, Vol. 16, No. 1 (April 2002), pp. 33–51.

50 MAKING MAKERS

position between history, security studies, and indeed strategic studies.[12] There is no doubting Earle's conviction that, as he wrote to Sir Charles Oman in 1944, 'the bitter lessons of the last twenty-five years will awaken students of politics to the fact that military strategy is an inherent part of statecraft and can be ignored only at our dire peril'.[13] Yet this increasing awareness of the exigencies of the present did not mean that Earle the scholar ever moved away from historical study. As we have seen in the previous chapter, the idea and significance of historical engagement that linked past to present had been established in the first decades of the twentieth century. By focusing here on the development and compilation of *Makers of Modern Strategy*, we gain a greater appreciation for Earle the historian, whose avowedly historical approach was key to the scrutiny of contemporary problems. Earle's collaborators, too, were for the most part historians, who brought their training to bear on the study of war, even if it sometimes meant moving into areas outside their comfort zones. In producing *Makers*, Earle was attempting to assemble a volume which could be used as a historical lens through which to better understand the demands of the war then in train, driven by the conviction that the expansion of war and strategy beyond the application of military force had brought the global war into the lives of all citizens. Moreover, since Earle considered that strategy had become an inherent part of statecraft, as apparent in peacetime as it was in wartime, greater civilian engagement with war was now crucial, both in terms of public exposure to debates on war and civilian academic involvement in the same. In this sense, those contributing to *Makers*, whilst not the first civilian academics to concern themselves with the study of war, were nonetheless important in further legitimizing the civilian study of war and strategy into the second half of the twentieth century.

Equally, in terms of the broader *Makers* project, Earle and his team were—albeit unbeknownst to themselves—setting important precedents for those whose professional careers would see them interact with the project in decades to come. In this sense, bringing the historical mode of scrutiny to the challenges of war would become an important element in understanding the genesis of the book beyond the Second World War, both in terms of the relationship between past and present and what the history of war encompassed and excluded. As the first editor of *Makers*, Earle himself would serve as the first in a line of individuals who would grapple with such challenges in the context of attempting to remake and reshape the work. As the final part of this chapter demonstrates, those challenges became increasingly insurmountable for Earle as he turned his attention towards a revised second edition, motivated by the realization that some of the chapters which were most explicitly rooted in contemporary concerns and developments

---

[12] M. Cox 'Foreword', in Schmidt (ed.), *International Relations*, p. xiv.
[13] MLP, Earle Papers, MC020/Box 36/Makers of Modern Strategy 1943 [2 of 5], Earle to Oman, 4 January 1944.

would not stand the test of time, even in the shortest of terms. Earle, then, was the first to succeed in making *Makers* as well as the first to fail in revising it.

An Oddity in the School of Economics

When Edward Mead Earle was first offered employment at the Institute for Advanced Study he was not an eminent historian, he was not appointed to a post within the school of historical studies, and he was not even well enough to take up the post immediately. In overcoming these potential obstacles, he owed a great deal to his friendship with the institute's founding director, Abraham Flexner, and the nascent state of the institute that the latter was in the process of creating.

Over the course of a career spanning half a century, Flexner (see Figure 2.2) forged a unique path as both a critic and an innovator in American education. After founding and running an innovative school in Louisville, Kentucky in 1892, he would go on to undertake important commissioned work for the Carnegie

Figure 2.2 Abraham Flexner, c.1943. As the foundational director of the Institute for Advanced Study, Flexner was a crucial figure in bringing Earle to Princeton.
Source: Shelby White and Leon Levy Archives Center, Institute for Advanced Study, Princeton, NJ, USA. Photograph collection—Trustees—Directors—Flexner Abraham [Marie Eichelser] folder.

52 MAKING MAKERS

Foundation for the Advancement of Teaching, which would lead in turn to a place on the General Education Board of the Rockefeller Foundation, which he held between 1912 and 1928. During this time Flexner earned his reputation with the production a series of surveys, particularly in the field of medical education, which garnered international attention for their forthright and penetrating observations. By the late 1920s, with his departure from the Rockefeller Foundation, Flexner's critical gaze moved from medical education to the university system itself, which he made the subject of his Rhodes Lecture series delivered at Oxford University in 1928, as well as his book *Universities: American, English, German*, published two years later.[14] Although many of Flexner's views on education were long-held, now armed with a broader and deeper knowledge of the US education system and a comparative understanding of European systems, Flexner was able to articulate bolder criticisms.[15]

The American university, he believed, was not fit for purpose. It was a hybrid product of nineteenth-century developments, which created for the most part an unhappy fusion of training and employment-focused undergraduate colleges and advanced learning-oriented graduate schools. What was necessary for the 'modern university' to flourish was to separate the undergraduate college and the graduate school, so that the latter might become a true incubator of new knowledge. Flexner had initially thought that the Johns Hopkins University—the pioneering research university of the late nineteenth century and Flexner's *alma mater*—might become such a 'modern university', since at the time of his pronouncements its governing body was considering a proposal to scrap the first two years of college along with the bachelor's degree. To Flexner's mind, success in this endeavour would have been:

> a godsend to serious students, who will be enabled to work out their own salvation, free from all the academic red tape which a graduate school partially identified with a college cannot, perhaps, help employing; and it will be a paradise for creative scholars and scientists who—still teachers, to be sure—will be free of all parental responsibility for their students.[16]

Rather than witness Johns Hopkins create such a 'paradise', however, Flexner was able to work towards the realization of his own vision. At the time of writing his *Universities*, he was introduced to siblings Louis Bamburger and Caroline Bamburger Fuld. The pair had made a fortune from the department store in

---

[14] For a detailed account of Flexner's life and work see T. N. Bonner, *Iconoclast: Abraham Flexner and a Life in Learning* (Baltimore, MD: The Johns Hopkins University Press, 2002).

[15] For example, his belief in the superiority of small classes, personalized learning, and proactive teaching stretched back to his days running the Flexner School in Louisville, and would inform his philosophy of education regarding the IAS. Ibid., p. 36.

[16] A. Flexner, 'A Modern University', *Atlantic Monthly*, Vol. 136 (October 1925), p. 540.

MEAD EARLE, THE IAS, AND THE SECOND WORLD WAR 53

Newark, New Jersey which they had established in 1892 with business partners Louis M. Frank and Felix Fuld. Caroline, who had been married to Frank until his death in 1910, married Fuld three years later. After Fuld's death in 1929, the siblings sold their business to R. H. Macy and Company with the intention thereafter of devoting themselves to philanthropic causes.[17] Although they had originally hoped to focus their efforts on the city of Newark through the establishment of a medical school, Flexner was able to persuade them to make an initial $5 million bequest in 1930 to create a dedicated research establishment in Princeton.[18] The institute that resulted from this endowment represented a scaled-down version of Flexner's original vision of a small university, but this was a triumph for him nonetheless, since allowed him to put his ideas into practice. Nine years into the project, with three schools established and Fuld Hall—the institute's central building—newly opened, Flexner described it as 'a paradise for scholars who, like poets and musicians, have won the right to do as they please and who accomplish most when enabled to do so'.[19]

This idealistic picture masked the more taxing reality of Flexner's travails of the 1930s. When Flexner began working in earnest to create the IAS, he approached the task with the assumption that in creating an institution which freed exceptional scholars from the 'red tape' which bound them elsewhere—which included the formal demands of governing the institution as well as giving pastoral care to students—they would find little need or opportunity for political intrigue. In reality, his near decade as director was consistently marked by disputes and struggles between himself, the benefactors, and the academics, which encompassed all manner of issues relating to the staffing, building, and governance of the new institute. The global depression of the same decade added further complications, placing unforeseen limits on Bamburger and Bamburger Fuld's additional financial contributions, thereby creating a persistent element of uncertainty which compelled Flexner and his board to grow the institute in piecemeal fashion, establishing the three original constituent schools of the institute in a sequential fashion and staffing the institute ahead of the completion of its physical edifices.[20]

Flexner's experience of founding the first of these schools, the School of Mathematics, would have significant consequences for the two schools that followed, and so for the manner in which Earle was hired. In choosing to begin with mathematics, Flexner was able to create significant publicity for the fledgling

---

[17] B. Stern, 'A History of the Institute of Advanced Study' (unpublished mss, 1964), pp. 13–17. E. Shore, 'Carrie Bamberger Frank Fuld', *Jewish Women: A Comprehensive Historical Encyclopedia*, 27 February 2009. Jewish Women's Archive, accessed 27 July 2020, https://jwa.org/encyclopedia/article/fuld-carrie-bamberger-frank.

[18] Stern, 'A History of the Institute of Advanced Study', pp. 1–13, 44–72. Bonner, *Iconoclast*, pp. 233–240.

[19] A. Flexner, 'The Usefulness of Useless Knowledge', *Harper's Magazine*, No. 179 (June/November 1939), p. 552.

[20] Bonner, *Iconoclast*, pp. 239–40, 269–72.

54   MAKING MAKERS

institute by appointing established scholars on generous salaries. The announcement in October of a first tranche of hires that included the famous Nobel prize winner Albert Einstein, alongside Herman Weyl and Oswald Veblen, brought exactly the kind of attention Flexner desired.[21] Over the longer term, however, the mathematicians came to form a powerful bloc within the institute, whose numbers swelled with the arrival of temporary members, overseas visitors, and research assistants, reaching a high of fifty-eight in 1936.[22] Unsurprisingly, the faculty quickly outgrew the space allotted to them in Fine Hall, home to the Princeton University Mathematics department. Moreover, Flexner quickly came to realize that Veblen, in particular, was determined to act as a leading voice in pursuing his own interests, as well as those of the mathematicians and the wider faculty, in a manner that frequently set him at odds with the director. Almost from the moment of his appointment, Veblen emerged as Flexner's most consistent and formidable opponent.[23]

In light of these experiences, when the time came to create the School of Economics and Politics, Flexner resolved to follow a different approach. This time he would hire younger, less established scholars, who he believed would prove more inclined to focus their energies on their immediate research projects, rather than institute politics. At the same time, the turn towards lesser-known scholars was also a matter of necessity. Since financial support from the benefactors for the second and third schools was not as generous as it had been for mathematics, Flexner was unable to appoint scholars with the levels of salary that were sufficient to secure Einstein and Veblen.[24] Earle was a principal beneficiary of this development. As Flexner explained to him in October 1933, 'we cannot begin in economics and history with a group of seasoned and distinguished persons as we have begun in mathematics [...] we shall have to take younger men and give them opportunity to show what is in them'.[25]

For Earle, the prospect of joining the IAS was an opportunity too good to turn down. He may even have seen it as something of a last chance in academia. After graduating from Columbia University in 1917, Earle first joined the US Army and then took a banking job in New York at the war's end. In 1920 he decided to return to Columbia to further his studies, working as a lecturer whilst undertaking his PhD, which he completed in 1923.[26] The doctoral study that he researched formed the basis for his book *Turkey, the Great Powers, and the Bagdad Railway*, which was published to a warm reception the following year, and he subsequently rose to become full professor at Columbia by 1926. Soon after this, however, he was struck by a bout of tuberculous which compelled him to give up his job.[27]

---

[21] Ibid., pp. 249–50.   [22] Ibid., p. 256.   [23] Ibid., pp. 250–2, 272–5.
[24] Ibid., p. 269.   [25] Quoted in Stern, 'A History of the Institute of Advanced Study', p. 224.
[26] 'E. M. Earle Dead; Military Expert', *New York Times*, 25 June 1954.
[27] Stern, 'A History of the Institute of Advanced Study', p. 111.

It would be the first of multiple periods of illness which would beset him for the rest of his life. By the early 1930s he had returned to teaching, now at Barnard College in New York, but his health was still poor. These impediments had also taken their toll upon his research career, such that he had yet to produce another substantial work of historical scholarship.

When Flexner decided to hire Earle for the institute's second school, the younger man was also fortunate in one final respect. Although there was no prospect of establishing a School of Historical Studies at that time, the director had adopted an expansive view of economics, which could accommodate Earle the historian.[28] As such, Flexner made a case to the IAS board to hire Earle based on the credentials he had built as an economic historian thanks to his Baghdad railway book, to which Flexner could add a recommendation from the renowned historian Charles A. Beard, one of his key advisors during this period.[29] Although years later, Alfred Vagts contended that neither Beard nor Flexner was entirely happy with the choice of Earle, with Flexner concerned about the state of Earle's health and Beard convinced that 'no professors better qualified would at that time leave Columbia or Harvard jobs', these reservations were more likely a reflection of the broader approach taken towards hiring personnel after the experience with the School of Mathematics, rather than an indictment of Earle's scholarly credentials per se.[30] For Flexner, Earle was not a candidate of last resort. As early as May 1930 he made an unsuccessful attempt to involve him in the institute as a trustee.[31] Now confronted by the more realistic prospect of Earle joining as a faculty member, Flexner was able to address lingering doubts about his health by offering him an initial appointment on a one-year contract at half-pay, renewable subject to improvement in his condition. In late 1934, when positive reports were received from the sanatorium at which Earle was recuperating in Colorado Springs, Flexner moved to make his position permanent. This move proved to be premature, however, as soon after Earle suffered a relapse which would limit his involvement with the institute to a brief visit to the founders in the spring of 1936, before he took up his post in earnest in the autumn of 1937.[32]

Although Flexner continued to list Earle amongst the institute's 'publicists and economists' in public pronouncements, once engaged in a programme of study for the institute Earle's interests moved ever further away from that field of study.[33] In part, this was a consequence of the somewhat tenuous economic connections Flexner had drawn in justifying Earle's selection. Nevertheless, Earle's chosen

---

[28] The School of Historical Studies was created 1949 through the unification of the School of Economics and Politics and the School of Humanistic Studies, with Earle taking a leading role in the process. Stern, 'A History of the Institute of Advanced Study', pp. 660–1.

[29] Ibid., pp. 224–5.

[30] Vagts to Gilbert, 6 January 1970. Gilbert Papers, Box 8/A.Vagts, Hoover Institution Library & Archives (hereafter HI), Stanford, California.

[31] Stern, 'A History of the Institute of Advanced Study', pp. 111–12.

[32] Ibid., p. 224.   [33] Flexner, 'The Usefulness of Useless Knowledge', p. 550.

56 MAKING MAKERS

path was a source of chagrin to the older man, who had hoped that the secure birth he provided would convince Earle to commit to a focus on economics. Yet since Flexner had created in the institute the ultimate 'ivory tower' in which all members could do as they pleased, there was little he could do about it. Even in his attempts to corral Earle towards an economic programme he felt compelled to stress that only the professor could decide his future course. In late February 1938, for example, whilst emphasizing that developing the economic aspects of Earle's research questions would put him 'on the right track', and would go some way towards helping to 'make a unit of the School of Economics and Politics', he added that 'I do not want to dictate to you or to anybody else what he shall do...'.[34] It hardly helped matters that Earle was not the only professor within the school determined to chart his own course. None of Flexner's three principal appointments—Earle, David Mitrany, and Winfield Riefler—was a natural collaborator in economic research.[35] Indeed, as Beatrice Stern wrote, they were 'not only autonomous; they were actively disunited'.[36]

Through his own choices, Flexner had created the School of Economics and Politics as a fissiparous organization. This did not prevent the disappointment he felt with Earle opening up a rift between two men who had previously been firm friends. To make matters worse, in the summer of 1939 Earle colluded with Veblen in faculty machinations to force Flexner to stand down as director, serving, in Stern's words, as 'the tactician in the struggle' to Veblen's strategist.[37] With the success of those schemes, Earle attempted to maintain cordial relations. Flexner, who had done so much to resurrect Earle's career, found it harder to contain his bitterness. Shortly after Flexner announced his departure in September 1939, Earle wrote him a letter of effusive thanks. Flexner's reply carried a sharp rebuke. 'At great risk you were called to the Institute for the purpose of developing scholarship', he wrote:

> The ideas underlying the Institute and its relationship with Princeton University were never, and are not now, a part of your concern. What would happen to the Institute if sixteen men or more each felt himself free, in the babyhood of a new institution embodying a new ideal, to ventilate his views instead of concentrating on his subject? [...] All you need to know is that you were asked to join the Institute because of my confidence that, in cooperation with Princeton historians and publicists, you might add to the world's store of knowledge... You are here to advance scholarship and to conduct in good faith an educational experiment.[38]

---

[34] Quoted in Stern, 'A History of the Institute of Advanced Study', p. 252.
[35] Indeed, of the three, only Riefler was a true economist.
[36] Stern, 'A History of the Institute of Advanced Study', p. 251.
[37] Ibid., pp. 416–41. For the quote, p. 426. See also Bonner, *Iconoclast*, pp. 282–9.
[38] Quoted in Stern, 'A History of the Institute of Advanced Study', p. 425.

In time, Earle would contribute to the 'world store of knowledge', but not in the manner that Flexner, or perhaps even Earle himself, had imagined he would.

Earle against the Torrent

Flexner's allegation that Earle had capitalized on the 'babyhood of the institute' to meddle in internal politics contained an element of truth, but this was not the only and certainly not the most productive pursuit that he undertook at this time. With the staggered growth and gradual coalescence of activity around the IAS in the mid to late 1930s, Earle found himself endowed with a great deal of latitude in the conduct of his research. The agenda that he chose to pursue reflected this in the manner in which it departed from both his previous research and the IAS founder's vision. Whilst Flexner had originally conceived of the institute as a refuge for 'pure research' in which scholars would not be compelled to engage with the outside world, Earle found himself inexorably drawn to look outwards, rather than inwards.[39] In the first instance, as befitted a man whose health now seemed to be improving, this meant travel. During 1937–8, his first academic year fully engaged at the IAS, Earle once again spent little time in Princeton. Instead, he focused on reconnecting with old colleagues and forging new connections within the historical and broader academic community that he felt he had lost touch with during his prolonged illness. He also spent time at the Huntingdon Library in Pasadena, and subsequently made a trip to Europe.[40]

By the time he settled down to residency in Princeton, the substantive aspect of Earle's research had likewise taken a decidedly outward turn. For the rejuvenated Earle, the way ahead lay in tackling what he considered to be the most pressing issues of his time in the 'real world' of defence and security affairs as they related to American foreign relations. He considered that the rise of totalitarianism had created a fundamental challenge to the normal state of international relations, which sprang from the militarization of politics and society in totalitarian states. For such regimes, war represented 'both the supreme expression of human personality and the dominating consideration in all statecraft'.[41] As early as 1938 he argued that this state of affairs raised questions that could not be simply restricted to the internal affairs of those states. Rather, the external activities of such states had helped to ensure that 'war' itself had become a 'relative term'. With undeclared conflicts in progress between Nazi Germany, Austria, and Czechoslovakia, as well as between Japan and China, and with the scale of war preparations ever increasing, Earle was moved to ask whether 'peace exists in more than name'. 'In truth',

---

[39] Ibid., p. 252.   [40] Ibid., pp. 251–2.
[41] E. M. Earle, *Against This Torrent* (Princeton, NJ: Princeton University Press, 1941), p. 7.

58   MAKING MAKERS

he wrote, 'the world may now be said to be in various stages of mobilization for war, of which armed hostilities are merely the most aggravated form.'[42]

Arguments such as these put Earle at odds with the prevailing consensus within the United States in the late 1930s. Yet what Earle saw with more perspicacity than most was that the country could not afford to stand apart from the problem. Whereas in previous eras the geopolitical position of the USA had provided a shield that often appeared to render deep engagement with such problems in the service of military policy 'discretionary rather than imperative', in the climate of a looming global war this was no longer possible.[43] This did not mean that Earle advocated reciprocal activity that would inevitably lead to war. As he first engaged with these issues, he maintained hope that for the US at least, the possibility of averting conflict still remained.[44] The onset of open hostilities in Europe in 1939 and the eventual US entry into the conflict progressively dashed those hopes, yet they only served to deepen Earle's conviction in the strength of his diagnosis. At the most fundamental level, he carried the positions that he developed in the late 1930s—on the challenges of totalitarianism, the blurring of boundaries between war and peace, and the enlargement of war itself—into the Second World War unchanged.[45]

Just as he was confident in his diagnosis, Earle was also sure of his prescription. Whether in war or peace, what was necessary was a re-examination of the United States' 'whole policy of national defense in the light of historical traditions, the prevailing policies of other powers, and the basic elements in international relations'.[46] He was equally convinced that such an investigation was just as much a civilian responsibility as a military one, perhaps even more so. This was because, in line with the blurring of boundaries between the state of war and the state of peace, the reach of war and the scope of planning for war had now expanded far beyond what were considered its traditional confines. As he explained in 1940:

---

[42] E. M. Earle, *American Military Policy and National Security* (reprinted from *Political Science Quarterly*, Vol. 53, No. 1, March 1938) (New York: Academic of Political Science, 1938), p. 2.

[43] E. M. Earle, 'National Defense and Political Science', *Political Science Quarterly*, Vol. 55, No. 4 (December 1940), p. 495. Earle engaged with this issue in significant depth in *Against This Torrent*.

[44] Earle, *American Military Policy and National Security*, p. 4.

[45] An indication of the solidification of Earle's thought can be found in the repetition of particular ideas across pieces written in the period from 1938 through to the publication of *Makers*, which include verbatim or near verbatim duplication of passages. For example, Earle's consideration of war and peace in *American Military Policy and National Security* bears striking similarity to the discussion included in *Against This Torrent*. Similarly, passages from his argument about the importance of the layman in the analysis of military problems in 'National Defence and Political Science' are repeated in *Against This Torrent*. Likewise, the essence of the definition of strategy presented by Earle in his introduction to *Makers* can be found in 'National Defense and Political Science', in the passage 'Strategy is not merely a concept of war time but an inseparable element in statecraft at all times; as such it is a legitimate element in statecraft at all times; as such it is legitimate and, indeed, an unavoidable concern of the social scientist. Only a narrowly restricted terminology would define strategy as the science and art of military command.' See, Earle *American Military Policy and National Security*, p. 2. Earle, 'National Defence and Political Science', p. 483. Earle, *Against This Torrent*, pp. 8–9, 67. Earle, *Makers*, p. viii.

[46] Earle, *American Military Policy and National Security*, p. 4.

Figure 2.3 Edward Mead Earle being presented with the Presidential Medal for Merit by US Army Air Force General Carl A. Spaatz, 1946. U.S. Army Air Forces Photo.
Source: Shelby White and Leon Levy Archives Center, Institute for Advanced Study, Princeton, NJ, USA. Photograph collection—Faculty. Members SHS—Earle, Edward M.

No modern war can be waged without the national effort going far beyond the boundaries of technical military efficiency into almost every realm of civilian activity. The British and American officer of today is encouraged to widen his horizons of knowledge to include an understanding of social and economic questions. There is no reason, in turn, why the civilian should not bring military affairs, which so vitally affect the nation at large and even himself as an individual, into his purview.[47]

Contemporary circumstances did not merely suggest that civilians should engage in the problems of war, they compelled it. If within a democracy there was not 'the widest possible discussion of military problems, conducted on the highest possible plan' it would be impossible to 'formulate intelligent and practicable foreign policies or, for that matter, domestic policies'.[48] Moreover, Earle emphasized that scholars must play a special role with the civilian community of analysts.

[47] Earle, 'National Defence and Political Science', p. 483. [48] Ibid., p. 485.

60   MAKING MAKERS

'Only the scholar', he argued, 'is capable of maintaining a *continuous, objective and documented* study of the problem.' Through their engagement they might also create 'a vast reservoir of competence in the field' in the form of their students, 'the voters, teachers, reserve officers and statesmen of tomorrow', thereby expanding and sustaining a deeper understanding of conflict.[49]

Advocating such a course of action for scholars brought with it certain challenges, of which Earle was only too aware. For this reason, in his published writings of the period he underlined in strident terms the importance of a new approach to scholarly engagement. Political and social scientists, Earle contended, had hitherto exhibited wilful disengagement through their failure to undertake 'adequate systematic inquiry into the problems of defense and strategy'. This he saw as the continuation of a trend evident throughout the nineteenth century and into the near present whereby consideration of military affairs was 'left to soldiers writing for soldiers rather than civilians writing for civilians'.[50] It was wrong to consider that scholarly objectivity might be impossible to sustain in scrutinizing military affairs, even if they were 'closely bound up with powerful emotions' which were difficult to separate from 'patriotic or nationalistic bias'.[51] Similarly, scholarly flight from defence matters, informed by liberal democratic wariness of connections to 'imperialism, aggression, vested armament interests, political conservatism, and a potentially militarized society', did nothing to ameliorate those same problems. 'By abandoning the field to others', Earle affirmed, such academics 'solved none of the problems and resolved none of their fears'.[52] Only by addressing difficult, unsettling questions and by directing their findings towards influencing policy could scholars act in a manner which might bring resolution.

In making an appeal to scholars to devote their attention to the problems of war, and particularly to put aside liberal distaste for the subject matter in doing so, Earle both built on precedent and enunciated a broad line of argument that would come to be repeated with variations over subsequent decades, particularly by individuals connected with the *Makers* project. First, that war needed to be studied, no matter how repugnant an activity it might be considered, because it was 'a recurrent phenomenon which from time to time transcends all other human activity and assumes command of our lives, our fortunes and our destiny'.[53] Second, that war *could* be studied, because 'military problems do not dwell in the realm of the occult, the supra-temporal, or the recondite' and were 'susceptible of analysis, criticism and practical contributions'.[54] He made his appeal to a correspondingly broad community of academics, exhorting scholars as a whole to confront the problem, although his writings in the late 1930s and early 1940s

---

[49] Ibid., p. 494.   [50] Ibid., p. 487.

[51] E. M. Earle, 'National Defense: A Program of Studies', *The Journal of the American Military Institute*, Vol. 4, No. 4 (winter 1940), pp. 207–8.

[52] Earle, 'National Defence and Political Science', p. 487.

[53] Ibid., p. 481.   [54] Ibid., pp. 481, 483.

MEAD EARLE, THE IAS, AND THE SECOND WORLD WAR   61

laid particular emphasis on the responsibility of political and social scientists, rather than historians specifically.

Such developments in Earle's thinking might lead to the conclusion that by effectively relaunching his research career in conjunction with his appointment at the IAS Earle moved away from the study of history. There is a degree of truth in this notion. Evidently, the urgency of the present bred in Earle a desire to tackle contemporary problems. This appeared to lead him towards areas of study best described under the headings of 'security' or 'strategy'. Nevertheless, it is worth underlining the apparently porous qualities of the interdisciplinary environment that Earle inhabited. As previously noted, in joining the IAS Earle found himself occupying an important position at the foundation of a school of 'economics and politics' with loosely defined parameters. It is perhaps unsurprising, then, that when it came to describing the purview of his own research project he couched it under a variety of headings, encompassing 'American foreign relations', 'grand strategy', 'national security', 'defence and security affairs', 'military affairs', and 'military studies', without displaying much concern for defining and delineating them in disciplinary terms. In this respect, Earle's approach was more fluid than fixed.

Furthermore, despite the marked difference in the focus of his research, Earle's interest in contemporary affairs did not demand a fundamental departure from his historical approach. In terms of content, his research concerns of the 1930s were markedly different from those of his previous phase of research in the early 1920s, at which time empires and imperialism could be said to have been the unifying themes.[55] Yet his major research publication, *Turkey, the Great Powers, and the Baghdad Railway*, was both a work of international scope—incorporating Ottoman, German, Russian, British, French, Italian, and American perspectives— and an exercise in contemporary history. The latter point was especially significant given Earle's turn towards the present, since it distinguished him from those amongst his scholarly peers who considered that historical study should not extend to recent events, not least because of the likely absence of a sufficient archival base from which to draw upon.[56] Proximity to the present posed no such impediment for Earle, whose 1923 study considered developments in the Near East up to the year 1922.[57]

As Ekbladh notes, Earle's book can be understood—both for its international range and its conscious effort to integrate economic and social developments

---

[55] As well as his *Turkey, the Great Powers, and the Baghdad Railway* (New York: Macmillan, 1923), see also E. M. Earle, 'The Outlook for American Imperialism', *Annals of the American Academy of Political and Social Science*, Vol. 108 (July 1923), pp. 104–7. E. M. Earle, 'Problems of Eastern and Southeastern Europe', *Proceedings of the Academy of Political Science in the City of New York*, Vol. 12, No. 1 (July 1926), pp. 265–8.

[56] The establishment of the Stevenson Chair in International History at the University of London provides an illuminating illustration of this divergence in attitudes. See D. Stevenson, 'Learning from the Past: The Relevance of International History', *International Affairs*, Vol. 90, No. 1 (2014), pp. 5–11.

[57] See Earle, *Turkey, the Great Powers, and the Baghdad Railway*, especially pp. 314–50.

62 MAKING MAKERS

alongside political factors—as a product of the 'new history' which emanated from Columbia University during Earle's time engaged in undergraduate and graduate study.[58] Proponents of the 'new history' adhered to several key tenets, all of which found some echo in the approach to the study of war that Earle maintained through the 1930s and into the Second World War. First they contended, in the words of the chief spokesman for the movement and professor of history at Columbia from 1895 to 1919, James Harvey Robinson, that 'the historian [...] will aspire hereafter to find out not only exactly how things have been, but how they have come about'.[59] Casting themselves in contrast to the 'scientific' approach pioneered in the late nineteenth century, which sought to establish the empirical base that would lead to a full understanding of historical events in their own right, the new historians believed that history needed to play a useful role in the present. To that end, they believed that historical study should correspond to the needs of the moment. Equally, they reacted against the perceived narrowness of earlier historical enquiry, by embracing a broader purview encompassing economic and social developments, and looking towards mundane aspects of everyday life as well as higher-level political developments. They also embraced the work of the social sciences, whose engagement with the pressing concerns of the present had provided much of the stimulus for their own agenda, emphasizing that, in the words of John Higham, 'the special contribution of history lay not so much in its distinctive interest in the past, but rather in its ability to synthesize the results of more specialized sciences'.[60] In these respects, far from hindering his move towards contemporary issues, Earle's historical training provided a necessary foundation that aided him in particular ways: introducing a level of comfort in working with the social sciences, stressing the importance of taking a broad approach to the study of any issue, and, most important of all, emphasizing the importance of the past in thinking about the present.

The Seminar and the Book

With the broad contours of his research agenda established, and with financial limitations at the institute a perennial consideration, Earle searched for funding

---

[58] Ekbladh, 'Present at the Creation', pp. 112–14.

[59] J. H. Robinson, *The New History: Essays Illustrating the Modern Historical Outlook* (New York: Macmillan, 1932, first published 1912), p. 69. Robinson's book constitutes a manifesto for the new history, underlining Higham's characterization of the movement as 'a diffuse stimulus to action, a kind of yeast that worked for thirty years or more in an otherwise sluggish profession'. J. Higham, *History: Professional Scholarship in America* (Baltimore, MD: Johns Hopkins University Press, 1983), p. 115. See also P. Novick, *That Noble Dream: The 'Objectivity Question' and the American Historical Profession* (Cambridge: Cambridge University Press, 1988), pp. 86–108. D. Gross, 'The "New History": A Note of Reappraisal', *History and Theory*, Vol. 13, No. 1 (February 1974), pp. 53–8.

[60] Higham, *History*, pp. 110–16.

MEAD EARLE, THE IAS, AND THE SECOND WORLD WAR   63

from external sources. His principal sponsor in this respect was the Carnegie Corporation of New York, although he was unable to secure their backing until explosive events in Europe at the outset of the Second World War convinced them of the urgency of his cause. Earle's initial approach to the corporation to fund a project on 'military and foreign policy' in 1937 was turned down by a board out of step with the professor's vision. His second attempt, however, resulted in an award of $6,500 in early 1940 for work on a 'grand strategy for the United States'. Further wartime grants followed from the corporation's National Emergency Program, as Earle became a beneficiary of a broader surge in funding caused by the sudden turn towards questions of grand strategy and national security, questions which Earle had embraced several years earlier.[61]

The funding stream provided by the Carnegie Corporation was funnelled by Earle towards the seminar on the 'military and foreign policies of the United States' which he inaugurated in the autumn of 1939.[62] This forum would prove to be a staple of the early years of the institute, continuing with some interruption throughout the war years and beyond. In a 1942 article for *Military Affairs*, Earle explained how the seminar had run up to that point and how he understood its purpose and influence. He portrayed it as a continuous activity with a 'constantly changing' cast of participants. Although based at the IAS, it welcomed not only members of the institute but also interested faculty from Princeton University, as well as external invitees, for discussions across a broad range of topics, held ordinarily on a weekly basis during the academic year. The participants came from a variety of disciplinary backgrounds, including history, economics, and political science, but were united by their interest in 'the clarification of the several phases of national policy and a unified concept of Grand Strategy'. Because of the transient involvement of many of the participants, Earle considered that the influence of the seminar spread far beyond the confines of the institute, with scholars returning to academic jobs carrying 'new concepts of national problems and international relations' which would bring 'real and long-term influences on academic thinking and research in the social sciences'. In this manner, Earle went so far as to suggest that:

> The result is that there has been created in the Princeton community a *centre d'études militaires* which is not concerned with immediate technical military and naval problems but rather with broad questions of national strategy, military

---

[61] Ekbladh, 'Present at the Creation', pp. 118–24. Beatrice Stern notes that during the 1939–40 academic year Earle also became chairman of the American Committee for International Studies, charged with 'basic research which is necessary to the formulation of an intelligent foreign policy'. The committee was based at the institute with Earle afforded a secretary paid for by the Rockefeller Foundation. Stern, 'A History of the Institute of Advanced Study', p. 252.

[62] E. M. Earle, 'The Princeton Program of Military Studies', *Military Affairs*, Vol. 6, No. 1 (spring 1942), p. 23.

64 MAKING MAKERS

security, the elements of military and economic power, and the role of the United States in world politics.[63]

The establishment of the seminar certainly proved to be an important milestone in Earle's career at the IAS, and he doubtless saw it as a most welcome development, coming so soon after the unsavoury intrigues in which he had been embroiled over the summer of 1939. In the absence of the production of a solo-authored major research publication, it was also an important instrument in cementing for Earle an alternative position at the institute as a networker and facilitator.[64] In contrast to Flexner's reservations, subsequent IAS directors— Robert Oppenheimer in particular—would come to view the Earle seminar as an important and worthwhile endeavour that enriched the research culture of the institute.[65] The Carnegie Corporation also appeared to be satisfied with Earle's work. A survey conducted by the Columbia professor Nathaniel Peffer at the end of 1940 on behalf of the corporation gave cautious praise to the seminar, with the hope that it might develop into a permanent centre for the study of military affairs.[66]

The members of the seminar kept a busy schedule in the initial years of its existence. In a January 1940 application for funding from the William C. Whitney Foundation, Frank Aydelotte—Flexner's successor as director of the IAS— reported that Earle's seminar had already considered the historical origins of the American policy of isolation, was currently engaged in a study of the relation of American naval policy to world politics since 1890, and was about to undertake a critique of Alfred Vagts's book on the balance of power in Europe and its effects upon the United States.[67] By the time Earle came to publicize the work of his military studies programme in spring 1942 he reported that an extensive list of topics had been considered in detail:

> The elements of sea power and the balance of power in Europe and the Far East, not only as a phenomenon in itself, but as a factor in the defense of the United States; the "military potential"—that is to say, the basic factors in military strength; war as a social and economic institution; strategic factors in the foreign policies of the Great Powers, including the United States; the impact of war upon the economic and social structure; the meaning of terms like "security," "strategy," "defense," and "sea power," which are commonly used but not always with exactitude; *Wehrwirtschaft* and economic warfare; the spread of geo-political

---

[63] Ibid., p. 23.

[64] Beatrice Stern appraised him as a 'catalyst among men', who 'brought to the Institute through the following years some of the best non-mathematical members to come to it'. Stern, 'A History of the Institute of Advanced Study', p. 251.

[65] Ibid., p. 660.   [66] Ekbladh, 'Present at the Creation', p. 123.

[67] IAS, Faculty Files/Box 6/Earle, Edward Mead 1940–4, Aydelotte to Anne T. Bogue (William C. Whitney Foundation), 27 January 1940.

MEAD EARLE, THE IAS, AND THE SECOND WORLD WAR   65

doctrines in Europe, especially since 1919; changing power relationships in the Atlantic area and in the Pacific; the historical origins and development of the American doctrine of isolationism and non-entanglement; the European background of early American foreign policy; theories and practice of diplomacy; the rôle of the army in a democratic society; comparative methods of recruitment and discipline of military personnel; the concept of hemispheric defense and hemispheric solidarity; the historical development of American military policy; non-political—especially psychological—aspects of warfare.[68]

Whilst Earle contended that these studies were built around 'a single unifying objective: American security, its basic assumptions, its changing conditions, and its present imperatives', the range of issues under scrutiny suggested a looser grouping.[69] Even the name of the seminar shifted. It was variously referred to as the seminar on 'American Foreign Relations', 'the foreign and military policies of the United States', 'American Military Policy', before seeming to morph into the 'Princeton Military Studies Group' by the war's end. Under such circumstances it is perhaps unsurprising that what was generally presented as a coherent programme of studies did not seem so dynamic to all involved. For example, years later Richard Poate Stebbins remembered that he and the émigré German scholar Herbert Rosinski, both members of the IAS during the 1940–1 academic year, considered the seminar a series of 'remarkably unfocused conversations about the war and related matters', not to be taken terribly seriously.[70]

Alongside the regular schedule of seminar meetings, the work of the group gave rise to a substantial amount of publications. Many of these were individually authored pieces arising from particular interests and research paths, which Earle was keen to assemble in the periodic reports he passed to the IAS director as evidence of group productivity.[71] Other activities were essentially collaborative. Earle recorded in his 1942 article that the membership had been involved in the preparation of a syllabus in collaboration with scholars from Columbia University which was published under the editorship of Grayson Kirk and Richard Stebbins as *War and National Policy* in January 1941, and which would be followed by a complementary reader. A scholarly bibliography on war and defence, prepared in conjunction with the American Military Institute, was also underway, as well as a select analytical bibliography with critical annotations of works published between 1936 and 1941 on 'Problems of Sea Power in the Pacific', and a 'tentative

---

[68] Earle, 'The Princeton Program of Military Studies', pp. 23–4.   [69] Ibid., p. 24.

[70] R. Stebbins, *The Career of Herbert Rosinski: An Intellectual Pilgrimage* (New York: P. Lang, 1989), p. 42.

[71] For example, IAS, Institute for Advanced Study Princeton (N.J.), Director's Office, Faculty records, Box 6/Earle, Edward Mead 1940–4. Earle to Aydelotte, 5 July 1940. Institute for Advanced Study Princeton (N.J.), Director's Office, Faculty records, Box 6/Earle, Edward Mead 1940–4, Studies of the Foreign Relations and Military Policies of the United States at the Institute for Advanced Study, School of Economics and Politics. Princeton, New Jersey. Revised to December 1941.

bibliography' on 'Modern War—Its Economic and Social Aspects' for teachers of international relations.[72]

This atmosphere of collegial cooperation created the conditions under which an ambitious edited collection could be contemplated. Nevertheless the precise genesis of the volume that would become *Makers of Modern Strategy* is not entirely clear. As early as December 1940 the members of the seminar agreed to draft a syllabus for a 'proposed collaborative book on American foreign policy' which would seek to address certain fundamental issues: the basic assumptions of US foreign policy in the preceding century, the challenges to those assumptions during the previous decade, the alternative course of action opened by fundamental changes to those assumptions. Earle would write the introductory chapter: the rest of the content, arranged broadly to address the three guiding questions, would be supplied by the various members of the seminar that year. The draft syllabus provided a foundation for thinking about how to collate a volume, and its scope was more expansive than the title suggested, encompassing such matters as the changing balances of power in Europe and the Far East, British command of the seas, and changes in military technology.[73] However, the project did not progress beyond this rudimentary stage.

When a new volume was proposed in spring 1942, however, momentum gathered far more quickly. The proposed book, Earle explained, 'concerned not with military history but with military thought, as expressed by representative military men rather than by chronological classification', was expressly designed 'to answer important needs of the moment'. It would fill a gap in English-language scholarship, constituting 'collateral reading' for colleges and universities which were concerning themselves with military affairs, whilst also offering a tool for the training of soldiers, since 'officers in the army have urged the publication of the book as an aid to such instruction'. Yet it was also addressed to the general public, up to that point 'not trained to think and to judge in military and strategic matters'. Earle recognized that the book had to be a collaborative work, since 'a single author would have to work years before he could complete a work of such scope. Historical completeness cannot be attained in such an enterprise, nor is it desired.'[74] With the need to tie projects to American concerns seemingly weakened following US entry into the Second World War, the proposed volume was given the title 'The Foundations of Modern Military Thought'. This then morphed into the working title 'The Development of Modern Military Thought', which it would retain until a very late stage, becoming *Makers of Modern Strategy* only as

---

[72] Earle, 'The Princeton Program of Military Studies', pp. 24–5.

[73] MLP, Earle Papers, MC020/Box 33/Research Files—WWI–WWII. Security, 'Memorandum concerning a possible volume on the changing conditions of American security', 4 December 1940.

[74] IAS Institute for Advanced Study Princeton (N.J.), Director's Office, Faculty records, Box 7/ Earle, Edward Mead, Memoranda, 'Purposes and character of proposed volume on the development of modern military thought', 27 March 1942.

it moved into production. Upon learning of Earle's plans for 'The Foundations of Modern Military Thought', Aydelotte wrote to offer his 'hearty congratulations', stating that the book would be 'useful everywhere' and expressing the hope that 'it will not be long before you undertake it'.[75]

Yet the praise Aydelotte lavished on Earle obscured a more convoluted reality. Asked to recall the origins of the project in 1980, Felix Gilbert wrote that whilst he had no recollection of who had first suggested the idea of a collective volume, he was certain that he had produced the first outline. He took this to Alfred Vagts and Harvey DeWeerd, before taking it to Earle. Earle initially appeared hesitant, but then 'he became very enthusiastic and gave the plan his full support, helping by writing letters to prospective collaborators, negotiating with the publisher, etc., etc.'.[76] In this manner, whilst it is clear that 'The Foundations of Modern Military Thought' emanated from the work of the seminar, and so corresponded in turn to some of Earle's larger concerns, carried through from the late 1930s to the Second World War, the inception was not his. Nor was the proposal a product of the seminar in the sense that it was an object of discussion in that forum, with issues, ideas, and parameters debated and refined. Rather, the project was propelled by key individuals: from Gilbert, on to Vagts and DeWeerd, with Earle then taking up the reins.

At the same time as the book project was beginning to take shape, the character of the military policy seminar was also changing. Earle's report to Aydelotte in April 1943 indicated that during the academic year 1942–3 the work of the group 'centered in the preparation of a volume on the Development of Modern Military Thought'.[77] Insofar as various members of the group were actively engaged in writing contributions for the volume there was some truth in this. Nevertheless, this form of reporting obscured the fact that the seminar itself was put on hiatus at this time. Membership of the seminar—always a select group—had risen to a peak of fifteen for the 1940–1 academic year, declining to twelve the following year, before experiencing sharp decline thereafter (see Figure 2.4).[78] Looking back over his work during the war years in January 1945, Earle gave a more frank assessment, admitting that the 'seminar on military affairs had to be interrupted in the spring of 1942 because of the entry of all its members into the Armed

---

[75] IAS, Institute for Advanced Study Princeton (N.J.), Director's Office, Faculty records, Box 6/ Earle, Edward Mead 1940–4, Aydelotte to Earle, 15 April 1942.

[76] Gilbert to Ropp, 8 January 1980. Gilbert Papers. FG Papers, Box 68, correspondence 1968–88. HI. Although active at the inception of *Makers*, Gilbert explained that Vagts left the IAS soon after this episode and so did not participate in the project. Gilbert's and Vagts's roles in devising the volume are also noted by Christopher Bassford in his *Clausewitz in English: The Reception of Clausewitz in Britain and America 1815–1945* (New York and Oxford: Oxford University Press, 1994), pp. 174, 182–3.

[77] IAS, Stern Vertical File/Box 2/Economics & Politics (SEP), Memorandum for Dr. Aydelotte, 7 April 1943.

[78] These numbers do not include Earle himself.

68 MAKING MAKERS

Participant Name	1939–40	1940–1	1941–2	1942 and after
Robert G. Albion			X	
Thomas A. Bailey	X			
Bernard Brodie		X		
Gilbert Chinard *	X			
Pierre Cot		X (spring only)		
Gordon Craig ±				X
Etienne Dennery		X		
Harvey A. DeWeerd ±			X	
William T. R. Fox			X	
Felix Gilbert ±	X	X	X	X
Jean Gottmann ±				X
John H. Herz	X			
Deborah A. Hubbard			X	
Robert A. Kann			X	
Albert T. Lauterbach		X		
William W. Lockwood		X		
Etienne G. Mantoux ±			X	
Horst Mendershausen		X (autumn only)		
DeWitt Clinton Poole			X (autumn only)	
Stefan T. Possony ±			X	
Herbert Rosinski		X		
J. Rumney	X			
Harold Sprout *±	X	X	X	
Margaret Sprout ±	X	X	X	
Charles P. Stacey *±	X			
Richard P. Stebbins		X		
Alfred Vagts	X	X	X	
Maxim von Brevern		X		
Jean Sylvain Weiller		X		
Albert K. Weinberg	X	X		
Total	10	15	12	3

± = *Makers* chapter author
* = Princeton University faculty
** = Bibliographic and research assistant

Figure 2.4 Members of Earle's seminar, 1939–44.

Collated from: IAS, Institute for Advanced Study Princeton (NJ). Director's Office. Faculty records, Box 6/Earle, Edward Mead 1940–4. Aydelotte to Anne T. Bogue (William C. Whitney Foundation), 27 January 1940. Earle to Aydelotte, 5 July 1940. Members of Professor Earle's Seminar on American Military Policy, 10 February 1940. Studies of the Foreign Relations and Military Policies of the United States at The Institute for Advanced Study, School of Economics and Politics. Princeton, New Jersey. Revised to December 1941. Appendix A. Members of Professor Earle's Seminar on American Military Policy and Foreign Relations 1939–42. List appended to Earle to Captain Lewis L. Strauss, 1 June 1945.

Forces or other branches of Government service'.[79] In effect, whereas during the first years of the war the members of the seminar had discussed the problems of the global conflict, from 1942 onwards they engaged with them.

No one was more affected by this development than Earle himself. Already in early 1941 he had made visits to air force and naval bases in the Caribbean, as well

---

[79] IAS, Stern Vertical File/Box 2/Economics & Politics (SEP), Memorandum, 13 January 1945.

as US territories in the region, filing related reports. In July 1941 he assisted in the organization of the Division of Research and Analysis at the Office of Strategic Services (OSS), and from that point until the autumn of 1942 he served as a member of the Board of Analysts of the OSS. Finally, in December 1942 he was appointed Special Consultant to the Commanding General of the Army Air Forces with responsibility to help organize the Advisory Committee on Bombardment (later renamed the Committee of Operations Analysts), on which he served continuously from 1942 to 1944, then joining its successor body, the Joint Target Group.[80] These commitments laid an increasing claim on Earle's time and his person. As Gilbert recalled decades later, the result was that Earle was 'very frequently away in Washington during the time of the writing of this book'.[81] Absence from Princeton did not mean that Earle was unable to carry out his editorial role—just as was the case for other members of the project, writing, reviewing, and editorial tasks could be performed from a distance. It did mean, however, that he sought the assistance of others in order to compile the manuscript in a timely fashion.

The two men he relied upon most to accomplish this task were Felix Gilbert and Gordon Craig. Although neither was afforded the rank of 'co-editor', appearing in the final publication as 'collaborators' instead, both played important, if distinct, roles in the project. Gilbert (see Figure 2.5) had arrived at the IAS in 1937 as an assistant to Earle, just as Earle was in the full flourish of his research transformation.[82] He remained there throughout the war years, although like Earle he eventually entered into war service, working for the Central European Section of the Research and Analysis Branch at the OSS between 1943 and 1945.[83] He was a mainstay of Earle's seminar, one of a small number who participated throughout the period from 1939 to 1942. This, coupled with his politeness and his affable nature, made him an obvious choice to assist in preparing the book. Moreover, as noted above, he had been instrumental in conceiving the volume itself, and he appeared to exert influence in shaping the contours of the book as the months progressed. In this sense, his role was more significant than the label 'collaborator' suggested.

For Craig, meanwhile, the task was more straightforward. Unlike Gilbert, he had not been involved with the IAS in the period up to 1942, and he did not know

---

[80] IAS, Institute for Advanced Study Princeton (N.J.), Director's Office, Faculty records, Box 6/ Earle, Edward Mead, 1945–7, Earle to Aydelotte, 13 October 1945. His work with the Committee of Operations Analysts involved the production of surveys of the industries and resources of the Axis powers, to enable target selection for maximum damage on the enemy war effort.

[81] Gilbert to Ropp, 8 January 1980, Gilbert Papers, FG Papers, Box 68, correspondence 1968–8. HI.

[82] G. Craig, 'Insight and Energy: Reflections on the Work of Felix Gilbert', in H. Lehmann (ed.), *Felix Gilbert as Scholar and Teacher* (German Historical Institute, Washington, D.C. Occasional Paper No. 6), p. 20. F. Gilbert, *A European Past: Memoirs 1905–1945* (New York and London: Norton, 1988), pp. 174–6.

[83] Ibid., p. 20. Gilbert's work with the OSS involved moving to Washington, D.C., and eventually to London, Paris, and Wiesbaden. Gilbert, *A European Past*, pp. 177–204.

Figure 2.5 Felix Gilbert in 1981. Gilbert was an editorial assistant to Earle on the first *Makers*, and exerted a significant influence on that volume. He went on to assist Peter Paret with the successor volume.

Source: Shelby White and Leon Levy Archives Center, Institute for Advanced Study, Princeton, NJ, USA. Photograph collection—Faculty. Members SHS—Landshoff Portaits—Felix Gilbert folder.

Earle prior to his involvement with the project. After completing his PhD at Princeton University in the spring of 1941 he spent the rest of the year teaching at Yale, only to find that position abruptly terminated shortly after the attack on Pearl Harbor.[84] Craig returned to Princeton to teach classes in history, but by March 1942 he had relocated to Washington to take up a post as Associate Social Science Analyst in the Mediterranean Section of the Office of the Coordination of Information at the OSS, subsequently moving to the Africa Section, and then on to the State Department.[85] His experiences in these posts were mixed, but in any case the pull of government service was not strong enough to keep him in Washington when in February 1943 a new post opened up at Princeton as an

---

[84] J. Sheehan, 'Gordon Alexander Craig (1913–2005)', *Central European History*, Vol. 40, No. 1 (March 2007), pp. 134–5. W. Palmer, *Engagement with the Past: The Lives and Works of the World War II Generation of Historians* (Lexington, KY: University of Kentucky Press, 2001), p. 79. The university was, according to Craig, worried about the decline in enrolments that would follow the US entry into the war, and so fired faculty members who did not have a Yale connection.

[85] Craig Diaries, Vol. V, p. 18; Palmer, *Engagement with the Past*, p. 79.

assistant professor, charged with delivering courses for army officers.[86] When Craig returned to Princeton, Gilbert left for Washington. In this manner, the responsibility for overseeing the final months of the project was handed over from Gilbert to Craig.[87] By Craig's own admission, however, his contribution came at a point at which the book was close to completion. 'Everything was in order when I arrived,' he recalled in 1980; 'the manuscripts were coming in; and the job to be done was basically editorial.'[88]

Making *Makers*

Several months after the publication of *Makers* Henry Guerlac wrote to Earle to voice certain concerns. 'I am sure that all the contributors who did not have the privilege of sharing in the work of your seminar at Princeton regret the fact,' he wrote. 'But since many of us were in truth not there, it is probably better in the interests of accuracy not to convey that false impression.'[89] Guerlac, a young historian of science then working at the University of Wisconsin, owed his involvement with the project to the initiative of Gilbert. The two men had become friends in 1940, when they met at Ithaca and embarked on a sailing trip on Cayuga Lake.[90] In May 1942, several months into the *Makers* project, Gilbert wrote to Guerlac to ask whether he would be willing to contribute to the book. At this point R. R. Palmer, a specialist in eighteenth-century French history who had recently published his study of the committee of public safety in the era of the Terror, *Twelve Who Ruled*, had already been secured to write a chapter then listed as 'Frederick the Great, Marshal Saxe, Guibert, Napoleon'.[91] Gilbert was concerned, however, that since Palmer intended to concentrate on the later parts of the eighteenth century, a chronological gap would open up between this chapter and his own contribution on Machiavelli. To solve this problem he invited Guerlac to write a piece on the earlier part of the 1700s, although he also offered the option of writing the as yet unassigned chapter on Jomini. He stated openly that he had decided to contact Guerlac without Earle's prior knowledge. Earle 'has very much

---

[86] Craig Diaries, Vol. V, pp. 18–59.

[87] MLP, PUP, Box 344, Folder 3 (CO728), Gilbert to Ropp, 8 January 1980. Craig could not have begun his work on *Makers* prior to 12 April 1943, at which point Earle noted in correspondence that he was seeking to secure his services. Division of Rare and Manuscript Collections, Cornell University Library (hereafter CUL), Henry Guerlac Papers, Box 10, Folder 22—Makers of Modern Strategy, Earle to Guerlac, 12 April 1943.

[88] MLP, PUP, Box 344, Folder 3 (CO728), Craig to Ropp, 28 January 1980.

[89] MLP, Earle Papers, MC020/Box 36/Makers of Modern Strategy 1943 [1 of 5], Guerlac to Earle, 16 December 1943.

[90] Woolf, Gilbert to Woolf, 10 June 1981, Gilbert Papers, Box 44/H, Woolf. HI.

[91] The table of contents Gilbert sent to Guerlac approximated that shown in Figure 2.6, with a few contributors crossed out. Palmer's chapter would appear in print as 'Frederick the Great, Guibert, Bülow: From Dynastic to National War'.

72   MAKING MAKERS

his own ideas', Gilbert noted. 'However, he plans in general and in detail (with exception of the last 4 chapters which are a hodge podge and will have to be brought into a more chronological and systematic context).'[92] Guerlac agreed to contribute a piece centred on Vauban 'drifting over into the 18th century'.[93] Over the next few months he worked diligently on the chapter, exchanging drafts with both Gilbert and Palmer to avoid unwanted overlaps.[94]

Guerlac was right to suggest that many of the contributors to *Makers* did not share in the work of the IAS seminar. As well as underscoring the role of Gilbert in moulding the parameters of the volume, his experience was representative of many of those who produced chapters for the book. Of the twenty scholars involved in the project, twelve were not members of Earle's seminar, and this number included individuals such as Princeton University Professor Palmer, who were close at hand.[95] The high number of 'outsiders' amongst chapter authors demonstrates that although *Makers* was conceived within the intellectual environment of the IAS, in the first instance its editor and his principal assistant sought out those individuals whom they thought were the best authorities on a given subject. This process frequently led them beyond the confines of the institute.

This process resulted in as much disappointment as joy. As the outlines for 'The Foundations of Modern Military Thought' show (see Figures 2.6–2.8), a number of those slated as potential contributors were not secured for the final work. Alexander de Seversky, for example, appeared in the first tentative outline as the author of a chapter on air warfare. By April 1943 he had been replaced by Dr Ed Warner of the Civil Aeronautics Board. Whilst it is unclear how far engaging Seversky was seriously entertained, it is clear that more concerted efforts were made to obtain the services of the eminent—and elderly—Oxford don Sir Charles Oman.[96] At the outset of the project Earle was very keen that Oman write a chapter on 'the military historian' and wrote to him to that effect, but his letter went unanswered. Although he had met the older man on a visit to Oxford in 1938, Earle worried that Oman would not remember him. To this end, in April 1942 Earle asked Aydelotte to lobby on his behalf. 'It might be helpful if you were to write him a note telling him that you think this is a worthwhile enterprise,' Earle wrote; more so since 'I am not of his generation and may need a lift from someone like you.'[97] Although Aydelotte's letter was no more effective in swaying

---

[92]   CUL, Guerlac Papers, Box 10, Folder 23—Felix Gilbert, Gilbert to Guerlac, 6 May 1942.

[93]   CUL, Guerlac Papers, Box 10, Folder 23—Felix Gilbert, Gilbert to Guerlac, 15 May 1942.

[94]   CUL, Guerlac Papers, Box 10, Folder 22—Makers of Modern Strategy, R. R. Palmer to Guerlac, 21 August 1942.

[95]   Those scholars not involved with the IAS were Henry Guerlac, R. R. Palmer, Crane Brinton, Hans Rothfels, Sigmund Neumann, Hajo Holborn, Hans Speier, Irving M. Gibson (pseudonym for Arpad Kovacs), Derwent Whittlesey, Ed Warner, Theodore Ropp, and Alexander Kiralfy.

[96]   Oman was eighty-two at the time he was approached by Earle.

[97]   IAS, Institute for Advanced Study Princeton (N.J.), Director's Office, Faculty records, Box 6/ Earle, Edward Mead 1940–4, Earle to Aydelotte, 20 April 1942.

(Tentative Outline)
<u>FOUNDATIONS OF MODERN MILITARY THOUGHT</u>
General Editor, Edward Mead Earle, Institute for Advanced Study, Princeton, N.J.
Foreword by Professor Carlton J.H. Hayes, Columbia University
Section I: <u>The Origins of Modern War: From the 16th to the 18th Century</u>
Chapter 1. Machiavelli: The Renaissance of the art of war.
    Dr Felix Gilbert, Institute for Advanced Study
Chapter 2. Frederick the Great, Marshal Saxe, Guibert.
        Professor Robert R. Palmer, Princeton University.
Chapter 3. Adam Smith, Alexander Hamilton.
        Professor Edward Mead Earle, Institute for Advanced Study.
Section II: <u>The Classics of the 19th Century</u>.
Chapter 4. Jomini.
        Professor Hajo Holborn, Yale University, or
        Dr. Peter Viereck, Harvard University
Chapter 5. Clausewitz.
        Professor Hans Rothfels, Brown University.
Section III. <u>Military Thought from the Middle of the 19th Century to the First World War</u>.
Chapter 6. Moltke and Schlieffen: the Prussian-German school.
        Dr Alfred Vagts, Institute for Advanced Study, or
        Professor Hajo Holborn, Yale University
Chapter 7. DuPicq and Foch: the French school
        Dr. Stefan Possony and Dr Etienne Mantoux, Institute For Advanced Study
Chapter 8. Mommsen, Delbruck, Fortescue, Oman: the military historian.
        Sir Charles William Oman, All Souls College, Oxford, or
        Dr Alfred Vagts, Institute for Advanced Study.
Chapter 9. Modern Naval Thought
        1. Advocates of Fleet Action: Mahan and others.
        Mrs Margaret Sprout, Princeton, New Jersey.
        2. Advocates of the Guerre de Course.
        Dr. Theodore Ropp, Duke University.
Chapter 10. Marx, Engels, Malaparte: military concepts and revolution.
        Professor J. Rumney, University of Newark.
Chapter 11. Colonial and Frontier Warfare: Washington, Lyautey and others.
        As yet unassigned.
Section IV: <u>From the First World War to the Present</u>
Chapter 12. Lloyd George, Clemenceau, Churchill, Trotski: the emergence of the civilian.
        Professor Harvey A. DeWeerd, Denison University
        Granville, Ohio (now at the Institute for Advanced Study).
Chapter 13. Ludendorff, Rathenau, Hitler: German concepts of total war.
        Professor Hans Speier, New School for Social Research.
Chapter 14. The role of the journalist, military correspondent, and columnist.
        André Géraud (Pertinax)
Chapter 15. The problems of global warfare.
        Professor Harold Sprout, Princeton University.
Chapter 16. Air warfare: Douhet and others.
        Major Alexander P. de Seversky.
Chapter 17. Russian Military Theorists.
        Dr Jean Gottmann, Institute for Advanced Study.
Chapter 18. Japanese military and naval thought.
        Professor John Masland, Stanford University.
Chapter 19. American contributions to the theory and practice of war.
        Professor Edward Mead Earle, Institute for Advanced Study.

Figure 2.6 Tentative outline of *Foundations of Modern Military Thought* (likely spring 1942).

Source: IAS / Institute for Advanced Study Princeton (N.J.), Director's Office, Faculty records, Box 7, Earle, Edward Mead, Memoranda (Tentative Outline), <u>Foundations of Modern Military Thought.</u>

74   MAKING MAKERS

THE DEVELOPMENT OF MODERN MILITARY THOUGHT
Editor – Edward Mead Earle, Institute for Advanced Study, Princeton, New Jersey

Section I: The Origins of Modern War: From the 16th to the 18th Century

Chapter 1. Machiavelli: The Renaissance of the Art of War
(Dr. Felix Gilbert, Institute for Advanced Study)
Chapter 2. Vauban: Symbol of Science in War
(Dr. H.E. Guerlac, University of Wisconsin)
Chapter 3. Frederick the Great, Guibert, Buelow: From the Professional to the National Army
(Prof. R.R. Palmer, Princeton University)

Section II: The Classics of the 19th Century: Interpreters of Napoleon

Chapter 4. Jomini
(Prof. Crane Brinton, Harvard University)
Chapter 5. Clausewitz
(Prof. H. Rothfels, Brown University)

Section III: From the 19th Century to the First World War

Chapter 6. Adam Smith, Alexander Hamilton, and Friedrich List: The Economic Foundations of
Military Power
(Prof. Edward Mead Earle, Institute for Advanced Study)
Chapter 7. Moltke and Schlieffen: The Prussian-German School
(Prof. Hajo Holborn, Yale University)
Chapter 8. DuPicq and Foch: The French School
(Dr. Stefan Possony and Dr Etienne Mantoux, Institute for Advanced Study)
Chapter 9. Bugeaud, Gallieni, Lyautey: The Development of French Colonial Warfare
(Dr. Jean Gottmann, Institute for Advanced Study)
Chapter 10. Delbruck: The Military Historian
(Dr. Gordon Craig, Princeton University)
Chapter 11. Marx, Engels, Sorel: Military Concepts and Revolution
(Prof. Sigmund Neumann, Wesleyan University)

Section IV: From the First to the Second World War

Chapter 12. Churchill and Lloyd George: The Contribution of the Civilian
(Captain Harvey A. DeWeerd, Associate Editor, Infantry Journal)
Chapter 13. Ludendorff: The German Concept of Total War
(Prof. Hans Speier, New School of Social Research)
Chapter 14. Dragomiriv, Tuchachevski, Shaposnikov: Soviet Concepts of Total War
(Michael Berchin, New York City)
Chapter 15. Maginot, Liddell Hart: The Doctrine of Defense
(Prof. A. Kovacs, St. John's University)
Chapter 16. National Factor in Military Thought
(Dr. Herbert Rosinski, Fletcher School of Law and Diplomacy)

Section V: Problems of the Present War

Chapter 17. Modern Naval Thought
1. Mahan: His Followers and Opponents
(Dr. Theodore Ropp, Duke University)
2. Japanese Naval Thought
(Alexander Kiralfy, New York City)
Chapter 18. Douhet, Seversky, Mitchell: The Development of the Theory of Air Warfare
(Dr. Edward Warner, Civil Aeronautics Board)

Figure 2.7 Table of contents for *The Development of Modern Military Thought*,
7 April 1943.

Source: IAS, Stern Vertical File, Box 2, Economics and Politics, 'The Development of Modern Military
Thought', appended to Memorandum for Dr. Aydelotte, 7 April 1943.

THE DEVELOPMENT OF MODERN MILITARY THOUGHT
Editor – Edward Mead Earle, Institute for Advanced Study, Princeton, New Jersey

Section I: The Origins of Modern War: From the 16th to the 18th Century

Chapter 1. Machiavelli: The Renaissance of the Art of War
    (Dr Felix Gilbert, Institute for Advanced Study)
Chapter 2. Vauban: Symbol of Science in War
    (Dr H.E. Guerlac, University of Wisonsin)
Chapter 3. Frederick the Great, Guibert, Buelow: From the Professional to the National Army
    (Prof. R.R. Palmer, Princeton University, now with the Historical Section, War Department
      General Staff)

Section II: The Classics of the 19th Century: Interpreters of Napoleon

Chapter 4. Jomini
    (Prof. Crane Brinton, Harvard University)
Chapter 5. Clausewitz
    (Prof. H. Rothfels, Brown University)

Section III: From the 19th Century to the First World War

Chapter 6. Adam Smith, Alexander Hamilton, and Friedrich List: The Economic Foundations of
Military Power
    (Prof. Edward Mead Earle, Institute for Advanced Study)
Chapter 7. Moltke and Schlieffen: The Prussian-German School
    (Prof. Hajo Holborn, Yale University)
Chapter 8. DuPicq and Foch: The French School
    (Dr. Stefan Possony and Dr. Etienne Mantoux, Institute for Advanced Study)
Chapter 9. Bugeaud, Gallieni, Lyautey: The Development of French Colonial Warfare
    (Dr. Jean Gottmann, Institute for Advanced Study)
Chapter 10. Delbruck: The Military Historian
    (Dr. Gordon Craig, Princeton University)
Chapter 11. Marx, Engels, Sorel: Military Concepts and Revolution
    (Prof. Sigmund Neumann, Wesleyan University)

Section IV: From the First to the Second World War

Chapter 12. Churchill and Lloyd George: The Contribution of the Civilian
    (Captain Harvey A. DeWeerd, Associate Editor, Infantry Journal)
Chapter 13. Ludendorff: The German Concept of Total War
    (Prof. Hans Speier, New School of Social Research)
Chapter 14. Dragomiriv, Tuchachevski, Shaposnikov: Soviet Concepts of Total War
    (Michael Berchin, New York City)
Chapter 15. Maginot, Liddell Hart: The Doctrine of Defense
    (Prof. A. Kovacs, St. John's University)
Chapter 16. National Factors in Military Thought
    (Dr. Herbert Rosinski, Fletcher School of Law and Diplomacy)

Section V: Problems of the Present War

Chapter 17. Modern Naval Thought
    1. Mahan: His Followers and Opponents
      (Dr. Theodore Ropp, Duke University)
    2. Japanese Naval Thought
      (Alexander Kiralfy, New York City)
Chapter 18. Douhet, Seversky, Mitchell: The Development of the Theory of Air Warfare
    (Dr. Edward Warner, Civil Aeronautics Board)
Chapter 19. Haushofer: A Geopolitical School
    (Prof. Derwent S. Whittlesey)

Figure 2.8 Table of contents for *The Development of Modern Military Thought*.

Source: IAS, Institute for Advanced Study Princeton (N.J.), Director's Office, Faculty records, Box 6, Earle, Edward Mead 1940–4, 'The Development of Modern Military Thought'.

76 MAKING MAKERS

Oman, the correspondence ensured that he was very aware of Earle's endeavour.[98] After the book was published he wrote to the editor to express his favourable impression of the work.[99]

The inability to enlist first-choice authors illustrated by these examples does not simply offer a glimpse of what might have been. As Earle and Gilbert worked to secure alternative writers, the amended chapter titles that followed marked apparent shifts in coverage. Thus, Seversky became an explicit focus of the chapter on air power, which changed under the pen of Warner from 'Air warfare; Douhet and others' to 'Douhet, Seversky, Mitchell'. Similarly the chapter on 'military concepts and revolution' began with the triumvirate of 'Marx, Engels, Malaparte' when allotted to former seminar and IAS member Jay Rumney, but changed to 'Marx, Engels, Sorel' once Sigmund Neumann agreed to write it, and finally appeared in print as 'Marx and Engels'. The chapter that began life as simply 'Russian Military Theorists' also featured a changing triumvirate. Assigned to Michel Berchin in the table of contents of 7 April 1943, it was listed as 'Dragomirov, Tuchachevski, Shaposnikov'; it appeared in print with Earle as the author and the subjects changed to 'Lenin, Trotsky, Stalin'. In other cases, the compromises involved in settling on new authors resulted in a narrowing of the focus of particular chapters. This was case for the 'military historians' chapter, which began as a treatment encompassing Mommsen, Delbrück, Fortescue, and Oman. By the time Earle approached Gordon Craig as a possible author the focus had been narrowed to Oman and Delbrück. Craig offered to write the chapter on Delbrück alone, so the German historian became the sole exemplar.[100] Similarly, the chapter that appeared unassigned in the original tentative outline as 'Colonial and Frontier Warfare: Washington, Lyautey and others' became a chapter concerning only French experiences at the pen of Jean Gottmann. Still other chapters that appeared in the earliest outline of the book—on 'The role of the journalist, military correspondent, and columnist' and 'The problems of global warfare'— disappeared altogether from subsequent drafts.

Of course, in some cases IAS seminar members were the individuals best placed to write particular chapters. Gilbert's knowledge of the Italian Renaissance, for example, made him the ideal candidate to write on Machiavelli. Likewise, as co-author with her husband Harold Sprout of *The Rise of American Naval Power* and its second volume *Towards a New Order of Sea Power*, Margaret Tuttle Sprout was an obvious choice to write on Mahan.[101] A mainstay of Earle's group, Sprout

---

[98] IAS, Institute for Advanced Study Princeton (N.J.), Director's Office, Faculty records, Box 6/ Earle, Edward Mead 1940–4, Aydelotte to Oman, 27 April 1942.

[99] MLP, Earle Papers, MC020 Box 36, Makers of Modern Strategy 1943–7 [2 of 5], Oman to Earle, 6 December 1943.

[100] MLP, PUP, Box 344, Folder 3 (CO728), Craig to Ropp, 28 January 1980.

[101] IAS, Institute for Advanced Study Princeton (N.J.), Director's Office, Faculty records, Box 6/ Earle, Edward Mead 1940–4, 'Members of the Seminar in American Foreign Relations, The Institute for Advanced Study 1939-1940', appended to Aydelotte to Anna T. Bogue, 27 January 1940. Members of Professor Earle's Seminar 10/2/40.

MEAD EARLE, THE IAS, AND THE SECOND WORLD WAR 77

thus became the only woman to write for the book. Yet even here, it was not always possible to secure the services of those who had been active in the seminar. Alfred Vagts, for example, was mooted as a possible author for both the military historians chapter and the chapter on the Prussian-German school of the nineteenth century, although, as Gilbert noted, he left Princeton soon after the initial outline was put together and had no more to do with the project.[102] The future nuclear strategist Bernard Brodie offers another example. Brodie joined Earle's group at the IAS for the 1940–1 academic year as a naval specialist, looking to adapt his doctoral thesis for publication.[103] By 1942, with Earle's help, he had moved away from the Princeton circle.[104] As his commitments had rapidly mounted following the move, contributing to *Makers* was not possible. Earle later bemoaned the fact, writing to him that 'we had all hoped to have you as a contributor to the original volume but we knew that you were so busy with your Guide to Naval Strategy that we ought not to trouble you'.[105]

Another seminar member who was due to contribute to the volume did not make for an agreeable collaborator, despite being well suited to the task on paper. Herbert Rosinski, expelled from Germany on account of a Jewish grandfather, entered the USA in July 1940 on an initial six-month visa, having spent the previous four years in England. Aware that his expertise spanned such topics as Clausewitz, the German army, and naval warfare, Earle assembled funds for a $2000 stipend which would bring him to the IAS for the 1940–1 academic year. Once installed in Princeton, however, Rosinski cut a frustrating figure. Afforded a good deal of freedom to pursue his own research, Earle asked only that he actively participate in his seminar. Rosinski, however, did not take these meetings seriously. Unsurprisingly, then, as Earle grew disillusioned he came to see Rosinski as arrogant, and became increasingly irritated at Rosinski's constant lobbying of Earle and senior figures at the IAS for assistance in obtaining a visa for his wife, then resident in London. Relations between the pair deteriorated to such a degree that Rosinski's stipend was not renewed for the following academic year.[106] Despite this, when planning began for *Makers* Earle was still willing to include him and allotted him a significant task. He gave him responsibility for preparing a chapter on 'The National Factor in Military Thought', intended to draw a number

---

[102] MLP, PUP, Box 344, Folder 3 (CO728), Gilbert to Ropp, 8 January 1980. Gilbert also noted that he had wanted to write on Moltke and Schlieffen, especially because it was initially thought that Holborn would not be able to do so.

[103] It would subsequently appear as *Sea Power in the Machine Age* (Princeton, NJ: Princeton University Press, 1941).

[104] For Brodie's early career see F. Kaplan, *The Wizards of Armageddon* (Stanford, CA: Stanford University Press, 1991), pp. 11–19. For a discussion of his early academic work see B. S. Zellen, *State of Doom: Bernard Brodie, the Bomb, and the Birth of the Bipolar World* (London and New York: Continuum, 2012), pp. 13–34.

[105] MLP, Earle Papers, MC020/Box 13/Correspondence Brodie, Bernard 1944–5, Earle to Brodie, 15 November 1944.

[106] Stebbins, *Herbert Rosinski*, pp. 39–43, 48–9.

78 MAKING MAKERS

of themes from across the work to a satisfactory close but without retreading ground covered elsewhere in the volume.[107] He even gave him a $50 honorarium to encourage him to complete the piece in good time—a kindness made in view of Rosinski's continuing financial struggles and which was not extended to any other contributor. It did not achieve the desired results. Rosinski delivered a lengthy chapter three months late, which contravened Earle's direction by cutting across content covered elsewhere, and managed to do so within the narrow confines of a survey of military thought in France and Germany since the mid-eighteenth century. It was duly rejected.[108] The delays incurred by Rosinski left Earle with no time to rewrite the piece himself. As a result, the chapter was dropped entirely.

Earle's experience with the remaining seminar member-contributors was much happier and more productive. The eight members of the IAS seminar who contributed scholarly material to *Makers*—Earle, Felix Gilbert, Gordon Craig, Stefan Possony, Etienne Mantoux, Jean Gottmann, Harvey DeWeerd, and Margaret Tuttle Sprout—accounted for close to half of the content of the volume: nine of twenty chapters.[109] For many of them, however, the chapters they wrote were assignments of necessity rather than choice, governed by a looming manuscript deadline and the lack of alternatives. Gordon Craig, for example, was given the task of writing on Hans Delbrück after the attempt to solicit Oman had failed. Years later, he admitted to Christopher Bassford that he had never heard of Delbrück before that point.[110] Jean Gottmann, who had arrived in Princeton in 1942, was first slated to author the chapter on Russian military theorists before taking over the narrowed colonial and frontier warfare chapter. He would not write on French colonial warfare again, establishing his reputation as a leading geographer after the Second World War.[111] Similarly, although Etienne Mantoux's area of expertise was economics, he co-authored a chapter on the 'French school' of the nineteenth century with Stefan Possony. In these instances the relative youth and early career stage of the seminar members doubtless played a role in their willingness to take on subjects with which they were less familiar.

---

[107] IAS Stern Vertical File/Box 2/Economics & Politics (SEP), Memorandum for Dr. Aydelotte, 7 April 1943. Rosinski would have preferred to write on either Clausewitz or Mahan, but these were given to Hans Rothfels and Margaret Tuttle Sprout respectively. Stebbins, *Herbert Rosinski*, pp. 67–8.

[108] Stebbins, *Herbert Rosinski*, pp. 67–9. Discarded by Rosinski, the French portion of the manuscript was subsequently lost, but the German section was published in the *Naval War College Review* in 1976, fourteen years after his death.

[109] Of these, Gilbert and Sprout were the only two involved since 1939, the others joining at various points after 1940. The nine chapters mentioned here include a chapter co-authored by Stefan Possony and Etienne Mantoux, the chapter on Jomini listed as a collaborative effort by non-member Crane Brinton, Gilbert, and Craig, and the two chapters authored by Earle himself, as well as the introduction and epilogue.

[110] Bassford, *Clausewitz in English*, p. 178.

[111] After the war Gottmann made his name in the field of geography with his concept of the 'megalopolis'.

MEAD EARLE, THE IAS, AND THE SECOND WORLD WAR 79

Since Earle had created a hub for younger scholars, who might hope to move on to firmer positions thanks to Earle's patronage, it made sense for them to do what the professor required rather than plead a special case.

It should be noted, however, that Earle was equally willing to tailor his own contributions to meet the requirements of the volume. In his initial plan for the book Earle listed his contribution as two chapters, the first on 'Adam Smith, Alexander Hamilton' and the second on 'American contributions to the theory and practice of war', which was to be the final chapter (see Figure 2.6). By the time the revised table of contents was circulated in April 1943, the second chapter had disappeared. So too had a proposed foreword by Professor Carlton Hayes of Columbia University.[112] When the book was finally published it opened with an introduction by Earle, who also wrote a conclusion that shifted focus to 'The Nazi Concept of War', away from American contributions. In addition to his chapter on the economic foundations of military power, Earle appeared as the author of the chapter on Soviet concepts of war, following the late withdrawal of Berchin.[113]

Whilst a great deal of the efforts of the IAS members involved addressing gaps in coverage by writing specified chapters, the relationship between the authors, the seminar members, and the text was not passive. As well as being characterized by their relative youth, many of the academics drawn to Earle's group—and some who wrote for the book as outsiders—were migrants.[114] With the advent of the Second World War in Europe, large numbers of European academics made their way towards the United States. Under Flexner, the IAS had taken a leading role in seeking to assist scholars even before the war began. From 1933 to 1939, forty-five of the visiting scholars at the institute—around a quarter of the total visitors— were European refugees.[115] Once his research group was up and running, Earle too became an important figure in securing financial and scholarly lifelines for a number of refugee intellectuals, enabling them to take their first steps towards securing positions in US academia. Yet very quickly the requests for assistance became overwhelming. As early as January 1940, he reported being 'deluged with applications from German refugees as well as from Americans' at a session of the

---

[112] Earle held Hayes in high esteem, later editing a *festschrift* in his honour, describing him in its introduction as 'a public servant—a minister without portfolio concerned with educating the American people, through successive generations of American youth, to a sympathetic understanding of their European heritage and an intelligent appreciation of their responsibilities to European civilization', and later as 'the Meinecke of American historiography'. E. M. Earle (ed.), *Nationalism and Internationalism: Essays Inscribed to Carlton J. H. Hayes* (New York: Colombia University Press, 1950), pp. ix, xiv.

[113] Walter Lippmann papers, Sterling Memorial Library (hereafter SML), Yale University, New Haven, CT. MS 326/Series III/Box 68/Folder 675, Earle to Lippmann, 9 August 1943.

[114] P. Porter, 'Beyond the American Century: Walter Lippmann and American Grand Strategy, 1943–1950', *Diplomacy & Statecraft*, Vol. 22, No. 4 (2011), p. 565. An even higher number of contributors to the volume were either immigrants or first-generation descendants of immigrants.

[115] Bonner, *Iconoclast*, pp. 265–6.

80 MAKING MAKERS

American Historical Association in Washington.[116] The result was that Earle and the IAS became increasingly selective about who they could and could not help. As Earle affirmed several months later in a missive to Aydelotte, 'We must be highly selective in the matter of refugees, or we shall be submerged.'[117]

Those individuals who became involved with the book brought with them frameworks and understandings representative of their national groupings, which impacted on the development of *Makers* in a specific way. As Felix Gilbert recalled years later, the European aspect of the book was in fact its original core, added to which were the concerns of the war in progress, which became increasingly prominent with the deepening of US mobilization. He explained:

> originally the book was meant to show European, and particularly German stra-
> tegical theories of strategical thought with the purpose of some kind of explan-
> ation of what had been going on in the first years of the Second World War in
> Europe. Later on the happenings of the Second World War began to play a
> greater role and I think one can really distinguish two layers in the book, the one
> concerned with the general development of European strategical thought up to
> the end of the First World War, the second a consideration of the Second World
> War and the strategical approach of its participants.[118]

The migrant groups that most impacted the book fell under two categories: francophone and germanophone. Amongst the francophone constituency was Etienne Mantoux, who had served as an officer in the French Air Force during the campaign of 1940. After an unsuccessful attempt to sail to England with his two brothers in the wake of the French defeat, Mantoux secured a Rockefeller fellowship which took him to the IAS in the summer of 1941. His path was smoothed by the links between his father, the historian Paul Mantoux, and Aydelotte, who in turn introduced him to Earle.[119] Eager to join the forces of resistance but initially reluctant to rally to de Gaulle—Gilbert recorded that this was for personal not political reasons—Mantoux overcame his reservations and left to enlist in the Free French Forces in England in early 1943, fighting with them from Normandy to Germany, where he was killed on 29 April 1945.[120] Mantoux's *Carthaginian Peace*, guided through to publication by his father after his son's death, was a

---

[116] IAS, Institute for Advanced Study Princeton (N.J.), Director's Office, Faculty records, Box 6/ Earle, Edward Mead 1940–4. Earle to Aydelotte, 3 January 1940.

[117] IAS, Institute for Advanced Study Princeton (N.J.), Director's Office, Faculty records, Box 6/ Earle, Edward Mead, 1940–4. Earle to Aydelotte, 12 August 1940.

[118] MLP, PUP, Box 344, Folder 3 (CO728), Gilbert to Ropp, 8 January 1980.

[119] See correspondence in IAS, Institute for Advanced Study Princeton (N.J.), School of Economics and Politics, Member records, Box 91/Mantoux, Etienne G., 41–3.

[120] E. Mantoux, *The Carthaginian Peace or The Economic Consequences of Mr Keynes* (London: Oxford University Press, 1946), pp. ix–xiv. F. Gilbert, *A European Past: Memoirs, 1905–1945* (New York and London: Norton, 1988), p. 183.

MEAD EARLE, THE IAS, AND THE SECOND WORLD WAR   81

product of his work at the IAS. Psychological warfare expert Stefan Possony was another francophone. Although born in Vienna, Possony moved to France, where he worked for the French government before crossing the Atlantic in 1940. He was a member of the IAS for the 1941–2 year, working for the Columbia Broadcasting System as a newscaster on short wave to Central Europe after the expiry of his IAS stipend. After the war he became a fellow at the Hoover Institution and was heavily involved in the Star Wars programme during the 1980s.[121] Another such individual was Jean Gottmann. Ukrainian born and orphaned as an infant, Gottmann was taken to Paris by his uncle Michel Berchin. Motivated to flee France on account of his Jewish heritage, he followed an arduous route to the United States, where he made Earle's acquaintance at the beginning of 1942. He was able to join the IAS group soon after thanks to a Rockefeller Foundation grant for $1500. He worked in a political capacity with the Free French, and later returned to Paris to join the post-war administration.[122] As noted above, these individuals ultimately turned their hands to chapters focused specifically on French historical experiences, despite their varied academic specialisms.

The germanophone constituency was yet more significant. In addition to Rosinski, there were a number of German-speaking academics involved in the seminar and the book project. Unlike the francophone contingent, whose migration was largely a consequence of the war itself, several of the German speakers had arrived earlier in the 1930s. Alfred Vagts, for example, found his entry into the USA in 1933 and subsequent route to US citizenship smoothed by his marriage to the daughter of Charles Beard in 1927.[123] Gilbert, too, had arrived relatively early. His path from Germany had first taken him to London. In 1936, however, frustrated at the lack of British understanding of the nature of Nazism and unable to find an academic position in the UK, he decided to leave. After a year teaching in southern California he joined the IAS, and had acquired US citizenship by the time the Second World War began.[124] Alongside these, a number

---

[121] IAS, Institute for Advanced Study Princeton (N.J.), School of Economics and Politics, Member records, Box 111/Possony, Stefan Thomas 40–2. For an obituary see 'Stefan Possony', *The Times*, Tuesday 2 May 1995. See also Stebbins, *Herbert Rosinski*, p. 43. See also F. Bientinesi, 'An "Austrian" Point of View on Total War: Stefan T. Possony', in F. Bientinesi and R. Patalano, *Economists and War: A Heterodox Perspective* (London: Routledge, 2017).

[122] M. Finch, *A Progressive Occupation? The Gallieni-Lyautey Method and Colonial Pacification in Tonkin and Madagascar, 1885–1900* (Oxford: Oxford University Press, 2013), pp. 49–51. For the grant, see Bibliothèque Nationale de France, Site Richelieu, Paris, Gottmann Papers, Ge. Gottmann/Ear/444, Earle to Gottmann, 6 February 1942. Ge. Gottmann/Ear/448, Earle to Gottmann, 21 February 1942.

[123] E. Schulin, 'German and American Historiography in the Nineteenth and Twentieth Centuries', in H. Lehmann and J. Sheehan (eds.), *An Interrupted Past: German Speaking Refugee Historians in the United States after 1933* (Washington, D.C. and Cambridge: German Historical Institute and Cambridge University Press, 1991), p. 23.

[124] Gilbert, *A European Past*, pp. 158–77. Lehmann (ed.), 'Felix Gilbert as Scholar and Teacher', pp. 19–20, 25.

82   MAKING MAKERS

of individuals wrote chapters but were not seminar members: Hans Rothfels, Hajo Holborn, Sigmund Neumann, Hans Speier.[125]

The German constituency brought its own traditions in the study of history to the IAS, as much as to the American historical profession more widely, and played a substantial role in shaping the volume.[126] As has previously been noted, Gilbert and Vagts were key instigators of the idea of the book, alongside DeWeerd, and Gilbert also later explained that the collection was originally intended to be centred on German strategic theories. It is equally significant that three of the germanophone contributors to *Makers*—Gilbert, Rothfels, and Holborn—were former students of the eminent historian Friedrich Meinecke.[127] Anson Rabinbach goes so far as to trace a direct line from Meinecke to the form and approach adopted for the book, noting that 'in keeping with Meinecke's *Ideengeschichte* (history of ideas), *Makers* centers almost exclusively on the intellectual biographies of great personalities who represent and embody specific events and epochal shifts in military history'.[128] Such was the influence of Meinecke's students on the process that 'the creation of *Makers of Modern Strategy* might be described as the first reunion of the Meinecke seminar in Princeton'.[129] Additionally, it was likely due to Meinecke that the German contingent brought with them to Princeton an appreciation of the significance of Hans Delbrück, since the two professors had been colleagues and friends in Berlin until Delbrück's death in 1929.[130] Felix Gilbert, for one, remembered 'being told that Delbrück was an eccentric but important historian'.[131]

---

[125] Bassford, *Clausewitz in English*, pp. 174, 185, 262 (see footnote 89). Gilbert, *A European Past*, p. 72. For Holborn, see the introduction to L. Krieger and F. Stern (eds.), *The Responsibility of Power: Historical Essays in Honor of Hajo Holborn* (London: Macmillan, 1968), pp. x–xi. O. Pflanze, 'The Americanization of Hajo Holborn', in Lehmann and Sheehan, *An Interrupted Past*, pp. 170–9. Also the special edition of *Central European History*, Vol. 3, Nos. 1–2, in memory of Hajo Holborn, 1902–69 (March–June 1970), a journal which he co-founded. For the contested legacy of Rothfels in German historiography, see J. Eckel, 'Hans Rothfels: An Intellectual Biography in the Age of Extremes', *Journal of Contemporary History*, Vol. 42, No. 3 (July 2007), pp. 421–46.

[126] For German historians' migration to the USA in a broader context see the essays in Lehmann and Sheehan, *An Interrupted Past*, particularly pp. 73–93, 94–101, 116–35, 136–9. Also C. Epstein, *A Past Renewed: A Catalog of German-Speaking Refugee Historians in the United States after 1933* (Washington, D.C. and Cambridge: German Historical Institute and Cambridge University Press, 1993).

[127] G. Ritter, *German Refugee Historians and Friedrich Meinecke: Letters and Documents, 1910–1977*, trans. A. Skinner (Leiden: Brill, 2010) includes biographical sketches of all three, with special reference to their relationships with Meinecke. See pp. 23–32, 40–56. Gilbert observed that on account of the presence of Meinecke, the University of Berlin historical seminar was 'the center of gravity for history students with a democratic and intellectually adventurous outlook. This attitude was not popular among older, conservative historians still predominant in German academic life'. Adherents to the New History seemed to share a similar sentiment. Gilbert, *A European Past*, pp. 68–76, quote at p. 71.

[128] Rabinbach, 'The Making of Makers of Modern Strategy', p. 104.   [129] Ibid., p. 107.

[130] Although Meinecke was not always in agreement with Delbrück, and was amongst the professors who voted against his proposal for a chair in military history in 1921. A. Bucholz, *Hans Delbrück and the German Military Establishment: War Images in Conflict* (Iowa City, IA: University of Iowa Press, 1985), pp. 141, 145.

[131] H. Delbrück (ed. and trans. A. Bucholz), *Delbrück's Modern Military History* (Lincoln, NE: University of Nebraska Press, 1997), p. 37.

The German speakers were also crucial in bringing Clausewitz to bear on *Makers*. As Christopher Bassford notes, Earle compiled a volume in which half of the chapters made some form of reference to the Prussian military thinker.[132] This occurred because Earle facilitated the dissemination of the knowledge of a German contingent that brought an understanding of Clausewitz as an integral part of their historical training. Rothfels and Rosinski were notable exponents, having both written on the theorist in their native language prior to arriving in the USA, with the former going on to write a seminal chapter on Clausewitz for *Makers*. Rothfels was at the vanguard of an intellectual current that sought to reinterpret the writers' theories within the context of his own lifetime, with particular emphasis on the trials of Prussia at the hands of Napoleon and its subsequent national rejuvenation. Inspired by a renewed period of national peril during the period 1914–18, such an interpretation marked a transition in the understanding of Clausewitz, now placing emphasis on the relationship between war and policy rather than on strategy and tactics, in a manner that was more complementary to Earle's own understanding of the enlarged parameters of strategy.[133]

Succeeding, Revising, Failing

In the months after *Makers of Modern Strategy: Military Thought from Machiavelli to Hitler* was published in October 1943, it quickly became apparent that it was a success.[134] By 20 December 1943 Princeton University Press had only one thousand copies remaining of the first run of ten thousand, and with orders being received at a rate of more than fifty per day, a new run of five thousand copies was scheduled for printing the following week.[135] As 1944 began, Earle declared that he was 'amazed that we have had this sort of quantitative success'.[136] Whilst the reprint presented the contributors with an opportunity to make minor revisions to their chapters, the success of the book suggested to Earle 'that after we have had the advantage of more general scholarly criticism, we shall be in a position to bring out a complete revision of the work'.[137] The near unanimous praise he

---

[132] Bassford, *Clausewitz in English*, pp. 173–4.

[133] H. Strachan, 'Clausewitz and the First World War', *The Journal of Military History*, Vol. 75, No. 2 (April 2011), pp. 380–7.

[134] CUL, Guerlac Papers, Box 10, Folder 22—Makers of Modern Strategy, Earle to Guerlac, 7 September 1943.

[135] MLP, Earle Papers, MC020/Box 36/Makers of Modern Strategy 1943 [1 of 5], Earle to Guerlac, 20 December 1943.

[136] MLP, Earle Papers, MC020/Box 36/Makers of Modern Strategy 1943–7 [2 of 5], Earle to Oman, 4 January 1944.

[137] MLP, Earle Papers, MC020/Box 36/Makers of Modern Strategy 1943 [1 of 5], Earle to Guerlac, 29 November 1943. Earle wrote to contributors to request changes, with most responses resulting in minor requests: Possony asked for it to be made clearer that he had written the section of his chapter

84   MAKING MAKERS

received from his contributors contributed to his bullishness, with most echoing the sentiments of Guerlac that 'you deserve a great deal of credit for "getting thar fustest with the mostest men"'.[138] Arpad Kovacs (who wrote under the pseudonym Irving Gibson) affirmed that he would 'heartily cooperate' in efforts at revision, whilst Possony proposed that 'a revised and <u>augmented</u> edition be prepared at the earliest possible date'.[139]

As Earle considered the prospects of a new edition, however, he came to believe that it could not be achieved within the same swift time frame as the original. This time more formalized consultations would be needed. As such, Earle looked to hold 'round table discussions concerning the content and proportions of the revised edition'.[140] By the end of 1944 those discussions had yet to take place, leading him to admit that 'it will be sometime [sic] before the revised edition of our book will appear, as there is a great deal to be done and as it will be necessary to wait until some material, which is now classified as secret, can be released for publication'.[141] In this manner, the new *Makers* transformed into a project for the post-war era, whenever that might prove to be. To Earle's mind, this situation offered certain advantages. For one thing, the release of secret material would allow for better analysis of contemporary developments. Furthermore, the cessation of hostilities would be accompanied by a return to normal academic routine for many of the original or prospective new participants whose professional lives were increasingly consumed by the US war effort.

Yet if *Makers* mark two was to be a post-war publication, this did not prevent Earle from thinking over its future form. Indeed, there was plenty to reflect on. In this respect, one particularly important source were reviews. In the first few months Earle expressed frustration that these had been 'slow in coming'.[142] Once they did start to appear they were very positive, with tributes frequently paid to

---

on Du Picq, while Mantoux had written on Foch. Guerlac pointed out the unauthorized insertion of a manuscript into his bibliographical notes. Hans Rothfels, meanwhile, asked for a substantial increase in the length of his biographical notes and also offered corrections for the bibliographical notes to Palmer's chapter—a move which was not well received by the latter. See MC020/Box 36/Makers of Modern Strategy 1943 [1 of 5], Possony to Earle, 9 December 1943. MC020/Box 36/Makers of Modern Strategy 1943 [1 of 5], Guerlac to Earle, 16 December 1943. Earle to Guerlac, 20 December 1943. MC020/Box 36/Makers of Modern Strategy 1943–7 [2 of 5], Rothfels to Earle, 14 December 1943. Smith to Earle, 28 December 1943. MC020/Box 36/Makers of Modern Strategy 1943 [1 of 5], Rothfels to Earle, 22 October 1943. MC020/Box 36/Makers of Modern Strategy 1943 [1 of 5], Palmer to Earle, 28 October 1943.

[138] MLP, Earle Papers, MC020/Box 36/Makers of Modern Strategy 1943 [1 of 5], Guerlac to Earle, 16 December 1943.

[139] MLP, Earle Papers, MC020/Box 36/Makers of Modern Strategy 1943 [1 of 5], Kovacs to Earle, 5 December 1943. Possony to Earle, 9 December 1943.

[140] MLP, Earle Papers, MC020/Box 36/Makers of Modern Strategy 1943 [2 of 5], Earle to Neumann, 31 January 1944.

[141] MLP, Earle Papers, MC020/Box 36/Makers of Modern Strategy 1943 [2 of 5], Earle to Richmond, 20 December 1944.

[142] MLP, Earle Papers, MC020/Box 36/Makers of Modern Strategy 1943 [1 of 5], Earle to Guerlac, 29 November 1943.

Earle as editor, as author, or both.[143] Moreover, the reviews validated Earle's contention that the book responded to the urgent needs of the moment. The influential public intellectual Walter Lippmann gave early fulsome praise in his syndicated column 'Today and Tomorrow', writing that 'the book will establish the study of military history and the development of military doctrine as an indispensable subject in higher education and in the intellectual life of the nation'.[144]

Earle followed the reviews assiduously, even going so far as to rank those appearing in British journals on an A to C scale (see Figure 2.9).[145] He was not impervious to unfavourable comment, noting 'exasperating experiences' with a handful of reviewers.[146] Still, the reviews gave Earle pause for thought and for action. In a handwritten note, most likely written at the very end of 1943 or the beginning of 1944 and entitled 'Book Changes—General Comments for Second Edition', he brought some of these ideas together. The list of possible new inclusions

---

[143] P. J. Searles, for example, wrote that 'no one book in English (or probably in any language) approaches it in distinction, scope, lucidity and general excellence'. MLP, Earle Papers, MC020/Box 36/Makers of Modern Strategy 1943–5 [3 of 5], 'Men Who Analyzed the Meaning of War. A Brilliant and Authoritative Group of Essays on the Historic Students of Warfare' Review by Captain P. J. Searles in *New York Herald Tribune Weekly Book Review*, 5 December 1943.

[144] W. Lippmann, 'The Serious Study of War', *The Washington Post*, 30 October 1943. Lippmann's comments did not come as a surprise. Earle's views chimed with Lippmann's growing belief that history could serve as a guide for future policy, and his tendency to 'equate foreign affairs with military history and to talk of the two synonymously'. The pair kept abreast of each other's projects in the early 1940s and were not averse to mutual back-scratching. Earlier that year, Earle had written a favourable review of Lippmann's *Shield of the Republic*, which the latter described as 'an author's dream'. Two months later, Earle had galley proofs of selected chapters from *Makers* sent to Lippmann in the hope that he might provide a favourable quote for the advance advertising. Despite not getting round to reading them, Lippmann was happy to offer 'some kind of perfunctory remark such as "This is a necessary book on the most neglected subject in American learning"'. Nor did he object to Earle's further suggestion that 'scholarship and statecraft' be substituted for 'learning', on the grounds that both he and the Princeton University Press considered the latter 'as being a little bit formidable for the general reader'. F. Curro Cary, *The Influence of War on Walter Lippmann 1914-1944* (Madison, WI: State Historical Society of Wisconsin for the Dept. of History, University of Wisconsin, 1967), pp. 161, 170–4. See also Porter, 'Beyond the American Century'. SML, Lippmann Papers, MS 326/Series III/Box 68/Folder 675, Lippmann to Earle, 23 June 1943. SML, Lippmann Papers, MS 326/Series III/Box 68/Folder 675, Earle to Lippmann, 9 August 1943. SML, Lippmann Papers, MS 326/Series III/Box 68/Folder 675, Lippmann to Earle, 6 September 1943. Earle to Lippmann, 8 September 1943. Lippmann to Earle, 17 September 1943.

[145] MLP, Earle Papers, MC020/Box 36/Makers of Modern Strategy 1943–5 [3 of 5], Reviews of MAKERS OF MODERN STRATEGY in English journals.

[146] MLP, Earle Papers, MC020/Box 36/Makers of Modern Strategy 1943 [1 of 5], Earle to Guerlac, 20 December 1943. A review by the official historian of the First World War, Brigadier-General J. E. Edmonds, was the cause of particular anguish. Edmonds contended that the book was 'more academic than practical', lamented the lack of attention paid to 'books on strategy read by soldiers before 1914' by such authors as Hamley, Mordacq, and von Blume, and dwelt on the lack of direct military experience of the vast majority of chapter authors. The following year, still irritated by the accusation, Earle raised it when consulting with Sir Herbert Richmond, who expressed his surprise that 'so experienced and cultivated a man as Edmonds should have expressed such a sentiment' and dismissed the notion as 'a false doctrine'. MC020/Box 36/Makers of Modern Strategy 1943–5 [3 of 5], J. E. Edmonds review in *Army Quarterly*, XLIX October 1944. MC020/Box 36/Makers of Modern Strategy 1943 [2 of 5], Richmond to Earle, 10 March 1945.

86 MAKING MAKERS

National Review	April 1945	C
Spectator	2 February 1945	C
Contemporary Review	January 1945	A
World Review	December 1944	B
Royal Engineers Journal	December 1944	A (Although unfavourable)
Cambridge Review	2 December 1944	B (Critical of DeWeerd)
Yorkshire Post	3 November 1944	Perfunctory
Glasgow Herald	26 October 1944	B
The Scotsman	5 October 1944	B
Punch	4 October 1944	A (Short but very complimentary)
Observer	24 September 1944	A
John O'London's Weekly	8 September 1944	A (But very unfavorable especially of Gibson)
The Listener	7 September 1944	A (But critical)
Birmingham Post	22 August 1944	B (Although laudatory)
Belfast Telegraph		A

Note: A, B and C indicate the quality of the review, A being excellent.

Figure 2.9 Earle's ranking of reviews of *Makers of Modern Strategy* in 'English' journals.

Source: MLP, Earle Papers, MC020 Box 36 Writings: Correspondence and Related Materials, Folder: Books—Makers of Modern Strategy 1943–5 [3 of 5], Reviews of MAKERS OF MODERN STRATEGY in English journals.

ranged across the centuries, including the following: 'Chapter on Carnot?', 'Vauban to be supplemented by other data on military engineering. Trace connections between Vauban and Maginot (involving a discussion of historic French foreign and strategic policies)', 'Marshal Saxe?', 'Gneisenau and Scharnhorst', 'Fuller and de Gaulle', 'Mahan to be supplemented by other Americans. Fiske and Sims?', 'Petain to be in Chap 15 (including name in title)'.[147]

He made an early start in broaching some of these areas, with mixed results. In November 1943 he asked Palmer if he would write a chapter on Carnot 'sometime in the foreseeable future, building around him the idea that a political and social revolution always has its impact upon military affairs'.[148] Palmer's commitments to the Historical Section, Army Ground Forces now prevented him from accepting. Although he recognized the value of a piece on Carnot, he reasoned that 'the time doesn't exist, and what with my eyesight I can't work in the evening after a full day at the office'.[149] A few months later, Earle's attention was drawn to a review in *Survey Graphic* in which the author argued for the inclusion of the sixteenth-century cartographer Mercator.[150] He subsequently wrote to Derwent Whittlesey

---

[147] Chapter 15 refers to Gibson's 'Maginot and Liddell-Hart: The Doctrine of Defense'. MLP, Earle Papers, MC020 Box 36, Makers of Modern Strategy 1943 [2 of 5], Undated Handwritten Note.

[148] MLP, Earle Papers, MC020/Box 36/Makers of Modern Strategy 1943 [1 of 5], Earle to Palmer, 20 November 1943.

[149] MLP, Earle Papers, MC020/Box 36/Makers of Modern Strategy 1943 [1 of 5], Palmer to Earle, 22 November 1943.

[150] MLP, Earle Papers, MC020/Box 36/Makers of Modern Strategy 1943–1945 [3 of 5], 'War as a Science'. Review by Hans W. Weigert in *Survey Graphic*, January 1944.

to enquire whether he might augment his chapter on Haushofer—itself a very late addition to the book—with some appropriate reflections. Whittlesey felt that it was more appropriate to add a stand-alone 'short essay on the effect of maps upon military thinking' to be written in collaboration between a historian and a geographer, rather than himself.[151] As these examples demonstrate, in thinking about how to prepare a new *Makers* Earle almost immediately began to depart from his earlier assertion that historical completeness was neither desirable nor possible. Given more time to think about the parameters of the book, the historical omissions became more apparent.

More than the historical aspects, however, in the years after publication Earle's attention was increasingly drawn towards revisions related to contemporary events.[152] As well as being driven by the prospect of future access to official documentation which might be used to provide a solid basis for deeper post-war assessments, this was also a consequence of the events of the Second World War itself, which shone new light on particular domains. Those areas most in need of revision were underlined in the two reviews of *Makers* that Earle found most constructive, both of which came from the pens of former seminar members. Despite the acrimonious events earlier in the year, when Herbert Rosinski's review appeared in December 1943 Earle was pleased to discover that he had written a largely complimentary piece, although one which suggested some areas for improvement.[153] Bernard Brodie's review, meanwhile, did not appear until the following October. Since Brodie had already told Earle in late 1943 that the book was shaping up to be 'the outstanding symposium of the decade', it hardly came as a surprise to find that Brodie's published remarks were very positive, although like Rosinski he pointed out a few substantial shortcomings.[154]

One such shortcoming was in the domain of air power, the treatment of which Brodie considered to have been very limited.[155] Earle readily acknowledged this criticism and was already planning a new chapter for the post-war *Makers* which would focus on RAF Air Chief Marshal Sir Arthur Harris and USAAF

---

[151] MLP, Earle Papers, MC020/Box 36/Makers of Modern Strategy 1943 [2 of 5], Whittlesey to Earle, 10 February 1944. For Whittlesey see L. Ashworth, 'A Forgotten Environmental International Relations: Derwent Whittlesey's International Thought', *Global Studies Quarterly*, Vol. 1, No. 2 (June 2021), pp. 1–10.

[152] IAS, Institute for Advanced Study Princeton (N.J.), Director's Office, Faculty records, Box 7/ Earle, Edward Mead, Memoranda, 'Purposes and character of proposed volume on the development of modern military thought', 27 March 1942.

[153] MLP, Earle Papers, MC020/Box 36/Makers of Modern Strategy 1943–5 [3 of 5], 'The Evolution of Total War' (A review by Dr. Herbert Rosinski), *Infantry Journal*, December 1943. Earle described it as 'In many ways this is the most intelligent and the most satisfactory comment which has been made on the work.' MC020/Box 36/Makers of Modern Strategy 1943 [1 of 5], Earle to Rosinski, 26 November 1943.

[154] B. Brodie, review in *The American Journal of International Law*, Vol. 38, No. 4 (October 1944), pp. 754–5.

[155] Brodie review, p. 755, although he conceded in part that this was due to 'the paucity of sound and penetrating writings on the subject which have thus far appeared' and gave praise to the sole chapter on the subject, Ed Warner's 'Douhet, Mitchell, Seversky'.

General H. H. Arnold, 'making the central theme the divergent British and American viewpoints concerning strategic bombing'. He intended to write this chapter himself, and awaited with some excitement the declassification of material, 'so that I can really go to town'.[156] He was in an advantageous position to engage in such an analysis, on account of the significant role that he continued to play as special consultant to the USAAF and a member of the Joint Target Group. In the later years of the war these responsibilities increasingly required not only that he travel to Washington, but also that he travel abroad. In the late spring and early summer of 1944 he spent three weeks in the United Kingdom with the US Strategic Air Forces and the Eighth and Ninth Air Forces, predominantly advising on issues relating to the bombing of Europe before and immediately after the Normandy landings. This was followed by a two-month trip to Germany in the summer of 1945, on business relating to the Historical Division of the Army Air Forces.[157] The latter visit came after the authorization Earle received in April 1945 to prepare multiple volumes of a general operational history of the USAAF 'for publication as soon as possible after termination of hostilities'. This task would give him access to 'all Army Air Forces files available to officer historians', authorization 'to visit continental and overseas air forces and commands', and the guaranteed cooperation of all Army Air Forces personnel in the furtherance of his work.[158] When given this authorization from the USAAF Earle was elated. 'Naturally, I consider this a great opportunity,' he wrote to Aydelotte, 'one which lies entirely within the field of my academic interests.'[159]

The second area that received substantial attention was sea power. For Rosinski, Sprout's chapter on Mahan emphasized 'the political and historical aspects of his work and the influence of his ideas both upon American and foreign naval policy rather than his fundamental contribution to the establishment of a theory of naval strategy', whilst Ropp's contribution 'Continental Doctrines of Sea Power' 'hardly does justice to the very curious development of the German Navy's outlook from its real founder Tirpitz to the present conflict'.[160] Brodie was far less

---

[156] MLP, Earle Papers, MC020/Box 13/Correspondence Brodie, Bernard 1944–5, Earle to Brodie, 8 December 1944.

[157] IAS, Institute for Advanced Study Princeton (N.J.), Director's Office, Faculty records, Box 6/ Earle, Edward Mead, 1945–7, Earle to Aydelotte, 13 October 1945.

[158] IAS, Institute for Advanced Study Princeton (N.J.), Director's Office, Faculty records, Box 6/ Earle, Edward Mead, 1945–7, Memorandum for the Assistant Chief of Air Staff, Intelligence, 23 April 1945.

[159] IAS, Institute for Advanced Study Princeton (N.J.), Director's Office, Faculty records, Box 6/ Earle, Edward Mead, 1945–7, Earle to Aydelotte, 4 May 1945. For his wartime work with the USAAF Earle was subsequently awarded the US Presidential Medal for Merit and the French *Legion d'Honneur*. IAS, Institute for Advanced Study Princeton (N.J.), Director's Office, Faculty records, Box 6/Earle, Edward Mead, 1945–7, Abstract from Army Air Forces Recommendation for Medal for Merit for Edward Mead Earle. Ekbladh, 'Present at the Creation', pp. 126–7, 132–4.

[160] MLP, Earle Papers, MC020/Box 36/Makers of Modern Strategy 1943–5 [3 of 5], 'The Evolution of Total War' (A review by Dr. Herbert Rosinski), *Infantry Journal*, December 1943.

MEAD EARLE, THE IAS, AND THE SECOND WORLD WAR   89

critical of those chapters, but he was fully in agreement with Rosinski's contention that 'the great tradition of British naval thought is almost completely ignored'.[161]

For Brodie, the limited treatment of sea power was a matter of particular regret, 'since the editor and contributors are citizens of the country which has now become the premier sea power of the world'.[162] In private correspondence with Earle, he expanded on the 'notable hiatus in the absence of English naval thought' that the book presented:

> The British, after all, began at least as early as the Dutch Wars of the 17th century to fight according to the ideas which Mahan later developed and popularized. And it is inconceivable that in all the letters and memoranda, published and unpublished, of such figures as Barham, Anson, Rodney, Nelson and others it should not be possible to derive some sort of coherent doctrine. Your book clearly does not restrict itself to figures who wrote complete treatises for publication.
>
> Another British figure who I think should have a whole chapter is Mahan's great contemporary, Julian Corbett. Corbett would be especially interesting to you because he was a civilian scholar whose ideas clearly dominated British naval strategy in the last war.[163]

Once again, Earle was in full agreement. During 1944 he had been consulting with others as to how the treatment of naval theorists might be improved in the second edition.[164] His most important correspondent was Sir Herbert Richmond. After mentioning to Brodie that Richmond was equally keen to see a future chapter on Corbett, Brodie was quick to suggest that this offered 'an excellent opening to ask him to do the job', adding that 'you could find no better person. Richmond is in my opinion England's most distinguished naval writer today'.[165] The former commander of the Royal Naval War College and commandant of the Imperial Defence College, then Master of Downing College, Cambridge, had by now

---

[161] Brodie review, p. 755. He described Sprout's work as 'long and competent' and, contrary to Rosinski, considered Ropp's chapter 'a brilliant interpretation'. MLP, Earle Papers, MC020/Box 36/Makers of Modern Strategy 1943–5 [3 of 5], 'The Evolution of Total War' (A review by Dr. Herbert Rosinski), *Infantry Journal*, December 1943.

[162] Brodie review, p. 755.

[163] MLP, Earle Papers, MC020/Box 13/Correspondence Brodie, Bernard 1944–5, Brodie to Earle, 17 November 1944.

[164] As well as Richmond, Earle also solicited views from Allan Westcott of the US Naval Academy, who suggested a chapter on Corbett or Richmond, as well as 'a chapter perhaps on combined operations, or "triphibious" warfare'. He also believed there was 'a good deal of interest in the older British (and also Dutch) ideas on the functions of a fleet, from Sir Walter Raleigh on, and the gradual development of the idea of command of the sea'. MLP, Earle Papers, MC020/Box 36/Makers of Modern Strategy 1943 [2 of 5], Westcott to Earle, 8 January 1944.

[165] MLP, Earle Papers, MC020/Box 13/Correspondence Brodie, Bernard 1944–5, Earle to Brodie, 20 November 1944. MC020/Box 36/Makers of Modern Strategy 1943 [2 of 5], Brodie to Earle, 24 November 1944.

reached the twilight of his career.[166] He voiced concern about the difficulty of examining British naval theory in a cohesive manner, writing: 'It is not easy to define the British doctrines or theories of sea warfare. Certainly they never have been defined except perhaps in the form of some broad generalisations drawn from our practices, but it will take some hard thinking to make an analysis of them.' In any case, he was not the person to meet this challenge. He lamented that he could have obliged if he were 'twenty years younger and in the robust health I've been so fortunate as to enjoy throughout my life until my heart caved in four years ago', but he now found himself bound to too many existing projects, and so had to decline Earle's offer.[167]

Although Brodie appeared as the next obvious candidate for this task, Earle had other plans for him. These related to the most striking of *Makers*'s three chapters on war at sea, Alexander Kiralfy's 'Japanese Naval Strategy'. Kiralfy, who led a career in the film industry whilst maintaining a sideline as an observer and commentator on Pacific maritime affairs, was a second choice to author the chapter after Professor John Masland of Stanford University. He argued that Japanese naval thought was radically different from naval thought in the West, and that 'occidental terminology' was not a useful means to understand it. The Japanese adapted naval strategy and tactics to an aggressive 'spirit of the Samurai' and to the geography of the Far East, with the result that their navy did not subscribe to the idea of 'command of the sea', was not bound to the principle of annihilation of the enemy fleet, and subordinated its role to the land forces. This made it 'a floating wing of a powerful army occupied with offensive operations in an area militarily far weaker than Europe or North America'.[168] Brodie took exception to these ideas in his review, describing Kiralfy's chapter as 'an analysis of Japanese naval strategy which because of its many inaccuracies and misconceptions is of very dubious value and in this reviewer's opinion unworthy of its company in the book'.[169]

---

[166] For Richmond's Cambridge years see B. Hunt, *Sailor-Scholar: Admiral Sir Herbert Richmond, 1871–1946* (Waterloo, Ontario: Wilfrid Laurier Press, 1982), pp. 208–34. H. G. Thursfield, 'Richmond, Sir Herbert William (1871–1946)', rev. Marc Brodie, *Oxford Dictionary of National Biography* (Oxford University Press, 2004), http://www.oxforddnb.com/view/article/35743, accessed 5 September 2012. D. M. Schurman, *The Education of a Navy: The Development of British Naval Strategic Thought, 1867–1914* (London: Cassell, 1965), pp. 116–46.

[167] MLP, Earle Papers, MC020/Box 36/Makers of Modern Strategy 1943 [2 of 5], Richmond to Earle, 10 March 1945. The books to which Richmond referred include *Statesmen and Sea Power*, published shortly before his death in 1946, and *The Navy as an Instrument of Policy*, never completed but published posthumously and covering only the period from 1558 to 1727.

[168] A. Kiralfy, 'Japanese Naval Strategy', in Earle (ed.), *Makers of Modern Strategy*, pp. 457–84. Kiralfy presented the same ideas in an article for *Foreign Affairs*. See A. Kiralfy, 'Why Japan's Fleet Avoids Action', *Foreign Affairs*, Vol. 22, No. 1 (October 1943), pp. 45–58. Kiralfy's arguments echoed those of British military observers of the Russo-Japanese War of 1904–5, who contended that the Japanese had 'achieved a marriage of *Bushido* and modernity'. See P. Porter, *Military Orientalism: Eastern War through Western Eyes* (London: Hurst, 2009), pp. 88, 87–98.

[169] Brodie review, p. 755. Stefan Possony also refuted Kiralfy's reading of Japanese history at length in 'Japanese Naval Strategy', *United States Naval Institute Proceedings*, Vol. 70, No. 5 (May 1944), pp. 515–24.

This was not the first time Brodie had taken aim at Kiralfy. In the third edition of his *Guide to Naval Strategy*, published earlier the same year, he had offered forthright criticism of the 'current widespread tendency to exaggerate the peculiarities of Japanese thinking and behaviour', arguing that 'there is no use in going, as some writers do, into remote Japanese naval history to find precedents for a behaviour which does not in fact exist'. Japanese strategy had to be understood solely in the context of the modern Japanese navy, as a creation of the late nineteenth century. Whilst the Japanese navy was necessarily bound to a national strategy produced by a particular set of historical and geographical problems, it was in this respect no different from any other navy. Therefore the broader principles of naval strategy applied to the Japanese as much as to any other power.[170] Shortly after his review of *Makers* appeared, Brodie again took aim at Kiralfy in an article for *The Nation*. Without referring to him by name, he argued that the Second Battle of the Philippine Sea had claimed an intellectual casualty: 'the recently popular theory that the Japanese navy shunned the Nelsonian tradition of decisive actions for command of the sea, that it regarded itself as merely "a floating wing of a powerful army," existing exclusively for convoy escort'. The battle had been 'Trafalgar for Japan', proof of its commitment to the annihilation of the enemy.[171]

In correspondence, Brodie voiced his objections in even more forthright terms, writing:

> I always regretted the inclusion of the Kiralfy chapter in the book not only because I felt it unworthy of its company in a scholarly sense but especially because I felt that the inevitable and perhaps too-tardy exposure of its fallacies might tend to discredit the whole book. That appeared a particular danger when it early became clear that this chapter was being made the center of much of the publicity given the volume. It was the subject of much discussion, and Kiralfy was obliquely honored by being plagiarized by all sorts of writers. All that was not surprising, since the Kiralfy chapter was the most sensational one in the book as well as the one of most immediate popular interest. And it acquired an aura of authenticity from the scholarly quality of the whole volume.

> What Kiralfy did was rewrite history to conform to a doctrine conceived in solitude, something comparable to the Marxist "economic interpretation of history" but with even less justification. Naturally it could be implemented only by a kind of phony documentation. If it were necessary to offer any final refutation of his views, I would only have to quote several passages from an important document found on Saipan which recently came to my desk.[172]

---

[170] B. Brodie, *A Guide to Naval Strategy*, 3rd edn. (Princeton, NJ: Princeton University Press, 1944), pp. 131–2.

[171] B. Brodie, 'Trafalgar for Japan', *The Nation*, 11 November 1944, pp. 580–3.

[172] MLP, Earle Papers, MC020/Box 13/Correspondence Brodie, Bernard 1944–5, Brodie to Earle, 17 November 1944.

92 MAKING MAKERS

By the time Earle discussed the matter with Brodie, he was already very aware of the shortcomings of Kiralfy's chapter, and had decided that 'when we get out a second edition of "Makers of Modern Strategy" we shall need to have an entirely new discussion of Japanese naval policy, in the light of the developments of this war'. Having already displayed a zeal for refuting Kiralfy's arguments, Brodie would be the ideal candidate for the new piece.[173] He set about collecting materials immediately for a new chapter centred on Togo, who 'adapted to Japanese problems the ideas of Mahan', and Yamamoto, 'the modernizer who brought in the emphasis on air combat'.[174] Despite this initial burst of enthusiasm, at the end of the war Brodie rapidly reoriented his interests towards the implications of the nuclear age, thus ensuring that his chapter on Togo and Yamamoto was never completed.

The final episode in the unfinished genesis of Earle's revised edition of *Makers* came after the war was over. This time, the protagonist was a reader and a subject of a chapter, rather than the editor. When Basil Liddell Hart first obtained a copy of *Makers* in mid-1944, his initial appraisal was none too kind. 'It is a well-meaning, but rather half-baked production', he wrote. 'I found that most of the leading American soldiers I have met over here this year, have, by now, acquired a much better sense of realities, and inherent handicaps, than the authors of this book show.'[175] When he finally contacted Earle to voice his criticisms in April 1946, he was a little more generous but insisted that 'the middle of a great war is not the best time for an accurate assessment of currents of thought—especially the later currents', and that this held particularly true in reference to the chapter in which he was named: 'Maginot and Liddell Hart: The Doctrine of Defense'.[176]

Earle and Liddell Hart were not strangers. Acquainted in writing since 1934, they first met in person in 1938, and would meet again in the summer of 1948 when Earle travelled to All Souls College, Oxford.[177] Amicable relations were no barrier to strident criticism, however, and the critique Liddell Hart offered of

---

[173] MLP, Earle Papers, MC020/Box 13/Correspondence Brodie, Bernard 1944–5, Earle to Brodie, 15 November 1944.

[174] MLP, Earle Papers, MC020/Box 13/Correspondence Brodie, Bernard 1944–5, Brodie to Earle, 17 November 1944. Brodie quickly overcame his reservations concerning his inability to read Japanese. He noted that Kiralfy could not read the language either, and that there were at least three people that he could lay his hands on in his office with knowledge of the language, as well as 'in translation all sorts of documents which could be cited after the war and which could in fact silently guide an interpretation even now'.

[175] LHCMA, LH 1/255/5. Liddell Hart to Hilda Sloane, 5 August 1944. Liddell Hart's opinion of the book did not improve over time. In 1963 he described it as 'of very uneven quality, some of the chapters being very misleading'. Quoted in P. Lorge, *Sun Tzu in the West: The Anglo-American Art of War* (Cambridge: Cambridge University Press, 2022), p. 204.

[176] LHCMA, LH 1/255/6, Liddell Hart to Earle, 24 April 1946.

[177] LHCMA, LH 1/255/1, Liddell Hart to Earle, 30 November 1934. LH 1/255/7, Earle to Liddell Hart, 31 May 1946. LH 1/255/22, Earle to Liddell Hart, 5 June 1948. LH 1/255/24, Earle to Liddell Hart, 5 July 1948. LH 1/255/25, Liddell Hart to Earle, 15 July 1948.

Irving M. Gibson's chapter was lengthy and detailed.[178] Gibson's chapter used the twin reference points of the Maginot Line and Liddell Hart to argue for the development in France and Britain of doctrines of defence which were 'the result of the trend in national thought arising from a superior civilization which turned horror stricken away from the holocaust of war' and which had its roots in a post-First World War 'victory psychology'.[179] Perhaps surprisingly, Liddell Hart's critique was more concerned with the French section than the British, and rested on the notion that many of the author's 'deductions and judgements suffer from a lack of background knowledge—particularly of the European background'.[180] In his initial response, Earle admitted that 'we feared that you would dislike and probably take exception to a great deal of what we had to say concerning your work'.[181] Some months later, he wrote again to give a fuller response. At this point Earle revealed that the author of the chapter was Professor Arpad Kovacs of St John's University in Brooklyn, a historian of Czech origin, who had served in the Austro-Hungarian army during the First World War and had adopted a pseudonym in order to protect family in territory under German control.[182]

Kovacs, who had been forwarded Liddell Hart's critique, offered a feisty rejoinder, arguing that 'the famous author tries to make us believe that black is white, that the French army was offensive, that General Gamelin entertained aggressive schemes, and that the Maginot Line was merely the exception which usually proves the rule'.[183] Prepared to concede mistakes in the British section of the chapter, Kovacs was much less forgiving of criticisms of his argument about France in a repudiation that ran to thirteen pages.[184] Far from settling the matter, however, the missive only served to invite another lengthy reply from Liddell Hart, in which he dealt with Kovacs's response paragraph by paragraph, bemoaning the fact that his opponent had not done likewise, and arguing that this proved that he was 'fighting a defensive action to sustain his original thesis, so far as he

---

[178] LHCMA, LH 1/255/6, Liddell Hart to Earle, 24 April 1946. The full letter ran to twelve typewritten pages, identifying specific page numbers and paragraphs in Kovacs's chapter.

[179] I. Gibson, 'Maginot and Liddell Hart: The Doctrine of Defense', in Earle, *Makers of Modern Strategy*, pp. 365–87.

[180] LHCMA, LH 1/255/6, Liddell Hart to Earle, 24 April 1946.

[181] LHCMA, LH 1/255/7, Earle to Liddell Hart, 31 May 1946.

[182] LHCMA, LH 1/255/10, Earle to Liddell Hart, 22 May 1947. This revelation put paid to Liddell Hart's conviction that errors in the chapter stemmed from the author's unfamiliarity with the European background, and made his further assertion that 'it may be difficult for an American writer [...] to realise the inherent limitations on the strength of Britain and France' look rather foolish. LHCMA, LH 1/255/6, Liddell Hart to Earle, 24 April 1946.

[183] LHCMA, LH 1/255/11, Kovacs to Earle, 8 April 1947.

[184] After the Second World War Kovacs published two articles on the French military in the modern period. See A. Kovacs, 'French Military Institutions before the Franco-Prussian War', *The American Historical Review*, Vol. 51, No. 2 (January 1946), pp. 217–35. A. Kovacs, 'French Military Legislation in the Third Republic 1871–1940', *Military Affairs*, Vol. 13, No. 1 (spring 1949), pp. 1–13.

94   MAKING MAKERS

possibly can, rather than being ready to revise his judgements point by point in accord with fresh evidence.[185]

Harvey DeWeerd, to whom Earle had shown the correspondence, summed up the general feeling regarding Liddell Hart at this time when he wrote that he 'has developed a tendency to justify himself on all issues by reinterpreting what he once wrote or said.[186] Still suffering the damage done to his credentials by his pre-Second World War adherence to the doctrine of 'limited liability', and even allowing for the fact that, in the words of Brian Bond, 'Liddell Hart relished intellectual discussion and controversy both in conversation and in print', his correspondence during this episode conveyed a certain anxiousness to exert control over his own reputation.[187] For his part, Earle was keen to find a way to put the issue to bed as quickly as possible. To Kovacs, he speculated about the possibility of publishing the debate in article form, provided Liddell Hart was also willing.[188] The following year he told Liddell Hart that he was consulting with colleagues on an appropriate venue for the publication, although the correspondence was 'not likely to have very general interest.[189] DeWeerd, a former associate editor of the *Infantry Journal*, did not think the exchange worthy of publication as it stood, and suggested instead that Liddell Hart be invited 'to contribute a chapter to any revision of <u>Makers of Modern Strategy</u> restating his position on the questions at issue.[190] The idea did not appeal to Earle, who merely assured Liddell Hart that 'when we revise "Makers of Modern Strategy"—as we shall have to do shortly, because the present supply is approaching exhaustion—Kovacs will, of course, take your comments into account.[191] He reassured Kovacs, however, that 'I am committing you to nothing when I say that you will "take his comments into

---

[185] LHCMA, LH 1/255/13, Notes on the letter of Professor Kovacs ("Irving M. Gibson") to Professor Edward M. Earle, April 8th, 1947—with regard to my criticism of his chapter in "Makers of Modern Strategy", LHCMA, LH 1/255/12, Liddell Hart to Earle, 19 September 1947.

[186] MLP, Earle Papers, MC020/Box 36/Writings: Correspondence and Related Materials, Folder: Books—Makers of Modern Strategy 1943 [2 of 5], De Weerd to Earle, 10 June 1947.

[187] During the period in which Liddell Hart and Earle corresponded over *Makers*, Liddell Hart seriously considered a permanent switch from military writing to fashion writing, after having failed to secure the Chichele Professorship in the History of War in April 1946. See A. Danchev, *Alchemist of War: The Life of Basil Liddell Hart* (London: Weidenfeld and Nicolson, 1998), particularly pp. 187–242. B. Bond, *Liddell Hart: A Study of His Military Thought* (Aldershot: Gregg Revivals in association with Department of War Studies, Kings College London, 1991), p. 3. For the role of 'limited liability' in Liddell Hart's decline see pp. 88–115. For detail on Liddell Hart's post-war attempts at manipulating his own historical legacy, see J. Mearscheimer, *Liddell Hart and the Weight of History* (London: Brassey's Defence, 1988), pp. 178–217. For a wartime example of Liddell Hart's desire to protect and mould his reputation see his interactions with George Orwell in J. Stone, 'George Orwell on Politics and War', *Review of International Studies*, Vol. 43, part 2 (2016), pp. 233–7.

[188] MLP, Earle Papers, MC020/Box 19/Correspondence, Liddell Hart, B. H. 1946–52, Earle to Kovacs, 31 May 1946.

[189] LHCMA, LH 1/255/10, Earle to Liddell Hart, 22 May 1947.

[190] MLP, Earle Papers, MC020/Box 36/Makers of Modern Strategy 1943 [2 of 5], De Weerd to Earle, 10 June 1947.

[191] LHCMA, LH 1/255/10, Earle to Liddell Hart, 22 May 1947.

MEAD EARLE, THE IAS, AND THE SECOND WORLD WAR   95

account"' since Kovacs had made 'an effective case'. As for Liddell Hart, Earle noted, he had 'a lot to answer for to his country and to the world. And he learneth not, for he is back doing business at the old stand—this time in the guise of "limited war".'[192]

Conclusion

By the time Earle died in June 1954, his ambition of compiling a new edition remained unfulfilled.[193] Although he still entertained the notion into 1947, post-war events made it increasingly unlikely that he would achieve this goal. With the end of the war came the return of Earle's health problems. As had been the case before the war, Earle experienced periods of reprieve as well as suffering during the rest of the 1940s before things took a turn for the worse in the following decade. He spent the last academic year of his life seriously ill, particularly affected by 'a severe and somewhat mysterious gastro-intestinal disturbance'.[194] By early June 1954 he had been admitted to hospital in New York for special surgery and was suffering from an infection in his knee.[195] He died in his sleep soon after.[196]

Earle blamed the initial return of his ill health on the work that he had undertaken with the USAAF. 'Overwork and high altitude flying caused a recurrence of an old tuberculous lesion,' he wrote in 1947. He reasoned that with his medical history he should have stayed away from war service, but he found the offer too good to refuse.[197] Yet the opportunities afforded Earle by his work with the USAAF came to an abrupt halt with the war's end. Despite the authorization that was given to Earle to work on an official history of USAAF operations, and despite the alacrity with which he greeted this news, by November 1945 it was decided between Aydelotte and Earle that he would not move forward with the project.[198] With the end of the USAAF project came the end of Earle's privileged access to the sources he intended to use to write his chapter for the revised *Makers*. Just as was the case with Brodie's on Togo and Yamamoto, the chapter never materialized.

---

[192] MLP, Earle Papers, MC020/Box 19/Correspondence, Liddell Hart, B. H. 1946–52, Earle to Kovacs, 22 May 1947. Earle's correspondence demonstrates that Liddell Hart had not 'succeeded in convincing Earle that the chapter's author was fundamentally wrong', as Mearscheimer suggests. Mearscheimer, *Liddell Hart*, p. 217 note 123.

[193] For an obituary, see 'E. M. Earle Dead; Military Expert', *New York Times*, 25 June 1954.

[194] CUL, Guerlac Papers Box 4, Folder 57, IAS Correspondence, Earle to J. P. T. Bury, 19 April 1954.

[195] CUL, Guerlac Papers, Box 4, Folder 57, IAS Correspondence, Marion Hartz to Guerlac, 15 June 1954.

[196] CUL, Guerlac Papers, Box 4, Folder 57, IAS Correspondence, Marion Hartz to Guerlac, 1 July 1954.

[197] LHCMA. LH 1/255/14, Earle to Liddell Hart, 7 October 1947.

[198] IAS, Institute for Advanced Study Princeton (N.J.), Director's Office, Faculty records, Box 6/ Earle, Edward Mead, 1945–7, Joseph E. Johnson to Aydelotte, 23 November 1945.

96   MAKING MAKERS

The forces that had coalesced to facilitate both Earle's seminar and *Makers of Modern Strategy* seemed to dissipate once they had been drained of the urgency supplied by the war itself. Earle did try to give the 'Princeton Military Studies Group' a more permanent institutional form. In June 1945, for example, he wrote to Secretary of the Navy James V. Forrestal in the hope of persuading him to raise a fund of one million dollars for its future activities.[199] No such grant was made, however, and as a consequence the *centre d'études militaires* that Earle believed he was creating in the Princeton community remained an informal entity: a meeting of scholars drawn together by Earle and indelibly linked to his person. With Earle's death, such an ephemeral creation was bound to disappear.

In truth, Earle himself had also moved on to new areas of research in the years before his death, and seemed also to have given up remaking *Makers*. In a letter to Robert Oppenheimer sent in October 1948 he outlined two areas of interest on which he wished to focus seminars in the period 1949–51, both of which were distinctly European: first, a study of economics and politics in Europe during the second half of the eighteenth century, and second, a study of the political, economic, and international problems of modern France.[200] The latter eventually resulted in the second weighty tome that Earle edited during his lifetime.[201] He also found time to oversee a *festschrift* for Carlton Hayes.[202] These projects rendered it increasingly unlikely that Earle would ever return to *Makers*. So too did his continuing desire to travel, despite his health troubles. Oxford University, and All Souls College in particular, was his preferred destination. Earle enjoyed several residencies in Oxford in the late 1940s, culminating in his election to an associate membership of All Souls for two months in 1950, during which time he gave the Chichele Lectures on the subject of 'The American Stake in Europe, 1900–1950'.[203] He was sufficiently well known within the university at the time of his death to warrant a note in *The Oxford Magazine*, which emphasized that 'few of our American visitors have done more to build up ties of friendship between the academic communities on both sides of the Atlantic'.[204]

These words offered a suitable epitaph for a man who had begun his career as a researcher but ended as a networker and facilitator. Not that Earle would have

---

[199] IAS, Institute for Advanced Study Princeton (N.J.), Director's Office, Faculty records, Box 6/Earle, Edward Mead, 1945–7, Earle to Captain Lewis L. Strauss, 1 June 1945. Earle to James V. Forrestal, 1 June 1945.

[200] IAS, Institute for Advanced Study Princeton (N.J.), Director's Office, Faculty records, Box 7/Earle, Edward Mead, 1948–9, Earle to Oppenheimer, 22 October 1948.

[201] E. M. Earle (ed.), *Modern France: Problems of the Third and Fourth Republics* (Princeton, NJ: Princeton University Press, 1951). Henry Guerlac was the only contributor to *Makers* who also wrote for the *Modern France* volume. Guerlac and Earle became friends in the post-war period, with Guerlac joining the IAS as a member for a two-year term from 1953.

[202] Earle (ed.), *Nationalism and Internationalism*.

[203] IAS, Institute for Advanced Study Princeton (N.J.), Director's Office, Faculty records, Box 7/Earle, Edward Mead, 1948–9. Sumner to Oppenheimer (Director), 11 May 1949.

[204] *The Oxford Magazine*, Vol. 73, No. 2 (21 October 1954), p. 27.

MEAD EARLE, THE IAS, AND THE SECOND WORLD WAR 97

been happy with such a description. As early 1941 he could see the risks that his activities posed to his research career, writing to Aydelotte:

> It may well be that my greatest usefulness is in the continuation of my research and writing. Aside from the important work of my seminar during the past two years (which has been largely a <u>teaching</u> rather than a <u>research</u> job), I am frankly disappointed in my own achievements. I do not mean that they have not been considerable. But they are not what they would have been had I not been compelled to run an employment service, a real estate office, a visa bureau, and a thousand and one other extraneous things. I must ruthlessly give more of myself to my own work and less of myself to the work of others if I am going to realize my full usefulness to the Institute.[205]

But Earle's career was of his own making. In the pre-war years he turned the circumstances at the nascent IAS to his advantage in order to pursue the things that most interested him, and did so in the manner that he thought best to achieve this. His health struggles aside, if he never managed to produce a substantial piece of academic research to match his work on the Baghdad railway, this came not as a consequence of constraints placed upon him but as a result of choices freely made.

As for *Makers*, it stood as the most tangible legacy of Earle's collaborative research contribution as well as of his wider project at the IAS, although it was not a simple distillation of it. The volume emerged from the efforts of a small number of those involved in Earle's seminar: Vagts, DeWeerd, and especially Gilbert, before it was taken up by Earle. Thereafter, Gilbert appeared to exert as much influence over the contours and composition as Earle did, with Craig arriving only in the later stages of compilation. The book was also shaped by the concerns of its francophone and germanophone contributors. Indeed, there was a certain irony that Earle, so firm in his conviction that 'the education of the British and American peoples in military affairs is essential if we are to have a lasting peace or if, failing that, we are to survive a third world war', had overseen a work that said so little about both American experiences and British naval thought.[206]

Nevertheless, Earle's achievement, and that of his collaborators, was significant in enhancing the legitimacy of the civilian academic study of war in the anglophone sphere into the mid-twentieth century. Moreover, they had taken the book

---

[205] IAS, Institute for Advanced Study Princeton (N.J.), Director's Office, Faculty records, Box 6/Earle, Edward Mead, 1940–4, Earle to Aydelotte, 12 August 1941.

[206] MLP, Earle Papers, MC020/Box 36/Makers of Modern Strategy 1943 [2 of 5], Earle to Richmond, 20 December 1944. The lack of attention to American affairs was remarked upon by several reviews. See, for example, MC020/Box 36/Makers of Modern Strategy 1943–5 [3 of 5], Review by Colonel Ernest R. Dupuy in *The Saturday Review of Literature*, November 13, 1943, Vol. 26, p. 9. Review by Ralph Adams Brown in *Social Education*, Washington, D.C., November 1944.

from inception to print in little over a year. This was a remarkable turnaround, achieved against the backdrop of the dissolution of Earle's group in Princeton and the increasing demands that wartime service placed on contributors and editors alike. It was also ironic, then, that when faced with the prospect of undertaking a substantially revised edition, under conditions that allowed for fuller consideration of what had been missed and what needed to change, Earle was unable to rise to the task. As noted above, this was partly a consequence of Earle's own choices and his faltering health. Yet it was also a consequence of his commitment to consideration of both past and contemporary developments. Even before the end of the war, it was clear how quickly some of the chapters which seemed most revelatory had lost their lustre. In the rapidly changing strategic context of the post-war world it is easy to see how this task snowballed beyond Earle's control. Earle had both succeeded in making *Makers* and failed in revising it. The task of remaking the book would be left for others to undertake. He would not be the only one defeated by it.

Making Makers: The Past, the Present, and the Study of War. Michael P. M. Finch, Oxford University Press.
© Michael P. M. Finch 2024. DOI: 10.1093/9780191959257.003.0003

3

Revisiting *Makers*

Theodore Ropp and the Afterlife of the Book

The professional historian has only two reasons to venture onto the thin ice of contemporary history. Beneath it, Admiral Hindsight has repeatedly warned, lurk the whirlpools of contemporary social science. But somebody has to call attention to history's practical value. [...] We have freely criticized other haruspices for misreading their chicken livers, for theoretical prognostications which cost them their reputations and many others their lives. If historians try forecasting, it may add some charity to their judgements of stupidity or folly, or civic courage or timidity. Unlike Earle's writers, we must also counter the idea that only contemporary science and the social sciences are relevant.

—Theodore Ropp, 1980[1]

In the years immediately preceding his death, Edward Mead Earle appeared to have given up on his attempt to prepare a second edition of *Makers*. Travel opportunities, alternative research projects, and ultimately his poor health ensured that he never returned to the book after his correspondence with Liddell Hart ended in 1947. Yet the book did not die with Earle. As this chapter shows, *Makers* enjoyed an afterlife that began shortly after the editor's death and continued, albeit intermittently, up to the inception of Peter Paret's *Makers*. The first part of the chapter illuminates the interest of Franklin Publications in translating parts of the book during the 1950s as part of its efforts during the cultural Cold War. In this manner *Makers* continued to be a scholarly asset 'from the arsenal of democracy'—as Paret would later put it—beyond the Second World War. Alongside former Princeton University Press editor Datus C. Smith's involvement with Franklin, it also underlines the persistence of interest in the book on the part of Herbert S. Bailey, who would later become a pivotal figure in the genesis of the Paret edition.

The main focus of this chapter, however, falls on an individual whose career was yet more intertwined with the book: Theodore Ropp. In the late 1970s and early

---

[1] DSP, Theodore Ropp, 'The Present State of Strategy', 17 April 1980, 19 April 1980, 6.

1980s, Ropp, a long-serving professor at Duke University and a contributor to the original volume, embarked on the most concerted attempt to revise and update *Makers* between the publication of Earle's book and Paret's successor. This attempt can be understood as a bookend to a career pursued in parallel with the growth of academic military history in US higher education: Ropp's contribution to Earle's 1943 volume marked a key stage in his emergence as a military historian, while his own project came as he neared retirement in 1980. In the intervening decades his periodic contributions in print demonstrated a commitment to the teaching of military history and to the production of a body of scholarship that teachers might draw upon. By the late 1970s, however, still unsatisfied with efforts within his field towards the production of bibliographies and textbooks, Ropp turned his attention towards revisiting *Makers*. Afforded an opportunity to spend a trimester in Singapore, Ropp and his chief collaborator, the naval historian Donald Schurman, used that time to consider the viability of a new companion volume. Although they had already devised in outline how they would update Earle's book, the dedicated seminar series they created at the University of Singapore allowed them to consider the project at greater length and in close collaboration with each other, and to scrutinize a number of substantively new prospective chapters, intended not only to bring *Makers* up to date, but to extend the breadth of its historical purview. The book that Ropp hoped to publish, *Makers of Modern Strategy Revisited*, never appeared in print. For reasons both personal and professional, its editor was unable to see the task through. Yet despite this failure, scrutiny of Ropp's project is illuminating both for the alternate vision it offers of a successor to *Makers*, and for the insights Ropp's case gives into the development of military history and its deceptively complex relations with the *Makers* project.

Cold Warriors and Scholars

The first rumblings of a new wave of interest in *Makers* arrived almost exactly one year after Earle's death. In June 1955 the Princeton University Press requested permission from the IAS for an Urdu-language version of *Makers*, to be published in Pakistan. The envisioned translation would be an abridged version of the book, comprising about 50 per cent of the original work, with chapters such as Kiralfy's and Warner's removed on the grounds that they were already obsolete. In their stead, it was proposed that more up-to-date material might be included, such as an air power piece by Bernard Brodie.[2] In October of the same year a request was made for a complete and unabridged translation into Persian.[3]

---

[2] IAS, Institute for Advanced Study Princeton (N.J.). Director's Office. Faculty records, Box 7/Earle, Edward Mead, 1950–1970. Telephone note, 7 June 1955.

[3] IAS, Institute for Advanced Study Princeton (N.J.). Director's Office. Faculty records, Box 7/Earle, Edward Mead, 1950–1970. Herbert S. Bailey to Oppenheimer, 11 October 1955.

THEODORE ROPP AND THE AFTERLIFE OF THE BOOK 101

These requests demonstrated that the appeal of *Makers* had spread beyond the anglophone world. Yet the enquiries did not come directly to PUP from publishing houses in Pakistan and Iran. Rather, PUP acted as an intermediary on behalf of another institution: Franklin Publications. Franklin had been set up in June 1952 by a mixed group of book publishers, library directors, and academics, and received funding from both private and public sources, drawing support in particular from the US International Information Administration and the US Agency for International Development. With a mission to use print publications to promote American values outside the English-speaking world, Franklin opened local offices in many of the countries in which it operated, becoming a significant organization in carrying the cultural Cold War to Africa, the Middle East, and Latin America through to its closure in 1978.[4]

Much of Franklin's initial activity, of which the request to the IAS formed a part, involved seeking to secure translations of important works of non-fiction. If *Makers of Modern Strategy* was known in the offices of Franklin Publishing, however, it was likely thanks to its director, Datus C. Smith, Jr., the key figure in guiding Franklin through its formative years. Smith was a Princeton University graduate who had moved from writing and journalism in the 1920s to editing and publishing in the 1930s. In 1940 he joined PUP as an assistant editor. By the time *Makers* was undertaken Smith had become director of the press, a position that he would hold until he chose to leave after taking up his role with Franklin.[5] Although Smith enshrined a principle of local choice into Franklin's mode of operation—whereby local advisors in-country would select the desired books for publication, rather than Americans—Franklin's approach to the IAS in 1955 was not wholly reactive.[6] In addition to seeking permission for the Urdu and Persian translations, Franklin also moved to secure rights to other foreign-language versions of *Makers* in anticipation of future interest. These included Arabic and Turkish, and a range of South Asian languages: Hindi, Bengali, Punjabi, Marathi, Gujarati, Tamil, Telugu, Malayalam, and Kanarese.[7] As the rights holder to *Makers*, the IAS—through the authority of Oppenheimer—happily consented to all these requests.[8] In the years that followed, part-translations of the book were published in various languages. For example, in 1958 a thousand copies of a Persian-language *Makers of Modern Strategy* 'part one' were printed, as were three thousand copies

---

[4] See A. Laugeson, *Taking Books to the World: American Publishers and the Cultural Cold War* (Boston, MA: University of Massachusetts Press, 2017), particularly pp. 1–38.

[5] Ibid., pp. 31–2. Smith initially took a leave of absence from PUP but subsequently decided to resign in order to continue the role with Franklin.

[6] D. C. Smith, Jr., 'Ten Years of Franklin Publications', *ALA Bulletin*, Vol. 57, No. 6 (June 1963), p. 508. Laugeson, *Taking Books to the World*, pp. 32–4.

[7] IAS, Institute for Advanced Study Princeton (N.J.). Director's Office. Faculty records, Box 7/Earle, Edward Mead, 1950–1970. Herbert S. Bailey to Oppenheimer, 11 October 1955.

[8] IAS, Institute for Advanced Study Princeton (N.J.). Director's Office. Faculty records, Box 7/Earle, Edward Mead, 1950–1970. Oppenheimer to Bailey, 14 October 1955.

102 MAKING MAKERS

of an Arabic-language 'part two'.[9] In June 1962 the press notified the IAS of the receipt of 'part three' of the Arabic translation.[10] The following year an Indonesian translation appeared.[11]

During the first two post-war decades, sales of the book remained respectable, even if some of the available figures are contradictory. By 1960, PUP reported that the book had been through several reprints with more than fifteen thousand copies sold.[12] A decade later, the press relayed the news that the book was about to go into its ninth printing, having sold 10,930 copies by the end of August that year.[13] At the same time, the outdated elements of the volume, already apparent to Earle prior to the end of the Second World War, became more pronounced with the passage of years. Herbert S. Bailey, Datus Smith's successor as director of the press, had recognized as much when making the request for an Urdu translation in 1955. Yet *Makers* remained on his mind. Five years later, he wrote to Oppenheimer again, noting that the book was 'now, inevitably, somewhat out of date, and it is selling rather slowly'. Bailey, who saw it as 'still an important and valuable book', did not view this as the death knell for the volume. Instead, he proposed a new edition of the book, which would:

> discard a number of the chapters, such as the ones on Haushofer and on Air Warfare, and would include about 10 new chapters on Soviet Strategy, on Hitler, on MacArthur, on Marshall, on Coalition Strategy, on Nuclear Strategy, and the like. Partly because of the excellent reputation of the original edition, we believe that we could enlist the efforts of the leading experts in the various fields to contribute new chapters. We believe that the addition of such new material, and the omission of out-of-date material, would enhance the value of the older material and would result in a book of major importance.[14]

Bailey made this proposal having already discussed the matter with Gordon Craig. The pair envisaged that Felix Gilbert would also participate in an editorial capacity, with appropriate credit given to Earle. The new book would have a title

---

[9] IAS, Institute for Advanced Study Princeton (N.J.). Director's Office. Faculty records, Box 7/Earle, Edward Mead, 1950–1970. Bailey to Oppenheimer, 28 May 1958. Report of Publication MAKERS OF MODERN STRATEGY PART I (Persian). Report of Publication MAKERS OF MODERN STRATEGY PART II (Arabic).

[10] IAS, Institute for Advanced Study Princeton (N.J.). Director's Office. Faculty records, Box 7/Earle, Edward Mead, 1950–1970. Margaret L. Hopkins to Oppenheimer, 22 June 1962.

[11] IAS, Institute for Advanced Study Princeton (N.J.). Director's Office. Faculty records, Box 7/Earle, Edward Mead, 1950–1970. Gordon Hubel to Oppenheimer, 13 August 1963.

[12] IAS, Institute for Advanced Study Princeton (N.J.). Director's Office. Faculty records, Box 7/Earle, Edward Mead, 1950–1970. Bailey to Oppenheimer, 13 January 1960.

[13] IAS, Institute for Advanced Study Princeton (N.J.). Director's Office. Faculty records, Box 7/Earle, Edward Mead, 1950–1970. Roy E. Thomas to Carl Kaysen, 25 September 1970.

[14] IAS, Institute for Advanced Study Princeton (N.J.). Director's Office. Faculty records, Box 7/Earle, Edward Mead, 1950–1970. Bailey to Oppenheimer, 13 January 1960.

along the lines of 'MAKERS OF MODERN STRATEGY. 2nd edition edited by Gordon A. Craig and Felix Gilbert, based on the original edition edited by Edward Mead Earle.'[15]

In this manner Bailey became the first person, other than Earle himself, to attempt to revise *Makers*. Of note, however, was the prominence of Craig in the proposal. It was Craig whom Bailey had consulted about the new book, rather than Gilbert, and it was Craig who appeared most keen to remain associated with the project. When the press contacted the IAS about the Urdu translation, they also raised the possibility of publishing a shorter English-language version of the work. In response Oppenheimer suggested that Craig be made editor, and did not mention Gilbert.[16] Thus, although Gilbert had been the crucial figure of the two in shaping the first volume, in the post-war period Craig looked to assume a bigger role. His desire would be fulfilled, but not in the short term. Despite Bailey and Craig's apparent enthusiasm for the new edition, it did not progress beyond the initial stage. Nevertheless, the activity surrounding the various translations and the 1960 scheme for a revised edition attested both to the afterlife of Earle's *Makers* and to the desire of others to carry the project forward. Such developments marked the passing of the project from its central figure to others whose professional lives had become entangled with it, and who felt an abiding attachment to it.

Not all those who were involved in the wartime project developed such entanglements. After the war was over, a number of those who wrote for Earle's *Makers* settled quickly back into civilian academic life, resuming or building careers in research and teaching that intersected with the study of war to varying degrees, or not at all. Robert Palmer returned to Princeton, and later worked at Washington University and Yale, cementing his reputation as a distinguished historian of France. Henry Guerlac did the same at Cornell University, with a specialization in the history of medicine. Crane Brinton, a contributor to the chapter on Jomini, continued at Harvard, becoming McLean Professor of Ancient and Modern History in 1946. Hajo Holborn remained at Yale, where he was successively Randolph Townsend Professor of History and then Sterling Professor of History.[17] Even Craig and Gilbert, whose paths would eventually lead back to *Makers*, otherwise led fairly conventional academic careers, Craig at Princeton and then Stanford, Gilbert at Bryn Mawr College and then the Institute for Advanced Study.

---

[15] IAS, Institute for Advanced Study Princeton (N.J.). Director's Office. Faculty records, Box 7/ Earle, Edward Mead, 1950–1970. Bailey to Oppenheimer, 13 January 1960.

[16] IAS, Institute for Advanced Study Princeton (N.J.). Director's Office. Faculty records, Box 7/ Earle, Edward Mead, 1950–1970. Telephone note, 7 June 1955. Perhaps because the sense of Oppenheimer's response was unclear, when Bailey contacted Oppenheimer later in the year regarding the Persian translation he noted that 'I suppose in this, as in the proposed abbreviated Urdu translation, you would prefer to have me check with Gordon Craig before going ahead.' See Bailey to Oppenheimer, 11 October 1955.

[17] For biographies of all those involved in Earle's book as well as his seminar, see the appendix.

104 MAKING MAKERS

For others, however, involvement with *Makers* was a staging post on a pathway that led to a more sustained engagement with problems of war and strategy. This was particularly true of those connected to the project who sought to do so beyond the confines of the university through the RAND corporation, the Santa Monica-based think tank which became a key institution in the establishment of the post-Second World War 'military-intellectual complex'.[18] The lynchpin figure amongst this group, Hans Speier, had been a contributor to Earle's *Makers* but not a member of his seminar.[19] Speier left his native Germany for the USA in reaction to the Nazi assumption of power in 1933. Arriving in New York, he found an academic home at the New School for Social Research, but transferred to government service during the war years and continued his work in occupied Germany once the war was over. Returning to the New School in the autumn of 1947, Speier quickly became disillusioned with civilian academic life, and was excited by the prospects he glimpsed at a RAND symposium in the same year.[20] In June 1948 he became the head of the newly created RAND Social Science Division, where he showed himself to be 'fiercely devoted to RAND's mission of bringing scientific knowledge to bear on U.S. foreign policymaking'.[21]

In order to achieve this goal Speier was proactive in recruiting prominent scholars, many of whom were prior acquaintances who shared with him a record of wartime government service and an attraction to the access to high-level contacts and information that RAND, as the foremost think tank of the era, could provide. One such hire was Harvey DeWeerd. Though not a celebrated scholar, DeWeerd was central to the genesis of *Makers*. He came to the IAS from Denison University for the 1941–2 academic year at the invitation of Earle and quickly fostered good, productive relations with his seminar colleagues. Earle regarded him as 'one of the country's most able military historians, greatly valuing his enthusiasm and prominent role he played in the seminar's activities' such that he arranged for him to remain in Princeton for the 1942–3 academic year, although in the event DeWeerd joined the US Army instead, becoming an associate editor of *Infantry Journal*.[22] After the war, and despite his involvement in some of the first post-1945 military history courses in his new position at the University of Missouri, like Speier, DeWeerd found his return to university life unfulfilling. In 1952 he was persuaded to join RAND by Speier, whom he knew from at least

---

[18] On the early years of RAND see J. Farrell Brodie, 'Learning Secrecy in the Early Cold War: The RAND Corporation', *Diplomatic History*, Vol. 35, No. 4 (September 2011), pp. 643–70. Fred Kaplan, *The Wizards of Armageddon* (Stanford, CA: Stanford University Press, 1991), pp. 51–73.

[19] He wrote the chapter 'Ludendorff: The German Concept of Total War', which was not retained or directly updated in Paret's edition.

[20] For an intellectual biography of Speier see D. Bessner, *Democracy in Exile: Hans Speier and the Rise of the Defence Intellectual* (Ithaca, NY and London: Cornell University Press, 2018).

[21] Ibid., p. 147.

[22] T. Wolters, 'Harvey A. DeWeerd and the Dawn of Academic Military History in the United States', *The Journal of Military History*, Vol. 85, No. 1 (January 2021), pp. 105–10.

THEODORE ROPP AND THE AFTERLIFE OF THE BOOK   105

the time that *Makers* was compiled if not before. At the corporation he put his historical skills to use in the service of war gaming, but he also developed expertise on both limited war and British defence policy, as his work was drawn increasingly towards contemporary problems.[23]

Bernard Brodie was a more significant figure to make the transition to the RAND corporation and the life of the 'defence intellectual'. For Earle, Brodie had been the one figure whose absence, he quickly realized, had made the book a lesser publication than it might have been. Although his presence loomed large over potential revisions for *Makers*, the manner in which the Second World War ended also brought with it an end to Brodie's interest in naval affairs. On the day that he learned of the atomic bomb that had been dropped on Hiroshima, he is reputed to have told his wife that 'everything I have done up till now is obsolete'.[24] The swift publication of *The Absolute Weapon* in 1946 marked the reorientation of his research towards the implications of atomic weaponry and his emergence as a leading voice in a burgeoning field of strategic studies which quickly became dominated by the hypotheticals of nuclear strategy.[25] His Damascene conversion also marked a parting of ways with Earle. Once intimate, by the beginning of the 1950s the pair were so distant from each other that Earle apparently had no qualms about contributing to the events that saw Brodie lose a position as a consultant to the air staff in 1951.[26] In the same year Brodie left Yale to join RAND, remaining there for fifteen years.

The parting was not just personal, it was intellectual. In the last decades of his life, Earle expended much of his energy on championing public understanding of strategy. By contrast, Brodie's path in the immediate post-war years was emblematic of the broader trajectory of strategic studies. Civilian expertise remained essential—the non-military parameters of strategy underscored by the

---

[23] Ibid., pp. 123–8. Another former member of Earle's seminar, the economist Horst Menderhausen, joined RAND in 1956. Although he joined the IAS earlier than DeWeerd, he left the institute prior to the genesis of the *Makers* project.

[24] A lively account of Brodie's turn towards the bomb and the subsequent effect on his career can be found in Kaplan, *Wizards*, pp. 9–33. See also, B. Steiner, *Bernard Brodie and the Foundations of American Nuclear Strategy* (Lawrence, KA: University Press of Kansas, 1991), and Barry Scott Zellen, *State of Doom: Bernard Brodie, the Bomb, and the Birth of the Bipolar World* (London and New York: Continuum, 2012).

[25] B. Brodie (ed.), *The Absolute Weapon: Atomic Power and World Order* (Yale University: Institute of International Studies, 1946). It should be noted that although Brodie was responsible for writing the largest portion of the book, it was nevertheless an edited publication, which also included contributions by Frederick S. Dunn—the director of the Institute of International Studies—Arnold Wolfers, Percy E. Corbett, and William T. R. Fox, the last of whom had also been a member of Earle's seminar in 1941–2. During the late 1950s and 1950s Brodie cemented his reputation as a preeminent strategist, culminating the publication of his *Strategy in the Missile Age* in 1959.

[26] Earle disagreed with the way Brodie assessed the impact of bombing in the Second World War in relation to his arguments on nuclear war, and may have taken personal offence given his own role in devising air power plans. In 1951, at his own request, Earle visited the Secretary of the Air Force and the Air Chief of Staff to talk about Brodie's role in creating a Special Advisory Panel on Strategic Bombing Objectives. Shortly afterwards, Brodie was removed from his post. Kaplan, *Wizards*, p. 49.

106 MAKING MAKERS

Second World War and compounded by the dawn of the nuclear age demanded as much—but civilian understanding was not: strategy was to be an elite preserve.[27] Furthermore, for many of those concerned with the study of strategy, history could no longer serve as a guide. Indeed, Brodie was amongst the most vocal of those who proposed that strategic studies should look elsewhere for its methodological framework. In his 1949 article on 'Strategy as a Science' he proposed that economics could provide such a model, arguing that: 'what is needed in the approach to strategic problems is *genuine analytical method*. Formerly the need for it was not great, but, apart from the rapidly increasing complexity of the problem, the magnitude of disaster which might result from military error today bears no relation to situations of the past.'[28]

Theodore Ropp: Making a Military Historian

Of all the scholars who contributed to Earle's *Makers*, Theodore Ropp was the most affected. For Ropp, writing a chapter for the book proved to be a milestone in his development as a military historian. Yet despite having participated in the original volume, Ropp knew very little about how it had come about. Indeed, the air of mystery that developed around the book was such that in later years the attempt to uncover more about Earle's seminar and the reason why the book took the form that it did would become a source of fascination to him.

At the time he wrote the chapter, however, Ropp did not ask questions. As was the case for many of those involved, the offer to work on the *Makers* volume came at an early stage in Ropp's career, as he was looking to establish himself within the historical profession. In this, he had already fared better than many in the difficult economic climate of the 1930s, having taken a position at Duke University in 1938. Ultimately, he would remain at the university for the duration of his career. His encounter with Earle appears to have come by chance, rather than through connections. They met when Ropp was being interviewed for a position at Swarthmore College. Earle, he recalled, gave him 'no particular directions' for the piece he was asked to write, 'he was not very well, was getting ready to leave for Washington, and had probably already turned the job over to Felix and Gordon.'[29] Ropp's encounter with Earle was serendipitous for both parties. For Earle, it came at a point during the evolution of the project when external experts were needed. In retrospect Ropp wondered why Earle 'never picked up Brodie or

---

[27] Andrew J. Bacevich, 'Strategic Studies: In from the Cold', *SAIS Review*, Vol. 13, No. 2 (Summer–Fall 1993), pp. 11–15.

[28] B. Brodie, 'Strategy as a Science', *World Politics*, Vol. 1, No. 4 (July 1949), p. 484. On the development of strategic studies in the USA in the two decades after 1945 see G. Lyons and L. Morton, *Schools for Strategy: Education and Research in National Security Affairs* (New York: Praeger, 1965).

[29] MLP, PUP, Box 344, Folder 3, Ropp to Paret, 6 July 1982.

THEODORE ROPP AND THE AFTERLIFE OF THE BOOK   107

[Arthur] Marder, and picked on me, instead'.[30] He could not have known about the circumstances that made Brodie's participation untenable, or that Marder appeared never to have been considered, so that Ropp was needed to bring additional naval expertise. For Ropp, meanwhile, youthful and enthusiastic, it was an opportunity for him to make a scholarly mark.

In subsequent years, the chapter that Ropp wrote, 'Continental Doctrines of Sea Power', remained a key piece of his scholarship. As late as 1977, a biographical sketch for an article he wrote still described the chapter amongst his best-known works.[31] It remained so because his scholarly output was sparse. The doctoral thesis that Ropp completed at Harvard University in 1937 was a significant piece of scholarship which sought to explain the development of French naval policy in the late nineteenth century in terms that went beyond battles and sailors, incorporating diplomatic, economic, and social analysis, whilst also adopting a comparative framework that brought in Italian, Russian, and British aspects. The thesis qualified Ropp to write for Earle, and he drew from it to craft an essay that focused heavily on the French *jeune école* 'strategy of the weak'.[32] With the chapter published, however, he did not go on to prepare the doctoral study for publication. Instead, he devoted himself to a work of synthesis on the history of war, which would appear as *War in the Modern World* in 1959. This did not mean that his earlier research was entirely lacking in influence. Indeed, when his PhD thesis was belatedly published in book form in 1987 its editor declared that 'this book became a classic long before it was published'.[33] That this was so owed much to its place amongst specialists in naval history, as well as to its influence on Ropp's students.

Ropp, like Earle, forged a career that relied less on his personal research, and more on professional efforts focused elsewhere. For Ropp, however, that effort focused on his students. In the decades following the end of the Second World War, he built a reputation as a 'pioneer in the teaching of military history' encompassing education at all student levels.[34] Alongside his colleague Irving Brinton Holley, Ropp supervised forty-eight PhD students through to completion during the period from 1956 to 1982.[35] In so doing, he played a major role in turning Duke University into a leading centre for the study of military history by the

---

[30] MLP, PUP, Box 344, Folder 3, Ropp to Paret, 6 July 1982.

[31] Theodore Ropp, 'Military Historical Scholarship since 1937', *Military Affairs*, Vol. 41, No. 42 (April 1977), p. 74.

[32] See T. Ropp, 'Continental Doctrines of Sea Power', in Edward Mead Earle, *Makers of Modern Strategy: From Machiavelli to Hitler* (Princeton, NJ: Princeton University Press, 1943), especially pp. 446–53.

[33] T. Ropp (ed. S. Roberts), *The Development of a Modern Navy: French Naval Policy, 1871–1904* (Annapolis, MD: Naval Institute Press, 1987), p. v.

[34] Ibid., p. 74.

[35] E. Coffman, 'The Course of Military History in the United States since World War II', *The Journal of Military History*, Vol. 61, No. 4 (October 1997), p. 772.

108 MAKING MAKERS

1970s.[36] In this way, and despite the absence of a substantial legacy in published research, Ropp was nonetheless an important figure in the teaching and training of a generation of military historians. In the words of Peter Paret, he was one of a handful of figures without whom 'the history of war would hardly have had a continuous institutional presence in American higher education.'[37]

As a leading advocate of the study of military history, Ropp maintained an active interest in the state and scope of the sub-discipline within US universities, giving voice to his thoughts and concerns intermittently from the late 1940s through to the late 1970s. One of the first such interventions came just a few years after the end of the Second World War. Quoting Liddell Hart's admonition of academics in his *The Ghost of Napoleon* (1933) for their inability to incorporate the study of war 'as a branch of knowledge worthy of exploration', Ropp contended that this position held good for the post-war American university. Given the recent experience of the Second World War, both Ropp's generation and those who would follow could not 'ignore this branch of human activity because we do not like it, or believe in it, or because it is very difficult for us to understand'. Rather, it was incumbent on them to 'prove that war has been a recurrent—note that we do not have to commit ourselves by saying *normal* or *natural* or even *regular*—part of social intercourse in the western world', rendering the study of it crucial not just to historians, but also to students of political science, international relations and economics.[38]

In making this plea, Ropp echoed the motivations that had driven Earle in the late 1930s: that liberal sensitivities should not deter citizens of a democracy from the study of war, and that such study should be undertaken across disciplines. In the near term it appeared that this stance had achieved wide consensus: the experience of the Second World War, compounded by a shared sense of urgency in the emerging Cold War, had conveyed a new-founded acceptability on the study of war.[39] At the end of the 1950s, Wesley Frank Craven observed in his Harmon Memorial Lecture that if the First World War engendered indifference, even hostility, to military affairs, the reality of fighting in a major conflict 'for a second time within a generation' appeared to make this position seem untenable after 1945.[40]

As he approached retirement, Ropp reflected on the paucity of military historians working during his formative years. 'Before World War II,' he wrote, 'military historians were accidentals in American literary, academic, or government

---

[36] Maurice Matloff, 'The Nature and Scope of Military History', in R. Weigley (ed.), *New Dimensions in Military History* (San Rafael, CA: Presidio Press, 1975), p. 407.

[37] P. Paret, 'The New Military History', *Parameters*, Vol. 21 (Autumn 1991), p. 13.

[38] T. Ropp, 'The Teaching of Military History', *Military Affairs*, Vol. 13, No. 1 (Spring 1949), pp. 15, 19.

[39] Coffman, 'The Course of Military History', p. 765.

[40] W. Frank Craven, 'Why Military History?', in Harry R. Borowski (ed.), *The Harmon Memorial Lectures in Military History, 1959–1987* (Washington, DC: Office of Air Force History, United States Air Force, 1988), pp. 9–11.

THEODORE ROPP AND THE AFTERLIFE OF THE BOOK   109

circles.'[41] Ropp's own evolution was indicative of this state of affairs. After completing his PhD, he taught for a year at Harvard, before being hired 'sight unseen' by Duke University in 1938, the institution at which he would remain for more than forty years.[42] Ropp's background lay originally in diplomatic history. At Harvard he worked under the supervision of the renowned diplomatic historian William L. Langer. The breadth of his dissertation, however, lent him the credentials to teach across European, French, and Russian history, in addition to diplomatic history. His first courses were given on European and East European history, since more established faculty members reserved those in French and diplomatic history for themselves, and it was only during and after the war that Ropp was able to teach 'Duke's first courses in Russian, naval, military, and technological history'.[43] Ropp's course on modern warfare was first instituted 'during the days of the Marshall Plan and NATO', capitalizing on the new wave of acceptance of military history in American universities that followed in the immediate aftermath of the war.[44] (See Figure 3.1.)

Although military history benefitted from an expansion in the number of university courses that affected the whole of the higher education sector, the increases witnessed at this time were significant.[45] A study by John Bowditch on the availability of courses in the catalogues of thirty leading universities, for example, found that whereas in 1935–6 next to no military or naval history courses were offered, apart from those legally mandated for Reserve Officer Training Courses (ROTC) and taught predominantly by military personnel, in 1951–2 ten of the universities had introduced undergraduate or graduate courses on military or naval history, and a further two offered courses on the Second World War.[46] A 1954 study of 493 colleges and universities, meanwhile, found that thirty-seven institutions either offered or intended to create courses on military-related matters within their history departments.[47] This upward trended continued through to the 1970s. By 1975, Maurice Matloff noted that there were 'at least 110 institutions offering specialized courses of one kind or another in military history, not counting ROTC courses'. Matloff considered this to be 'a remarkable development' and one accompanied by a rise in the number of students undertaking

---

[41]   DSP, T. Ropp, 'History Disarmed. History 352'.
[42]   DSP, T. Ropp, 'Military Historians. History 352.1', 12 February 1981.
[43]   DSP, 'Military Historians: My Brilliant Career. Marcus's "What's My Line?"', Durham Rotarians, 16 March 1981.
[44]   DSP, 'Clio and her Daughters. History 352'.
[45]   Coffman, 'The Course of Military History', p. 765.
[46]   J. Bowditch, 'War and the Historian', in Henry Stuart Hughes, Myron P. Gilmore, and Edwin C. Rozwenc (eds.), *Teachers of History: Essays in Honor of Laurence Bradford Packard* (Ithaca, NY: Cornell University Press, 1954), pp. 322–3. At the time of the study Bowditch was Professor of History at the University of Minnesota. He would later take up a post as Professor of History at the University of Michigan, holding the position from 1960 to 1983.
[47]   Study by Brown, cited in L. Morton, 'The Historian and the Study of War', *The Mississippi Valley Historical Review*, Vol. 48, No. 4 (March 1962), p. 601.

Figure 3.1 Theodore Ropp teaching c.1950. After the Second World War Ropp became a prominent figure in the teaching of military history in American universities.

Source: Duke University Archives, Durham, North Carolina. UAPC-026-022-001. University Archives Photograph Collection, box 26.

PhD degrees. He estimated that around 10 per cent of recent history dissertations fell into military-related areas, with some even undertaken in institutions which did not offer military history courses.[48] Roger Spiller later calculated that whilst around a hundred doctoral dissertations in military history were produced between 1949 and 1953, more than five hundred were either completed or ongoing in the period from 1961 to 1970.[49]

As course enrolments and PhD student numbers grew, however, confidence in the acceptability of war as a legitimate area of study amongst academics seemed to decline. If during the 1940s and 1950s the proximity of the last global war tended to mute critics, the era of the Vietnam War in particular bore witness to the emergence of more vocal criticism from within the academy. In the words of

---

[48] M. Matloff, 'The Nature and Scope of Military History', in Russell Weigley (ed.), *New Dimensions in Military History* (San Rafael, CA: Presidio Press, 1975), pp. 406–7.

[49] R. Spiller, 'Military History and Its Fictions', *The Journal of Military History*, Vol. 70, No. 4 (October 2006), p. 1088.

THEODORE ROPP AND THE AFTERLIFE OF THE BOOK   111

Paul Kennedy, the 1960s and 1970s brought 'ideological, political, and methodological turbulence [...] from which few, if any, U.S. campuses escaped'.[50] The effects of this were somewhat paradoxical. Student demand for courses remained strong. Edward Coffman later recalled that whilst working in 'an epicenter of student protest' at the University of Wisconsin-Madison during the Vietnam War era, student numbers for his American military history course 'peaked at double what it would be later'. At the same time, the perception grew amongst many military historians that, faced with the reinvigoration of liberal suspicion regarding the study of war, they were now firmly on the defensive.[51]

Ropp was far from immune from such sentiments, writing in a 1971 article that 'as we won scholarly acceptance, modest course and paper growth statistics during a general educational boom could be too easily seen as signs of general intellectual progress and wider acceptability'.[52] The experience of the 1960s convinced him that military history remained 'a marginal academic subject'.[53] It was certainly the case that Ropp understood this marginalization in terms of history's relations to other areas of, and approaches to, historical enquiry. He shared a perception common to many of military history's lack of standing within the discipline.[54] Yet he also understood its marginality in relation to other disciplines concerned with the study of war. In the same period, political scientists, international relations theorists, economists, and others had all turned increased attention on the phenomenon, and had done so with such success that to many—including to those in uniform—they seemed to offer better and more appropriate solutions to the problems of the nuclear age. As such, by the 1960s they appeared to undermine the position of military history as a useful discipline, especially in relation to military education.[55]

For some, this situation appeared to herald the death of the field. In 1961, for example, Walter Millis concluded a pamphlet for teachers of history by remarking that 'military history as a specialty has largely lost its function [...] the old tales are increasingly irrelevant to modern international politics, to modern war and modern citizenship'.[56] Such was the power of the hypothetical nuclear

[50] Paul Kennedy, 'The Fall and Rise of Military History', *Military History Quarterly*, Vol. 3, No. 2 (1991), p. 10.

[51] Coffman, 'The Course of Military History', p. 769.

[52] T. Ropp, 'Forty Years of the American Military Institute', *Military Affairs*, Vol. 35, No. 3 (October 1971), p. 89.

[53] T. Ropp, 'Military History and the Social Sciences', *Military Affairs*, Vol. 30, No. 1 (Spring 1966), p. 8.

[54] P. Paret, *Understanding War: Essays on Clausewitz and the History of Military Power* (Princeton, NJ: Princeton University Press, 1992), p. 217.

[55] For example, the United States Air Force's annual Harmon Memorial Lecture in Military History, inaugurated in 1959, could have been wrapped up in 1963 when discussion arose over the series's usefulness, and a senior department member suggested the lectures be terminated. See Borowski (ed.), *The Harmon Memorial Lectures*, p. x.

[56] W. Millis, 'Military History' (Washington, DC: Service Center for Teachers of History Publication Number 39, 1961), pp. 17–18. See also R. Weigley, 'Review: Walter Millis and the Conscience of the Military Historian', *Reviews in American History*, Vol. 16, No. 3 (September 1988),

112 MAKING MAKERS

confrontation that even the record of conventional war in such places as Korea and Vietnam seemingly could not shake the position of those theoreticians who 'confidently offered solutions which appealed to the military'.[57] Here too, whilst not as despairing as Millis, Ropp shared a sense of frustration, bemoaning that:

> a fascination with gadgets—such as electronics and cost accounting—still grips both the military and the civilian components of the defense department. Our military intellectuals—who seem to be so admired in Britain—pander to this market for panaceas. Even the works of the abler ones [...] are so "solution-oriented" that they are quickly dated. Gresham's Law in this case is the lack of training in historical fundamentals by both consumer and producer in what is now a very flourishing industry.[58]

Yet Ropp's relationship with competitor disciplines was a curious one. Certainly, in his younger days he was not as suspicious of them as his older self would later suggest. In the immediate aftermath of the Second World War he displayed much greater willingness to seek out and to grow interdisciplinary collaboration. The principal vehicle for his efforts was the cross-campus Duke University–University of North Carolina National Security Policy Seminar. As his close colleague I. B. Holley later recalled, in the early 1950s, he and Ropp would host meetings with a group of graduate students to discuss work in progress: 'It was fun and productive. It was only after this custom had gone on for some time that Ted Ropp had the excellent notion of proposing a collaboration with UNC.'[59] The seminar that was instituted as a result of this proposal, commonly known as DUNC, was established between 1957 and 1958. In its first years it would meet on a fairly ad hoc and informal basis to discuss research-in-progress papers amongst a membership of faculty, students, and service members, with hosting duties alternating between the two campuses.[60] At this time, Ropp was enthusiastic about the programme, writing in *Military Affairs* that the interaction between disciplines was 'one of the seminar's most valuable features [...] Members can submit their ideas in their formative stages to informed and helpful criticisms

---

pp. 503–4. 'By the time he wrote *Arms and Men*, Millis was so utterly disillusioned about the prospects of using war as any sort of rational instrument of national policy that [...] Millis came close to warning his readers that there was no value in his own book. War had changed so drastically from being at least a partially rational instrument of policy, that understanding its history, he suggested, might have little applicability to dealing with its present and future. [...] So why bother learning that history? Why bother reading *Arms and Men?*'

[57] Coffman, 'The Course of Military History', p. 765.

[58] Liddell Hart Papers, Liddell Hart Centre for Military Archives, King's College London, London (hereafter LHCMA), LH 1/608. Correspondence with Theodore Ropp [1952–68], Ropp to Liddell Hart, 10 January 1964.

[59] Foreword by I. B. Holley in F. Blazich, Jr., *Fifty Years of Interdisciplinary Scholarship: A Brief History of the Triangle Institute for Security Studies* (February 2009), p. v.

[60] Ibid., pp. 1–4.

from members trained in other disciplines. The line between political science and history is quite unclear. Such criticism, for this reason, can be very stimulating.'[61]

By the late 1970s, however, Ropp had grown disillusioned with the initiative, remarking with some disdain that 'for political reasons we have allowed our political science colleagues to misname [it] as the DUNCE seminar.'[62] His disillusionment coincided with changes to the DUNC organization. By the end of that decade the seminar had secured funding from the Ford Foundation—funding which had eluded it in earlier years and which would facilitate more ambitious project work. By the early 1980s DUNC had established a pattern of holding annual spring and autumn conferences. In 1983, with the admission of North Carolina State University into the partnership, DUNC became the Triangle Universities Security Seminar, or TUSS.[63] Just as DUNC/TUSS began to take on the trappings of something more than a seminar, then, so Ropp charted a different course. He spoke at just one of the TUSS biannual conferences in subsequent years, in spring 1987.[64] His preference, rather, was to turn back towards history.

Military History and *Makers*

When Ropp thought about military history, he did not conceive of it as a long-established field of historical study, now under sustained attack from upstart rivals inside and outside the discipline. Quite the opposite. He thought of it as an emerging field seeking to distinguish itself amongst competitors, and to establish its own identity. In 1949 he wrote that the field was 'so new and involves so many problems that it seems to me our first cooperative effort might well be directed toward the sort of activity which historians in other fields carried on a generation or two ago.'[65]

This notion exerted an influence on Ropp's professional activities from a very early stage in his career. Indeed, he made it in the context of setting out a possible university syllabus for a broad survey of military history, to be built around three aspects: political, technological, and organizational/professional. It was his belief that the overriding aim of such a broad education in military history should not be 'the sprouting of future graduate students', or even 'the technical training of a military reserve', so much as the formation of 'a broadly informed public opinion'.[66] In tandem with this, he implored military historians to direct their

---

[61] T. Ropp, 'Duke University—University of North Carolina National Security Policy Seminar', *Military Affairs*, Vol. 27, No. 1 (Spring 1963), p. 9.

[62] DSP, Ropp, 'MMS I 31/1/79—Introductory Remarks'.

[63] Blazich, Jr., *Fifty Years of Interdisciplinary Scholarship*, pp. 9–20, 38–9. In 1995 TUSS rebranded itself as the Triangle Institute for Security Studies, in overdue recognition of the fact that the work of the organization had transcended that of a seminar.

[64] Ibid., p. 63.   [65] Ropp, 'The Teaching of Military History', p. 19.

[66] Ibid., pp. 15, 19.

114   MAKING MAKERS

attention towards the production of the bibliographies, textbooks, handbooks, atlases, and encyclopaedias on which the modern field could be built. He maintained this stance for the next thirty years, in part because he felt that the task remained only partially complete. Thus in a 1977 piece for *Military Affairs* on the best historical scholarship produced since 1937, he also offered thoughts on areas for future research, and closed his article with a list of one hundred essential works on war for graduate students.[67]

Whenever Ropp considered the matter of essential works in military history, Earle's *Makers* was never far from his mind. Throughout his career he considered it a crucial reference point in thinking about military history. In 1949 he described it as 'a pioneer work', the best one-volume history of modern warfare whose bibliographies were 'the indispensable starting point for any serious course in military history'.[68] In 1977 he still considered it 'the only work of its kind'.[69] The esteem in which he held the book was shared by others within the profession during these decades. For Walter Millis, *Makers* was 'a broad but creative view of the role of military strategy and military history in the modern world'.[70] John Bowditch rated it as 'a provocative, highly competent collection of essays', which still awaited 'a supply of integrated, balanced works' to expand and complement it.[71] The closest equivalent throughout most of the 1950s could be found in the form of a three-volume reader compiled by the Princeton Military History Project to meet the requirements of its combined ROTC and military history paper.[72]

It is easy to see why *Makers* appealed to Ropp. He was enculturated by his own experience of writing for the book, and his approach to the understanding and teaching of military history in the post-war world can be understood as descended from the approach in evidence in the book. His repeated calls for history to be used for the purposes of creating 'a broadly informed public opinion' echoed Earle's appeal that *Makers* should inform not just soldiers and students, but also the general public.[73] His conception of military history as a broader area of enquiry, rather than a narrowly pitched subject focused only on military strategy and operations, echoed Earle's understanding that the study of war had to be broad-based and wide ranging. Such concerns were carried through to Ropp's most significant publication, *War in the Modern World*. Early on in its genesis he explained it to Liddell Hart as an attempt 'to treat the history of warfare in

---

[67] T. Ropp, 'Military Historical Scholarship since 1937', *Military Affairs*, Vol. 41, No. 42 (April 1977), pp. 68–74. It seems that Ropp was also speaking publicly on similar areas at the same time. On 14 March 1977, for example, he gave a talk to a USMA history colloquium entitled 'Forty Odd Books for Military Historians', which included many of the same titles as his *Military Affairs* piece.

[68] Ropp, 'The Teaching of Military History', p. 16.

[69] Ropp, 'Military Historical Scholarship since 1937', p. 68.

[70] Millis, 'Military History', p. 14.   [71] Bowditch, 'War and the Historian', p. 322.

[72] *A History of Military Affairs in Western Society since the Eighteenth Century* (1953). Millis, 'Military History', pp. 14–15.

[73] Earle, 'Introduction', in *Makers*, p. xi.

modern times as one would treat the history of medicine or some other science'.[74] By time of its publication in 1959 he described it as 'written for civilians with some knowledge of history and for military men interested in the ways in which their profession has been changed by political, social, and economic developments'.[75] Ropp intended that *War in the Modern World*, a broad survey of the history of war from the Renaissance to the Second World War, serve not only as a textbook, but also as a means to draw readers towards the most important and accessible studies indicated in both the text and the bibliographical footnotes.[76] In this manner, the book went some way towards answering Ropp's call for the production of bibliographic and textbook material. In its scope, meanwhile, it could be considered as an intellectual heir to *Makers*. As Coffman noted, 'Ropp's book, in a sense, complemented Earle's collection'.[77]

War in the Modern World was Ropp's most successful work. It was revised in 1962, then reprinted several times, with the most recent reprint appearing in 2000. Yet if it was seen by others an intellectual heir to *Makers*, for Ropp it was not an adequate successor. With the passing of decades his thoughts continually returned to Earle's book. Whilst he held it in high esteem, he also recognized—in common with many other scholars—that it was far from flawless. In the words of John Bowditch, the book was produced to satisfy the needs of the moment, which 'the contributors would be the first to recognize as falling short of the ideal solution'.[78] As a contributor, Ropp concurred, noting as early as 1949 its 'errors of omission—it is weakest on British and American military thought'.[79] By 1979, approaching the age of seventy and on the cusp of becoming emeritus professor, Ropp decided that it was time for him to engage directly with *Makers*. (See Figure 3.2.)

Operation Military History Singapore

The opportunity came from an unexpected quarter. In 1978 Ropp's employer, Duke University, entered into an arrangement with the University of Singapore and the Singapore Ministry of Defence with the aim of bringing officers of the Singapore Armed Forces (SAF) to Duke to study for an MA in military history.[80] As a preliminary move towards this goal, Ropp was invited to take up a visiting

---

[74] LHCMA, LH 1/608, Ropp to Liddell Hart, 11 September 1952.

[75] T. Ropp, *War in the Modern World* (Durham, NC: Duke University Press, 1959), pp. v, xii.

[76] Ropp, *War in the Modern World*, p. v.

[77] Coffman, 'The Course of Military History', pp. 767–8. The lineage from *Makers* to *War in the Modern World* is also noted in Millis, 'Military History', p. 16.

[78] Bowditch, 'War and the Historian', p. 322.

[79] Ropp, 'The Teaching of Military History', p. 16.

[80] DSP, 'First Session of Makers of Modern Strategy Seminar. Introduction by Professor Wong Lin Ken' [n.d.].

Figure 3.2 Theodore Ropp, August 1979. Of all those who tried to create a version of *Makers* Ropp was the most explicit in describing his efforts as military history.
Source: Duke University Archives, Durham, North Carolina. NSBF-TRopp-p01. News Service Biographical Files, box 139, Duke University Archives.

fellowship at the University of Singapore at the beginning of 1980, which he planned to use to work his on *Makers* project.

He was joined on the trip and in the endeavour by Donald Mackenzie Schurman. Ten years Ropp's junior, Schurman was young enough to see active service with the Royal Canadian Air Force towards the end of the Second World War. He began his studies once the war was over, moving to Cambridge University to pursue a PhD on 'Imperial Defence, 1868–1887', which he completed in 1955.[81] Greg Kennedy and Keith Neilson identify Schurman as 'one of the major practitioners' of a 'lost school' of historians of British imperial defence, whose career prospects had been partially scuppered by the decline of their specialism in the face of the new imperial history that emerged in tandem with the decline of the British Empire after 1945.[82] It was certainly true that in terms of the scholar

---

[81] G. Kennedy and K. Neilson, 'Introduction', in G. Kennedy and K. Neilson (eds.), *Far Flung Lines: Studies in Imperial Defence in Honour of Donald Mackenzie Schurman* (London: Frank Cass, 1996), p. 5.
[82] Ibid., pp. 1–4.

THEODORE ROPP AND THE AFTERLIFE OF THE BOOK   117

that he was to become, Schurman would have comfortably fit the Harmsworth chair in its guise as a naval *and* imperial specialism. When he undertook his doctoral project, however, his knowledge of empire was decidedly more developed than his understanding of naval matters. In the latter regard he was fortunate in making the acquaintance of Brian Tunstall, formerly a lecturer at the Royal Naval College, Greenwich, and also secretary of the Navy Records Society between 1932 and 1937. By Schurman's own admission Tunstall 'discerned very quickly that I knew no naval history and that I was trying to write a thesis about the sea and the British Empire, so he began to teach me'.[83] The connection with Tunstall proved to be a significant and long-lasting one, which ended only with the latter's death in 1970. It played a major role in Schurman's move towards naval history, a pragmatic as well as intellectual choice that led to employment at the Royal Military College of Canada and latterly Queen's University, Ontario.

Tunstall, who was the posthumous son-in-law to Julian Corbett by virtue of marriage to Corbett's daughter Elizabeth, became custodian of Corbett's archive.[84] In affording Schurman access to Corbett's archive and discussing naval history with him, Tunstall also came to play a role in shaping Schurman's most influential book.[85] *The Education of a Navy*, published in 1965, concentrated on a set of naval 'makers of strategy' of particular relevance to the development of British naval strategic thought. The book, which Schurman had rather tellingly wanted to call 'The Pens behind the Fleet', offered intellectual portraits of major figures in British naval thinking across the second half of the nineteenth century and into the twentieth century, encompassing the Colomb brothers, Mahan, Laughton, Richmond, and Corbett.[86] It was indicative of Schurman's intellectual approach to his research, which concentrated on 'individuals, their ideas and the institutional memory that ensured that these ideas became part of British imperial defence policy' and so 'shaped his writing and teaching'.[87] The book also corresponded to a number of aspects of naval history and strategy recognized as deficient in Earle's *Makers*.[88]

---

[83] 'Discussion of papers written by Professor Donald M. Schurman, Dr Barry Hunt and Commander James Goldrick', in J. Goldrick and J. Hattendorf (eds.), *Mahan Is Not Enough: The Proceedings of a Conference on the Works of Sir Julian Corbett and Admiral Sir Herbert Richmond* (Newport, RI: Naval War College Press, 1993), p. 103.

[84] Andrew Lambert, *The British Way of War: Julian Corbett and the Battle for a National Strategy* (New Haven, CT: Yale University Press, 2021), p. 3.

[85] Andrew Lambert, *The Foundations of Naval History: John Knox Laughton, the Royal Navy and the Historical Profession* (London: Chatham Publishing, 1998), p. 230.

[86] *The Education of a Navy* was the title chosen by Schurman's publisher. D. Schurman, 'Julian Corbett's Influence on the Royal Navy's Perception of Its Maritime Function', in Goldrick and Hattendorf (eds.), *Mahan Is Not Enough*, p. 51.

[87] Kennedy and Neilson, 'Introduction', in Kennedy and Neilson (eds.), *Far Flung Lines*, p. 4.

[88] In addition to *The Education of a Navy*, Schurman also wrote a concise biography of Corbett. D. Schurman, *Julian S. Corbett, 1854–1922* (London: Royal Historical Society, 1981).

118   MAKING MAKERS

Thus, like Ropp, Schurman had made his own contribution to the *Makers* legacy, albeit not by design, which rendered him a suitable partner in the putative Singapore project. Like Ropp, he was also awarded a visiting fellowship. Over the period between 1979 and 1981 he served as Ropp's sounding board, co-editor, and the author of several chapters for the new work. The partnership was certainly beneficial to Ropp. Although Ropp had his own long-standing credentials in naval history, by the time their work began Schurman had established himself as 'the founder of the serious study of maritime history in Canada', an 'ideas man' who also brought 'the study of personality and ideology' to other significant projects.[89] The synergy that existed between the pair on naval warfare would also afford Ropp greater latitude to direct his attention to theories of land warfare once the project was underway.

Ropp's decision to co-opt his Singapore trip for the purposes of the *Makers* project was doubtless an exercise in opportunism, but it was also reflective of the limits of what he believed was attainable in North Carolina. Despite the efforts he and Holley had made in turning Duke into a national hub for the study of military history, the university still lacked a dedicated seminar which might have lent itself to the task.[90] In this regard, he later surmised that 'the subject is so vast that it has no special methodology'.[91] His disillusionment with DUNC, meanwhile, weighed against that forum as a potential alternative. The Singapore fellowship, by contrast, afforded him the freedom to consider the project through a uniquely historical lens, whilst also allowing him to avoid the 'growing obsession with the contemporary and parochial problems of American military power' which he saw as a significant deficiency in contemporary American military studies.[92]

Ropp and Schurman arrived in Asia in mid-January 1980 to commence what Schurman described as 'Operation Military History, Singapore'.[93] Shortly after their arrival, Ropp penned a brief note underlining the purpose of their four-month residency:

Subject: What Goes on Here?

Or: Why are we subjecting Olive and Betty to shop talk, when they are putting up with colonial living and driving in order to experience the sights and sounds of Singapore?

---

[89] Schurman was a founder of the Disraeli Project in 1972, which was dedicated to the locating, collection, and publication of the papers of the nineteenth-century British prime minister. He also published research on the Anglican Church in Canada. Kennedy and Neilson, 'Introduction', in Kennedy and Neilson (eds.), *Far Flung Lines*, p. 4.

[90] In notes made for the *Makers* project in 1979, Ropp indicated that there were a number of reasons why no seminar existed, although he did not give specifics. DSP, Ropp, 'MMS I 31/1/79—Introductory Remarks'.

[91] DSP, 'Military Historians: My Brilliant Career. Marcus's "What's My Line?"', Durham Rotarians, 16 March 1981.

[92] DSP, Ropp, 'MMS I 31/1/79—Introductory Remarks'.

[93] DSP, 'Commentary on Draft Introduction to Makers Revisited, or to use a "Fisherism" Makers Redivivus', by D. M. Schurman [n.d.].

THEODORE ROPP AND THE AFTERLIFE OF THE BOOK   119

Because we are:

1. Turning out a history of strategic thought, in the form of a commentary on the best history of that subject in English which

   a. May sell, but, in any case, will give its readers something to think about,

   b. Will say some things both of us have long wanted to say,

   c. Will give some other people a chance to say something on their subjects, and

   d. Will give Singapore students of military history a chance to practice the art of historical criticism.[94]

As Ropp's note suggested, their plan did not involve rewriting the book in its entirety. In a letter to Gilbert and Craig he explained that he and Schurman hoped 'to reinterpret <u>Makers of Modern Strategy</u>, rather than to reedit it'.[95] Elsewhere, he justified this approach in terms that reflected the high level of deference that he still felt in regard to Earle's volume, pointing to 'the continued usefulness of its essays and bibliographies in the teaching of military history'. To his mind, this meant that it was better 'to comment and to supplement rather than to revise', or to ask those original authors still living to do so, since 'our own revisions would surely be no better than theirs, and would relegate their work to an honoured obscurity which it does not yet deserve'.[96] The draft preface for the new book gave a further indication of how this would work. Instead of supplanting 'that classic English history of strategic thought' the editors would add 'several new chapters on classical and contemporary strategy' and review the other chapters 'in the light of nearly forty years of new ideas and scholarship'.[97]

Although the contours of Ropp's vision conveyed a certain vagueness, expressed in the various descriptions of the project that he would use—'reinterpretation', 'commentary', 'companion'—he approached his trip to Singapore with a relatively firm idea of what he intended to do. With the outline and structure of the new volume in place as early as September 1979, as well as the majority of authors (see Figure 3.3), he would run a seminar series from late January to mid-April 1980 (see Figures 3.4 and 3.5) to assess the viability of the project. The seminar would consist of approximately forty members, of whom ten would be full members expected to submit papers on a designated subject. These would be cir-culated in advance of each session for critical discussion.[98] In this way, although his trip was ostensibly geared towards teaching military history to SAF personnel, the substantial attraction for Ropp lay in the chance that it gave to focus on the

---

[94] DSP, Ropp to Schurman, 20 January 1980.

[95] DSP, Ropp to Craig and Gilbert, 20 December 1979.

[96] DSP, 'Draft Introduction. Makers of Modern Strategy Revisited', Theodore Ropp, 31 January 1980, p. 12.

[97] DSP, 'Draft Preface for <u>Makers of Modern Strategy Revisited</u>' [n.d.].

[98] DSP, Ropp to 'Strategy Revisitors', 3 September 1979. Ropp to 'Friends', 28 January 1980.

120   MAKING MAKERS

I.   Introduction.
II.   Classical Western Theorists. Wheeler.
III. Classical Chinese Theorists. Singapore.
IV.   Early Modern Western Strategists.
V.   Napoleonic Concepts of Warfare.
VI.   Traditional Naval Strategists. Schurman.
VII. The Search for Mobility on Land.
VIII. The New Naval Strategists. Schurman.
IX.   Air Power. MacIsaac.
X.   Revolutionary Warfare. Singapore.
XI.   A Small Power in a Violent World. Singapore.
XII. A Middle Power in a Violent World.
XIII. The Present State of Strategy.

Figure 3.3 New chapters for *Makers of Modern Strategy Revisited* as of September 1979.
Source: Ropp to 'Strategy Revisitors', 3 September 1979.

Date	Subject	Place
Thurs 31 Jan. 1980	Introduction	Room C, History Dept, 3 pm
Fri 14 Mar. 1980	Western Classical and Early Modern Strategic and Military Thought	Room C, 3 pm
Tues 18 Mar. 1980	Classical Chinese Strategic and Military Thought: the Sun Tzu	Room C, 3 pm
Fri 21 Mar. 1980	Western Classical and Early Modern Maritime and Colonial Thought	Room C, 3 pm
Tues 25 Mar. 1980	Napoleon and his Interpreters	Room C, 3 pm
Fri 28 Mar. 1980	Nineteenth Century Maritime and Colonial Thought	Room C, 3 pm
Tues 1 Apr. 1980	The Great War: New Theories of Land Warfare	Room C, 3 pm
Thurs 3 Apr. 1980	New Theories of Sea Power	Room C, 3 pm
Tues 8 Apr.1980	The Rise of Air Power	Room C, 3 pm
Fri 11 Apr. 1980	Revolutionary Warfare	Room C, 3 pm
Tues 15 Apr. 1980	Small Powers in a Dangerous World	Room C, 3 pm
Fri 18 Apr. 1980	Group Critique	Room C, 3 pm
Sat 19 Apr. 1980	The Present Makers and State of Strategy	Room C, 3 pm

Figure 3.4 Revised schedule for the National University of Singapore seminars, 1980.
Source: Seminar Schedule: Makers of Modern Strategy. Appended to 'Summary Introduction: Makers of Modern Strategy Revisited' Theodore Ropp, 23 January 1980.

Due Date	Session Date	Subject and Comments
26/2/80	11/3/80	Classical Western Military Thought – Wheeler; Neoclassical Western Military Thought – Ropp. Two essays, two book chapters.
29/2/80	14/3/80	Classical Chinese Military Thought – Ong
4/3/80	18/3/80	Classical and Early Modern Naval Thought: One chapter in two sections by Schurman and Ropp. Schurman should have three-fourths of the space.
7/3/80	21/3/80	Napoleon and his Interpreters – Ropp
11/3/80	25/3/80	Nineteenth Century Maritime and Colonial Thought. Mahan saw them as closely connected, Schurman may say as much or as little about the Bugeaud chapter in Earle as he likes.
14/3/80	28/3/80	The Great War: New Theories of Land Warfare – Ropp.
18/3/80	1/4/80	New Theories of Sea Power – Schurman
21/3/80	4/4/80	The Rise of Air Power – MacIsaac. This, like the two previous chapters, can come up to the present.
25/3/80	8/4/80	Revolutionary Warfare: Prof. Ernest Chew.
28/3/80	11/4/80	Small Powers in a Dangerous World. Taped and transcribed student discussion, to be edited – with the approval of the participants – for publication. This format, suggested by Professor Wong, may prove to be attractive for the Australian session I am hoping to get on Medium Powers in a Dangerous World.
	15/4/80	Group Critique, need not be published.
4/4/80	18/4/80	The Current Makers and State of Strategy – Ropp.

Figure 3.5 New schedule for the National University of Singapore seminars, 1980.
Source: Ropp to 'Friends', ref.: <u>Makers of Modern Strategy Revisited</u>. 28 January 1980.

book that—for want of a better title—he had decided to call *Makers of Modern Strategy Revisited*.[99]

The introductory session of the Singapore series afforded Ropp the opportunity to give voice to his fascination with Earle's terminology. The purpose of the seminar was to ask 'for some thought on makers, modern, and strategy, topics on which Earle's original seminar seems simply to have accepted contemporary definitions'.[100] In his draft introduction, Ropp set this issue out in more detail:

The modern world was assumed to have begun with the Renaissance, the French monarch's "invasion" of "Italy" in 1494, or Europe's "discovery" of America in 1492. Strategic thought was assumed to be Western, or that of the Western great powers and a Westernized Japan who were then fighting all over and to

---

[99] DSP, Ropp to 'Strategy Revisitors', 3 September 1979. In correspondence he confessed that he was not satisfied with this title as it sounded 'a bit like visiting a scholarly graveyard'.

[100] DSP, 'MMS I 31/1/79—Introductory Remarks / First Session: Makers of Modern Strategy Seminar. Introductory Remarks by Professor Theodore Ropp' [n.d.].

122 MAKING MAKERS

dominate the world. The makers of strategy were those ideological, political, and professional administrative and military advisers who, since the Renaissance, had increasingly aided more powerful princes in allocating their societies' increasing resources to preparing for and conducting military operations.[101]

Ropp's preoccupation with these matters was such that, prior to departing the USA, he had written to Gilbert and Craig to ask for more information, since he could 'find no correspondence whatever with Prof. Earle which might relate to his definition of modern, makers, or strategy, let alone why particular strategists were selected'.[102] Neither Gilbert nor Craig could provide the answers Ropp was looking for. Gilbert did explain something of the process by which the book was made, however, disclosing his part in compiling the first chapter outline and explaining the dual-layered development of the book, whereby the focus on European strategic thought gave way to consideration of the Second World War itself.[103] Gilbert's references were perhaps oblique, and he wrote nothing to alert Ropp directly that he might have been asking the wrong question. Nevertheless, read carefully, his letter might have given Ropp certain clues.

In some respects, Ropp was sensitive to the way in which contemporary circumstances helped shape the book that Earle's *Makers* became. He was alert to its Western-centric focus, as well as to the peculiar manner in which it placed emphasis on allies and enemies ahead of the United States itself. From his vantage point on the cusp of the 1980s, he also saw in the attitude of that generation, forged by the legacy of the First World War and focused on the conduct of the Second, greater assurance over 'how to win a war than those military historians who were searching for certainty in the 1900's or the 1960's' or indeed the 1970s.[104] But he did not fully appreciate—or perhaps could not bring himself to accept— the implications of the lack of debate over definitions. The title of the book was a red herring, concocted after completion for the purposes of marketability. Gilbert's explanation of the process was the key, which also alluded to the distance between the seminar and the book. Ropp was looking for a simpler answer, or perhaps merely a complete one, where no such answer existed.

Nevertheless, Ropp's ruminations on 'makers', 'modern', and 'strategy' played a role in shaping his *Makers of Modern Strategy Revisited*, and the new chapters needed in the uncertain climate of the ongoing Cold War 'to fill what now seem

---

[101] DSP, 'Draft Introduction. Makers of Modern Strategy Revisited', Theodore Ropp, 31 January 1980, p. 1.
[102] DSP, Ropp to Craig and Gibert, 20 December 1979.
[103] MLP, PUP, Box 344, Folder 3 (CO728), Gilbert to Ropp, 8 January 1980. Craig to Ropp, 28 January 1980.
[104] DSP, 'Draft Introduction. Makers of Modern Strategy Revisited', Theodore Ropp, 31 January 1980, p. 12.

THEODORE ROPP AND THE AFTERLIFE OF THE BOOK   123

like gaps in the general history of modern military strategy'.[105] Those chapters also went beyond the limitations that Ropp had identified in the 1940s concerning British and American thought, to encompass a broader chronological and global scope. In terms of chronology, this meant considering the link between the classical and the modern world, since Earle's 'conventional definition of modern did not take the maxims of the soldier's trade in traditional Western societies back to that antiquity which Machiavelli saw himself reviving'.[106] To this end, Everett L. Wheeler, a classicist colleague of Ropp's at Duke University, was asked to write a new chapter on 'The Classical Western Theorists'. In global terms this meant looking beyond the Western experience, principally towards the Chinese experience. As Ropp explained, Earle's book gave no room for 'the equally sophisticated and even longer-lived military tradition of a China which, while Makers of Modern Strategy was being written, was producing one of the most influential military and political strategists of the next era of dogma and doubt'.[107] Two academics at the National University of Singapore, Ong Chit Chung and Ernest C. T. Chew, were asked to address these issues by contributing chapters on 'Classical Chinese Thought: Sun Tzu's "Art of War"' and 'Revolutionary Warfare à la Mao Tse-Tung' respectively. Finally, *Makers Revisited* would also devote space to the experience of smaller powers. Although Earle's *Makers*, Ropp wrote, 'considered all strategy to be great power strategy', during the 1950s and 1960s 'chickens and eaglets, individually or collectively, began to play an increasingly important role in international organizations, in military and political affairs, and in strategic thought'. As such, contemplating the longer history of small and middle powers seemed necessary 'for studying what security has come to mean to everyone in a still violent and complex, but increasingly interdependent world'.[108]

Alongside these new directions, *Makers Revisited* also looked to update and augment the 1943 book in ways that Earle had intended too. As befitted the backgrounds of its editors, in the first instance this meant establishing a much greater focus on naval history and strategy. Since Ropp had decided to devote most of his attention to land-focused pieces—under such titles as 'Early Modern Western Strategists', 'Napoleon and his Interpreters', and 'New Theories of Land Warfare' after the First World War, alongside his concluding essay on 'The Present State of Strategy'—the maritime burden fell most heavily on his junior partner. Schurman was slated to take responsibility for pieces on 'Classical and Early Modern Naval Thought', 'Nineteenth Century Maritime and Colonial Thought', and 'New Theories of Sea Power'.[109]

---

[105] Ibid.   [106] Ibid.   [107] Ibid.

[108] DSP, 'Draft Introduction. Makers of Modern Strategy Revisited', Theodore Ropp, 31 January 1980, pp. 12–13.

[109] See Figures 3.3–3.5.

124   MAKING MAKERS

Nevertheless, Ropp took on a smaller part of the first of these papers. His initial section, in a mirror to the purpose of Wheeler's chapter, considered maritime thought from antiquity in an attempt to explain the historical reasons for division between military and naval thought, and in particular later continental land theorists' limited comprehension of the maritime domain. This was epitomized in the figure of Jomini, 'the islander who had become Modern Europe's greatest land captain' who 'did not understand the art of the admiral'.[110] Schurman, meanwhile, brought his naval and imperial bearing to the treatment of the early modern period, emphasizing the emergence of naval strategy in its relations to trade, diplomacy, and, most importantly, national policies founded on overseas expansion. He was equally keen to emphasize that pre-nineteenth-century naval strategy could not be fully understood in relation to individuals. 'The mariner's instinctive reaction', he wrote:

> [...] when faced with rules of strategy is to reach for his Rutter—not for Mahan or Corbett or anyone else like them. In fact, before the nineteenth century they did not do so in any comprehensive way.
>
> Sea strategy existed, however it was decided, in the event by the changing relationship between developing traditions of national seamanship and the always changing but situationally defined sea purposes of the State.[111]

In making this observation, moreover, Schurman emphasized one of the key aspects which Ropp hoped to draw out across the new chapters in *Makers Revisited*. The largely biographical approach that Earle had adopted, Ropp wrote, 'was both practical and appealing for a quick collective survey of modern military thought' written under conditions that militated against longer debate over form.[112] By thinking less in terms of individuals and more in terms of time periods, Ropp hoped that a fuller sense of the continuum of military thought might emerge, bringing with it a sharper picture of movements, groupings, and national experiences. Nevertheless, in practice the heavy emphasis on key thinkers could not be entirely avoided, nor was it wholly unhelpful to Ropp and Schurman's collective purpose. For example, in their draft work for later chapters they demonstrated their intent to undertake deeper scrutiny of Mahan and to give Corbett much greater prominence than he had been allotted in Earle's book.[113]

---

[110] DSP, T. Ropp and D. Schurman, 'Western Classical and Early Modern Maritime and Colonial Strategy', p. 4.

[111] Ibid., p. 15. Of note, and as a complement to Chung and Chew's papers, Schurman's manuscript also paid some attention to developments in China during the Ming Dynasty, p. 16.

[112] DSP, T. Ropp, 'Napoleon and His Interpreters', p. 1.

[113] See, for example, DSP, D. Schurman, drafts for 'Mahan and the Classical Age of Sea Power Writing'.

THEODORE ROPP AND THE AFTERLIFE OF THE BOOK   125

Since the significance of air power had only increased in the decades after 1945, Ropp sought the means to address this area as well. From that point, he wrote, air strategists had 'advanced their claims for air power and air forces, not just to co-equality, but to strategic and policy paramountcy. When bombers were armed with absolute weapons, they transformed, or threatened to transform all strategy, diplomacy, and policy in the 1950's and 1960's.'[114] To account for these developments, Ropp reported in September 1979 that he had 'persuaded Col. [David] MacIsaac, who was passing through on his way from Washington to the Air War College, where he is joining the faculty, to do the air power piece, a subject on which he knows much more than I do.'[115] Of all the chapter drafts for *Makers Revisited*, MacIsaac's contribution on air power was most explicit in using the original chapter as a guide, although he did so in an historically sensitive manner. He noted that Ed Warner's background as an aeronautical engineer and vice chairman of the Civil Aeronautics Board 'set him apart from most of the contributors to the original edition, but uniquely qualified him to analyse the theoretical practical limitations applicable to the existing tools of war in the air', even if his 'technical remarks tended to be predictive and therefore fallible'. He also pointed to three areas in which Warner could be '(unfairly) criticized at this date': his neglect of Blitzkrieg, the lack of treatment of US and Japanese carrier-borne naval aviation, and 'the work of the U.S. Army's Air Corps Tactical School during the thirties' in translating 'Douhet's and Mitchell's broad concepts into an elaborated doctrine of employment for operations against the enemy's industrial net'. He closed his offering with a summary theorizing about air and space power in the atomic age, pointing to the prevalence of 'games theorists, statistically oriented behavioral [sic] scientists, economists and other social scientists,—most of whom are addicted to a horrendus [sic] jargon subconsciously aimed at making the unthinkable appear rational', whilst underlining the paucity of 'truly new ideas' that had appeared.[116] Such overt criticisms of ahistorical theorizing were doubtless well received by Ropp.

Where Ropp had been fortunate to bring MacIsaac on board, and had very willing collaborators in his University of Singapore colleagues, he encountered more difficulties finding authors for his proposed pieces on middle powers.[117] In part, this was because he did not appear to have a clear idea of which powers to choose. As far as small powers were concerned, once again, Singapore presented

---

[114] DSP, 'Draft Introduction. Makers of Modern Strategy Revisited', Theodore Ropp, 31 January 1980, p. 12.

[115] DSP, Ropp to 'Strategy Revisitors', 3 September 1979.

[116] DSP, David MacIsaac, 'Voices from the Central Blue', pp. 3–4, 7.

[117] Wong Lin Ken, head of the History Department at the university, was keen to emphasize in his opening remarks to the seminar series the way in which 'post-war developments have rendered Euro-centric thinking less relevant—perhaps even irrelevant', emphasizing also that 'the two global powers are not European powers'. DSP, 'First Session of Makers of Modern Strategy Seminar. Introduction by Professor Wong Lin Ken' [n.d.].

126   MAKING MAKERS

the obvious solution since a University of Singapore academic could tackle this. Yet by the time Ropp compiled his draft chapter structure in September 1979 the 'middle power in a violent world' was unspecified. Consequently, he and Schurman continued to seek an appropriate case study, and appropriate authors, during their stay in Singapore. They ended up with two prospective 'middle power' chapters rather than one. In late 1979 and early 1980 Ropp made reference to 'a possible Australian chapter'.[118] Since Ropp intended to travel on to another fellowship in Canberra after the completion of his seminar series in Singapore this made good practical sense, as the likelihood of finding a willing individual appeared high. By February 1980 he had received agreement from Professor Robert O'Neill, head of the Strategic and Defence Studies Centre at the Australian National University, to write 'a chapter on Small and Middle powers'.[119] At the same time, however, Schurman had approached a Swedish academic, K. R. Bohme, for a chapter on Sweden, since 'it would add to the book to have a Eurocentric chapter on Small and Middle Powers with Sweden as the focus' in order to speak to 'the general middle power predicament in Europe' since 1789.[120] Two months later, Ropp received a letter from Bertil Johansson, an associate of Prof Bohme, proposing that he, along with a military colleague, write the chapter on Sweden instead.[121] These moves seemed to leave no room for a dedicated seminar paper on middle powers. Similarly, small powers were considered only via the medium of a 'taped and transcribed student discussion' in one of the final sessions (see Figure 3.5).[122]

Although the additional chapters led to areas of enquiry not considered in Earle's volume, not all of them added as much to the sense of continuity in strategic thought that Ropp seemed to have hoped to achieve. Wheeler, for example, devoted much of his paper to establishing the differences between the classical and modern world, especially in terms of strategy, noting also that technological developments had greatly diminished the utility of ancient military theory in the modern era. Nevertheless, he did affirm linkages in terms of tactics and stratagems, particularly into the eighteenth century, and underlined the debt that modern military thinkers owed their ancient counterparts for the very idea of encapsulating

---

[118] DSP, Ropp to 'Strategy Revisitors', 3 September 1979. Ropp to 'Friends', Ref: Makers of Modern Strategy Revisited, 28 January 1980.

[119] For O'Neill's tenure of the centre, see R. O'Neill, 'From Childhood to Maturity: The SDSC, 1972–82', in D. Ball and A. Carr (eds.), *A National Asset: 50 Years of the Strategic and Defence Studies Centre* (Acton ACT: ANU Press, 2016), pp. 49–71. O'Neill went on to direct the International Institute for Strategic Studies from 1982 to 1987 and then held the Chichele chair in the History of War at the University of Oxford from 1987 to 2001.

[120] DSP, Schurman to Professor K. R. Bohme, 5 February 1980. Schurman also noted in this letter that 'Ropp is writing a new chapter on land war technology', presumably a reference to the chapter 'The Search for Mobility on Land' (see Figure 3.3).

[121] DSP, Bertil Johansson to Ropp, 14 April 1980.

[122] Although the same schedule suggested that Ropp intended to run a similar session on 'medium powers' it is not clear whether he managed to do so or not.

military theory in writing.[123] Other chapters revealed things that could not realistically have been understood by Earle's contributors. As Chew noted, when that book was compiled 'the West wind had been prevailing over the East wind for more than two centuries', and the only Asian great power—Japan—had transformed itself militarily in imitation of the West. So it was no surprise that developments in China and the ideas of one Mao Tse-Tung were overlooked. In 1943, 'it was still not apparent that the Yenan War in Revolutionary China or Peasant Nationalism and Communist Power during the Sino-Japanese War of 1937–1945 would lead Chairman Mao and his comrades to Peking by 1949'. Within a decade circumstances had changed dramatically with the diffusion of Mao's thought on revolutionary warfare into Southeast Asia and beyond, so that by the end of the 1960s the Maoist theory of revolutionary war 'was taken seriously, if not always sympathetically, by most writers on revolution, guerrilla insurgency and counterinsurgency'. As such, Chew came to the reasonable conclusion that if *Makers* had been revisited even ten years after 1943 Mao would have merited inclusion, although he conceded that the climate of McCarthyism and the 'loss of China' might have led to his exclusion once more.[124] Perhaps Chew was too generous: there was no mention of Mao amongst Bailey's proposed revisions for *Makers* in 1960.

In a similar vein, Chung was relatively sympathetic to the lack of attention paid to Sun Tzu prior to 1945. His prominence in the post-Second World War era could be ascribed in large part to Mao, who could be considered a 'devout disciple' of the ancient strategist. Mao's revolutionary warfare was in keeping with 'Sun Tzu's philosophy of war or the spirit in which Sun Tzu would conduct his wars', and showed particular similarities at a tactical level.[125]

After Singapore

When Ropp left Singapore in April 1980 his spirits were high. During his residency he and Schurman had been able to consider the major gaps that their new chapters needed to cover, and they had also drafted a number of the commentaries that would complement the original and bring the work up to date. On the eve of his departure, Ropp wrote to his contributors to inform them that:

> By February 1981 we will have a publishable manuscript. It will be the only recent history of military thought in English. It will allow students to use Earle's

---

[123] DSP, Everett L. Wheeler, 'The Classical Western Theorists' (Preliminary Draft), pp. 1, 17.

[124] DSP, Ernest C. T. Chew, 'Revolutionary Warfare a la Mao Tse-Tung', pp. 1–3, 6.

[125] DSP, Ong Chit Chung, 'Classical Chinese Military Thought: Sun Tzu's "Art of War"', pp. 1, 72. Later in his career Chung, who died in 2008, would write a book on the defence of Singapore, in the preface of which he included Ropp as one of his 'teachers'. O. C. Chung, *Operation Matador: Britain's War Plans against the Japanese, 1918–1941* (Singapore, 1997), xi.

128 MAKING MAKERS

articles and bibliographies to show themselves how strategy has changed during the forty years since the publication of that work, and to place the subjects selected by Earle in a somewhat more continuous historical context. The supplementary chapters—including Don Schurman's reassessment of the history of maritime and colonial thought—will cover fields which have simply not been covered in general histories of military thought. The interest shown by Singapore's historians and soldiers in this project suggests that the book has a market in people interested in military affairs in any country in which one of the major international languages is English. The audience here and presumably elsewhere ranges from undergraduates in universities and military academics to staff and war colleges.

Since the contours of the book were now better understood, and to reinforce the point that 'this is a history and not a collection of Great Strategists or Basic Works on Warfare', Ropp amended the title to *A History of Military Thought: Makers of Modern Strategy Revisited*. 'We are leaving out Machiavelli to Hitler', Ropp explained, 'partly because we have no candidate for replacement. Sun Tzu to Henry sounds a bit trendy.'[126] With the seminar series complete, Ropp moved ahead with a suggestion made by Wong Lin Ken in January that the editors submit the manuscript to the Singapore University Press.[127] 'Singapore Press is interested in this project', Ropp wrote, 'and, because of the financial and other support given the project by the University and the Ministry of Defence, must have the right to buy or to sell a pig in a poke at this stage.'[128] Despite discussions with the editor of the press, however, no contract had been signed at the point of departure.

After Singapore, Ropp flew first to New Zealand, and then on to Australia to take up his Canberra fellowship.[129] From 21 to 24 July 1980, he participated in a conference at the Australian National University run by the Strategic and Defence Studies Centre, carrying news of his project to the other participants.[130] When the resulting publication, *New Directions in Strategic Thinking*, appeared the following year Ropp's preoccupation with *Makers* was still very much in evidence. His contributors notes made explicit reference to the 'expansion and commentary on E. M. Earle's *Makers of Modern Strategy*' that he and Schurman were preparing, and which took precedence over the revisions that he intended to make in preparation for a new edition of *War in the Modern World*.[131] The chapter he offered also made explicit use of both Earle's book and his own proposed work,

[126] DSP, Ropp to 'Authors and Critics of Makers of Modern Strategy Revisited', 25 April 1980.
[127] DSP, Ropp to 'Friends', 28 January 1980.
[128] DSP, Ropp to 'Authors and Critics of Makers of Modern Strategy Revisited', 25 April 1980.
[129] For Ropp's itinerary see DSP, 'Professor Theodore Ropp's Seminar, 1980. Schedule as Revised by History Dept, SU'.
[130] R. O'Neill, 'Introduction', in R. O'Neill and D. M. Horner (eds.), *New Directions in Strategic Thinking* (London: Allen and Unwin, 1981), p. xiii.
[131] O'Neill and Horner (eds.), *New Directions in Strategic Thinking*, p. x.

THEODORE ROPP AND THE AFTERLIFE OF THE BOOK   129

using 'cycles of strategic thinking' drawn from his assessment of the development of war and strategy since 1789 to 'chart those developments which made Makers, Modern, and Strategy look rather different in 1980 than in 1943'.[132]

This was the high point for Ropp's project, and the closest that *Makers Revisited* ever came to print. Nevertheless Ropp continued to cling to his proposed book past the point of culmination. The rest of 1980 and 1981 went by without any discernible progress. Yet as late as July 1982 Ropp was planning a visit to Singapore in October in order to discuss publication options with Professor Wong and representatives of the Singapore University Press.[133] In April of the same year, however, he learned through Princeton University Press of Peter Paret's plans for a new *Makers*.[134] In response, Ropp made no attempt to conceal his activities. He sent copies of parts of the draft manuscript both to Paret and to the press. In his correspondence, however, he seemed inclined to downplay his efforts and to defer to Paret's superior knowledge. He emphasized to Paret that his work was not a replacement for *Makers*, only a companion to it, or 'a commentary and supplement'. It was not, 'and is not intended to, supersede it', nor was it 'wholly dependent on Earle's remaining in print'. In his attempt at explanation, the same fuzziness that had surrounded his project since its inception could be detected. *Makers Revisited* had become no better defined in the two years since Singapore. Ropp even admitted that he had delayed sending his material by several months, 'until I could be a bit more certain of what our project was, and where and how fast it was going'.[135]

At the same time, he had to admit that where his project could not supersede the original, Paret's might. To the press he acknowledged that Paret was:

> surely the best person in this country who could be chosen to do, or to super-
> vise, a full scale revision of <u>Makers of Modern Strategy</u> [...] As naval historians,
> who have spent too much of our careers dealing with other subjects and with
> graduate students, Don and I would be quite incapable of working our way
> through the vast accumulation of stuff since Earle's book appeared.[136]

It was a sad end for Ropp's project. While he pressed on with his efforts for several months, the prospect of a fully revised *Makers* pushed *Makers Revisited* ever further towards redundancy. His words betrayed a hint of understanding that a project that had defeated him would now be pursued by someone who stood a much better chance of success. For their part, Princeton University Press decided to

---

[132] T. Ropp, 'Strategic Thinking since 1945', in O'Neill and Horner (eds.), *New Directions in Strategic Thinking*, p. 2.
[133] MLP, PUP, Box 344, Folder 3 (CO728), Ropp to Paret, 6 July 1982.
[134] MLP, PUP, Box 344, Folder 3 (CO728), Hoekzema to Paret, 2 April 1982.
[135] MLP, PUP, Box 344, Folder 3 (CO728), Ropp to Paret, 6 July 1982.
[136] MLP, PUP, Box 344, Folder 3 (CO728), Ropp to Sandford Thatcher, 6 July 1982.

130 MAKING MAKERS

deal with the matter with rigorous politeness. Upon receipt of Ropp's materials, Herbert Bailey delivered an unfailingly polite response: 'I understand that you are going to publish your material in Singapore [...] perhaps it would be worthwhile to consider an American edition here. I should be glad if you would keep me informed.'[137] No Singapore publication ever emerged. Ropp's *Makers Revisited* ended not with a bang, but with a whimper.

Conclusion

There were a number of reasons why Ropp's *Makers Revisited* appeared doomed to failure from the outset. As with Earle, ill health may have played a part. Ropp was approaching seventy by the time he turned his attention to the book, and although he did not seem to be suffering from any ailments during his stay in Singapore, he did later report having suffered from seizures around the time of the AHA conference in December 1981.[138] More significant were those reasons that related directly to the approach he had taken. First, there was the issue of Ropp's clarity of vision, or rather his lack thereof. The various ways in which he described what he was trying to achieve—a commentary, a supplement, an expansion of certain areas—spoke to a lack of clarity in his own mind over the ultimate goal, which became more pronounced with the passage of time, despite his insistence that he was not making a successor to Earle's volume. His quasi-contradictory assertions that his book would be a companion to the 1943 work, but that it did not rely on the continued availability of Earle's book in print or even 'the availability of copies in military and other libraries overseas', were also indicative of this tendency.[139] His deference towards the original only exacerbated the problem. Caught between his recognition of the continued value of much of the book and the pressing need to revise a substantial portion of it, he conceived a half-way solution that was neither full revision nor successor volume, and which ultimately did not warrant publication in its own right. Nor had he thought seriously about the viability of publication with the Singapore University Press, or whether the Princeton University Press or the Institute for Advanced Study— who, after all, had direct links to the original—had plans of their own. Indeed, when he learned of Paret's activities he seemed to have been taken by surprise.

Then there was the issue of using the Singapore seminar series as a proving ground for his book. This idea was founded in a certain logic, since it allowed for an alignment of the larger goal of teaching military history to SAF officers with

---

[137] MLP, PUP, Box 344, Folder 3 (CO728), Bailey to Ropp, 14 July 1982.
[138] The seizures prevented him from reading his paper. PUP, Box 344, Folder 3, Ropp to Paret, 6 July 1982.
[139] MLP, PUP, Box 344, Folder 3 (CO728), Ropp to Paret, 6 July 1982.

Ropp's personal goal of working on his scholarly project. It also seemed to appeal to him as a means to emulate how he thought the original volume had been produced, with members dissecting and criticizing pre-circulated papers in order to hone the future publication. But this was an inaccurate view of how Earle's *Makers* was made.

Although he was involved in the first iteration of *Makers*, Ropp was an outsider to the project. He had no connections to the Princeton group, was not part of either Earle or Gilbert's circle of friends, and so his participation was a product of good fortune as much as qualification.[140] The consequences of this played out in later years, as the limited view he had in 1943 gave way to a tenacious fascination with the production of the book and an unfulfilled desire to discover the rationale behind particular choices. Yet when presented with partial answers from Gilbert and Craig—who had been central to the process—his curiosity did not abate. As late as July 1982 he told Sandford Thatcher at the Princeton University Press that he was considering making a grant application to the Shelby Cullom Davis Center to fund a research trip to Princeton in order to search for records concerning Earle's seminar and the sales figures for *Makers*, but that he was 'not supposed to drive far without my wife'.[141] In this sense, there was an irony regarding Ropp's *Makers Revisited*. In his approach to the seminars and his attempt to tie analysis more stringently to definitions of 'Makers', 'Modern', and 'Strategy', he sought to frame his project in terms which he believed were comparable to Earle's approach. In fact, his project bore more accurate comparison to Earle's more consultative, but failed, attempt to revise *Makers* after 1943.

There was also the issue of how Ropp thought about *Makers* in relation to military history. Writing his chapter for Earle's volume proved to be a transformative experience for Ropp. As was the case for many of those associated with the book, his early historical training had not been explicitly focused on war. Recollecting his career from the vantage point of 1980, Ropp credited reading Liddell Hart's *The Ghost of Napoleon* and 'academic chance'—of which writing for *Makers* played a major part—with setting him on the path to becoming a military historian.[142] Taking his own experience as representative, he tended to view the work uniquely through the lens of military history. In the same manner, he ascribed the oversights and deficiencies of the original to the fact that some of the contributors, himself included, 'were not trained as military historians', with the implication that had they been trained as such some of these lapses may have been avoided.[143]

---

[140] In his letter to Ropp, Gilbert explained the invitations to write for the book in terms of three groups: members of the seminar; external experts such as Ropp, Hans Speier, and Derwent Whittlesey; and finally personal friends of Earle and himself, amongst whom he listed Guerlac, Palmer, Neumann, Holborn, and Craig. MLP, PUP, Box 344, Folder 3 (CO728), Gilbert to Ropp, 8 January 1980.

[141] MLP, PUP, Box 344, Folder 3 (CO728), Ropp to Thatcher, 6 July 1982.

[142] DSP, Theodore Ropp, 'The Present State of Strategy: Part II', 19 April 1980, p. 3.

[143] DSP, Theodore Ropp, 'The Present State of Strategy', 17 April 1980, 19 April 1980, p. 9. Theodore Ropp, 'The Present State of Strategy: Part II', 19 April 1980, p. 3.

132   MAKING MAKERS

Only Schurman saw with clarity that Ropp's identity as a military historian set firm after the Second World War rather than during it, writing that 'it seems to me that he is much more the product of Tricky [Nixon] and his Chinese moves now than he was a product of FDR in 1942–3'.[144]

Ropp, meanwhile, projected his own course onto his co-authors, when in truth few were as committed to the study of military history as he was, and none underwent the same kind of transformation. It was also to misunderstand what Earle's *Makers* really was. When Earle described the purpose and character of his volume he made an explicit distinction between military history and military thought, stressing that the book would be demonstrative of the latter rather than the former.[145] Furthermore, while Earle brought an historical approach to the study of war, he remained favourably disposed towards interdisciplinarity. For Ropp, disillusioned—disgruntled even—with the challenges posed by the 'whirlpools of contemporary social science', things were quite different.[146] 'In August 1945,' he explained, 'some people felt that [time] had outmoded all previous military history. Every historian of military strategy since then has had to begin by convincing his audience that relating military strategy to military thought and practice is more than mere "intellectual dilettantism." '[147] As a maritime specialist working at the opening of the nuclear age—and who chose to stick to his specialism with the advent of the bomb, rather than depart from it in the manner of Bernard Brodie—Ropp appeared to feel this need more than most. He saw Earle's era as blessedly free from disciplinary competition. 'Unlike Earle's writers,' he contended, 'we must also counter the idea that only contemporary science and the social sciences are relevant.'[148]

After this fashion, of all the iterations of the *Makers* project *Makers Revisited* was the most invested in an idea of military history, and it was the least successful. Nevertheless, it would be wrong to suggest that this was due to limitations in the military historical purview that Ropp brought to bear on the work. On the contrary Ropp sought to situate military history in relatively broad terms, thinking of himself as a 'Delbrückian scholar, with a wide-ranging view of the world'.[149] He did not sit at the forefront of methodological innovation within the field, but at the same time his commitment to a broad conception of military history was long-standing: as apparent in his writings of the 1940s as it was in the

---

[144] DSP, 'Memorandum to T. Ropp regarding the Americanocentric [sic] nature of Makers Redivivus in relation to the Predominance of Europeans featured in both Makers and Makers Redivivus', Donald Schurman, 18 April 1980.

[145] IAS Institute for Advanced Study Princeton (N.J.). Director's Office. Faculty records, Box 7/ Earle, Edward Mead, Memoranda. 'Purposes and character of proposed volume on the development of modern military thought', 27 March 1942.

[146] DSP, Theodore Ropp, 'The Present State of Strategy', 17 April 1980, 19 April 1980, p. 6.

[147] DSP, Theodore Ropp, 'New Theories of Land Warfare', 3 April 1980, p. 1.

[148] DSP, Theodore Ropp, 'The Present State of Strategy', 17 April 1980, 19 April 1980, p. 6.

[149] DSP, Theodore Ropp, 'Clio and Her Daughters. History 352' [n.d.], p. 5.

1980s. As he wrote in 1977, 'Historians must continue to be as concerned as the AMI's [American Military Institute] founders were with these wider aspects of military history and affairs. To revise Delbruck, we must see the art of war not only within the framework of political history, but also within social, economic, intellectual, technological, and, eventually, psycho history.'[150] If anything, this was a position that Ropp held with more passion than ever in the later stages of his career.

His *Makers Revisited* also bore witness to this in the alternative vision that it presented to Paret's successor volume. His revisions were not without limitations. For instance, in an attempt to account for gaps in Earle's treatment as they had emerged since the end of the Second World War, it was a strange choice to omit a dedicated chapter on nuclear strategists. It is also hard to discount the influence that circumstances played in driving some of Ropp's choices: the correlation between his itinerary in 1980 and the selection of Singapore and Australia as exemplars of the predicaments of small and middle powers is readily apparent. Still, there were valid justifications for focusing on these states, to which Ropp could easily give voice: 'Australia, as a middle power far more exposed to international dangers than Canada; and Singapore, a small power still capable of a measure of self-defense, in a less dangerous situation over the short term than Israel.'[151] Moreover, in giving them prominence Ropp made a serious effort to redress the Euro-centrism that he saw in Earle's book, even if the effort to redress the balance between great and lesser powers also meant bringing Sweden into the fold. The inclusion of the new chapters on Chinese experiences, ancient and modern, also served this purpose, and ensured that in Ropp's envisioned publication there would have been non-Western scholars writing on non-Western matters.[152] For all these bright spots, however, Ropp's project book never amounted to enough of a cohesive whole. Whilst it pushed towards a more all-encompassing scope, in global and chronological terms, its editor could not drive it to completion. It would not be long before a new *Makers* emerged, however, edited by one who could.

Making Makers: The Past, the Present, and the Study of War. Michael P. M. Finch, Oxford University Press.
© Michael P. M. Finch 2024. DOI: 10.1093/9780191959257.003.0004

---

[150] Ropp, 'Military Historical Scholarship since 1937', p. 72.
[151] MLP, PUP, Box 344, Folder 3 (CO728), Ropp to Paret, 6 July 1982.
[152] As recently as 2008 John Lynn remarked that 'there may *not* be a Western way of war, but there seems to be a Western way of military history, and translating non-Western military experience into it is a challenging, but potentially very rewarding, path along which we are only starting to advance'. Whether by accident or design, Ropp seemed to appreciate the potential of that path some years earlier. Lynn, 'Breaching the Walls of Academe: The Purposes, Problems, and Prospects of Military History', *Academic Questions*, Vol. 21 (2008), p. 28.

4

Remaking *Makers*

Peter Paret and the Genesis of a New Edition

'War is too serious a subject to be left to the conventional military historian.'

—Peter Paret, 1967[1]

At the same time as Ropp's *Makers Revisited* was unravelling, work began on the project that would eventually result in the publication of *Makers of Modern Strategy: From Machiavelli to the Nuclear Age*. The genesis of that publication was in many ways a more prosaic affair than was the case for both Earle's and Ropp's projects. As this chapter demonstrates, the editorial team which coalesced around Peter Paret—with Gordon Craig and Felix Gilbert returning as associate editors in a mirror to the original edition—adopted a pragmatic approach to the task at hand. Using the structure of Earle's book as a guide, Paret and his collaborators crafted a new edition which reflected upon developments in war after 1945, gave a fuller account of the Second World War itself, and sought to place a greater emphasis on the role of the United States. At the same time, in attempting to bring these changes to bear upon the next *Makers* it quickly became apparent to the editors that the publication they envisaged would be substantially new and substantially longer than its predecessor, such that Paret, in particular, was insistent that the book be viewed as a 'successor' and not a revised edition. As the vision for *Makers II* expanded, the time needed to complete the project increased in turn, with the result that, from conception to publication, Paret's book took far longer to emerge than its wartime predecessor.

During the time in which the book was made Paret, Craig, and Gilbert also had to negotiate a variety of obstacles that stood in the way of a smooth route to production. Many of these concerned the problems inherent in assembling an appropriate cast of contributors and steering them through to the delivery of chapters. Indeed, the difficulties that they encountered in finding authors for certain parts of the book, and the subtle shifts in coverage and emphasis that resulted from changes in prospective contributors, echoed the process that Earle and his

---

[1] LHCMA, LH 1/566 338. Peter Paret to Louis Morton, 4 January 1968. 'Report on the session "Contemporary History and War," held at the AHA Meeting in Toronto on 28 December 1967'.

team had experienced in the 1940s. In other respects, however, Paret's *Makers* experienced its own peculiar challenges, which included encountering Ropp's project and, still more significantly, negotiating with the IAS, with whom the original contract for the book had been signed. As well as illustrating the manner in which the IAS, through the person of its then director, Harry S. Woolf, cemented its connection to the original book alongside the seminar-to-book notion, this process of arbitration also underscored the most significant difference between Earle's *Makers* and its successor. Whereas the 1940s edition had been presented to the Princeton University Press as a finished product, ready for the production stages, the 1980s edition was instigated not by academics but rather by the publisher, and by its director, Herbert S. Bailey, in particular. Bailey, whose personal affinity for *Makers* stretched back to the Second World War, played a key role in bringing together the editorial team and ensuring that the Princeton University Press would play a more integral role in overseeing and shaping the volume during its prolonged gestation.

This is not to suggest that the academic role in establishing the parameters of the work diminished as a consequence. On the contrary, close scrutiny of the production process illuminates that, aside from the editorial team, Michael Howard also played an influential role in determining what would be considered and who would be invited to contribute. As for the three central editorial figures, only Gilbert, quietly influential in bringing Earle's book into being, now appeared reluctant to assume duties beyond the minimum required. For Craig and Paret, on the other hand, the project resonated on a deeper level. As will be seen, Craig brought to the endeavour a keen sense that the new book was a timely response to the grave absence of strategic thinking in the early 1980s, although his attempts to make such connections explicit in the text were largely blunted in collaboration with Gilbert. Paret, meanwhile, had realized some years before the *Makers* opportunity presented itself that he was less concerned with the specifics of the present than he was with the past. As far as the successor volume was concerned, his interests lay more in developing the notion of the continuum of strategic thought from the early modern era through to the twentieth century, and in situating the historical treatment of conflict in relation to broader currents of historical study, rather than to what he perceived as the narrower constraints of military history.

Peter Paret and the Limits of Military History

Peter Paret was nineteen years old when Earle's *Makers* was first published. As was the case for many of those involved in the first incarnation of the book, the year 1943 saw him move from civilian life to war service. Unlike most of those

136 MAKING MAKERS

individuals, however, Paret saw the war at the sharp end.[2] Drafted into the US Army infantry, he served in New Guinea and the Philippines, ending the war stationed in Korea with the rank of staff sergeant. Where Earle's younger collaborators had completed their education by the time they were drawn into the war, Paret's education was interrupted. It was only following his discharge in 1946 that he was able to return to the University of California, Berkeley to recommence study for his degree, which he completed in 1949.

If participation in the Second World War was the first trait that the future editor of *Makers* shared with many of the original makers, the second was his immigrant background. Born in Berlin in 1924, Paret's parents divorced when he was eight years old. In the five years that followed he went with his mother, first to Vienna in 1933, then on to Paris the following year, before making the journey across the Atlantic in the summer of 1937. With his military service and his undergraduate days behind him, he decided to make the reverse journey, returning to Europe in order to reconnect with his paternal family, and particularly his ailing father. He was not immediately drawn to postgraduate study. It was only after six years working as a journalist that he joined King's College London as a PhD student. Certain that he would pursue a course in history, Paret's intention was to develop a thesis focused on literature and the fine arts. Once enrolled, however, he found himself drawn back to war, fuelled by the realization that his engagement with it as a historical phenomenon was not complete. Much later in his life, he reflected on how his military service had:

> raised questions that did not disappear when the fighting stopped. How men faced danger; how the course of fighting could be described and interpreted with some accuracy; how a country's social and political energies were transformed into organized violence—these were matters to investigate and understand.[3]

At King's he found an agreeable supervisor in Michael Howard, then lecturer in war studies and laying the foundations for the establishment of the War Studies Department. In certain respects, Howard and Paret were more like contemporaries than supervisor and student. Only two years separated them, with the Englishman the elder. Like Paret, Howard had served as an infantryman—although he was a junior officer rather than an NCO—with a record of distinguished service in the Italian campaign.[4] And although Howard would supervise Paret through to

---

[2] Of the original slate of authors for Earle's *Makers*, Etienne Mantoux's return to a front-line role is noted in Chapter 2. In August 1944 Gordon Craig joined the US Marine Corps as an intelligence officer, but he did not see combat. At the time the atomic bombs were dropped on Hiroshima and Nagasaki he was at sea, en route to Pearl Harbor. See Gordon Craig Diaries, Stanford University Archives, Stanford Calif. Box Box 1, reel 1: Tagebuch Vol. V, pp. 163–6.

[3] P. Paret, 'Crossing Borders', *Historically Speaking*, Vol. 4, No. 2 (November 2002), p. 8.

[4] For Howard's experiences in Italy see M. Howard, *Captain Professor* (London: Bloomsbury, 2006), pp. 61–119.

PETER PARET AND THE GENESIS OF A NEW EDITION   137

successful completion of his PhD, he did not hold the degree himself. In his memoirs Howard wrote that he 'cooperated with' Paret in his doctoral studies, since 'it would be impertinent to say "supervised"'.[5] It was a fruitful partnership, which would lead to further collaboration in later years. In 1960 Paret submitted his doctoral study on the transformation of Prussian infantry tactics in the late eighteenth and early nineteenth centuries. By now in his mid-thirties, it was only at this point that he felt sure about an academic career, and decided to turn his energies towards securing an academic post.[6]

His trajectory thereafter was the inverse of Earle's path. Whereas Earle had become increasingly drawn to contemporary issues as his career progressed, for Paret his initial years working on current problems in the study of war served to underline that his real passions lay further in the past. Whilst still a PhD student at King's College London, he was made a member of the International Institute for Strategic Studies, of which Michael Howard was one of the founders.[7] In addition to this he made his only sustained foray into military education in 1959 when he took a position as a resident tutor in the Delegacy of Extra-Mural Studies at Oxford University, lecturing on military history to officers of the US armed forces stationed in England.[8] At around the same time, Paret worked on two articles examining aspects of the French army's conception and practice of *guerre révolutionnaire*, both of which were published in the *RUSI Journal*.[9] These were perspicacious analyses that highlighted the internal contradictions and implications of the theory, written at a time when the extent of the French army's willingness to intercede in domestic politics during the Algerian War had not yet played out in full. They provided the basis for the expanded analysis that Paret would publish as *French Revolutionary Warfare from Indochina to Algeria* in 1964. These experiences laid the groundwork for Paret's relocation across the Atlantic.

His career in the United States began in 1960, when he accepted a position as a research associate at the Center of International Studies at Princeton University. He got the job, in part, due to good fortune when, having delivered a paper on 'internal war' at a conference in Oxford, he met the political scientist Klaus Knorr. Knorr offered him a one-year renewable post on his newly commenced project on the theory and problems of internal war, which Paret accepted.[10] As one of two full-time members of the research group, Paret used his two years in Princeton effectively, producing a study of pacification in the Vendée for the research

---

[5] Howard, *Captain Professor*, pp. 202–3.   [6] Paret, 'Crossing Borders', p. 8.

[7] Founded as the Institute for Strategic Studies.

[8] LHCMA, LH1/566 64, Paret to Liddell Hart, 19 January 1959. The Delegacy of Extra-Mural Studies became the Department of Continuing Education in 1990.

[9] P. Paret, 'The French Army and la Guerre Révolutionnaire', *Journal of the Royal United Services Institution*, Vol. 104 (February 1959), P. Paret, 'A Total Weapon of Limited War', *Journal of the Royal United Services Institution*, Vol. 105 (February 1960). The latter was originally published in the German-language journal *Wehrwissenschaftliche Rundschau* the previous year.

[10] Paret, 'Crossing Borders', p. 8. LHCMA, LH 1/566 144, Paret to Liddell Hart, 24 November 1959.

138 MAKING MAKERS

monographs series of the Center, and collaborating with John Shy, another newly
minted doctor, on the monograph *Guerrillas in the 1960s*.[11] Yet whilst this was a
productive period for Paret, the time he spent working with Knorr's group only
served to sharpen his identity as a historian. He later reflected that whilst a 'fixation
on the tangible and specific' precluded him from gaining as much as he had
hoped from 'the variety of abstract orientations' on display, his projects at least
provided confirmation of his preference for exploring the historical development
of phenomena, not their present-day incarnations.[12] At the time, however, this
realization manifested in more frustrated tones. In September 1961 he explained
to Liddell Hart—with whom he had become acquainted on the basis of his work
on French revolutionary war theory—that whilst he was enjoying his time at
Princeton, 'the intellectual atmosphere of the Center is not to my taste'. His
colleagues operated 'with theories and statistics', he wrote, 'but their analyses
suffer from a lack of historical knowledge. They have no real understanding to
what extent the past impinges on the present, they are not really interested in
what has gone before.'[13] Two months later, he described his attempts to achieve a
balance between history and contemporary issues, whilst lamenting that 'the
Center of course is really interested only in the latter.'[14]

His reprieve from contemporary problems came in 1962, when he was
appointed as visiting assistant professor in history at the University of California,
Davis, a post which was made permanent the following year. At around the same
time he also made acquaintance with Felix Gilbert and Gordon Craig, who would
both play important roles in supporting and advising him during the 1960s.
Indeed, Paret gave Gilbert, who had read his dissertation and a variety of written
work he had completed on German history and historiography, particular credit for
recommending him for jobs in European history.[15] Once installed at Davis, Gilbert
gave Paret assistance and encouragement in helping him see *Yorck and the Era of
Prussian Reform*—the book based on his PhD study—through to publication.[16]
In the same year that the book was published, Gilbert also played a role in bringing Paret to the IAS for the academic year.[17] This was to be Paret's first association
with the institute prior to his joining on a permanent basis following the publication of *Makers*. During this period Paret also began work on a Clausewitz project,
which would lead in the following decade to the publication of a new translation

---

[11] P. Paret, *Internal War and Pacification: The Vendée, 1789–1796*, Research Monograph No. 12,
Center of International Studies (Princeton University, Princeton, 1961).

[12] Paret 'Crossing Borders', p. 9.

[13] LHCMA, LH 1/566 208, Paret to Liddell Hart, 26 September 1961.

[14] LHCMA, LH 1/566 211, Paret to Liddell Hart, 13 November 1961.

[15] Paret 'Crossing Borders', p. 9.

[16] See letter of thanks sent by Paret. Paret to Gilbert, 27 November 1965, Gilbert Papers, Box
14/P. Paret. HI.

[17] Gilbert to Paret, 6 May 1966. Gilbert Papers, Box 14/P. Paret. HI. Paret was a member for the
year 1966–7. Gilbert had been a fellow of the IAS since 1962.

of *On War*, which he co-edited alongside Michael Howard, as well as to *Clausewitz and the State*, Paret's intellectual biography of the Prussian theorist.[18]

Paret would later write that his major historical works of the 1960s and 1970s 'confirmed my identity as a military historian'.[19] Yet this judgement belied the nuances of his intellectual development during that time. Just as Paret's experiences at the Center of International Studies had furnished him with visceral proof that he was 'not cast for a career as a defence analyst', his career path in the mid-1960s took him in a direction that suggested he was uncomfortable with the label 'military historian'.[20] Part of the reason for this was his desire to maintain a broader focus in the study of history. Ever since his undergraduate days, Paret's interests had encompassed more than the study of war. Indeed, his interest in the history of art and culture pre-dated his interest in military thought, and the initial attraction of further study and research lay in the former rather than the latter. The draw of studying war, which appeared as unfinished business in the 1950s, developed into a career-long specialism, but it never entirely superseded his interest in art and culture. Consequently, Paret sought throughout his career to balance these interconnected, but often competing, research interests.[21]

Yet his discomfort can also be understood in relation to his thoughts on military history itself. A key episode in this respect came in 1968, when Paret was offered the chair in War Studies at King's College London as a replacement for Michael Howard, who had left to take up a fellowship in Higher Defence Studies at All Souls College, Oxford.[22] When Paret first became aware of the possibility that he might be offered the role in 1967, Gilbert and Craig once again played the role of advisors, although they were hardly impartial.[23] As well as writing letters of recommendation in an attempt to facilitate alternative offers of employment, they worked behind the scenes to increase the chances of Paret remaining in the United States. As Gilbert wrote to Craig in November that year, 'I also would be very unhappy if Peter would go to England, and if I can do anything to prevent this, let me know'.[24] Ultimately, Paret chose not to return to London. Instead, in 1969 he joined Gordon Craig at Stanford University, where he was later appointed Raymond A. Spruance Professor of International History, a position he held from 1977 to 1986 (see Figure 4.1).[25]

---

[18] The translation of *On War* and *Clausewitz and the State* both appeared in 1976.

[19] Paret 'Crossing Borders', p. 9.   [20] Ibid., p. 9.

[21] 'Peter Paret: Narrative Account of My Career', annexed to Paret to Gilbert, 13 September 1985. Gilbert Papers, Box 14/P. Paret. HI.

[22] Ibid. See also Howard, *Captain Professor*, pp. 194–6, 200–1.

[23] Paret to Gilbert, 11 November 1967. Paret to Gilbert, 27 November 1967. Paret to Gilbert, 15 December 1967. Gilbert Papers, Box 14/P. Paret. HI. Paret first became aware that he might be offered the role in spring 1967, see LHCMA, LH 1/566 324, Paret to Liddell Hart, 15 April 1967.

[24] Gilbert to Craig, 1 November 1967. Gilbert Papers, Box 63/G.Craig. HI. Gilbert attempted to recommend Paret to Lawrence Stone at Princeton, as well as George Mosse at Wisconsin-Madison. In the case of the former he reported little interest.

[25] 'Peter Paret: Narrative Account of My Career', annexed to Paret to Gilbert, 13 September 1985. Gilbert Papers, Box 14/P. Paret. HI.

Figure 4.1 Peter Paret in his office at Stanford University, 1986. As editor of the 'successor' volume of *Makers of Modern Strategy*, Paret was keen to stress the ways in which his book should explore the place of war in general history.

Source: Stanford University, News Service, Records (SC0122). Dept. of Special Collections and University Archives, Stanford University Library, Stanford, CA.

Paret's reasons for declining the opportunity presented by King's College London were diffuse. In correspondence with Liddell Hart, although acknowledging that it was a 'magnificent and undeserved offer', he underlined family considerations, his desire to take up a short-term fellowship at Stanford—which would not have been possible had he left the USA—and even the notion that the chair should be taken up by an Englishman. Significantly, however, he also cited 'a feeling that my work was moving away from the history of military thought and policy'.[26] Years later, he put the matter more starkly: the move 'would have demanded an exclusive commitment to the study and teaching of military history'.[27] Even the terms in which he described his decision in 1968 were sufficient to cause deep anxiety in Liddell Hart, who replied that he was 'disturbed by your remark that you feel that your work is moving away from this field, and would welcome some further explanation of your point'.[28] Paret duly offered clarification, explaining that:

---

[26] LHCMA, LH 1/566 337. Paret to Basil and Kathleen Liddell Hart, 31 January 1968.
[27] 'Peter Paret: Narrative Account of My Career', annexed to Paret to Gilbert, 13 September 1985. Gilbert Papers, Box 14/P. Paret. HI.
[28] LHCMA, LH 1/566 339, Liddell Hart to Paret, 12 February 1968.

PETER PARET AND THE GENESIS OF A NEW EDITION   141

I intend to continue working on military problems, but more and more in relation with social, intellectual, and political factors. I am also increasingly interested in problems of historical method—just now, particularly in comparative history; and all this suggested to me that within a few years I would not be the most suitable man for the Chair at King's.[29]

By opting to remaining in the United States, then, Paret signalled not only his resolve to maintain a research profile that encompassed more than war, but also his reservations about the study of war itself. As a student of Michael Howard in the 1950s, it is easy to see the link between Paret and his supervisor in advocating for the study of war across multiple dimensions—social, intellectual, political— which in turn was part-product of Howard's own encounter with *Makers*. It is also worth underlining that Paret's approach bore a resemblance to the arguments made by Theodore Ropp throughout his decades of commentary on the study of military history. Where Paret differed, however, could be seen in his inclination towards expressing himself in terms that were overtly critical of military history, and which tended to position him outside of that field.

Paret's interventions in this area were forthright. In December 1967, for example, he participated in a session on 'Contemporary History and War' at the annual meeting of the American Historical Association. Although the purpose of the session was to bring together historians working across a variety of fields so that all might learn from each other, 'the message of the commentators', Paret wrote, 'and perhaps I may include myself in their group—was that war is too serious a subject to be left to the conventional military historian'. Whilst part of the emphasis of the session was to suggest that war and military institutions deserved the attention of 'sophisticated scholars', more emphasis appeared to be placed on exposing the conventional military historian's 'frequently narrow approach to the criticism of [their] colleagues'.[30] These were charges that Paret replicated in print in equally strident terms. In a 1966 article, for example, he asked pointedly:

Is there another field of historical research whose practitioners are equally parochial, are as poorly informed on the work of their foreign colleagues— particularly those publishing in languages other than English—and show as little concern about the theoretical innovations and disputes that are today transforming the study and writing of history?[31]

Five years later, he considered that little had changed. 'Far too much military history is being written in America' he wrote; '[...] with few exceptions, the character of the

---

[29] LHCMA, LH 1/566 342, Paret to Liddell Hart, 7 March 1968.
[30] LHCMA, LH 1/566 338, Paret to Louis Morton, 4 January 1968. 'Report on the session "Contemporary History and War," held at the AHA Meeting in Toronto on 28 December 1967'.
[31] P. Paret, 'Hans Delbrück on Military Critics and Military Historians', *Military Affairs*, Vol. 30, No. 3 (November 1966), p. 148.

142 MAKING MAKERS

work produced is extremely conventional—descriptive history, centering on leading figures, campaigns, and climactic battles, often with a strong antiquarian bent'.[32]

On one level, such claims served as a straightforward critique of the quality of much of the work being produced at that time, but they were also launched against the backdrop of the emergence of the 'new military history', which adopted and advocated for a broader-based approach to the subject, linking war to the societies in which it was waged and locating itself further from the battlefield.[33] The rise of the new military history led to a first wave of internecine disputes within the field. For those critical of the new approach, much of their concern centred on the very distance that it put between itself and the battlefield. As Dennis Showalter noted, studying everything about war but the fighting would be 'as though historians of science chose to disregard Newton's laws, or students of modern political history overlooked the conduct of elections'.[34] For those on the other side of the divide, meanwhile, the new military history offered an alternative position to military historians, who 'too often contribute to the "process of militarizing minds" by serving us up a policy-oriented, chronological "art of war" hash frequently designed for future military leaders'. The new military history gave the student of war the ability to 'use history to "understand," *not* simply to "arm," themselves'.[35]

Yet whilst Paret's comments appeared to align him with the new military historians, his own position was more nuanced. His appreciation of the parameters of the historical study of war bred in him a scepticism towards the novelty ascribed to such an approach. As he observed in 1991, 'the word "new" in the New Military History is inaccurate if it is used in an absolute sense to signify something that did not exist before'. He noted also that 'the New Military History has not yet been able to equal certain works written generations ago, which if they were written today would certainly be considered part of the new wave. Put differently, the New Military History is a continuation, in some cases perhaps an expansion of what has gone before'.[36] Like Ropp, Paret was 'Delbrückian' too. This broad-based approach to the history of war, coupled with an understanding of its deeper historical roots, would serve him well when the opportunity arose to take on *Makers*.

The Origins of a New *Makers*

The opportunity did not come at Paret's instigation. Although we can suppose that Earle's *Makers* played a part in his education, and it is certainly the case that

---

[32] P. Paret, 'The History of War', *Daedalus*, Vol. 100, No. 2 (spring 1971), p. 381.

[33] P. Paret, 'The New Military History', *Parameters*, Vol. 21 (autumn 1991), p. 11.

[34] Dennis Showalter, 'A Modest Plea for Drums and Trumpets', *Military Affairs*, Vol. 39, No. 2 (April 1975), p. 71.

[35] Peter Karsten, 'Demilitarizing Military History: Servants of Power or Agents of Understanding?', *Military Affairs*, Vol. 36, No. 3 (October 1972), pp. 88–9.

[36] Paret, 'The New Military History', pp. 11, 15.

PETER PARET AND THE GENESIS OF A NEW EDITION 143

he understood both its significance and its continued utility in the classroom, the book did not constitute an overt reference point for him in the manner that it did for Ropp. It dovetailed with his research interests and his approach to the study of war, but it did not dominate them. Rather, the impetus for the new volume came from the Princeton University Press, and specifically from Herbert S. Bailey.

In the two decades that elapsed after he made a proposal for a new edition under the aegis of Gilbert and Craig, Bailey's longstanding interest in *Makers* did not decline. Indeed, he held a deep-rooted interest in the book that stretched back to his own wartime service. After graduating from Princeton University in 1942, Bailey joined the navy and was assigned to a role instructing officers in the use of radar. The job took him first to Harvard, then back to Princeton.[37] His first encounter with Earle's volume in 1944 was, by his own admission, a formative experience. Once Paret's project was underway he explained that Earle's book was 'one of the things that made me want to come to Princeton University Press. I thought that it would be a good thing to be able to work on books like that. I still feel that way.'[38]

Fuelled by the possibilities of working on books like *Makers*, Bailey joined the press in 1946 as science editor. Thereafter, he ascended rapidly, becoming the youngest director of the press at the age of thirty-two when he succeeded Datus C. Smith.[39] In this capacity he oversaw the process that led to the IAS granting translation rights into Arabic, Persian, and a variety of Indian subcontinental languages to Franklin Publications, which he followed in 1960 with his idea for a new edition. That proposal had not been developed further, but it was a signal of Bailey's personal investment in the book. Bailey developed a reputation for his 'hands-on' approach to the publishing process as director, 'right down to walking the floor of the printing plant and discussing issues of book production with the staff directly', and when he returned to the idea of updating *Makers* in 1982 he was keen to emphasize his desire for direct involvement.[40] He wrote to Paret that 'this is a project that I want to handle personally, as much as possible'.[41] It was clear, then, that the thought of a new edition thrilled him no less than it had two decades previously. As he wrote to Felix Gilbert, the prospect was

[37] S. Thatcher, 'Herbert S. Bailey, Jr. 12 July 1921–28 June 2011', *Proceedings of the American Philosophical Society*, Vol. 161, No. 1 (March 2017), p. 76.
[38] MLP, PUP, Box 344, Folder 3 (CO728), Bailey to Paret, 3 June 1982. Bailey repeated this assertion two years later, writing to Paret that 'I really am excited about the prospect of this new edition; I think I told you that it had something to do with my coming to this Press in the first place.' Bailey to Paret, 18 May 1984.
[39] Thatcher, 'Herbert S. Bailey, Jr', pp. 70, 77. 'Publisher Herbert S. Bailey, Jr., Dies at 89', *Publisher's Weekly*, 13 July 2011.
[40] Thatcher, 'Herbert S. Bailey, Jr', p. 72. PUP retained an in-house printing plant until 1965, at which point the plant was relocated. It was sold to an outside company in 1993, after Bailey's tenure as director was over.
[41] MLP, PUP, Box 344, Folder 3 (CO728), Bailey to Paret, 6 October 1982.

144   MAKING MAKERS

'exciting'.[42] At the same time, it was not entirely clear what form a revised edition of Earle's book would take—or even whether Paret would take the helm—when discussions began between Paret, Bailey, and Bailey's assistant for Special Projects, Loren Hoekzema, in the spring of 1982.

By the early 1980s Earle's *Makers* continued to sell. Indeed, during the 1970s and early 1980s it appeared to have sold at a better rate than it had during the 1950s and 1960s. In June 1982 Bailey noted the sale of some 27,000 copies in hardback, and a comparable number in paperback, 'in the past few years'.[43] Such healthy figures continued into the mid-1980s. In the three years prior to 1985 the press sold an additional 9,000 copies of the paperback edition.[44] The expansion of US military education in the post-Vietnam period, which incorporated a renewed embrace of history, appeared to have played a significant role in this upward trend.[45] As Bailey acknowledged, military colleges and service academies constituted the biggest consumers in the figures he gave.[46] It was doubtless also a consequence of a broader reinvigoration of strategic studies that took place in the late 1970s and early 1980s.[47]

Yet whilst these sales numbers were substantially higher than those of earlier decades, and so brought very welcome income to the press, Bailey had recognized as early as 1960 that the press was selling a partially outdated product. As such, when Bailey requested that Paret give his views of the extent of revisions needed on the book, he must have known that the recommendation would be substantial. The assessment that Paret returned in March 1982 noted that of the twenty-two elements of the book (a figure which included the introduction and the epilogue), nine were fit for reprinting, five or six could be maintained with revisions, and the final five or six were 'useless'. Although Paret noted that the longevity of much of the book was 'a remarkable testimony to the quality of the enterprise', he was equally firm in stating that two decades of university teaching had demonstrated that a third of the book was not usable.[48]

---

[42] MLP, PUP, Box 344, Folder 3 (CO728), Bailey to Gilbert, 9 July 1982.

[43] MLP, PUP, Box 344, Folder 3 (CO728), Bailey to Paret, 3 June 1982.

[44] This figure is derived from the figure of 3,000 per annum indicated in the three-year sales of comparable books in the publication plan, of which Earle's *Makers* was one. MLP, PUP, Box 344, Folder 1 (CO728), Publication Plan for MMS, 2 July 1985.

[45] On this issue see R. Hart Sinnreich, 'Awkward Partners: Military History and American Military Education', in W. Murray and R. Hart Sinnreich (eds.), *The Past as Prologue: The Importance of History to the Military Profession* (Cambridge: Cambridge University Press, 2006), pp. 60–4.

[46] MLP, PUP, Box 344, Folder 3 (CO728), Bailey to Paret, 3 June 1982.

[47] R. Betts, 'Should Strategic Studies Survive?', *World Politics*, Vol. 50, No. 1 (October 1997), pp. 17–21.

[48] MLP, PUP, Box 344, Folder 3 (CO728), Paret to Hoekzema, 25 March 1982. The essays which could be retained and revised were: Neumann on Marx and Engels (which could also be replaced), Holborn on the Prussian-German School (which could also be replaced), Gottmann on French Colonial Warfare, DeWeerd on the Emergence of the Civilian, Speier on the German Concept of Total War, Whittlesey on the Geopoliticians (which might also be deleted). The essays he recommended deleting and replacing with new essays were: Possony and Mantoux on the French School, Earle on Soviet Concepts of War, Gibson on the Doctrine of Defence, Kiralfy on Japanese Naval Strategy, Warner on Theories of Air Warfare, the Introduction, and the Epilogue.

The question that arose from this initial assessment was what to do in response. The first suggestion came from Hoekzema rather than Paret. Hoekzema noted the press's decision to reprint a two-and-a-half-year supply of the Earle volume, and proposed using the time afforded by this move to create three 'companion volumes'. The first of these, *Makers of Modern Strategy II*, would showcase new essays on the same topics as Earle's tome. The second, *Makers of American Strategy*, would cover the colonial to the modern period in the USA. The third volume would be called *Makers of Strategy in the Nuclear Age*, and would carry matters to the present. In addition, he suggested that once the final run of Earle's *Makers* was sold, the press could then issue the first five chapters—that is, those chapters concerned with the early modern period and the run of military thinkers from Machiavelli to Clausewitz—as a stand-alone publication. 'Then', he concluded, 'we would have the best of the Earle work, along with three companion volumes.'[49]

Paret did not agree. Although he acknowledged that the timing was right for a revision of the book, which could be targeted to a large market, he favoured the creation of a single volume, arguing that this 'would have the great advantage of revealing the development of strategic thought, of connecting the remote past and the present, and thus of providing the college instructor with a unique teaching tool'.[50] In response, Bailey asked him to undertake a more detailed assessment of Earle's book, with a view to suggesting revisions, augmentations, and excisions. As Paret completed this task, however, it was not a foregone conclusion that he would become the lead editor, although it was quite apparent that Bailey hoped for such an outcome. The views of the two original 'associates', both active scholars, still needed to be taken into account. 'I think', wrote Bailey:

> we should ask Gordon and Felix whether they would jointly want to undertake the editorship of a revised edition; if so we would of course want to respect their wishes. Or they might prefer to ask another person, very likely yourself, to undertake this. I don't know how you would view that, but that would be a welcome alternative for us.[51]

Bailey's suggestion caused no problems for Paret, who replied that he would be happy for the pair to be involved in any way they saw fit.[52] He could hardly have said otherwise, since in addition to the link to Earle's volume that they represented, they had played such a significant role in supporting, encouraging, and promoting him at a crucial stage in his career. Moreover, the close links that he had maintained with them since the 1960s augured well for an academic collaboration.

---

[49] MLP, PUP, Box 344, Folder 3 (CO728), Hoekzema to Paret, 2 April 1982.
[50] MLP, PUP, Box 344, Folder 3 (CO728), Paret to Bailey, 6 April 1982.
[51] MLP, PUP, Box 344, Folder 3 (CO728), Bailey to Paret, 29 April 1982.
[52] MLP, PUP, Box 344, Folder 3 (CO728), Paret to Hoekzema, 6 April 1982. Paret to Bailey, 6 April 1982.

146 MAKING MAKERS

Paret's first approach, facilitated by proximity, was to his colleague at Stanford. Craig, who had long appeared more enthusiastic towards potential new work on the book, needed only cursory persuading. Early in April, Paret reported having broached the subject with him, at which point Craig had agreed that a number of the original essays were now redundant, but added that deciding how to change the work and who should be enlisted to that end would be a significant task.[53] Craig made no record of this conversation in his diary. The following month, however, he noted after lunching with Paret that the latter had 'become very interested in doing a new edition of <u>Makers of Modern Strategy</u>. Not a bad idea...'[54] Soon afterwards, he agreed to join the project.

Securing Gilbert's participation was a different story. Even with Craig's commitment, both Paret and Bailey doubted that Gilbert would be interested. 'My guess', Bailey wrote in June, 'is that he will not want to participate but will be delighted if you want to go ahead.'[55] Since Gilbert was travelling at that time, Paret resolved to pick up the matter with him once he returned to Princeton, and in the meantime decided to forge ahead on a revised table of contents with Craig.[56] In early July, however, Bailey instead established contact with Gilbert and reported his qualified consent for the new plan. 'He remarked that he was willing to help but that he hoped he wouldn't have to do too much work', Bailey wrote, 'and that he would agree to any arrangement that you and Gordon thought was appropriate.'[57] On the latter issue, by the time Gilbert agreed Craig had already proposed the arrangement that would eventually be agreed upon: Paret would assume the position of editor, with Gilbert and Craig once again acting as collaborators 'so that the old titlepage [sic] would in a sense be repeated'.[58] In this manner, the editorial team for the new *Makers* coalesced, thanks to the efforts of both Paret and Bailey.

Sticking Points

Securing Gilbert's involvement was not just important for maintaining a legacy of the original editorial arrangement. It was also important because, of the three men, only Gilbert had a direct connection to the IAS, where he had been a fellow since leaving Bryn Mawr College in 1962.[59] Bailey understood how significant

---

[53] MLP, PUP, Box 344, Folder 3 (CO728), Paret to Hoekzema, 6 April 1982.

[54] Craig Diaries, Tuesday 18 May 1982.

[55] MLP, PUP, Box 344, Folder 3 (CO728), Bailey to Paret, 3 June 1982. In April Paret had written that 'Felix is unlikely to be interested in the revisions'. Paret to Bailey, 6 April 1982.

[56] MLP, PUP, Box 344, Folder 3 (CO728), Paret to Bailey, 7 June 1982. Paret to Bailey, 16 June 1982.

[57] MLP, PUP, Box 344, Folder 3 (CO728), Bailey to Paret, 9 July 1982.

[58] MLP, PUP, Box 344, Folder 3 (CO728), Paret to Bailey, 16 June 1982.

[59] Gilbert went to Bryn Mawr from the IAS in the autumn of 1946. Although he returned to the institute in 1962, Oppenheimer had attempted to bring him back in 1949. At that time, Gilbert had turned down the offer because he did not want to abandon his teaching role. B. Miller Lane, 'Felix Gilbert at Bryn Mawr College', in Lehmann (ed.), *Felix Gilbert as Scholar and Teacher*, p. 11.

this would be if the project was to succeed, writing to Paret in June that Gilbert's support 'would be important in getting the Institute to agree' to a new edition.[60] The agreement of the institute was needed because the contract for Earle's *Makers* was not made between the press, Earle, and his authors, but rather between PUP and the IAS. Bailey reasoned that this was because 'the Institute financed the writing of the essays', or at least that Earle had gone to the trouble of securing releases from individual chapter authors.[61] Yet this reasoning was only partially correct, in the sense that the IAS had provided a base for the core group of seminar members, but not for those who worked elsewhere and were invited to contribute. None of those who had written for the volume received payment for their contributions at the time, and the stipulations of the contract meant that after publication royalties accrued to the institute and not to the authors.

Bailey already knew something of the potential sticking point that this situation created, since it had figured in his considerations for the mooted Gilbert and Craig revised edition in 1960. At that time, he had noted that a number of contributors had raised with Craig the possibility of receiving a share of the royalties from the book in light of its continued sales. To address this situation, he made retroactive payment to those individuals part of his proposal, whilst also requesting that the institute permit that all royalties from a revised edition be paid to the authors.[62] Since this situation remained unresolved as plans for the Paret-led edition took shape, it was imperative that some kind of arrangement be agreed upon. Bailey understood that the original contract made sense insofar as the major work towards the production of the book had been undertaken from within the IAS and the role of the press came 'only in publishing the book when it had been put together'.[63] By the spring and summer of 1982 it was already clear, however, that PUP would take a much more proactive role in the production of the new volume, and that there were no plans for the active involvement of the IAS as an institution. Nevertheless, it was equally apparent from a very early stage that any future edition would look to carry over some of the original chapters while introducing a larger proportion of new content.

To this end, Bailey entered into discussions with the director of the IAS, Harry S. Woolf. The pair were able to come an arrangement that would see the editor, associate editors, and chapter authors remunerated, including those authors whose chapters were to be reprinted, or their beneficiaries where those authors had died. The press would also make a one-off payment to the institute,

---

[60] MLP, PUP, Box 344, Folder 3 (CO728), Bailey to Paret, 3 June 1982.

[61] MLP, PUP, Box 344, Folder 3 (CO728), Bailey to Paret, 3 June 1982.

[62] IAS, Institute for Advanced Study Princeton (N.J.), Director's Office, Faculty records, Box 7/ Earle, Edward Mead, 1950–70, Bailey to Oppenheimer, 13 January 1960. Since Bailey made this a *sine qua non* for the revised edition, writing that 'unless we are able to do this, I do not see how we can go ahead', it is quite possible that this proved to be one of the key reasons why the 1960 project did not progress further.

[63] MLP, PUP, Box 344, Folder 3 (CO728), Bailey to Ropp, 14 July 1982.

148   MAKING MAKERS

after which it would receive no further royalties. A by-product of this negotiation, however, came with Woolf's request for some form of acknowledgement of the role of the institute in creating the original *Makers* in the new edition. As Bailey surmised in an account of one of their discussions: 'you are anxious to retain the relationship of the Institute to the project because of course it is a classic work which does credit to the Institute (and to everyone associated with it), and particularly because it exemplifies the Institute's interest in modern history'. In July Bailey agreed to the inclusion of a note to this effect, with the result that when the book was published the following appeared before the title page:

> The editors and Publisher wish to acknowledge the cooperation of the Institute for Advanced Study in the publication of this volume, the successor to the first *Makers of Modern Strategy*, which originated in a seminar in American foreign policy and security issues at the Institute and Princeton University in 1941.[64]

Bailey's diplomacy achieved counter-intuitive results. Although he had considered that by bringing Gilbert into the fold he would be better able to secure an agreement with the institute on the contractual issues, in fact, Woolf's generally positive attitude towards the project helped convince Gilbert to throw his weight behind it. As he wrote to Bailey in early August, 'this is one of the reasons why, against my original intention, I agreed to become an associate editor'.[65] For his part Woolf, who as a former doctoral student of Henry Guerlac had his own minor connection to *Makers*, declared that he looked forward 'to the development of the book with great enthusiasm and, of course, to its success'.[66] After the initial enthusiasm faded away, however, the editorial team came to believe that Woolf's interest in the project remained more financial than intellectual. They bristled quietly at the inclusion of the credit line but acquiesced for the sake of pragmatism. Three years later, Gilbert noted that Woolf 'was not overly supportive' of their work, and that he 'wanted to have the role of the Institute emphasized because (to my regret) he expects to get still some money out of this edition'.[67]

The long-standing contractual issue with the IAS was not the only problem that needed to be resolved in the initial months of the project, but it was at least foreseeable. By contrast, the discovery of Theodore Ropp's *Makers Revisited* came as a surprise, at least to Paret and Bailey. Although Gilbert and Craig had both

---

[64] MLP, PUP, Box 344, Folder 3 (CO728), Bailey to Woolf, 15 July 1982. Paret, *Makers*, p. ii.

[65] MLP, PUP, Box 344, Folder 3 (CO728), Gilbert to Bailey, 6 August 1982.

[66] MLP, PUP, Box 344, Folder 3 (CO728), Woolf to Bailey, 6 August 1982. For the relationship between Woolf and Guerlac see CUL, Guerlac Papers, Box 12, Folders 45–7. This collection includes a significant amount of correspondence between Guerlac and Woolf, who studied under his supervision in the early 1950s. Woolf was well liked and much favoured by Guerlac, who consistently ranked him highest amongst his doctoral students and made many favourable remarks to third parties about his academic and personal attributes.

[67] Gilbert to Paret, 15 March 1985, Gilbert Papers, Box 14/P, Paret. HI.

PETER PARET AND THE GENESIS OF A NEW EDITION   149

been contacted by Ropp in December 1979, at which time he had explained his project and sought information from them on the activities of Earle's group in the early 1940s, and despite the fact that both men had responded to him, neither appear to have talked about it with Paret.[68] So when on 24 March 1982 Paret received a mailgram alluding to the undertaking from Dr Jean Tashjean, a political scientist working in the Washington area, he was taken by surprise.[69] The form of Tashjean's missive only served to deepen his confusion. 'As Ropp unresponsive', Tashjean wrote, 'must ask you are you doing Clausewitz for Ropp revision of Earle Makers.'[70] Understandably perturbed at the prospect that a new book might already be underway, Paret requested clarification from Hoekzema.[71]

Hoekzema was equally confused. In the following days, however, he was able to establish contact with both Tashjean and Ropp and to make some kind of sense of what was happening. From his conversations he gathered, correctly, that Ropp was planning a companion volume which was intended to 'fill in some of the gaps of the Earle volume' and, incorrectly, that 'the new book appears to be single-author work'.[72] Ropp promised to send further information on his activities but did not do so until July. At that point, he managed to sow confusion once again when, perhaps misremembering the name of his interlocutor, he sent the material instead to Sandford Thatcher, assistant director of the press. 'I don't know why this came to me,' Thatcher wrote to Bailey, 'I have never had any contact with Ropp on this, despite what he says. Did you? Or Loren?'[73] As the aims and scope of Ropp's plan became clearer, Bailey clarified to Paret that the press had never sought Ropp's manuscript: 'in fact we didn't know about it. There is confusion somewhere.' He noted also that Ropp's essay had been excluded from Paret's tentative plan for the new book, and wondered if they should be 'seriously interested' in Ropp's Singapore publication.[74] Paret was not unduly concerned. Ropp was 'a pleasant man and an energetic scholar, though of somewhat limited outlook', he replied, 'and I should be surprised if his new work were of great interest to us.'[75]

---

[68] If Gilbert and Craig were not brought into discussions in March and April 1982, which given the manner in which they agreed to join the project is quite likely, their knowledge of Ropp's project cannot have remained hidden for very long, since Ropp included their letters to him amongst the various documents he passed on to Paret and to PUP in July 1982. For his part, Ropp did not appear to have been aware of Gilbert and Craig's involvement in the Paret project.

[69] Obituary: John Eugene Tashjean, *The Washington Post*, 12 October 1994, https://www.washingtonpost.com/archive/local/1994/10/12/obituaries/a1ff0624-4219-4cb0-b257-641aea662dba/.

[70] MLP, PUP, Box 344, Folder 3 (CO728), Tashjean to Paret, Mailgram 24 March 1982, annexed to Paret to Hoekzema, 25 March 1982.

[71] MLP, PUP, Box 344, Folder 3 (CO728), Paret to Hoekzema, 25 March 1982.

[72] MLP, PUP, Box 344, Folder 3 (CO728), Hoekzema to Paret, 2 April 1982.

[73] MLP, PUP, Box 344, Folder 3 (CO728), Handwritten note attached to Ropp to Thatcher, 6 July 1982.

[74] MLP, PUP, Box 344, Folder 3 (CO728), Bailey to Paret, 14 July 1982.

[75] Paret's view of Ropp was long established. As early as 1960, in response to Liddell Hart's disappointment over Ropp's failure to include the former's suggested corrections in his *War in the Modern World*, Paret wrote that Ropp was 'more of a magpie than a historian'. LHCMA, LH 1/566 190, Paret to Liddell Hart, 27 January 1960. Several years later, remarking on the state of military history in the US

150 MAKING MAKERS

Nevertheless, after the shock of the revelation, it likely came as a relief to Paret to note, as he did on 19 July 1982, that 'Apparently no real obstacles stand in the way of our project.'[76]

As it transpired this was a slightly premature judgement, since the final editorial hurdle would appear several months later. In early October Paret and Hoekzema discussed the possibility that Michael Howard might be made a third associate editor on the project, since, in Hoekzema's words, 'Howard has acted as the British agent of sorts for the revised edition.'[77] By the end of the month, Paret had changed his mind, explaining that Howard was 'fully committed to the project in any case, and it may be easier to perform the final editorial tasks when there are only three of us.'[78] Unfortunately, Hoekzema, with full support from Bailey and keen to have Howard's name attached to the project, had already issued an invitation.[79] An apologetic missive from Hoekzema to Howard soon followed, as well as a delicately phrased letter from Paret, who noted that whilst the prospect of Howard joining the team was enticing, it was not something that had been discussed with either Craig or Gilbert. He added that it would be more work than Howard needed to undertake, and that having four editors—who would need to maintain a transatlantic line of communication in addition to operating coast to coast—would be one too many.[80] Howard appeared to bear no malice for the rescinded invitation. The incident was embarrassing nonetheless, especially for Craig, who would shortly be meeting with Howard in person and privately expressed relief at the resolution of the episode.[81] It would not be the last time that Howard's participation caused headaches for the editors.

Scoping the Project

Even before the various editorial and contractual hurdles had been overcome, Paret had initiated the process of scoping for a new volume. The assessment that he gave Bailey in March identified one particular imbalance in Earle's book: the lack of focus on the USA. This was a calculation that was at least partly aligned to the genesis of the book as a European-focused volume, and it also mirrored some

---

universities, he observed that with the exception of Jay Luvaas, 'Ropp's students have been unable to break into the better institutions.' LHCMA, LH 1/566 367, Paret to Basil and Kathleen Liddell Hart, 6 December 1968.

[76] MLP, PUP, Box 344, Folder 3 (CO728), Paret to Bailey, 19 July 1982.

See MLP, PUP, Box 344, Folder 3 (CO728), Craig to Ropp, 28 January 1980, Gilbert to Ropp, 8 January 1980. Both attached to Ropp to Paret, 6 July 1982.

[77] MLP, PUP, Box 344, Folder 2 (CO728), Hoekzema to Bailey, Memorandum, 14 October 1982.

[78] MLP, PUP, Box 344, Folder 2 (CO728), Paret to Hoekzema, 29 October 1982.

[79] MLP, PUP, Box 344, Folder 2 (CO728), Hoekzema to Howard, 28 October 1982.

[80] MLP, PUP, Box 344, Folder 2 (CO728), Paret to Howard, 2 November 1982.

[81] Craig Diaries, Tagebuch, Vol. 37 Journal July 1982–April 1983, 23 November 1982, p. 150.

of the changes proposed by Bailey in 1960. In this manner, Paret immediately addressed a long-standing criticism of the original volume. Yet Paret did not think that the relative absence of considerations regarding the United States could be wholly explained by the increasing importance of the USA in the post-Second World War era. He found unconvincing Earle's explanation that the limited presence of American figures in his volume was because 'our significant contributions to warfare have been in the fields of tactics and technology, rather than strategy'.[82] Consequently, Paret decided at the very outset that the next *Makers* would need to say much more about American strategic thought and include several essays on strategic thinking during the Second World War. He added that it should conclude with an essay on the first generation of nuclear war theorists.[83]

In May, as they waited for confirmation of Gilbert's involvement, Paret and Craig held further discussions over the form of the proposed book. The result was a detailed appraisal of every chapter in the Earle volume (see Figure 4.2), which Paret conveyed to PUP. Adopting such a method enabled Paret to give substance to the observations that he had made in March by highlighting what should remain and what should change. In terms of the overall form of the book he suggested that the first three parts, covering warfare from the sixteenth century to the First World War, should remain largely unaltered. The final two parts, however, covering conflict from the First to the Second World War as well as air and sea power, should be replaced by a new section focused on post-Second World War developments, with a particular emphasis on American strategy. He proposed new chapters on Napoleon and American strategic thought in the nineteenth century for parts two and three respectively, and suggested that other chapters be removed completely. The proposed deletions included Derwent Whittlesey's piece on the geopoliticians—the significance of which both Paret and Craig thought overstated even in the context of the 1940s—and two chapters on French military thought: Possony and Mantoux's 'Du Picq and Foch' and Gottmann's 'Bugeaud, Gallieni, Lyautey'. In the case of the former, Paret proposed a piece on Foch and Haig as a replacement. The latter, meanwhile, was now judged superfluous in its own right. Instead, a new essay on guerrilla and counter-revolutionary warfare in the twentieth century would take its place, to include 'a section dealing with colonial warfare and its recent development into counter-revolutionary strategy'.[84]

The following month, Paret refined his plans further with the production of a new table of contents composed of twenty-three chapters, nine of which would be carried over from the original volume with revisions, and a further fourteen of which would be entirely new, as would the introduction (see Figure 4.3).

---

[82] Earle, *Makers*, p. ix.
[83] MLP, PUP, Box 344, Folder 3 (CO728), Paret to Hoekzema, 25 March 1982.
[84] MLP, PUP, Box 344, Folder 3 (CO728), Paret to Bailey, 19 May 1982.

152 MAKING MAKERS

Makers of Modern Strategy – Appraisal of Contents, Craig & Paret.

I The Origins of Modern War

1. Felix Gilbert: Machiavelli. Excellent. A fine discussion of Machiavelli, and a very useful introduction to the rest of the volume.

2. Henry Guerlac: Vauban. This essay is uneven. A better treatment of the influence of science on war, and of the increasing professionalization of war, would be desirable. But in a pinch, it could be retained.

3. R.R. Palmer: Frederick. A good discussion that brings out the major essential points. Palmer should be asked if he would like to revise the piece.

II The Classics of the Nineteenth Century

4. Brinton, Craig, Gilbert: Jomini. A good discussion. It might perhaps be revised slightly to point up Jomini's timebound quality in contrast to Clausewitz's universality.

5. Rothfels: Clausewitz. Although somewhat complex, this is basically a first-rate discussion of Clausewitz's theories. Perhaps the editors should simplify this text somewhat.

III From the 19th Century to the First World War

6. Edward Mead Earle: The Economic Foundations. This is still a good discussion of its subject.

7. Sigmund Neumann: Engels and Marx. Although specialists in Marxist theory might disagree, we think that this is still an adequate discussion. But since so much on the subject has appeared in the past forty years, there may be a case for a thorough revision.

8. Hajo Holborn: Moltke and Schlieffen. The literature in this field has grown enormously; in particular, we have a far better understanding of the strengths and limitations of the Schlieffen Plan than was possible in the 1940s. A new essay could certainly be written on Moltke and Schlieffen. But Holborn's discussion is still good in many respects; perhaps a thorough revision of the final section might suffice.

9. Stefan Possony & Etienne Mantoux: Du Picq and Foch. Just barely satisfactory. It covers the essential points, but is insufficiently critical. A strong candidate for deletion. Its place might be taken by a new essay on Foch and Haig.

10. Jean Gottmann: Bugeaud, Gallieni, Lyautey. Should be deleted because today French colonial warfare scarcely deserves a separate essay. Instead a section dealing with colonial warfare and its recent development into counter-revolutionary strategy should be added to a new essay on guerrilla and counter-revolutionary warfare in the 20th century.

11. Gordon Craig: Delbrück. Nothing in English has been written on Delbrück since this essay appeared. It continues to be an excellent introduction to Delbrück's work and significance, as well as to modern military history in general.

IV From the First to the Second World War

12. Harvey deWeerd: The Emergence of the Civilian. Outdated and insufficiently analytical. Should be replaced.

13. Hans Speier: Ludendorff. Although the discussion of the Wilhemine system is somewhat dated, overall this essay is still more than adequate.

14. Edward Mead Earle: Soviet Concepts of War. pp. 322–47 might still be acceptable, but the rest of the essay, dealing with the 30s and the early years of the Second World War, must be replaced by a new analysis. Alternately, the entire piece should be replaced.

15. Irving Gibson: Maginot and Liddell Hart. Probably the weakest piece in the volume. It should be replaced with an essay on land strategy in the 20s and 30s, which concludes with an analysis of blitzkrieg doctrines.

16. Derwent Whittlesey: Haushofer. The significance of the geopoliticians was overrated in the 1940s. This essay is no longer necessary.

V Sea and Air War

17. Margaret Sprout: Mahan. We have insufficient knowledge to judge this piece.

18. Theodore Ropp: Continental Doctrines of Sea Power. Not an essential contribution, but an adequate treatment of the subject. Ropp might be asked to revise and update the piece.

19. Alexander Kiralfy: Japanese Naval Strategy. This essay, largely dealing with the Second World War, should be replaced by a new treatment.

20. Edward Warner: Theories of Air Warfare. Adequate for the time, this essay is now totally outdated. It should be replaced by a new essay that includes a discussion of air strategy in the second World War.

Epilogue

Edward Mead Earle: Hitler. A brave and not unsuccessful attempt at instant history and prediction. It does not belong in a study of the history of strategy published in the mid-1980s.

Figure 4.2 Paret and Craig's assessment of Earle's *Makers of Modern Strategy*.

Source: MLP, PUP, Box 344, folder 3, Paret to Bailey, 19 May 1982.

PETER PARET AND THE GENESIS OF A NEW EDITION   153

A possible table of contents of <u>Makers of Modern Strategy</u>

New Introduction

I The Origins of Modern War

 1. Gilbert: <u>Machiavelli</u>.
 2. NEW ESSAY on the influence of science and the professionalization of war in the 17th century
 3. NEW ESSAY warfare as a branch of political economy 1648–1789; maritime and colonial warfare. Possible author: Piers Mackesy
 4. Palmer: Frederick

II The Classics of the Nineteenth Century

 5. NEW ESSAY on Napoleon. Desirable but not essential. Possible author: Paret
 6. Brinton, Craig, Gilbert: Jomini
 7. Rothfels: Clausewitz

III From the Nineteenth Century to the First World War

 8. Earle: Economic Foundations
 9. Neumann: Marx and Engels
 10. Holborn: Moltke and Schlieffen
 11. NEW ESSAY on the growth of American strategy. Possible author: Weigley
 12. Craig: Delbrück
 13. Sprout: Mahan. Revised by Phil Crowl?

IV From the First to the Second World War

 14. NEW ESSAY on the political leader as strategist. Author: Craig
 15. NEW ESSAY on French and British strategy during the first World War. Author: Howard
 16. NEW ESSAY on German strategy from the first to the second World War. Possible author: Michael Geyer.
 17. NEW ESSAY on Russian strategy. Possible author: John Erickson.
 18. NEW ESSAY on Japanese strategy. Possible author: Akire Iriye.
 19. NEW ESSAY on strategy of Western allies.
 20. NEW ESSAY on airpower from Billy Mitchell to Dresden.

VI Since 1945

 21. NEW ESSAY on conventional warfare in the nuclear age. Possible author: John Keegan.
 22. NEW ESSAY on revolutionary and counter-revolutionary war. Authors: John Shy and Tom Collier.
 23. NEW ESSAY on the first generation of nuclear strategists. Possible author: Lawrence Freedman.

Total: New Introduction

 9 essays taken over from the original version. Several of these will have to be significantly revised.
 <u>14 new essays</u>
 24 chapters

Figure 4.3 Paret's proposed table of contents, June 1982.
Source: MLP, PUP, Box 344, folder 3, Paret to Bailey, 16 June 1982.

In addition to the aforementioned changes, his plan for the new essays now included a chapter on 'the influence of science and the professionalization of war in the 17th century' to replace Henry Guerlac's chapter on Vauban, and a chapter on 'warfare as a branch of political economy 1648–1789', both to augment part one. Part four would include chapters on the 'strategy of the Western allies' and 'air power from Billy Mitchell to Dresden', whilst part five comprised three entirely new pieces including one on 'conventional warfare in the nuclear age' to complement the chapters on nuclear strategy and revolutionary war.[85]

---

[85] MLP, PUP, Box 344, Folder 3 (CO728), Paret to Bailey, 16 June 1982.

154   MAKING MAKERS

Thus over the course of three months, during which time it became clearer that he would be the chief editor, the extent of the revisions and additions that Paret envisaged for *Makers* increased dramatically. Where in late March he had suggested that one third of the book was unusable, by mid-May he made it clear to Bailey that he and Craig were proposing 'very substantial revisions' which would result in over 50 per cent of the book needing to be rewritten, with all the remaining chapters revised and updated to some degree.[86] The extent of the revisions only increased further when in July Paret produced an amended table of contents, which now consisted of twenty-five essays (a figure which included the introduction), of which only seven or eight would be carried over from the original, with a total of sixteen or seventeen entirely new pieces (see Figure 4.4). The burden on the editorial team would be 'considerable, in some respects greater than if we started from scratch', such that he wondered openly in May if the press really had the will to sanction such an expansive book.[87] With Bailey's personal investment in the project, however, its future was never seriously in doubt. For Paret, meanwhile, in light of the changes that he proposed, it became important to him from an early stage to emphasize that the new *Makers* would not be a revision of Earle's work, but a 'successor' to it.[88]

In taking planning in such a direction, Paret displayed some of the qualities that positioned him well to bring the book project to completion. In contrast to the overly deferential stance adopted by Ropp, Paret's approach was pragmatic and methodical, even ruthless. He adjusted the parameters of the book to account for what had been over-emphasized and what appeared to have been missed and had no compunction in recommending that cuts be made. His plan would see the least changes to those parts focused on the early modern period and the nineteenth century, with more attention required the closer the twentieth-century chapters drew to the present. In so doing he was able both to recognize the enormity of the project and to reconcile this with the impossibility of achieving definitive results. He was absolutely clear on the latter point, writing to Bailey that 'I believe quality is more important than coverage; we will never be able to deal with all aspects of this enormous subject, and some deletions or combinations of topics may be necessary'.[89]

At the same time, Paret exhibited a clear affinity for the Earle volume, an understanding of what made that publication effective, and a sense of what the successor project should aim to emulate. As he explained to contributors:

---

[86] MLP, PUP, Box 344, Folder 3 (CO728), Paret to Bailey, 19 May 1982. Paret's volume eventually came in at 942 pages, compared to Earle's 563 pages.

[87] MLP, PUP, Box 344, Folder 3 (CO728), Paret to Bailey, 19 May 1982.

[88] Paret maintained this stance through to the production and marketing phase, at which point he argued that since he now calculated that 80 per cent of the volume was new, the terms 'revised edition' and 'new edition' did not 'do justice to the book' and that instead he used 'the original MMS' and 'successor volume'. MLP, PUP, Box 350, Folder 2 (CO728), Paret to Bailey, 23 April 1985.

[89] MLP, PUP, Box 344, Folder 3 (CO728), Paret to Bailey, 16 June 1982.

MAKERS OF MODERN STRATEGY II

NEW INTRODUCTION Author: Paret

I The Origins of Modern War

1. Gilbert: Machiavelli. With some additions by Gilbert.
2. NEW ESSAY on the influence of science and of the professionalization of war in the 17th century.
3. NEW ESSAY on warfare as a branch of political economy, 1648–end of the 18th century. Maritime and colonial warfare. Possible author: Piers Mackesy.
4. Palmer: Frederick

II The Classics of the Nineteenth Century

5. NEW ESSAY on Napoleon. Author: Paret.
6. Brinton, Craig, Gilbert: Jomini. Revised by Shy.
7. NEW ESSAY on Clausewitz. Author: Paret.

III From the Nineteenth Century to the First World War

8. Earle: Economic Foundations
9. Neumann: Marx and Engels.
10. Holborn: Moltke and Schlieffen. Revised by Paret.
11. NEW ESSAY on the growth of American strategy. Author: Russell Weigley.
12. Craig: Delbrück
13. NEW ESSAY on Mahan. Possible author: Phil Crowl. Or revision of Sprout's essay on Mahan by Crowl?

IV From the First to the Second World War

14. NEW ESSAY on the political leader as strategist. Author: Craig.
15. NEW ESSAY on French and British strategy during the first World War. Author: Michael Howard.
16. NEW ESSAY on German strategy from the first to the second World War. Possible author: Michael Geyer.
17. NEW ESSAY on Russian strategy.
18. NEW ESSAY on Japanese strategy.
19. NEW ESSAY on strategy of Western allies.
20. NEW ESSAY on airpower from Billy Mitchell to Dresden.

V Since 1945

21. NEW ESSAY on conventional warfare in the nuclear age.
22. NEW ESSAY on revolutionary and counter-revolutionary war. Authors: John Shy and Tom Collier.
23. NEW ESSAY on the first generation of nuclear strategists. Possible author: Lawrence Freedman.
24. NEW ESSAY: A summing up. The role and demands of strategy in the present and future.

Bibliographical Notes. Each chapter is accompanied by an annotated bibliographical note, one to two printed pages in length.

Total contents: New Introduction. 7 or 8 essays taken over from the original version. Several of these will be significantly revised. 17 or 16 new essays. 25 essays (including the introduction).

Figure 4.4 Paret's amended table of contents, July 1982.
Source: MLP, PUP, Box 344, folder 3, Paret to Bailey, 31 July 1982.

The best essays in the original <u>Makers of Modern Strategy</u> combined the history of ideas with analyses of political, social, and technological developments, and with the history of war. By revealing interactions between external factors and some men's thinking about strategy, which in turn affected subsequent events, the book in its most useful sections fulfilled the program expressed in its title. We would hope that the essays in our new volume will again aim at the fullest possible integration of ideas and reality.

156   MAKING MAKERS

That this is most easily done in essays on a particular individual goes without saying. But authors of chapters dealing with developments in a particular country or war might also keep this goal in mind. It can never be the object of a chapter to give merely an account of campaigns. Instead we should try to trace the reciprocal relationship between campaigns, theory, and in some cases subsequent historical and theoretical analysis, by which societies try to understand previous wars and learn from them.[90]

In this manner, the holistic ambitions of the old volume echoed back into the new. Paret's articulation of the purpose and scope of *Makers* aligned him more closely to Earle than Ropp had ever been. In large part, this was a consequence of Paret's appreciation that the book was an examination of the history of war, rather than military history. In line with the understanding that Paret had developed over the course of prior decades, he continued to view military history as too narrow and insufficiently analytical to capture the true scope of the book. At its core, he thought about *Makers* in terms of ideas and their nexus with society, politics, and technology, more than campaigns. These were parameters that Paret underlined consistently through the period during which *Makers* was remade. Thus, during planning he stressed that the finished volume would lay emphasis on '1) the development of strategic thought, and 2) the interaction of politics, society, and war'.[91] Similarly, as the book approached publication he remained wary of any attempt to market it based on an appeal to a narrower conception, insisting that 'the book is not just about war, but about the way people thought and think about war (strategy). Beyond that, most of the essays attempt to integrate the history of war with general history'.[92]

Remaking *Makers*

It took four years to bring Paret's *Makers* from conception to publication. This was more than twice as long as it took Earle's team in wartime. It was also longer than Paret and the press had anticipated. In June 1982 Paret suggested an autumn 1983 deadline for the receipt of manuscripts.[93] Once he began planning with Craig this target came to appear unrealistic. The following month he reported Craig's scepticism that the viability of the original date could be met, and proposed instead a new deadline of summer or autumn 1984. Despite his reluctance

[90] MLP, PUP, Box 344, Folder 3 (CO728), Bailey to Paret, 24 May 1983. Guidance to authors appended to letter.

[91] MLP, PUP, Box 344, Folder 3 (CO728), Paret to Bailey, 19 May 1982.

[92] MLP, PUP, Box 344, Folder 2 (CO728), Paret to Hoekzema, 24 June 1985. This intervention came as a reaction to reading draft material prepared for the marketing campaign.

[93] MLP, PUP, Box 344, Folder 3 (CO728), Paret to Bailey, 7 June 1982.

PETER PARET AND THE GENESIS OF A NEW EDITION   157

to extend the writing period, he recognized that Craig's assessment was more reasonable: 'since we shall have to sign up a dozen authors', he wrote, 'I am bound to agree'.[94] Given the difficulties that they would encounter securing authors for a number of the chapters, this proved to be a prudent course of action.

The impediments to filling the roster became more apparent, and more pressing, with the passage of time, however. In the initial stages, things were rather more straightforward. In the first instance this was because a significant portion of the book could be written by the editorial team themselves. Here, the extent of activity matched the level of enthusiasm that each of the three brought to the enterprise. Paret's commitment increased over the course of summer 1982, as he first indicated that he would write the introduction and a new chapter on Napoleon and that he would revise Hajo Holborn's essay on Moltke and Schlieffen. Perhaps because of the self-acknowledged debt that he felt towards Rothfel's work on Clausewitz, and because he viewed his chapter for Earle as 'a first-rate discussion of Clausewitz's theories', Paret was initially reluctant to change it.[95] By July, however, he had decided to write a replacement.[96] Craig, meanwhile, committed not only to revising his contribution on Delbrück, but also to pen a new piece on 'the political leader as strategist' to replace Harvey deWeerd's contribution. In keeping with his more reticent approach, Gilbert's initial contribution consisted only of making amendments to his Machiavelli chapter. Both he and Craig, however, would eventually come to write a chapter on the present and future state of strategy, which first appeared as a concluding piece in the July chapter listing.

Whilst the editorial group were making these decisions, Paret decided that 'we are far enough along, I think, to contact a few possible contributors—those whom I know well enough to approach even before a contract is signed'.[97] Amongst this group of personal friends could be counted Russell Weigley, whom Paret managed to secure to write a chapter on American strategy through to the First World War.[98] John Shy was another significant figure brought onboard at this stage. Shy, whose association with Paret stretched back to their time working together at the Princeton Center of International Studies, offered to write the chapter on revolutionary and counter-revolutionary warfare that Paret had identified as a necessary addition, although at his suggestion he would do so with his colleague Tom Collier, an expert on US involvement in Vietnam. In addition to this, Shy agreed to revise the chapter on Jomini that had resulted from the combined efforts of Crane Brinton, Craig, and Gilbert, with the intention to 'integrate it more

---

[94] MLP, PUP, Box 344, Folder 3 (CO728), Paret to Bailey, 31 July 1982.

[95] MLP, PUP, Box 344, Folder 3 (CO728), Paret to Bailey, 19 May 1982, Paret to Bailey, 16 June 1982. For Paret's intellectual debt to Rothfels, see Bassford, *Clausewitz in English*, pp. 185–6.

[96] MLP, PUP, Box 344, Folder 3 (CO728), Paret to Bailey, 19 July 1982, Paret to Bailey, 31 July 1982. Gilbert, in particular, encouraged him to do so.

[97] MLP, PUP, Box 344, Folder 3 (CO728), Paret to Bailey, 7 June 1982.

[98] MLP, PUP, Box 344, Folder 3 (CO728), Paret to Bailey, 19 July 1982.

158   MAKING MAKERS

effectively with the discussions of Napoleon and Clausewitz.'[99] Shy's revisions eventually transformed into an entirely new piece of work, although he did not inform Paret of this development. In July 1982, he wrote to Paret that the necessary revisions were extensive.[100] Thereafter his lack of communication caused Paret anxiety, until, to Paret's surprise, he delivered a full chapter in the summer of 1984.[101] Thankfully, the editors were united in their positive appraisal of the piece: Gilbert thought it 'a brilliant article', while Paret considered it 'the best analysis of J I have ever read'.[102]

The most important person within this group of friends, however, was Michael Howard. Howard's role during the early planning for *Makers* was of such significance that it eventually led to the debacle of his invitation to join the editorial team. This came about not only because he agreed to contribute, but also because he helped to bring other contributors into the fold, such that Hoekzema and Bailey came to see him as *Makers*'s 'British Agent'. When first notified of Paret's intention regarding the book, Howard's reaction was unsurprisingly gleeful: 'Nothing has come out to replace the original edition, which is still mandatory reading for students and is sadly out of date', he responded. 'The news that you and Gordon are interested in doing a revision is the best that I have heard in years.' Yet whilst he was eager to be involved in the project he did not agree with Paret's proposal that he write the chapter on the first generation of nuclear war theorists. Instead, he proposed his former PhD student and newly appointed head of the War Studies Department at King's College London, Lawrence Freedman, since 'he is now the leading specialist on that particular field'.[103] By June, Freedman's name appeared on the chapter listing.

Having ruled himself out of contention to write on nuclear strategists, Howard was considered as a possible author for the chapter on the present and future of strategy, before settling on the First World War.[104] In part, this situation developed as a consequence of Howard's advice that Paret avoid inviting John Terraine, who he viewed as 'a monomaniac on the subject of Haig' with 'no real understanding of continental strategy', and that he might consider Howard himself.[105] By October this chapter, which had transformed from 'British and French strategy during the First World War' to 'the strategists of 1914', still lacked an author.

---

[99] MLP, PUP, Box 344, Folder 3 (CO728), Paret to Bailey, 16 June 1982. Brinton had left the chapter unfinished in 1943, so Craig and Gilbert worked together to complete it. PUP, Box 344, Folder 3 (CO728), Craig to Ropp, 28 January 1980.

[100] MLP, PUP, Box 344, Folder 3 (CO728), Paret to Bailey, 19 July 1982.

[101] MLP, PUP, Box 344, Folder 1 (CO728), Paret to Elizabeth Gretz, 20 August 1984.

[102] Gilbert Papers, Box 14/P, Paret, Gilbert to Paret, 18 November 1985. Gilbert to Paret, 20 February 1985. Paret to Gilbert, 9 March 1985.

[103] MLP, PUP, Box 344, Folder 3 (CO728), Howard to Paret, 19 May 1982. Howard wrote, 'his new book on the development of nuclear strategy seems to me definitive, and I would be drawing heavily on it in anything I wrote'.

[104] MLP, PUP, Box 344, Folder 3 (CO728), Paret to Hoekzema, 2 September 1983.

[105] MLP, PUP, Box 344, Folder 3 (CO728), Howard to Paret, 19 May 1982.

PETER PARET AND THE GENESIS OF A NEW EDITION   159

At this point, Howard suggested two candidates, Douglas Porch and John Gooch, before again offering himself as a possibility.[106] This time Paret accepted.

While conditioning his own role, Howard's advice shaped *Makers* in other ways. As well as shepherding Paret away from John Terraine, Howard also dissuaded him from his original choice for a new author on air power, Anthony Noble Frankland, since Howard believed Noble Frankland had not been active enough in the field over the previous twenty years to justify an invitation.[107] The search for an alternative would lead to David McIsaac, who held the distinction of being the only contributor to Ropp's *Makers Revisited* to contribute also to Paret's *Makers*. His chapter for the latter volume was written under the same title, although in a revised and expanded form. Howard's views were also significant in changing plans for the chapter on conventional warfare after the Second World War. In early consideration John Keegan was associated with this piece (see Figure 4.3). By July, however, his name had been removed from the chapter listing (see Figure 4.4).[108] In the autumn, Howard suggested that rather than seek an academic for this piece, Paret might think instead of enlisting a practitioner. His initial suggestion was General Sir John Hackett, former head of NATO Northern Army Group and former principal of King's College London. Howard cooled on this idea in October, however, since conversations had shown him to be 'completely tied up with his nonsense over the Third World War and I do not think we could get him to produce a serious piece of work'.[109] In his stead he proposed 'his great rival' Field Marshal Lord Carver, 'a very serious and learned soldier who is doing a great deal of writing now and did indeed produce a very solid and able book on Conventional War since 1945'.[110] Following Howard's advice, Paret brought Carver to the project.[111]

---

[106] MLP, PUP, Box 344, Folder 3 (CO728), Howard to Paret, 5 October 1982. As late as January 1984, Howard's chapter was listed as 'Militarism and the First World War'. See chapter listing for 8 January 1984, appended to Paret to Hoekzema, 9 January 1984.

[107] For Noble Frankland see MLP, PUP, Box 344, Folder 3 (CO728), Howard to Paret, 19 May 1982.

[108] It seems that Keegan was never asked to write by Paret. Others who were touted as potential contributors to the project by one or more of the editors, but who were ultimately not asked to join, included Edward Luttwak, Tom Etzold, William McNeill, and George Herring. See Craig Diaries, Tagebuch Vol. 37, Journal July 1982–April 1983, 16 December 1982, p. 186 and 2 January 1983, pp. 206–7.

[109] MLP, PUP, Box 344, Folder 3 (CO728), Howard to Paret, 5 October 1982. In 1982 Hackett published a sequel to his 1978 book *The Third World War*. A global bestseller translated into multiple languages, the 1978 book envisioned a conflict scenario between NATO and Warsaw Pact forces that included a limited nuclear exchange. For the genesis of the book, see J. Michaels, 'Revisiting General Sir John Hackett's *The Third World War*', *British Journal for Military History*, Vol. 3, No. 1 (November 2016), pp. 88–104. A. Seipp, '"Visionary Battle Scenes": Reading Sir John Hackett's *The Third World War*, 1977–85', *The Journal of Military History*, Vol. 83, No. 4 (October 2019), pp. 1235–57. Since Hackett's book had first appeared in 1978, it is possible that Howard had now tired of the project. In a qualified review upon its release, he described it as 'a careful, detailed, expert but at the same time imaginative account of the course which a war with the Soviet Union might take in seven years' time' which was 'remarkable as much for its political subtlety as for its military expertise'. M. Howard, 'Can the West Win the Next World War?', *The Sunday Times*, 16 July 1978.

[110] MLP, PUP, Box 344, Folder 3 (CO728), Howard to Paret, 5 October 1982.

[111] Carver's eighteen-thousand-word draft, delivered very promptly, required some careful editing to bring it down to a more appropriate length. MLP, PUP, Box 344, Folder 3 (CO728), Paret to Hoekzema, 9 January 1984.

160 MAKING MAKERS

As these developments showed, even in its early stages Paret's *Makers* underwent a degree of transformation, which was somewhat analogous to the process
that conditioned Earle's book, as plans were moulded to the interests and abilities
of prospective authors.[112] This continued as planning for the book progressed.
Michael Howard's suggestion in May 1982 that Brian Bond could write a piece on
Liddell Hart, for example, sowed the seed for the chapter that would become
'Liddell Hart and de Gaulle' which Bond would co-author with the French historian Martin Alexander.[113] This piece, which served as a replacement for the Arpad
Kovacs/Irving Gibson chapter on Maginot and Liddell, had not been included in
Paret's prospective chapter outlines of June and July 1982, although he had noted
in his May appraisal of the Earle volume that the original 'should be replaced with
an essay on land strategy in the 20s and 30s, which concludes with an analysis of
blitzkrieg doctrines.'[114] In a similar vein, a stand-alone chapter on Japanese strategy included in early chapter listings transformed into a treatment of American
and Japanese strategy in the Pacific War, authored by D. Clayton James.[115] In
other instances, Paret reversed his decisions. A case in point was Henry Guerlac's
chapter on Vauban, which Paret had initially sought to replace on the grounds
that 'a better treatment of the influence of science on war, and of the increasing
professionalization of war, would be desirable'.[116] In January 1984, he reported to
Hoekzema that he was undecided as to whether the chapter should be retained.[117]
By the time the book was complete, Guerlac's chapter was one of the few to be
republished without significant alterations, under the justification that it was
good enough to stand the test of time.[118] Similarly Paret changed his mind on the
superfluity of a chapter on French colonial warfare, reporting in January 1984
that he had asked Douglas Porch, whose name had earlier been suggested in connection with the First World War, to write the essay.[119]

---

[112] Away from Paret, Gilbert and Craig also discussed several chapter possibilities that never materialized. These included a chapter on wars of national liberation and the preparation for war in peacetime. Gilbert to Craig, 5 January 1983, Gilbert Papers, Box 63/G, Craig. HI.

[113] MLP, PUP, Box 344, Folder 3 (CO728), Howard to Paret, 19 May 1982. Bond was a long-serving
colleague of Howard's at the War Studies Department at King's College London, having joined as a
lecturer in 1966 'by interview but without competition'. He was only the second hire for Howard's
fledgling department, which was set up following his promotion to professor in 1963. Bond would
remain with the War Studies department for the rest of his career, rising to professor by 1986.
See B. Bond, *Military Historian: My Part in the Birth and Development of War Studies* (Solihull: Helion,
2018), pp. 24–9, 32–40.

[114] MLP, PUP, Box 344, Folder 3, Paret to Bailey, 19 May 1982.

[115] In 1983 the editors also considered adding a chapter on economic aspects of strategy to the
final section. In September 1983 Paret reported that he had been negotiating with the economist
Gavin Kennedy about the piece. MLP, PUP, Box 344, Folder 3 (CO728), Paret to Hoekzema,
2 September 1983.

[116] MLP, PUP, Box 344, Folder 3 (CO728), Paret to Bailey, 19 May 1982.

[117] MLP, PUP, Box 344, Folder 3 (CO728), Paret to Hoekzema, 9 January 1984.

[118] Paret, *Makers*, p. 6. The others were Earle's chapter on economics and Palmer's on dynastic and
national wars. Guerlac died in May 1985.

[119] MLP, PUP, Box 344, Folder 3 (CO728), Paret to Hoekzema, 9 January 1984.

PETER PARET AND THE GENESIS OF A NEW EDITION   161

The availability of Paret's first-preference authors also played a part in shaping the book, especially once the editor was no longer contacting 'old personal friends'.[120] As he began to establish contact with scholars outside of his immediate circle, his fortunes varied. There were some successes—Philip Crowl and Michael Geyer agreed to join, with Crowl agreeing to write a replacement chapter on Mahan, rather than a revision of the original.[121] This second round of invitations, however, bore witness to more frequent disappointment. Attempts to secure contributions by Piers Mackesy, John Erickson, and Akira Iriye, for chapters on eighteenth-century warfare, Russian, and Japanese strategy respectively, were unsuccessful.[122] In early 1983, Paret made a concerted attempt to persuade Geoffrey Parker to write a chapter on science and the professionalization of war in the seventeenth century, but Parker's unwillingness to commit to producing work in time for the original manuscript deadline proved insurmountable. In July 1983, Paret instead asked that Gunther Rothenberg of Purdue University take charge of the piece.[123]

Two chapters in particular caused difficulties that were not fully resolved until early in 1984. Over a year after the project had begun, Paret wrote to Hoekzema to explain that the essays on Marx and Engels and on Russian strategy had been 'extraordinarily difficult to place'. Although he was at that point negotiating with potential authors for both chapters, he conceded that if the attempt fell through 'we shall have to make do with Neumann's 1943 essay'.[124] In response, Hoekzema wrote that 'it would be a mistake to rely solely on the 1943 essay, since so much has changed in both Marxist studies and in Russian strategy in recent years' and that he would rather delay the schedule slightly, especially if it meant that the Russian chapter could be updated.[125] The Russian chapter had been the cause of consternation for several months. In April 1983, Craig recorded in his diary having pulled Gilbert out of a session of the American Philosophical Society to discuss the matter, with the two men agreeing 'that we must have a chapter on the Soviet Union, even if we couldn't find an absolutely first class person'.[126]

---

[120] MLP, PUP, Box 344, Folder 3 (CO728), Paret to Bailey, 19 July 1982. Paret did not want to approach scholars he was less familiar with until he knew with more certainty that the project would go ahead.

[121] Geyer wrote the chapter on German strategy from the First to the Second World War.

[122] All three were noted as possible authors in the June chapter listing. Erickson's and Iriye's names did not appear in the July listing.

[123] MLP, PUP, Box 344, Folder 3 (CO728), Paret to Hoekzema, 20 March 1983. Paret to Hoekzema, 28 July 1983. Ironically, Parker's involvement was curtailed because of his inability to produce his chapter before the autumn of 1984. In the event, some of the manuscripts for the book would not be received until around this time. Rothenberg also provided an additional chapter, 'From Moltke to Schlieffen', to complement Hajo Holborn's piece, revised by Paret, and to bring the German narrative through to the First World War. MLP, PUP, Box 344, Folder 3 (CO728), Paret to Hoekzema, 20 March 1983.

[124] MLP, PUP, Box 344, Folder 3 (CO728), Paret to Hoekzema, 4 August 1983.

[125] MLP, PUP, Box 344, Folder 3 (CO728), Hoekzema to Paret, 15 September 1983.

[126] Craig Diaries, Tagebuch Vol. 38, Journal April 1983–May 1984, 23 April 1983.

162   MAKING MAKERS

After Paret's failed attempt to secure their first preference, John Erickson, the next candidate was Raymond Garthoff, although here too there was no success.[127] A slew of suggestions from Hoekzema followed: Fritz Ermath, Benjamin Lambeth, Ty Cobb, David Holloway, William Culkowitz, William C. Potter, Jim Valenta.[128] It was only in January 1984 that Paret was finally able to report that Walter Pintner had agreed to contribute. Paret underlined how fortunate they were 'that a senior scholar with his reputation is prepared to undertake the work at such short notice', yet Pintner's participation came with a twist.[129] The original chapter outlines for the new *Makers* had situated the chapter on Russia in the 1914 to 1945 section. Pintner, however, would only consent to write on the subject up to the First World War. The solution, facilitated in part by the extra time that Pintner would need to write his piece, was to include an additional chapter specifically focused on Soviet strategy.[130] This time it was Craig rather than Paret who found the author, thanks in large part to good fortune. On 31 January he lunched with future Secretary of State Condoleezza Rice, then an assistant professor of political science at Stanford, working on 'arms control and also on the contemporary Staff system'. 'I was so impressed by Condoleezza', wrote Craig, 'that, after consulting Paret, I invited her to write the piece on Soviet strategy.'[131] Like Margaret Tuttle Sprout before her, Rice thus became the only woman to write for Paret's *Makers*. As for the essay on Marx and Engels, the editor's attempts in 1983 to secure 'the outstanding man in the field', Jurgen Kocka, came to nought.[132] It was not until April 1984 that Paret reported that Mark von Hagen, a Stanford PhD student on the cusp of completion, would revise the essay 'in return for some help I have given him in his work', adding, 'This finally solves a problem that has given us a lot of concern.'[133]

Gordon Craig and the Urgency of the Present

Despite the gradual onset of delays caused by the difficulties of finding authors for parts of the book and the decision to add new chapters, *Makers II*—as it was

---

[127]   MLP, PUP, Box 344, Folder 3 (CO728), Paret to Hoekzema, 2 September 1983. Erickson seemed strongly favoured by the press, such that even in September 1983 Hoekzema was moved to ask Paret whether he was 'still out of the question?' PUP, Box 344, Folder 3 (CO728), Hoekzema to Paret, 15 September 1983.

[128]   MLP, PUP, Box 344, Folder 3 (CO728), Hoekzema to Paret, 7 December 1983.

[129]   MLP, PUP, Box 344, Folder 3 (CO728), Paret to Hoekzema, 9 January 1984.

[130]   MLP, PUP, Box 344, Folder 3 (CO728), Paret to Bailey, 14 February 1984. This was also the period in which Paret asked Bond to write on inter-war strategy and reversed his decision on French colonial warfare and invited Porch. Paret described Porch's and Rice's essays as 'a kind of speculation. Nevertheless, Porch has written widely on the subject, and Rice is a very able young woman—I believe PUP is publishing her first book this August. So they seem reasonable bets.'

[131]   Craig Diaries, Tagebuch Vol. 38, Journal April 1983–May 1984, 31 January 1984, p. 293.

[132]   MLP, PUP, Box 344, Folder 3 (CO728), Paret to Hoekzema, 2 September 1983. At this time Paret relayed that Kocka 'cannot deliver the ms until the last months of 1984. Felix Gilbert will see him early next month and discuss the matter with him. Perhaps he is somewhat more flexible than I assume.'

[133]   MLP, PUP, Box 344, Folder 3 (CO728), Paret to Hoekzema, 30 April 1984.

PETER PARET AND THE GENESIS OF A NEW EDITION   163

sometimes referred to during the writing period—took shape largely in accordance with Paret's no-nonsense approach. Earle's *Makers* provided the model to which it partly conformed, diverging in more significant ways as it progressed to issues beyond the chronological and geographical purview of the contributors of the early 1940s. In working to this model, Paret was creating a volume which exhibited similar sensitivity towards the linkages between past and present as the original. As he later explained to Hoekzema, he felt that *Makers* stood out from other works because it presented 'a continuum of ideas on the use of military force from the Renaissance to the present'.[134] Yet unlike Earle, who understood his endeavours in the context of contemporary urgency, Paret showed little sign that he was particularly motivated by the significance of the moment. In part this can be explained by circumstances, since the challenges of the Second World War presented themselves in a visceral, immediate, and widespread sense that did not fully translate to the Cold War environment of the early 1980s. But it was also a reflection of Paret as an historian, and particularly of the clear realization he had experienced decades earlier that the past was of more interest to him than the present.

This was not the case for Gordon Craig. In addition to having been more invested in *Makers* than Gilbert in the decades after its first appearance, Craig was also the most eager of the three members of the new editorial team to link the successor volume to the needs of moment. As he wrote to Bailey in August 1982:

> It is good to be getting back under the wings of the Press, particularly in a new and long-overdue edition of MMS. Or perhaps <u>not</u> overdue, for it strikes me that this is precisely the right time to awaken the American people to the importance of a national strategy, which we have not had since Carter's time.[135]

When Paret first raised the prospect of collaborating on *Makers II* with him, Craig had been emeritus professor at Stanford for three years (see Figure 4.5).[136] Far from slowing down in his retirement, however, the early 1980s marked something of a late-career revival for Craig. This was all the more remarkable since he had begun the decade with surgery for a heart condition. Once recovered, he seemed to approach his work with renewed vigour. As he explained to a student reporter, he considered retirement 'a poor excuse to "slack off"', arguing that: 'The country

---

[134] MLP, PUP, Box 344, Folder 1 (CO728), Paret to Hoekzema, 5 June 1984.

[135] MLP, PUP, Box 344, Folder 3 (CO728), Craig to Bailey, 25 August 1982.

[136] After leaving the Marine Corps in 1946, Craig joined Princeton University as associate professor. In 1961 he joined Stanford as the J. E. Wallace Sterling Professor of History. The Stanford professorship allowed him to switch the focus of his teaching for the first time from diplomatic to German history. Gordon Craig Diaries, Stanford University Archives, Stanford CA, Box 1, reel 1: Tagebuch Vol. 6—Journal 1945–6, 11 March 1946, p. 131. The salary offer helped stave off a rival bid for him from Cornell University. W. Palmer, *Engagement with the Past: The Lives and Works of the World War II Generation of Historians* (Lexington, KY: University of Kentucky Press, 2001), pp. 101, 142–3.

164 MAKING MAKERS

Figure 4.5 Gordon Craig at Stanford University. Like Gilbert, Craig worked on both the 1943 and 1986 editions of *Makers of Modern Strategy*, although his impact on the latter was more substantial.
Source: Stanford Historical Photograph Collection (SC1071). Dept. of Special Collections and University Archives, Stanford University Libraries, Stanford, CA.

is peopled with old dodderers trying to pretend that a little golf every day will keep them busy. Really they're bored [...] They don't last as long as they should.'[137] He continued to teach enthusiastically until the end of the 1984–5 academic year, enjoying the experience as much for the performance as for the mental stimulation.[138] During the same period he also experienced considerable scholarly success. His standing within the profession was recognized with his appointment as president of the American Historical Association in 1982. Meanwhile, his synthesis of modern German history, *The Germans*, published in 1981, garnered critical acclaim and international commercial success.[139]

---

[137] T. Wheeler, 'Teacher, Scholar, Historian Adds Life to Academics', *The Stanford Daily*, 16 April 1982.
[138] See Craig Diaries Tagebuch Vol. 39, Journal May 1984–June 1985, pp. 350–2. As he told the same reporter: 'As a lecturer approaches the podium, he should be keyed up for the lecture. There should be a sense of anticipation [...] he should really want to do what he is about to do.' Wheeler, 'Teacher, Scholar, Historian'. See also Palmer, *Engagement with the Past*, p. 159.
[139] The success of the book in Germany was such that Craig made a number of publicity trips to Germany during this period. The attention, which extended to public recognition, was something that Craig relished. Whilst undoubtedly vain, and very preoccupied with his own appearance, Craig was

PETER PARET AND THE GENESIS OF A NEW EDITION   165

The *Makers* project, then, came at a time when Craig appeared energized on multiple fronts. It was also a time when concerns for the present state of the USA—manifest in a perceived deficit in national strategy, strategy making, and statecraft—were foremost in his mind. This perceived deficit provided a deep source of motivation which sustained him throughout the years of the book's production. He was keen to emphasize the role that the book could play in reversing this trend, noting in April 1983, for example, that he had addressed a dinner of the Humanities and Sciences Council 'on our plans to do a new <u>Makers of Modern Strategy</u> (and some recollections about the first one) and our hopes that it might correct or alleviate the dangerous lack of strategical thinking in high places'.[140]

Craig associated this lack of strategic thinking directly with the Reagan administration. As an individual whose left-leaning credentials stretched back to his youth, and to the particular affection he felt for Franklin Roosevelt, this was hardly surprising.[141] Nevertheless, he believed that the Reagan presidency marked a nadir for the US approach in world affairs that went beyond partisan politics. Over the period in which *Makers II* was created, he recorded numerous lamentations in his diary on this subject. The US invasion of Grenada in 1983, for example, provoked an anguished response from Craig, who wrote that: 'All our allies are angry with us, because (true to form) we consulted none of them [...] It is a mess, and one can take no pleasure in the fact that it is the Republicans who are being discomforted. It's our country, dammit!, and its foreign policy is maladroit beyond description and apparently wholly bereft of strategical plan'.[142] Several days later he railed against the regime once more, writing: 'Have these people no knowledge of our recent history? Have they no sense of connectedness?'[143] These sentiments did not dull over time. In August 1985, for instance, he launched another tirade, lamenting that:

> We have—at least in our public attitudes and pronouncements—become the most dangerous and reactionary country in the world. We are seeking to

also self-aware. As he noted in his diary in 1982—in reference to the process of keeping his diary: 'In my own journal, the element of vanity is strong, and I make little effort to overcome the self.' Craig diaries, Tagebuch Vol. 39, Journal May 1984–June 1985. Entry for Wednesday 29 August 1982, p. 101.

[140] Craig Diaries, Tagebuch Vol. 37, Journal July 1982–April 1983, Saturday 9 April 1983, p. 300.

[141] In July 1945 Craig had celebrated the Labour victory in the United Kingdom general election with drinks and revelry. The year before he had been deeply affected by the death of Franklin Roosevelt, noting that it was a 'dreadful tragedy [...] Ever since I went to college FDR has been president—always the chief—and I think he always will be for me.' Craig Diaries, Journal Vol. 5, 28, 12 April 1944, p. 72, July 1945, p. 150.

[142] Craig Diaries, Tagebuch Vol. 38, Journal April 1983–May 1984, 28 October 1983, pp. 151–3. The US action occurred while Craig was on a trip to Zurich, giving him a more direct sense of reactions amongst ostensible allies. One of his former students asked how it could be believed that a government that supported Marcos in the Philippines would establish democracy in Grenada. Craig agreed that 'the breach of treaty and the invocation of one we hadn't even signed is hurting us; and it is clear that more and more people in West Germany are beginning to think there is nothing to choose between us and the Soviet Union—and that adds up to a growing neutralist sentiment'.

[143] Craig Diaries, Tagebuch Vol. 38, Journal April 1983–May 1984, 31 October 1983, p. 162.

166 MAKING MAKERS

overthrow Nicaragua through the agency of a gang of Somozists, while in neighbouring Guatemala we support a government that murders opposition leaders without even the pretense [sic] of a trial. To all intents and purposes, we are supporting apartheid in South Africa [...] The President's insistence upon the unrealizable Star Wars "defense" threatens to defeat all hopes of arms control, in which the Administration is not interested in any case. All of this—and the phony patriotism rhetoric that accompanies it ("standing tall" etc., and talk of our heroic conquest of—Grenada!) the great American public tolerates and perhaps approves and the mass media embellish.[144]

If Craig was inclined to bemoan the actions of the administration, however, it was equally clear to him that they stemmed from a deeper failure of education. As he noted in connection to these complaints, at least part of the problem was 'the decline of humanistic education and the fixation on computers'.[145] For Craig, this was a broad issue, encompassing the absence of literary models as a means to teach values, and an overreliance on numbers and accumulation as a measure of success and satisfaction, but it was equally a product of lack of historical knowledge, and of the history of war in particular.[146]

In this manner, Craig provided a bridge to the importance of broader education and the need to address contemporary concerns, which linked to the original conception of *Makers*, fleshed out in dimensions that Paret was less inclined to emphasize.[147] Such postures could be seen in the division of labour between the editors towards the opening and closing of their volume, where Paret took sole responsibility for the introduction and Craig, along with Gilbert, co-wrote the final chapter on contemporary strategy. Paret's introduction did not ignore the link between past and present. Indeed, in framing the volume explicitly with reference to the original and against the backdrop of enhanced scrutiny of historical contributions in the post-Second World War era, Paret went so far as to suggest that 'the need to understand war is, if possible, even greater now than it was in 1943' and that 'the new *Makers of Modern Strategy* raises the question of relevance even more forcefully than did its predecessor'.[148] Yet his overriding inclination was to stress the 'continuum' of strategic thought that extended beyond 1945, even if the conditions of the nuclear age made it harder to discern the connections.

---

[144] Craig Diaries, Tagebuch Vol. 40, Journal July 1985–August 1986, 18 August 1985, pp. 43–5.

[145] Ibid.

[146] Craig had an abiding interest in literature, as well as music, stretching back to high school. Prior to university he took no history classes but focused on literature instead. His diaries show that he continued to maintain a varied literary diet well into his retirement. Palmer, *Engagement with the Past*, p. 12.

[147] Nor was *Makers* the only project of this type that Craig was involved with at this time. Similar motivations had provided the impetus for another project, *Force and Statecraft: Diplomatic Problems of Our Time*, published in 1983 and co-authored with Alex L. George, Professor of Political Science and Craig's colleague at Stanford.

[148] P. Paret, 'Introduction', in Paret, *Makers*, p. 7.

Moreover, in framing the volume, his piece was concerned with generalities rather than specifics.

The same restrictions did not apply to Gilbert and Craig's co-written effort 'Reflections on Strategy in the Present and Future', which served, in effect, as the volume's conclusion. Here, the two survivors of the original volume addressed in more substantive terms the question that had been posed in Paret's introduction: 'Has the experience of the past any real bearing upon the problems that confront us in the nuclear age?'[149] In so doing they used early twentieth-century parallels to illustrate the dynamics of arms races and the inevitability (or otherwise) of war, mused on the potential for developing technologies such as precision-guided munitions to shape the character of war away from mutual annihilation and towards something more reminiscent of the eighteenth century, whilst also illuminating the various claims of historical offensive-mindedness used to underpin NATO strategy against the Warsaw Pact. Such examples, they noted, 'are perhaps enough to show that the strategical experience of the past is by no means irrelevant to our current thinking about battlefield problems'.[150] Beyond the battlefield, meanwhile, multiple historical examples reinforced that 'the broader form of strategy' could be informed by 'cases for study and reflection and models against which to measure present practice'.[151]

It should be noted, however, that even in this enterprise Craig's desire to reach into the present was tempered by Gilbert's reticence. As befitted a personal and professional relationship that spanned four decades, Gilbert and Craig worked effectively together in producing the piece. Craig took the lead. Having completed his new chapter on the civilian as statesman, as well as the revisions to his chapter on Delbrück, in July 1984 he turned his attention to the concluding chapter.[152] At this stage, he envisaged:

> beginning with some definitions of strategy, then discussing the requirements of sound strategy (what is strategical vision? A proper assessment of interests, capabilities, and priorities? And what else?), and then, after some discussion of the strategical gifts of the Founding Fathers, reflecting on the ways in which the military, scientific and industrial revolutions have militated against sound strategic assessments—indeed, made them increasingly meaningless—ever since the turn of the century.[153]

[149] G. Craig and F. Gilbert, 'Reflections on Strategy in the Present and Future', in Paret, *Makers*, p. 863.

[150] Ibid, p. 869. It is important to note that the authors conceived of such historical examples as 'models and admonitions', not simple endorsements or validations for contemporary decisions and practice.

[151] Ibid, p. 871.

[152] Of his Delbrück chapter after revision, Craig wrote, 'It was a very solid piece of work when I wrote it, but it's better now.' Craig Diaries, Tagebuch Vol. 39, Thursday 14 June 1984, p. 29.

[153] Craig Diaries, Tagebuch Vol. 39, Friday 27 July 1984, pp. 70–1.

168 MAKING MAKERS

By 14 August he had finished his draft and sent it to Gilbert, who received it enthusiastically.[154] 'You will see from the enclosure', Gilbert responded, 'that I see as much danger to strategic thought and to fear in general in the present irrationalism and that I also fear the domination of military armament in economic life.'[155] When he came to rewrite the conclusion, however, Craig decided that 'Felix's notes are not helpful.' Consequently, he was forced to adopt an entirely different approach to the chapter, so that the new draft was completed only in January 1985.[156]

Despite Gilbert's overall positive assessment, points of difference inevitably emerged between the two men. Gilbert, for example, announced that he was 'somewhat astonished about your calling the years 1949–1971 the years of the Cold War', since he considered that 'at least in its most acute phase' it ended sooner.[157] Nor could he understand why Craig was so adamant to include an anecdote about Wilhelm II and Moltke the younger, and to tie this point about war by timetable to a gripe concerning computerized banking systems. More significantly, Gilbert had also early indicated his discomfort with those parts of Craig's draft which moved to the present day in explicit ways, writing that 'the reference to contemporary events, like Reagan's scandalous remark about bombing the Russians, but also the remarks on American and Soviet foreign policy might be removed. Since we hope that the book will last for a long while people soon won't understand such allusions any longer.'[158] After the draft was complete, Craig also pushed for the inclusion of comment on the Reaganite 'Star Wars' programme, which Gilbert argued against.[159] Craig, forthright but not unwilling to compromise, ceded some ground. In the end, Gilbert's chronology of the Cold War—1949 to 1969—was preferred, Craig's anecdotes remained, but the overt references to Reagan, to US and Soviet foreign policy, and to 'Star Wars' were removed.[160]

Final Hurdles

As *Makers II* marched towards production, its editors felt confident that their successor volume would constitute a fitting replacement for the original. As early as

---

[154] Craig Diaries, Tagebuch Vol. 39, Tuesday 14 August 1984, p. 90.

[155] Gilbert to Craig, 10 September 1984. Gilbert Papers, Box 63/G. Craig. HI.

[156] Craig Diaries, Tagebuch Vol. 39, Tuesday 8 October 1984, p. 150. Wednesday 2 January 1985, p. 246.

[157] Gilbert to Craig, 20 November 1984. Gilbert Papers, Box 63/G. Craig. HI.

[158] Gilbert to Craig, 10 September 1984, Gilbert Papers, Box 63/G. Craig. HI.

[159] Gilbert Papers, Box 14/P. Paret, Gilbert to Paret, 8 March 1985.

[160] Gilbert remained troubled by Craig's anecdotes, writing to Paret the following year: 'I still remain unhappy that we couldn't persuade Gordon to leave out the remark about the confusion in his personal bank records, nor do I really think that the story about William II and the younger Moltke is very important.' Gilbert to Paret, November 18, 1985, Gilbert Papers, Box 14/P. Paret. HI.

PETER PARET AND THE GENESIS OF A NEW EDITION   169

January 1984, at which point not all the chapters had even been assigned, Paret noted that 'the standard of the essays we have received so far is very high'.[161] By June, he felt emboldened to pronounce that 'On the whole, I think that the quality of the essays is superior to that of the original volume.'[162] His assessment was echoed by Craig, who noted in his diary entry for 13 May that he had been reading papers for the book: 'the standard high as far as content goes. The style in most cases leaves a lot to be desired.'[163] On the latter point, Craig and Paret shared common views. 'Some of our authors obviously don't know how to write,' Paret wrote. 'Others are careful writers, and some—like Gordon and myself—seek not only precision and clarity, but also an aesthetic impact.'[164] Fortunately, the editors who had set such elevated standards for their own prose had instituted a thorough editorial process intended in part to impose their standards on the work of their contributors. Before sending a manuscript to the press, Paret would send a duplicate to his associate editors, so that each man could make changes and suggestions on the copy. Once this was complete, Paret would combine the amendments into one copy to be returned to the author, who would then act on the suggestions. Only after Paret had scrutinized the author-corrected version would he send it on to the press. 'All this takes time,' Paret wrote 'but should ensure a better book.'[165]

Nevertheless, a labour-intensive process such as this could not entirely prevent the emergence of further problems, even after the editors considered their vetting complete. For example, issues arose concerning the length of contributions by Michael Geyer and Michael Carver, and differences of opinion also opened up between the editors and PUP staff over Rothenberg's chapters, particularly his piece on Maurice, Gustavus Adolphus, and Montecuccoli. On receipt of the draft, Paret described it as 'a first-rate revisionist study, which breaks a lot of new ground'.[166] Craig, too, viewed it as 'very good'.[167] Hoekzema, however, was disappointed, and thought it needed a stronger analytical focus.[168] Bailey also

---

[161]   MLP, PUP, Box 344, Folder 3 (CO728), Paret to Bailey, 14 February 1984.

[162]   MLP, PUP, Box 344, Folder 1 (CO728), Paret to Hoekzema, 5 June 1984.

[163]   Craig Diaries, Tagebuch Vol. 39, Wednesday 13 May 1985, p. 9.

[164]   MLP, PUP, Box 344, Folder 1 (CO728), Paret to Bailey, 4 June 1984. Paret added, 'Gordon, as I know from experience, is the kind of writer who will fight over a comma.' This was very true. When revising his Delbrück chapter, Craig noted 'changing about 60 "whiches" to "that's" in the course of it. Apparently no one in the Princeton Press in 1943, and neither Ed Earle nor I ever heard of the "that/which rule."' Equally in his entry for 22 March 1983, Craig noted, 'In reading my Marshall piece in The New Republic, I was infuriated to discover that, after I had corrected the proofs, someone had changed two of my "likes" to "such as's" Sent a wrathy [sic] letter to Jack Beatty.' Craig Diaries, Tagebuch Vol. 39, Thursday 14 June 1984, p. 29. Tagebuch Vol. 37, 22 March 1983, p. 290.

[165]   MLP, PUP, Box 344, Folder 3 (CO728), Paret to Hoekzema, 4 August 1983. He later added that this process also included readings by 'one, two, or more specialists in the field'. MLP, PUP, Box 344, Folder 1 (CO728), Paret to Hoekzema, 5 June 1984.

[166]   MLP, PUP, Box 344, Folder 3 (CO728), Paret to Hoekzema, 9 January 1984.

[167]   Craig Diaries, Tagebuch Vol. 38, Journal April 1983–May 1984, 9 January 1984, pp. 276–7.

[168]   MLP, PUP, Box 344, Folder 3 (CO728), Memorandum from Loren [Hoekzema] to Herb [Bailey], 22 May 1984.

170   MAKING MAKERS

considered Rothenberg's chapters 'weaker than the others' he had read by May 1984.[169] In response, Paret launched a partial defence of his contributor, noting that Rothenberg's earlier chapter 'has the great merit of dealing in an objective and realistic manner with complex material that is still largely unexplored' and that 'his treatment of the issue of the military revolution is quite original' and would create discussion.[170] For the rest, the issues were hardly insurmountable. He could work with the author to shape the essay into an acceptable form.

A more significant problem arose in the early summer of 1984, when the editors were faced with an 'unhappy surprise' from Michael Howard. In June Howard published an article in *International Security*, 'Men against Fire: Expectations of War in 1914', which was based on a talk that he had given at Stanford in April and which he had told Paret was 'an early version of his essay for Makers of Modern Strategy'. Since Howard had given no indication of his intention to publish the piece elsewhere, Paret was upset at the duplication. He was also concerned over the quality of the work. He viewed the argument as 'simplistic and far from original', the analysis of material as 'superficial', and added that he was 'beginning to think that his work on contemporary issues has interfered with his historical work'. A promise from Howard that he would rework the piece for publication in *Makers II* went some way towards assuaging Paret, who hoped that the finished piece would be 'significantly different and appreciably better'.[171] When the revised essay arrived a few months later, however, Paret could only bring himself to describe it as 'adequate: nothing very original or profound, but an intelligent, balanced treatment of questions that still arouse a great deal of interest'.[172] No further changes were offered by Howard, but the essay was accepted nonetheless. Reflecting on the debacle two years later, Paret was forced to concede that 'for once he [Howard] had behaved rather unprofessionally'.[173]

Although unwelcome, this episode proved to be the last major hurdle that needed to be overcome prior to publication. As the summer of 1984 gave way to autumn, with submissions coming in and the copy-editing beginning, Paret increasingly turned his attention towards the details of the book's form and presentation. This was in keeping with Paret's personality. Just as he took a precise interest not only in what his contributors wrote, but *how* they wrote, so too he

---

[169] MLP, PUP, Box 344, Folder 1 (CO728), Bailey to Paret, 24 May 1984. The essays Bailey had read included Paret on Napoleon and works by Crowl and Weigley.

[170] MLP, PUP, Box 344, Folder 1 (CO728), Paret to Bailey, 4 June 1984.

[171] MLP, PUP, Box 344, Folder 1 (CO728), Paret to Hoekzema, 5 June 1984.
For the article, M. Howard, 'Men against Fire: Expectations of War in 1914', *International Security*, Vol. 9, No. 1 (summer 1984), pp. 41–57.

[172] MLP, PUP, Box 344, Folder 1 (CO728), Paret to Hoekzema, 3 September 1984.

[173] MLP, PUP, Box 350, Folder 3 (CO728), Paret to Hoekzema, 25 April 1986. Paret's comment in full: 'I am afraid it's pretty clear what happened: Howard passed off the same essay to two different editors. He never once mentioned International Security to me. My position was that we had priority, and I counted on the changes he said he would make. When they didn't come and we were ready to go to press, I realized that for once he had behaved rather unprofessionally.'

PETER PARET AND THE GENESIS OF A NEW EDITION   171

looked to exert a degree of control over how the book would appear when published. At the same time, Paret's interventions were also a reflection of the care he took to ensure that *Makers* was positioned and marketed in a manner which was apposite to the broader parameters he had set for the work.

First, there was the title. In late June 1984 Bailey raised the issue, explaining that the press wished to retain the 'close connection with the earlier version' whilst emphasizing the extent of changes in the new publication. He suggested keeping the main title 'because it is indeed a classic book' but also offered 'THE MAKING OF MODERN STRATEGY (A Complete Revision of Earle's MAKERS OF MODERN STRATEGY)' as an alternative.[174] Three months later, Paret shared his thoughts. He agreed that *The Making of Modern Strategy* was a fairer reflection of the new book—indeed, he went so far as to note as much in his published introduction—but he concluded that it was 'not as effective a title as Makers of Modern Strategy'.[175] The issue then became how to use the subtitle to better reflect the scope of the work. Paret rejected the original subtitle on the grounds that ' "Military" is too narrow because we also deal with naval and air war, and "Thought" is too narrow because almost every essay contains as much on what actually happened as on ideas'. In its place, he offered two rather cumbersome possibilities: 'Essays on the Theory and Practice of War from Machiavelli to the Nuclear Age' or 'The Theory and Practice of War from Machiavelli to the Nuclear Age'. Paret favoured the first suggestion, not least because he insisted on a distinction between 'essays' and 'chapters':

> Chapters imply a high degree of integration of the contents, while essays suggest somewhat more independent works within a general framework. I have always felt that the use of "chapter" in the original volume was wrong, and I suggest that we do not use "chapter" in the table of contents and in the heading of each piece.[176]

In response, Hoekzema was able to convince Paret that his second suggestion was more appropriate, since in his experience books with 'essays' in the title tended not to sell very well.[177]

With the wording of the title almost settled—'the theory and practice of war' would also be removed prior to publication—Paret's attention turned to the cover design. In January 1985 he responded to a request for his opinions on the matter from the copy editor, Elizabeth Gretz, agreeing with her view that 'the design for the original edition strikes us now as rather awful'. Given the 'changed and

---

[174] MLP, PUP, Box 344, Folder 1 (CO728), Bailey to Paret, 25 June 1984.
[175] MLP, PUP, Box 344, Folder 1 (CO728), Paret to Hoekzema, 20 September 1984. Paret, 'Introduction', in Paret, *Makers*, p. 7.
[176] MLP, PUP, Box 344, Folder 1 (CO728), Paret to Hoekzema, 20 September 1984.
[177] MLP, PUP, Box 344, Folder 1 (CO728), Hoekzema to Paret, 28 September 1984. MLP, PUP, Box 344, Folder 1 (CO728), Paret to Hoekzema, 1 October 1984.

172 MAKING MAKERS

expanded character' of his book, Paret considered 'such symbols of military action and movement as arrows are no longer appropriate. The book is not primarily about offensive thrusts and defensive maneuvers, about strategic combinations that can be traced on the map; its approach is far more encompassing, and it would be a pity if the design did not convey this to the reader.' He proposed an alternative which he believed would better express the broader dimensions of the book:

> A jacket of light-colored coated stock—perhaps white like the jacket of <u>On War</u>, or pale grey—with a typographical design, using a simple strong typeface—for instance Janson or Garamond capitals—printed over a faintly reproduced 18th-century map. The subject of the map is unimportant. Its towns, roads, rivers, mountains merely provide a representation of the objects of war, which at the same time are its setting. Against the background of the faint map, the letters of the title stand out, and the tension between map and typography indicates the range of the book's contents from the more remote past to the present.[178]

Paret's idea was not taken up by the press. Rather, they favoured a design that emphasized the chronological spectrum of the work: a composite image bringing together detail from Albrecht Dürer's 'Triumphal Arch of Maximilian I' of 1515 and the mushroom cloud produced by the atomic bomb dropped on Nagasaki (see Figure 4.6).[179]

Nevertheless, Paret carried through to the marketing of the book his concern that the dimensions of his *Makers* and the circumstances of its creation be correctly conveyed. In April 1985, for example, he wrote to Bailey that he thought it 'important to avoid whenever possible the terms "first edition," "revised edition," even "new edition"' since 'they do not do justice to the book', and to use instead ' "the original MMS" and "successor volume"' to distinguish between the two.[180] When a flyer was produced later on in the year which failed to conform to these standards, he expressed his frustration to Gretz in abrupt terms: 'I thought we had agreed not to use the phrase: extensively revised. The book should be announced as the successor to the first MMS, just as it is described in the front matter. I really think this needs to be made clear to everyone.'[181] Similarly, in June 1985 he reacted strongly against some of the imagery used in a brochure to market the book. 'I <u>don't</u> like the rocket launcher or whatever it is in the lower right-hand corner,' he wrote Hoekzema, 'It may be a convenient symbol for war (of the most modern variety), but it has nothing to do with strategy. This is the wrong

---

[178] MLP, PUP, Box 350, Folder 2 (CO728), Paret to Elizabeth Gretz, 25 January 1985.
[179] MLP, PUP, Box 350, Folder 2 (CO728), Memo from Susan Halligan to Mardi Considine, Kate Wheeler, Trudy Glucksberg, 11 December 1985.
[180] MLP, PUP, Box 350, Folder 2 (CO728), Paret to Bailey, 23 April 1985.
[181] MLP, PUP, Box 350, Folder 2 (CO728), Paret to Elizabeth Gretz, 24 July 1985.

PETER PARET AND THE GENESIS OF A NEW EDITION 173

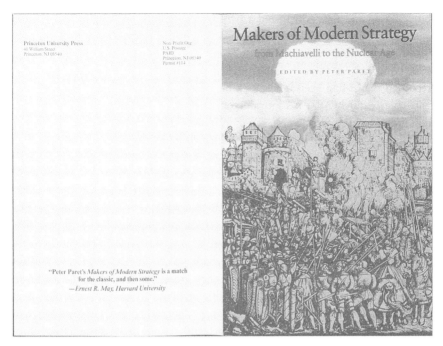

Figure 4.6 Jacket design for Paret's *Makers of Modern Strategy*.
Source: MLP, PUP, Box 350, folder 2.

kind of device to publicise the book.' Given that over half of the book was devoted to war prior to 1914, Paret argued, a more 'timeless' image would be fitting. To replace it, he suggested either 'A 17th or 18th century trophy (a decorative arrangements of helmets, lances, banners, swords, etc.)' or 'A Greek or Renaissance helmet and the diagram of an atom'. Whilst these suggestions were arguably just as tendentious in presenting the book through a particular lens, Paret's insistence was, nonetheless, driven by his desire to see the work presented in an appropriate manner. 'It is important to keep in mind', he finished, 'that the book is not just about war, but about the way people thought and think about war (strategy). Beyond that, most of the essays attempt to integrate the history of war with general history. If at all possible, that very broad perspective ought to be indicated.'[182]

Conclusion

Makers of Modern Strategy: From Machiavelli to the Nuclear Age was published by Princeton University Press on 31 March 1986.[183] To mark the publication of the

---

[182] MLP, PUP, Box 350, Folder 2 (CO728), Paret to Hoekzema, 24 June 1985.
[183] MLP, PUP, Box 350, Folder 2 (CO728), Susan Halligan to Paret, 10 March 1986.

174 MAKING MAKERS

book, Craig and Paret organized a two-day conference on 'War in History and War Today'. Over 7–8 March 1986, the event at the Hoover Institution brought together a number of the contributors and a range of additional invitees to discuss issues across three broadly pitched sessions.[184] The following day Craig recorded that it had been 'a considerable success' but noted that Paret had been particularly quiet: 'After his introductory speech, he was away much of the first day and mute at my session.'[185] Paret's mind was elsewhere. At the end of 1985 he confided to Craig that he had been invited to join the faculty of the School of Historical Studies at the IAS. While Craig could not see why anyone would trade California for the cold winters of the east, he conceded that 'a professorship at the Institute is perhaps the juiciest plum that academia has to offer' and rated Paret's chances of leaving at 65 to 35 per cent.[186] Nevertheless, the negotiating process ran through the winter, and it was only on 17 March, shortly after the conference, that Paret announced his decision to leave.[187]

Reflecting on the offer, Craig considered it was 'richly deserved, and the fact that it is in cultural history makes the honor greater'.[188] By choosing to take up the position Paret underlined the breadth of his historical interests. His next book, *Art as History* (1988), focused not on war but rather on art in its relations to social and intellectual change in nineteenth- and early twentieth-century Germany. Indeed, it should be stressed that for Paret the *Makers* project, although important to him, was but one publication amongst many solo-authored works. The same was true for Gilbert and Craig. The latter, for example, noted in his diaries that both the 1943 and 1986 editions constituted highlights of those respective years, but his entries during the mid-1980s showed that he was far more concerned with the progress of his own *The Germans*.[189] Thus while *Makers* became a major career milestone for Earle, and an ultimately unproductive preoccupation for Ropp, for Paret it was neither of these. In a sense, being relatively less invested in the project in comparison to his predecessors seemed to help him come to terms with it.

In other respects, his approach carried echoes of the past. For example, early on in the planning process his clear-eyed assessment that quality would be more

---

[184] The contributors to *Makers* comprised Paret, Craig, and Gilbert, alongside Maurice Matloff, Douglas Porch, John Shy, David MacIsaac, Michael Carver, and Phil Crowl. Also invited to speak were Richard Staar, Gordon Wright, Walter Emil Kaegi, Jr., Lewis Gann, Harry Summers, Peter Duignan, Edward Luttwak, Tom Wicker, Gerd Schmückle, and Bart Bernstein. The sessions were 'War before 1945', 'War since 1945', and 'Strategy and Politics'. There was also an evening talk by Luttwak. MLP, PUP, Box 344, Folder 2 (CO728), 'Conference "War in History and War Today," March 7 & 8, 1986'.

[185] Craig Diaries, Tagebuch Vol. 40, Journal July 1985–August 1986, 9 March 1986, pp. 267–9.

[186] Craig Diaries, Tagebuch Vol. 40, Journal July 1985–August 1986, 16 December 1985, pp. 202–3.

[187] Craig Diaries, Tagebuch Vol. 40, Journal July 1985–August 1986, 17 March 1986, p. 277.

[188] Craig Diaries, Tagebuch Vol. 40, Journal July 1985–August 1986, 16 December 1985, pp. 202–3.

[189] For MMS I: Craig Diaries, Journal Vol. 5, entry for period April 1943–August 1944, p. 67. For MMS II: Craig Diaries, Tagebuch Vol. 41, Journal August 1986–December 1987, 31 December 1986, p. 111.

important than coverage and that it would be impossible to deal comprehensively with the issues at hand was closely aligned with Earle's advice in 1942 that 'historical completeness cannot be attained in such an enterprise, nor is it desired'.[190] It was also significant that Paret brought to the project a defined view on war as an aspect of historical scholarship which, although more disciplinary-bound that Earle's position, was less restrictive than Ropp's allegiance to military history. And if Paret's disinterest in bringing his scholarly faculty directly to bear on contemporary quandaries might have worked to his disadvantage, he was fortunate that, in the person of Craig, he had a collaborator who thought more explicitly in those terms. Moreover, Craig and Gilbert's involvement in the successor edition helped maintain a line of authenticity from the original edition, although in the case of Gilbert and his ongoing connection with the IAS this was more symbolic than it was for the more proactive Craig. In this sense, for the two associate editors the roles of the 1940s had reversed by the 1980s. Indeed, although Gilbert's interest in the *Makers* project waned somewhat over time, Craig's longer-term investment, shared to a greater or lesser extent by such figures as Michael Howard and Herbert Bailey, attested to the enduring influence of the book across the academic and publishing spheres.

Making Makers: The Past, the Present, and the Study of War. Michael P. M. Finch, Oxford University Press.
© Michael P. M. Finch 2024. DOI: 10.1093/9780191959257.003.0005

---

[190] IAS Institute for Advanced Study Princeton (N.J.), Director's Office, Faculty records, Box 7/ Earle, Edward Mead, Memoranda, 'Purposes and character of proposed volume on the development of modern military thought', 27 March 1942.

5

Scholarship from the Arsenal of Democracy

The Reception of Paret's *Makers* and the Legacy of the Book

Makers of Modern Strategy was a scholarly contribution from the arsenal of democracy in the best sense of that contemporary term; a serious and fundamentally optimistic response to important intellectual needs of America at war and at the threshold of world power.

—Peter Paret, 1986[1]

In his introduction to the 1986 edition of *Makers*, Paret described Earle's *Makers* as 'a scholarly contribution from the arsenal of democracy [...] a serious and fundamentally optimistic response to important intellectual needs of America at war and at the threshold of world power'.[2] Although the comment was intended to contextualize the genesis of his predecessor's book and so contained clauses specific to it, Paret's own effort carried something of the same sense. So too did Ropp's unfulfilled alternative. Each part of the broader *Makers* project developed such scholarship in its own way, seeking to grapple with the history of military thought and the theory and practice of strategy, whilst also navigating a path between past and present that inevitably raised the issue of contemporary challenges. This was so even if such challenges manifested in a manner less visceral than those of the Second World War, and if the editors and their editorial assistants varied in their willingness to engage with them. Having examined the origins and development of each version of *Makers* in the preceding chapters, this chapter explores the parameters of that contribution and the legacy of the book.

The reception of Paret's *Makers* provides the lens through which to begin such an examination. Although the 1986 edition was favourably received, the reviews which appeared in press outlets and scholarly journals exhibited a marked range of assessments as to how well the book had covered its brief and where its omissions lay. Whilst some of these judgements were the mutually contradictory result

---

[1] P. Paret, 'Introduction', in P. Paret, *Makers of Modern Strategy: From Machiavelli to the Nuclear Age* (Princeton, NJ: Princeton University Press, 1986), pp. 4–5.

[2] Ibid.

THE RECEPTION OF PARET'S *MAKERS* AND ITS LEGACY   177

of differing scholarly perspectives, others pointed to less defensible shortcomings on the editors' part, as well as to a fragmenting of consensus as to how a book such as *Makers* might tackle its subject. At the same time, assessing Paret's *Makers* also played a role in cementing the status of the broader project, giving reviewers the opportunity to emphasize the importance of the first book and the need for the second. This process tended to cast the successor in a subtly lesser light, however, and played a part in providing the wellspring for another weighty book, 1994's *The Making of Strategy*. It also led to criticism of Paret for probing the concept of strategy in a less fulsome manner than Earle. As this chapter shows, the two scholars' engagement with strategy was intimately related to their scholarly formation, which contributed to markedly different approaches. These differences also help clarify how the limitations of Paret's thinking diverged from scholarly thinking in strategic and security studies.

Paret was more influential in shaping the 'canon' of strategic thinkers. Thus this chapter underlines Paret's importance, along with Michael Howard, in contributing to the rising acclaim for Clausewitz and his *On War*, in contrast to his disinterest in conceptualizing strategy. This chapter also underlines the broader pattern by which the changing parameters of the books, aligned with prevailing concerns at the points at which they were devised and the scholarly interests of those who contributed most to those processes, shaped their continental European and American focus. Although Basil Liddell Hart became a constant, exceptional, feature of the volumes, British thinkers such as J. F. C. Fuller, Charles Callwell, and Julian Corbett were notable for their near total absence. The lack of interest in Corbett in particular underscored the land-centrism of the books, to which Ropp's *Makers Revisited* would have provided a remedy, whilst also denying avenues for the exploration of strategy that a thinker such as Earle would surely have found most germane. Finally, this chapter explores the relationship between *Makers* and the exploration of the makers of strategy from earlier times. Redressing the absence of such thinkers began with Ropp's *Makers Revised*, found partial published form in *The Making of Strategy*, and a fulsome representation in the 2010 collection *Makers of Ancient Strategy*. At the same time, the rise in significance of thinkers such as Thucydides and Sun Tzu came from quite distinct lineages in the post-Second World War era, and—particularly in the case of the former—distinct disciplinary developments.

The Reception of Paret's *Makers*

Once published, Paret's *Makers* soon began to garner positive reviews. Amongst the editorial team, Gordon Craig followed the initial press reviews with great interest. By early July 1986 he noted positive write-ups in the *Wall Street Journal* and the *Christian Science Monitor*, and he made particular note of an astute piece

178   MAKING MAKERS

in the *New York Times*, which he credited to Edward Luttwak but which was in fact written by John Gooch, then a senior research fellow at the Naval War College.[3] Of most interest to him, however, was the review by John Keegan which appeared in the 17 July issue of *The New York Review of Books*. Whilst recognizing that *Makers* was an 'enormous, fascinating, and immensely important book', Keegan cast a critical eye on several aspects of the work. Moreover, he contrasted Craig and Gilbert's concluding essay, which he viewed as 'of the highest quality and value', with Paret's introduction, which he considered 'disappointingly short' and lacking in any attempt to define strategy itself, and further critiqued Paret's essay on Napoleon as conventional.[4] Craig surmised that Keegan had 'written his review with an eye to using every opportunity to take a cut at Peter, and he has managed it adroitly and with elegance'. He suspected 'that there is some secret history behind this'.[5] Given the speed with which Keegan's name had disappeared from early planning for the book and Paret's lack of interest in contacting him, it is certainly possible that an animus existed between the pair. Earlier in the year PUP had sent Keegan a copy of the book in the hope that he might review it, only to find that he had already been contacted by the *The New York Review of Books* to that effect.[6] Craig recorded in his diary that Paret had wanted someone other than Keegan to do the job, and had tried to persuade him to appeal to the editor of the NYRB, Robert Silvers, to make the change.[7]

Keegan's barbs against Paret notwithstanding, the tenor of other press reviews was generally positive. The reviewer for the *Wall Street Journal* was Colonel Harry G. Summers, senior military correspondent for U.S. News & World Report, who had been a speaker at the 'War in History and War Today' launch conference in March, and was the author of the influential book *On Strategy: A Critical Analysis of the Vietnam War* (1981).[8] He gave *Makers* plaudits, whilst offering little real criticism, lending the project a degree of strategic coherence that it had never really enjoyed by claiming that it 'had been published to coincide with the re-emergence of conventional military strategy'.[9] Gooch, meanwhile, offered more tempered views but nevertheless asserted that 'inevitably, Peter Paret's new version of an old classic will displace its predecessor on the strategy shelf'.[10] The

---

[3] Craig Diaries, Tagebuch Vol. 40, Journal July 1985–August 1986. 8 July 1986, pp. 338–40. J. Gooch, 'The Men in the Size 10 Helmets', *New York Times*, 13 April 1986.

[4] J. Keegan, 'Grand Illusions', *The New York Review of Books*, 17 July 1986.

[5] Craig Diaries, Tagebuch Vol. 40, Journal July 1985–August 1986. 8 July 1986, pp. 338–40.

[6] MLP, PUP, Box 344, Folder 1 (CO728), Joanna Hitchcock to John Keegan, 6 March 1986. Hitchcock to Keegan, 17 March 1986. Keegan to Hitchcock, 15 March 1986.

[7] Craig Diaries, Tagebuch Vol. 40, Journal July 1985–August 1986. 8 July 1986, p. 340.

[8] Christopher Bassford identifies *On Strategy* as a significant Clausewitzian work of the post-Second World War era, which played a role in preparing the intellectual groundwork for the Weinberger Doctrine. C. Bassford, *Clausewitz in English: The Reception of Clausewitz in Britain and America 1815-1945* (New York and Oxford: Oxford University Press, 1994), pp. 203–4.

[9] H. Summers, Jr., 'Bookshelf: New Lessons from Old Wars', *Wall Street Journal*, 9 May 1986.

[10] Gooch, 'The Men in the Size 10 Helmets'.

THE RECEPTION OF PARET'S *MAKERS* AND ITS LEGACY 179

reviews that appeared subsequently in academic journals were equally positive, tending to herald the arrival of a new classic to replace the old one.

Evidently, the publication of *Makers* was timely. It struck a chord for academic and military readers who felt that a revised and updated version of Earle's book was much needed, and this much was reflected in the reviews. Just as had been the case for Earle's volume, however, the reviews also brought criticism, and pointed to the gaps and inconsistencies which were an inevitable consequence of such an ambitious undertaking. Daniel Headrick, for example, observed that 'the sensitivity of the authors to technological change varies considerably', and that readers interested in such matters 'will be disappointed to find little discussion of weapons and arms manufacturing in this volume'.[11] Both David Yost and Hew Strachan, meanwhile, underlined deficiencies in the coverage of intelligence and deception as a strategic factor in the Second World War.[12] Strachan, in particular, noted the contrast between D. Clayton James's treatment of the war in the Pacific, which accounted for the intelligence contribution and incorporated contemporary research on Japan, and Maurice Matloff's account of the European theatre, which 'makes no mention of the Enigma machine and the contribution of Ultra to Allied decision-making in Europe in the same period'.[13] This oversight on the part of the editors was curious given that the secrecy surrounding Ultra had been definitively swept away after the publication of F. W. Winterbotham's *The Ultra Secret* in 1974, even if its integration into the scholarship on intelligence and deception in the Second World War was uneven by the mid-1980s.[14] It was more surprising still on account of the proximity of Sir Michael Howard to the project as a quasi-editor and his longstanding relationship with Paret. Howard had spent much of 1970s engaged in research for the fifth volume in the 'Intelligence Histories' series of the British Official History of the Second World War, which was concerned with deception and brought him into direct contact with the sources on Ultra, such that he was well aware of its significance in abetting strategic success. Although he completed the volume in 1979, it was blocked from publication by Prime Minister Margaret Thatcher, and did not appear in print until 1990.[15] Despite this, it seems unlikely that Paret had failed to gain some insight into Howard's work in this area over the course of the 1970s.

---

[11] D. Headrick, review of Paret, *Makers* in *Technology and Culture*, Vol. 29, No. 1 (January 1988), p. 140.

[12] D. Yost, review of Paret, *Makers* in *The Wilson Quarterly*, Vol. 10, No. 4 (Autumn., 1986), p. 144.

[13] Strachan, review of Paret, *Makers* in *The English Historical Review*, Vol. 103, No. 406 (January 1988), p. 159.

[14] See J. P. Campbell, 'An Update on the Interpretation of the Ultra Documentation', *Archivaria* Vol. 26 (summer 1988), pp. 184–8. A. S. Cochran, Jr., '"MAGIC," ULTRA," and the Second World War: Literature, Sources, and Outlook', *Military Affairs*, Vol. 46, No. 2 (April 1982), pp. 88–92. Harold C. Deutsch, 'The Historical Impact of Revealing the Ultra Secret', *Parameters*, Vol. 7, No. 3 (January 1977), pp. 16–32.

[15] M. Howard, *Captain Professor* (London: Bloomsbury, 2006), pp. 188–92. Howard remarked that 'Understandably, she [Thatcher] felt that the less the world knew about the activities of the security services, the better. It was too late to stop the publication of the Hinsley volumes [the first three volumes], but she could, and did, stop mine' (p. 191).

180   MAKING MAKERS

Strachan, along with Keegan, also offered sharp critiques of the decision to retain chapters from the original edition—those by R. R. Palmer, Henry Guerlac, and Earle himself—arguing that reprinting the older essays ignored advances in scholarship which had significant repercussions for the arguments made in those pieces. 'A book that aspires to a certain status', wrote Strachan, '[...] ought to take account of recent scholarship, even if only to discount it.'[16] This was most evident in relation to Palmer, whose principal argument about the disconnection between professional militaries and civil society in the eighteenth century now had to contend with research by scholars such as André Corvisier and John Childs, which suggested much to the contrary. Equally, Palmer's observations on supply needed to be qualified in light of Martin Van Creveld's argument on the importance of requisition, and his views on Guibert might have been amended to take account of the work of Robert S. Quimby.[17] Keegan agreed, writing on Palmer's chapter that 'much work, particularly on logistics, has been done since it was written'. He also extended his criticism to Guerlac's chapter on Vauban, noting that his Sandhurst colleague Christopher Duffy was 'now the world's leading expert on fortification, of which Vauban [...] was the Palladio, and he is the author of a definitive military life of Frederick the Great', so could have offered an updated essay on either topic.[18] These observations may well have stung the editor, since they underscored options for potential improvement that Paret had simply not taken. In the case of Guerlac, who had died during the period in which the new book was compiled, Paret had originally assessed the chapter as in need of replacement, only to later convince himself that it was of a sufficient standard to republish.[19] As for Palmer's chapter, the shortcomings were a direct consequence of the author's disinterest in the subject matter in the years since writing it. When contacted about the possibility of revising his essay in 1982, he replied that 'I have not really thought about military history in a serious way since I turned in my contribution in 1941 nor had I looked at what I then wrote for many years until yesterday.'[20]

In other respects, assessments of the constituent parts of the new *Makers* volume could be mutually contradictory. This was especially so where reviewers exercised their judgement on the quality of the various essays. Thus where Keegan saw MacIsaac's 'essay on the democratic powers' espousal of strategic bombing' as 'a splendid investigation of the politics of hypocrisy', Strachan thought it the 'most

---

[16]   Strachan, review of Paret, *Makers*, p. 159.

[17]   Ibid., p. 159. Strachan also noted that although Craig's revised essay on the political leader as strategist listed important later works by Fritz Fischer and David Woodward in his bibliography, there was no acknowledgement in the essay itself of the implications of these works for his assessment of Bethmann Hollweg and Sir William Robertson respectively.

[18]   Keegan, 'Grand Illusions'.   [19]   See Chapter 4.

[20]   MLP, PUP, Box 344, Folder 3 (CO728), R. R. Palmer to Bailey, 15 September 1982. Note that Palmer incorrectly thought that he had submitted the essay in 1941. The volume was not devised until the following year.

THE RECEPTION OF PARET'S *MAKERS* AND ITS LEGACY 181

disappointing essay in the book', which was 'so elliptical about Douhet and Mitchell that the reader must be assumed to have prior knowledge of their theories'.[21] And whilst Keegan accepted that Paret offered a 'succinct, authoritative, and down-to-earth' appraisal of Clausewitz, which 'rises to the occasion', Colin McInnes thought the piece 'a bit of a disappointment', which treated its subject solidly enough 'without ever stirring the reader into a realization that this was a central figure in the development of strategic thought'.[22] Gooch wrote that 'a notably vigorous revision of the history of French colonial warfare' was one of the highlights of the book.[23] Brian Holden Reid, by contrast, thought that a whole chapter on the subject was excessive, when British and French inter-war military developments had not been deemed of sufficient importance to warrant a chapter each.[24] Strachan appraised Walter Pintner's chapter on Russian military thought positively, as part of a group of chapters—alongside those by Russell Weigley, Condoleezza Rice, John Shy, and Thomas Collier—which succeeded in illustrating schools of thought which could not be attributed to a single emblematic figure.[25] William Fuller, on the other hand, placed the same piece amongst the 'uneven' contributions, on the grounds that it 'is not actually about strategy but rather about operations'.[26] Strachan also thought that Pintner's piece, as well as Shy and Collier's essay on revolutionary war, were 'original contributions in their own right'.[27] Conversely, McInnes thought that the latter 'never really convinces that the heart of the revolutionary warfare has really been exposed', particularly with regard to the thoughts of Mao Tse Tung.[28]

Alongside these mixed judgements, a few essays received near unanimous praise. One such essay was Shy's analysis of Jomini, which Strachan thought was 'now the definitive statement on the subject,' which 'above all, demonstrates Jomini's claim to be *the* maker of modern strategy, even in the German army', and which also drew plaudits from Holden Reid, Fuller, Gooch, and Stephen Walt.[29] The essay which drew the most consistent praise across the reviews, however, was Michael Geyer's piece on German strategy in the first half of the twentieth century, which Walt claimed 'brilliantly dissects the logical contradictions within German strategy in both world wars' and which Fuller described as a 'subtle and provocative examination of the forces that molded German strategy'

[21] Keegan, 'Grand Illusions'. Strachan, review of Paret, *Makers*, p. 160.

[22] Keegan, 'Grand Illusions'. C. McInnes, 'Strategic Doctrine and Political Practice', *Review of International Studies*, Vol. 14, No. 2 (April 1988), pp. 154–5.

[23] Gooch, 'The Men in the Size 10 Helmets'.

[24] B. Holden Reid, review of Paret, *Makers* in *History*, Vol. 73, No. 237 (February 1988), p. 90.

[25] Strachan, review of Paret, *Makers*, p. 160.

[26] W. Fuller, Jr., review of Paret, *Makers* in *The Journal of Modern History*, Vol. 61, No. 1 (March 1989), p. 134.

[27] Strachan, review of Paret, *Makers*, p. 160.

[28] McInnes, 'Strategic Doctrine and Political Practice', pp. 155–6.

[29] Strachan, review of Paret, *Makers*, p. 160. Holden Reid, review of Paret, *Makers*, p. 90. Gooch, 'The Men in the Size 10 Helmets'. S. M. Walt, 'The Search for a Science of Strategy: A Review Essay', *International Security*, Vol. 12, No. 1 (summer 1987), p. 145. Fuller, review of Paret, *Makers*, p. 162.

182 MAKING MAKERS

distinguished by 'mastery of sources and profound analysis'.[30] Similarly, Strachan applauded Geyer's ability to 'say something stimulating on almost every facet of a now-hackneyed subject'.[31] Keegan went further still, describing it as a 'theme essay' for the relationship between politics and war that ran throughout the volume:

> since he does indeed succeed in demonstrating how strategic necessity, or more properly the perception of such a necessity, came to permeate a nation's world outlook at a moment when it was crucially placed to affect the world's well-being. Overthematic [sic] though the essay is, it is by far the most coherent piece of argument in the book, cleaves nearest to its informing idea, and promises to be the foundation of a larger and even more impressive work in the field.

Geyer's thesis 'that external war came to seem to the Germans the solution of their internal problems', whilst not a novel one, '[...] does yield a plethora of insights, not least in explaining how the Germans came to consign their destiny to a man whose claim to lead derived, as much as anything else, from his status as a "front fighter," a common soldier'.[32]

The success of Geyer's chapter was achieved despite his editors, who had spent most of their time worrying first about whether the piece would be delivered in time for their deadline and subsequently about its length. Indeed, on the day he received his copy of the new *Makers*, Craig's only substantive comment about the book aside from its fine appearance was 'why did we ever permit Michael Geyer to go on for 70 pages?'[33] It was unsurprising, then, that Craig found Keegan's selection of Geyer's essay as the best in the volume, alongside Rothenberg's two pieces, 'a somewhat surprising judgement'.[34] Yet what Geyer had shown, and what several reviewers remarked upon, was the capacity to develop more coherent appreciations of national experiences and schools of strategy in longer, more expansive, essays. The contrast with other, more episodic, chapters was instructive. McInnes, for example, highlighted the disjointed character of the two essays—by Holborn and Rothenberg—that dealt with Germany's post-Napoleonic nineteenth-century experience, remarking that they needed to be taken as a whole rather than read and understood in isolation.[35] This was consistent with the decisions that Paret had taken as editor concerning the two pieces, but once again demonstrated the pitfalls of retaining material from the original edition—in this case, a portion of Holborn's 1943 essay. In a similar vein, Strachan pointed

---

[30] Walt, 'The Search for a Science of Strategy', pp. 134–5. Fuller, Jr., review of Paret, *Makers*, pp. 134–5.

[31] Strachan, review of Paret, *Makers*, p. 160.   [32] Keegan, 'Grand Illusions'.

[33] Craig Diaries, Tagebuch Vol. 40, Journal July 1985–August 1986. Wednesday 5 March, p. 267.

[34] Craig Diaries, Tagebuch Vol. 40, Journal July 1985–August 1986. 8 July 1986, p. 339.

[35] McInnes, 'Strategic Doctrine and Political Practice', p. 155.

THE RECEPTION OF PARET'S *MAKERS* AND ITS LEGACY 183

out that one consequence of organizing the book to include chapters on Soviet military thought and nuclear strategists was that 'Soviet thinking on nuclear weapons has fallen between the essays of Rice and Freedman', a gap that was also noticed by McInnes.[36]

Makers in the Shadow of Its Predecessor

Whatever the nuances of their assessments, almost all reviewers found it impossible to understand the new *Makers* in isolation from its predecessor. In this sense, the publication of Paret's book cemented the legacy of the original. Earle's *Makers* provided the comparative framework that helped to make sense of a book whose form and purpose still carried a degree of ambiguity—'(is it that of a textbook?)' Strachan wondered in parenthesis.[37] Collectively, they exhibited varying levels of sensitivity in relating the new book to the old. For example, Yost's conviction that the new *Makers* 'retains Earle's laudable goal—to underline both the importance of war in history' and to integrate the history of military thought into general history, was closer to Paret's vision than to that of his predecessor.[38] McInnes's appreciation of the book as more 'a linear descendant of Earle than a second edition' was nearer the mark.[39] Either way, it was notable that comparisons between the two books carried the sense, however sympathetically put, that the new edition was a somewhat diminished product: that it was 'in some ways less satisfying' than its predecessor, or that it was 'at once broader in scope and more modest in vision'.[40]

In part, this appeared as a consequence of the notion that the first *Makers* was the dramatic product of a historical moment: a searing and swift response to intellectual needs that came at just the right time. This convergence of circumstances and import its successor could not hope to emulate. Equally, and as a consequence of the first consideration, the original *Makers* inspired a degree of reverence which was rooted in its status as an intellectual starting point—whether for the disciplinary study of strategy itself, or more simply in corralling a set of 'makers' into a single binding, thereby promoting them within the canon of strategic thinkers. No matter that Earle's *Makers* carried certain continuities from earlier decades, reflecting concerns inherent to the 'scientific' scholarly study of war almost from its inception, from the vantage point of the 1980s the apparent

---

[36] Strachan also noted that Bernard Brodie appeared 'only incidentally'. Strachan, review of Paret, *Makers*, p. 160. McInnes, 'Strategic Doctrine and Political Practice', p. 155.

[37] Strachan, review of Paret, *Makers*, p. 159.   [38] Yost, review of Paret, *Makers*, p. 142.

[39] McInnes, 'Strategic Doctrine and Political Practice', p. 153.

[40] Gooch, 'The Men in the Size 10 Helmets'. D. Showalter, review of Paret, *Makers* in *Military Affairs*, Vol. 51, No. 2 (April 1987), p. 100.

184 MAKING MAKERS

challenges wrought by the expansion in the scope and complexity of that study since the 1940s, as much as of war itself, seemed inescapable.

Nevertheless, such challenges were all the more apparent as a consequence of Paret and his collaborators' decision to apply a framework to their book that mimicked that of the 1943 edition more than it departed from it. Yet although, as Holden Reid wrote, the weaknesses revealed by the book emanated from the 'structure of its predecessor which has been replicated faithfully in the second edition', this only told half the story, since Paret's replication was not as complete as it may first have seemed.[41] In choosing to present his book as another collection of 'makers' Paret reinforced the idea that the selection of individuals, or small numbers of associated individuals, and the presentation of their strategic ideas, lay at the core of the work. He departed from Earle, however, by emphasizing that the roster of such individuals could include those whose record for posterity was purely practical. Earle had not entirely excluded the practical art of strategy from his volume. Indeed, the majority of the individuals considered in the 1943 version had direct experience of war at some level, but they married this to a legacy in writing, by their own hand, which became the most important criterion for inclusion. Recognizing that this led to the exclusion of so prominent a figure as Napoleon, represented only by proxy primarily through the works of Jomini and Clausewitz, Paret argued that his approach would better illustrate that 'strategy is not exclusively—or even mainly—the work of great minds, interested in spelling out their theories'.[42] Whilst this was a logical position to take, it tended to reinforce a tension between men of theory and men of action which was detectable in the original but yet more apparent in Paret's book. As Strachan wrote, the 'direction and focus' given by Earle's individualist, theory-driven approach had been lost in a volume which had 'swung more towards the practice of strategy'.[43]

At the same time, Paret was unable, or perhaps unwilling, to sustain Earle's structure throughout the entirety of his volume.[44] This was most apparent in the final part of the book, on war since 1945. All four of the chapters in this section—on nuclear strategists, conventional warfare after 1945, revolutionary war, and strategy in the present and future—departed from the stated conventions of the work by presenting broader appraisals of forms of war and strategy, in a manner that invited comment. Thus, McInnes noted that Paret's organization of the book into

---

[41] Holden Reid, review of Paret, *Makers*, p. 90.

[42] P. Paret, 'Introduction', in Paret, *Makers*, p. 6.

[43] Strachan, review of Paret, *Makers*, pp. 159–60. Nevertheless, it was still possible for some to see the work primarily as an exposition of theory. Hence, Keegan wrote, somewhat confusingly, that 'The title [...] is, of course, a misnomer. Strategy is made by men of war, often without the benefit of book learning. Strategic *theory*, which is what this work is about, by contrast reeks of books, often written by scholars who never smelled powder.' Keegan, 'Grand Illusions'.

[44] Earle, too, had not entirely managed to sustain the technique throughout his volume, as attested to by the chapters on 'Continental Doctrines of Sea Power' and 'Japanese Naval Strategy', which referred to broader groupings.

THE RECEPTION OF PARET'S *MAKERS* AND ITS LEGACY   185

five chronological parts 'increasingly lose touch with Earle's original as they approach the modern day'.[45] This observation carried an implication that the inability to sustain a focus on select individuals was deeply impacted by the rupture opened up with the dawn of the nuclear age, which Earle had not had to confront, and which introduced additional layers of complexity that confounded attempts to understand strategy through a method that seemed too closely allied to a 'great man' approach. Yet there was ample evidence elsewhere in the volume of the erosion of the commitment to individual 'makers'. The third part of Paret's book, on the century after 1815, included essays such as those on 'Russian military thought' and 'American strategy' which were predicated on national experience, and the fourth part included similar essays on German and Soviet strategy, alongside the broad treatments of air power theorists, political leaders, and the cult of the offensive. The prevalence of such chapters pointed to an equivocation over the lens that should be applied to the study of strategy that the editors of the 1986 edition seemed never to have addressed directly. It also underlined the deeper limitations of the approach adopted by Earle's book, and spoke to the inherent tension between the individual and the nation, school, or collective that neither volume had been fully able to resolve. In the context of the 1980s, however, it was noteworthy that much of the comment on the new book dwelt on the positives and negatives of the latter approaches more than the former, which likely appeared in tune with the development of such explanatory concepts as 'strategic culture' and a renewed focus on 'ways of war'.[46]

Dissatisfaction with these limitations in Paret's *Makers* found its most direct legacy in the creation of another book, Williamson Murray, MacGregor Knox, and Alvin Bernstein's *The Making of Strategy*. Although not published until 1994, the book had its origins in informal discussions on strategy and policy between a number of the contributors which had taken place at the US Naval War College during the 1985–6 academic year and so coincided with publication of the new *Makers*. Those discussions had yielded dissatisfaction with existing literature on the subject, which was considered to be too concerned with 'the influence of individual thinkers or dwelled exclusively on a single polity' and so did not 'provide much insight into the factors that have actually molded the strategies of rulers and states'. Both editions of *Makers* were cited as exemplars of this tendency, particularly the first count. Consequently, the new publication sought to lay emphasis on 'the *making* of strategy as the element crucial to understanding the ultimate

---

[45] McInnes, 'Strategic Doctrine and Political Practice', p. 154.
[46] See, for example, J. Snyder, *The Soviet Strategic Culture: Implications for Limited Nuclear Operations* (Santa Monica, CA: RAND Corporation, 1977). C. Gray, 'National Style in Strategy: The American Example', *International Security*, Vol. 6, No. 2 (autumn 1981), pp. 21–47. R. Weigley, *The American Way of War: A History of the United States Military Strategy and Policy* (Bloomington, IL: Indiana University Press, 1973).

186   MAKING MAKERS

meaning of that elusive word'.[47] As a critique of Paret's volume, this charge was only partially valid. Paret had been sufficiently aware of the contours of his volume to think seriously about changing its title to the *Making of Modern Strategy*, as a reflection of what the book was really about. It was only the caché of the *Makers* name and the lineage that it reinforced which prevented him from doing so.[48] Reviewers of the book itself were perceptive enough to sense this too, with Showalter, for example, writing that 'this edition might have more aptly been titled *The Making of Modern Strategy*'.[49] Nevertheless, in organizing their collection of essays across a grander historical span of some two thousand years—thereby obviating the need to define the 'modern'—and grouping them around proto-national, national, and imperial collective experiences, Murray, Knox, and Bernstein took a logical step on from the *Makers* approach.

Making Modern Strategy?

The most significant area in which the successor version of *Makers* appeared less 'modest in vision' than its predecessor, however, was in its editors' presentation of strategy itself. Paret's reluctance to engage in prolonged analysis of the meaning of strategy was remarked upon by a number of reviewers of the book, notably forming Keegan's most pointed jab. Paret's introduction, he wrote:

> is disappointingly short and makes little effort to define for the general reader how "strategy" is to be understood. The word is, of course, a catchall, whose many meanings are best grasped by reading the book as a whole. Some analytical definition ought, nevertheless, to have been offered, if only as a baseboard against which the varied offerings of the individual contributors might be bounced.[50]

Short though Paret's introduction was, however, it was not entirely devoid of definition, although it was true that the editor was reluctant to commit himself to prolonged discussion much beyond the application of military force. Unsurprisingly for a scholar who had devoted much of his professional career to the study of Clausewitz, he leant heavily towards *On War* in presenting strategy as 'the use of armed force to achieve the military objectives and, by extension, the political purpose of the war'. Whilst this constituted his most definitive statement

---

[47] W. Murray and M. Grimsley, 'Introduction: On Strategy', in W. Murray, M. Knox, and A. Bernstein (eds.), *The Making of Strategy: Rulers, States, and War* (Cambridge: Cambridge University Press, 1994), p. 2. Amongst the contributors for the book were Geoffrey Parker, whom Paret had pursued for an essay in 1984, and John Gooch, who was recommended to Paret by Howard.

[48] See Chapter 4.   [49] Showalter, review of Paret, *Makers*, p. 100.

[50] Keegan, 'Grand Illusions'.

THE RECEPTION OF PARET'S *MAKERS* AND ITS LEGACY   187

on the issue, it should be noted that he further qualified this with the observation that strategy could be understood in terms of Moltke's 'system of expedients', and could equally incorporate 'the development, intellectual mastery, and utilization of all of the state's resources for the purpose of implementing its policy in war'. Consequently, he wrote, his book would encompass both senses of the term: 'the narrower, operational meaning, and its broadly inclusive implications'.[51]

The contrast with Earle's engagement with the concept was illuminating. Unlike Paret, the essence of Earle's discussion lay in the degree to which he believed strategy had departed from an understanding grounded solely in the use of force. 'Only the most restricted terminology would now define strategy as the art of military command,' he explained. Rather, 'as war and society have become more complicated—and war, it must be remembered, is an inherent part of society—strategy has of necessity required increasing consideration of nonmilitary [sic] factors, economic, psychological, moral, political, and technological'.[52] This was a conceptualization rooted in a certain understanding of the history of warfare which culminated in the peril and the urgency of a war still unresolved: a narrative of total war that brought conflict increasingly and inexorably into all areas in the life of the nation. Equally, it was allied to a particular American experience. Thus Earle emphasized the need for a 'national strategy' to be 'formulated by the President and the General Staff and implemented by acts of Congress', which arose from the palpable sense that 'the American nation is in the process of becoming the foremost military power of modern times', and that consequently the global implications of American power required serious thought into the future.[53]

Despite the immediacy of the world crisis to Earle's presentation of strategy, the expansive tones he struck were not solely conditioned by the Second World War. Rather, their roots could be found in his concerns for the parlous state of international affairs and their implications for strategy and national security during the late 1930s. The war then in progress was the ultimate test of an effective strategy, but Earle's insistence on the imperative for strategy emanated from prewar reflections that brought the concept of strategy itself into peacetime. In *Makers* Earle stressed that 'strategy deals with war, preparation for war, and the waging of war', but he was equally forthright in asserting that strategy is 'not merely a concept of wartime, but it is an inherent element of statecraft at all times', which might give states the ability to obviate the recourse to war as well as to prevail once war was undertaken. Consequently, strategy had to be understood as 'the art of controlling and utilizing the resources of a nation—or a coalition of

---

[51] Paret, 'Introduction', in Paret, *Makers*, p. 3.
[52] E. M. Earle, 'Introduction', in E. M. Earle, *Makers of Modern Strategy: From Machiavelli to Hitler* (Princeton, NJ: Princeton University Press, 1943), p. viii.
[53] Ibid., pp. vi, viii.

nations—including its armed forces, to the end that its vital interests shall be effectively promoted and secured against enemies, actual, potential, or merely presumed'.[54] That is to say, it could be understood in terms much broader than military power, but need not be directed against a defined competitor or adversary.[55] This represented the refinement of positions he had taken prior to US entry into the Second World War. Thus at the annual meeting of the Academy of Political Science in November 1940 he suggested that the inadequacy of the military-oriented definition of strategy was due in no small part to 'the fact that, under existing conditions, it is virtually impossible to draw any clear-cut line between war and peace', asking, 'How, for example, could we at any period since, say, 1935 decide whether the world was in a state of peace or a state of war?'[56] Arguing instead for 'a new definition of strategy', he offered an interpretation very close to that which he would set down in his introduction two years later, but one which incorporated a more pronounced aspect on the blurring of boundaries. 'The line dividing peace from war is no longer definite,' he wrote, 'if indeed it may be said to exist at all; it has been finally cut through and obliterated by the doctrines and activities of the totalitarian powers.'[57]

Prior to December 1941, Earle laid greater store in arguments about the distinction between war and peace, in part to underline the urgency of the situation and the costs of inaction. It was better to think in this way, he was sure, than to insert new categories or quasi-states between war and peace that only served to obfuscate. Consequently, he poured scorn on the phrase 'short of war' because he thought it was 'an anaesthetic that has been applied to our intelligence and our capacity to judge the situation now facing us'.[58] Once the USA joined the war, however, these aspects of his thinking became less pronounced, as active participation in the conflict rendered them less important than prosecuting the war at hand, at least in the short term. At the same time, Earle did not completely abandon them, not least because they were imbued in his concept of 'grand' or 'national' strategy—terms that he used interchangeably. In his introduction, Earle wrote that 'grand strategy' was the focus of *Makers*, explaining that it referred to 'the highest type of strategy [...] which so integrates the policies and armaments of the nation that the resort to war is either rendered unnecessary or is undertaken with the maximum chance of victory'.[59] This definition retained the continuity of strategy as perpetual necessity and as activity existing beyond war, but carried with it less suggestion that the state of war had bled into peacetime. It, too,

---

[54] Ibid., p. viii.   [55] Ibid.
[56] E. M. Earle, 'Political and Military Strategy for the United States', *Proceedings of the Academy of Political Science*, Vol. 19, No. 2 (January 1941), pp. 5–6.
[57] Ibid., p. 7.
[58] 'Discussion: The Bases of an American Defense Policy: Armed Forces', *Proceedings of the Academy of Political Science*, Vol. 19, No. 2 (January 1941), pp. 53–4.
[59] Earle, 'Introduction', in Earle, *Makers*, p. viii.

THE RECEPTION OF PARET'S *MAKERS* AND ITS LEGACY   189

was the product of Earle's earlier thinking, developed from his consideration of the historical bases of national security in an American context. As he explained to the Academy of Political Science:

> throughout our history, we have conceived national defense as being something more than mere resistance to attack. We have been fortunate in having in our early days, and even in our later history, a remarkable group of statesmen who believed that defense or security was not merely a crisis phenomenon, but an obligation of statecraft at all times, and that political as well as military maneuvers on our part and on the part of other nations in this hemisphere, and indeed in Europe and Asia, must be judged with relevance to their effect upon the security of these United States.[60]

After the conclusion of the war Earle was no less attached to a concept of 'Grand Strategy' extant beyond war itself. Indeed, the international environment of the early Cold War served to revalidate his previous arguments and bring back to the foreground the notion of the dissolution of the boundary between war and peace. Thus, in a lecture of 1951 he returned to the period prior to US entry into the Second World War, proposing that 'the real war began with the economic and military aid which the United States extended to Britain immediately after the fall of France, supplemented by the destroyers-for-bases deal and, later, by supporting naval operations and lend-lease'.[61] And just as there had been an undeclared world war in the recent past, so too was something analogous unfurling in the years since 1945. 'It must be admitted', Earle insisted in 1949, 'that we are participants in an undeclared civil war in Europe. If we are thereby involved in an ideological struggle with the Soviet Union it is because we are an integral part of Western European civilization and have a vital interest in its survival'.[62] As a result, he considered that 'the critical question at the moment' was 'whether strategy is a concept which operates only in wartime or is a concept which is applicable to times of peace as well'.[63]

Earle's answer to the question was stridently affirmative. In reflections delivered to the Naval War College in the summer of 1949, he set out his stall in direct contrast to the position of his former close associate Bernard Brodie. In his article 'Strategy as a Science', published just a month beforehand, Brodie had proposed 'security policy' as the best term 'to cover the total preparation for war as well as

---

[60] Earle, 'Political and Military Strategy for the United States', p. 5.

[61] E. M. Earle, 'The American Stake in Europe: Retrospect and Prospect', *International Affairs*, Vol. 27, No. 4 (October 1951), pp. 423–4.

[62] E. M. Earle, 'A Half Century of American Foreign Policy: Our Stake in Europe, 1898–1948', *Political Science Quarterly*, Vol. 64, No. 2 (June 1949), p. 175.

[63] E. M. Earle, 'Notes on the Term Strategy', *Naval War College Information Service for Officers*, Vol. 2, No. 4 (December 1949), p. 4.

the waging of it.'[64] Earle disagreed, arguing that 'one of the reasons why I prefer to use the term, "national strategy", or if you like, "grand strategy", even as applied to peacetime, is that if we use the term, we will be less likely than we otherwise would be to overlook the strategic factors in policy, as we have so often overlooked them in the past.'[65] For Earle, 'security' drained the urgency and direction from consideration and action outside of a military clash. 'If you want to call "national strategy," "security policy", I think you are using a somewhat undramatic term, to put it mildly,' he concluded; '[...] you are running the risk that you will, in the use of that term, depart from one of the things that is of principal consideration; namely, that political decisions would be made with constant reference to their strategical implications'.[66]

Earle was not the first person to discuss strategy in terms of 'grand strategy'. Even within the pantheon of American grand strategic thinkers he had a near predecessor in US Navy Captain Georges Meyers, who also made explicit claims in the late 1920s about the imperative for strategy in peace as well as war.[67] It is also important to underline the work of Earle's seminar in contributing to his conceptual thinking and helping him to refine it.[68] Nevertheless, by incorporating statecraft explicitly into the realm of strategy, and allying it to a story of US success in seeking security, Earle applied a sheen of historical continuity to a transformation in thinking about strategy. His contributions constituted a significant historical milestone in the expanding conceptualization of strategy. Such a transformation was not devoid of intellectual inconsistency or confusion, however, and Earle often seemed comfortable in conflating grand strategy, national strategy, and national security. Moreover, as Strachan underlines, the expansion of strategy to which Earle was a key contributor gave rise to a conflation of strategy and policy which would result in 'particular problems for strategic theory shaped in the Anglo-American tradition since 1945'.[69]

Yet despite the conceptual pitfalls of Earle's approach to strategy, it could not be denied that the older editor succeeded in producing a more multifaceted engagement with strategy than his successor would offer four decades later. Earle's introduction was just as concise as Paret's, but he put forward his case with a greater degree of conviction, arguing for an expanded conception of strategy which broke

---

[64] Brodie, 'Strategy as a Science', p. 477.   [65] Earle, 'Notes on the Term Strategy', p. 4.

[66] Ibid., p. 7. This represented something of a revision of his earlier adherence to the importance of national security. See A. Preston, 'National Security as Grand Strategy: Edward Mead Earle and the Burdens of World Power', in E. Borgwardt, C. McKnight Nichols, and A. Preston (eds.), *Rethinking American Grand Strategy* (Oxford: Oxford University Press, 2021), pp. 238–53.

[67] For the place of Meyers and Earle in American thinking on grand strategy see L. Milevski, *The Evolution of Modern Grand Strategic Thought* (Oxford: Oxford University Press, 2016), pp. 68–73, 77–8.

[68] See Preston, 'National Security as Grand Strategy', pp. 243–7.

[69] H. Strachan, *The Direction of War: Contemporary Strategy in Historical Perspective* (Cambridge: Cambridge University Press, 2013), pp. 33–5. See also H. Strachan, 'The Lost Meaning of Strategy', *Survival*, Vol. 47, No. 3 (autumn 2005), pp. 33–54.

THE RECEPTION OF PARET'S *MAKERS* AND ITS LEGACY   191

the temporal boundary between the states of war and peace, and engaged explicitly with a hierarchy of strategic levels in a manner that Paret did not. Unsurprisingly, then, those searching for a complex and nuanced conceptualization of strategy have found it in Earle's words, not Paret's, and it is to Earle that scholars turned as a key reference point in the resurgence of grand strategy in the late twentieth and early twenty-first centuries.[70]

Paret's reluctance to engage in more prolonged conceptualization of strategy was equally unsurprising, however, since it can be understood as a direct consequence of his own approach to the scholarship of war. His concerns were not for theoretical abstraction so much as contextualization, and the importance of understanding the theory of strategy in conjunction with its practice. Equally, they were born of an interest that was directed towards the broader historical phenomenon of war more than the phenomenon of strategy, and which he thought, moreover, it was important to understand on its own terms and for its own sake. 'Historians', he stressed, 'have sometimes been reluctant to acknowledge this necessity.'[71] This marked his approach as distinct from that of Earle, for whom the significance of the moment was everything at the time of writing. In truth, Earle had little choice but to confront the implications of contemporary war in his scholarship. It would have seemed perverse for him to write about strategy at that time and to refuse to do so. At the same time, if there was something of a generational divide between Earle and Paret, it was also imbued in the markedly different approaches to the study of history that existed between them, which can be understood as reflective of developments within the historical profession. For Earle, as we have seen, much of the purpose of history lay in its use to inform the present. It was this present focus that enabled him to lead a scholarly life that at times took him far from the 'ivory tower' into government service, and which provided the wellspring for his role in the foundation of more contemporary-focused disciplines. Paret, by contrast, was wary of present-focused pursuits as a matter of scholarly boundaries, not just personal discomfort. Reviewers of Paret's *Makers* read this stance as an implicit tendency 'to question the extent to which history has anything to offer the study of strategy as science', or as a loss of 'faith in the value of the past for understanding the present',

---

[70] See, for example, P. Kennedy, 'Grand Strategy in War and Peace: Toward a Broader Definition', in P. Kennedy (ed.), *Grand Strategies in War and Peace* (New Haven, CT: Yale University Press, 1991), p. 2. M. Howard, 'Grand Strategy in the Twentieth Century', *Defence Studies*, Vol. 1, No. 1 (spring 2001), pp. 1–2. L. Freedman, 'The Meaning of Strategy. Part II: The Objectives', *Texas National Security Review*, Vol. 1, No. 2 (March 2018), pp. 55–6. H. Brands, *What Good Is Grand Strategy? Power and Purpose in American Statecraft from Harry S. Truman to George W. Bush* (Ithaca, NY: Cornell University Press, 2014), pp. 2–3. W. Murray, 'Thoughts on Grand Strategy', in W. Murray, R. H. Sinnreich, and J. Lacey (eds.), *The Shaping of Grand Strategy* (Cambridge: Cambridge University Press, 2011), p. 7. An exception can be found in N. Silove, 'Beyond the Buzzword: The Three Meanings of "Grand Strategy"', *Security Studies*, Vol. 27, No. 1 (2018), pp. 27–57. Where the other examples tend to juxtapose Earle with Liddell Hart, Silove concentrates solely on the latter.

[71] Paret, 'Introduction', in Paret, *Makers*, p. 8.

192 MAKING MAKERS

which, if did not entirely break the links in the 'dialectical continuum [...] in strategy to the present day', ensured that 'the threads are somewhat slender'.[72] Yet it could equally be understood in relation to a historical profession which was, by the time Paret came of scholarly age, generally more wary of the perils of instrumentalizing the past for the purposes of the present.

In this respect, the contrast between Paret and his older collaborators, Gilbert and Craig, is pertinent. Unlike Paret, they had undertaken the entirety of their scholarly training before the United States' entry into the Second World War, and it was they—and Craig in particular—who brought something of Earle's stance to the 1986 edition through their willingness to comment on contemporary developments in their concluding essay on strategy in the present. In the same manner Ropp, another pre-war-trained historian, brought to his *Makers Revisited* an overt willingness to ruminate on the development of strategy in terms that Paret sought to avoid. 'Our history of strategy', he wrote, 'can—by using and supplementing Earle's Makers of Modern Strategy—help soldiers and citizens look at the past, ask the present what it is preparing for the future, and decide how best to spend their time, blood, and treasure.'[73]

The tension between the focus on strategy or war, and past or present, also spoke to another issue. In choosing Paret, Gilbert, and Craig as the editorial team for the new edition, Herbert S. Bailey and the Princeton University Press ensured that *Makers* was remade under the direction of historians, rather than scholars of strategic or security studies. This decision followed a certain logic. Gilbert and Craig offered continuity from the 1940s, and despite his scholarly differences Paret could still be seen as something of an inheritor of Earle's mantle. Yet this organizational continuity contrasted with the divergent paths trodden by historians of war and scholars in strategic studies, or security studies more generally, in the years since Earle's *Makers* was published, and this brought consequences for how the book was understood. If the first *Makers* contributed to the establishment of strategic studies in an environment more accommodating to the historical method as an approach to the study strategy, albeit one that was that was challenged by the implications of the dawn of the nuclear age, its successor was liable to be seen by those outside historical studies as more of an adjunct to the scientific study of strategy than its core.[74]

Nowhere was this more apparent than in the reception it received from Stephen Walt, writing—appropriately—for *International Security*. For Walt, the book was 'a worthy successor to the original edition' as a description of the development of strategic thought, but less compelling 'as an *evaluation* of these men and their

---

[72] Showalter, review of Paret, *Makers*, p. 100. McInnes, 'Strategic Doctrine and Political Practice', p. 156.

[73] DSP. Ropp, 'The Present State of Strategy', p. 1.

[74] On this issue, see Strachan, 'The Future of Strategic Studies', pp. 149–66.

THE RECEPTION OF PARET'S *MAKERS* AND ITS LEGACY   193

ideas'.[75] His critique fell into two major parts. The first, and the most substantial of the two, was that Paret and his contributors had shied away from the evaluative obligation of their task. Although they had, in his view, put forward the notion that a study of the past would provide lessons for the future, they 'do not devote much effort to identifying what those lessons might be'. A number of contributors appeared to him 'reluctant to offer a critical judgment', and even Gilbert and Craig's chapter, which he thought contained 'a number of wise observations', was criticized for failing to 'go much beyond Clausewitz's well-known dictum that military policy be controlled by political leaders in the service of political objectives'.[76] Walt's desire for substantial judgements and evaluations of strategy, however, lay beyond the limits of specificity to which the historians were willing to push their conclusions. Thus his critique served to illustrate the impasse between the two camps. It was redolent of Ropp's anxiety over the willingness of 'competitor disciplines' in the study of war to offer solutions, relegating the more circumspect historian who was brought in 'only at the beginning of most contemporary strategy studies' to provide background, before the serious business of addressing 'strategy concepts' might begin.[77] Paret's *Makers* may have formed part of what Richard Betts describes as the 'second cycle' of strategic studies, in which 'the most novel research and theoretical development took an empirical turn', but it was also suggestive of the tendency of some historians to stand apart from strategists.[78] It also appeared to presage a broader uneasiness regarding some social scientists' attitudes to history which became more palpable by the 1990s, described by Paul Schroeder as:

> an unconscious disdain for it, a disregard for its complexity and subtleties and the problems of doing it well or using it wisely; an unexamined assumption that its lessons and insights lie on the surface for anyone to pick up, so that one can go at history like a looter at an archaeological site, indifferent to context and deeper meaning, concerned only with taking what can be immediately used or sold.[79]

The second part of Walt's critique was that Paret's *Makers* overemphasized the military role in strategy. With its focus on the thinking and action of military figures, which was 'less the story of their accomplishments than a record of their recurring failures', the book reflected 'some of the problems that have impeded the development of strategy as a whole', such that it amounted to 'a powerful but

---

[75] Walt, 'The Search for a Science of Strategy', pp. 140–1.   [76] Ibid., pp. 141, 160.

[77] DSP. T. Ropp, 'The Present State of Strategy: Part II', p. 9.

[78] R. K. Betts, 'Should Strategic Studies Survive?' *World Politics*, Vol. 50, No. 1 (October 1997), pp. 17–20.

[79] P. Schroeder, 'Historical Reality vs. Neo-Realist Theory', *International Security*, Vol. 19, No. 1 (summer 1994), p. 148.

194   MAKING MAKERS

veiled indictment of much of its subject'.[80] The remedy to this would have involved the incorporation of approaches beyond the active application of force: Walt suggested, for example, a focus on men such as George C. Marshall, George F. Kennan, and Ernest Bevin, who 'helped create the security arrangements that have enabled the industrial democracies to enjoy unprecedented security at low cost for four decades'.[81] To his credit, Walt recognized that his major contentions were 'somewhat unfair' and openly regretted that Paret and his collaborators 'did not write a different book'.[82] At the same time, the point spoke to an issue applicable to both the Paret and the Earle editions. Yet where for Paret the emphasis on the application of military power across the volume was consistent with the definition of strategy with which its editor framed the work, this was less the case for Earle. Earle's framework rested on a broader definition of strategy, drawn in part from earlier work and other academic engagements, which made explicit reference to non-military elements and activity beyond war. With a few notable exceptions, however—including his own chapter on the economic foundations of military power—his book kept the military instrument front and centre.

Curating the Canon

If Paret showed little interest in innovative approaches to the conceptualization of strategy it was also because his interests lay in historical theorists rather than in developing his own theory. This was especially true of his interest in Clausewitz. Here was yet another instance in which the chief editors of *Makers* I and II held inverse positions. Earle may have been instrumental in bringing Clausewitz to a broad English-speaking audience—'the American who probably did the most to stimulate an American interest in Clausewitz' in the judgement of Christopher Bassford—but his role in that process was passive.[83] The German contingent of his seminar—principally Gilbert, Rosinski, and Vagts—were responsible for ensuring that Clausewitz gained prominence as a central figure of the book, in line with its original conception as an explanation of European and especially German strategic thought. Earle himself never displayed any substantial interest in Clausewitz, and the Prussian's writings did not inform his research work. He reached his conclusions on strategy and security outside of an engagement with Clausewitz, which might well have led him towards a more bounded purview.

Paret's relationship with Clausewitz was different. Unlike Earle, he played an active role in advancing and disseminating knowledge of the Prussian and his writings through decades of research, and in particular the translation of *On War*

---

[80] Walt, 'The Search for a Science of Strategy', pp. 141, 144, 160.   [81] Ibid., p. 164.
[82] Ibid., p. 165.   [83] Bassford, *Clausewitz in English*, pp. 173–4.

THE RECEPTION OF PARET'S *MAKERS* AND ITS LEGACY   195

that he edited with Michael Howard.[84] Although it was published in 1976, the genesis of the translation extended back into the late 1950s. At that time, Howard recalled, 'Paret was particularly concerned with the inaccuracies and misinterpretations in the existing English translations', whilst his own concerns lay in 'the continuing value of the text as a didactic tool for both civilian and professional students of war'.[85] Paret became the driving force in working towards a translation, which was originally just one element of a more ambitious project aimed at publishing the entirety of Clausewitz's political and military writings across six volumes. In 1962 he organized a conference in Berlin that brought together a group of scholars to undertake the work, including several whose past or future trajectories connected them to *Makers*: not only himself and Howard, but Gordon Craig, Bernard Brodie, and John Shy.[86] Despite the demise of the broader project, Paret and Howard pressed on with *On War*, engaging the services of Angus Malcolm, a retired British Foreign Office official, who completed a draft of the translation before his death.[87] Thereafter, they worked from different sides of the Atlantic, meeting only twice to collaborate in person, with Paret spending a summer in London and Howard just a week in Stanford.[88] When the book was finally published, it became a great success, 'arriving on the market just as the Vietnam War became history and the subject of military and political postmortems', to which it was applied.[89] Clausewitz spoke to the needs of the moment. 'It was our good fortune', wrote Howard, 'to be able to present his work in a text that was accessible both to military colleges and to university students.'[90]

In a preface to a later collection of Clausewitz's writings, Paret and his collaborator, Daniel Moran, explained their approach to translation. 'All translation is, in the end, interpretation', they wrote:

> The translators have tried to preserve or at least reflect those elements of Clausewitz's style that are most distinctive of his way of thinking [...] But there has been no hesitation in settling for less than literal equivalence, when to do otherwise would have resulted in preciousness or evasiveness. Nor has it seemed

---

[84] Up to the final years of his life Paret continued to publish research notes on Clausewitz in multiple issue of *The Journal of Military History*.

[85] M. Howard, 'Clausewitz *On War*: A History of the Howard-Paret Translation', in H. Strachan and A. Herberg-Rothe (eds.), *Clausewitz in the Twenty-First Century* (Oxford: Oxford University Press, 2007), p. v.

[86] Ibid., p. v. See also Bassford, *Clausewitz in English*, pp. 207–8.

[87] Howard, 'A History of the Howard-Paret Translation', p. vi.

[88] H. Strachan, 'Michael Howard and Clausewitz', *Journal of Strategic Studies*, Vol. 45, No. 1 (February 2022), p. 145.

[89] Bassford, *Clausewitz in English*, p. 208.

[90] Howard, 'A History of the Howard-Paret Translation', p. vi. See also Howard, *Captain Professor*, pp. 202–3. In his autobiography Howard gives the date of the Berlin conference as 1964. Given the association of Princeton and Klaus Knorr with the project, 1962 seems the more accurate date, and a June conference would have preceded Paret's move to UC Davis that later year.

196   MAKING MAKERS

advisable to translate the same words in the same way in every instance [...] Clausewitz put no stock in rigid or artificially systematic terminology. Language always took second place to thought.[91]

These contentions were just as applicable to Paret's approach to translating *On War*. As he wrote in 2014, translation is 'a very imperfect, if at times inspired, activity. The translator must serve the author, even as—especially as—the need to depart from the precise verbal equivalent of the original text becomes apparent.'[92] Evidently, translation is a distinct activity from historical research, but as a skill frequently exercised as part of the historian's craft it is related to it nonetheless. Consequently, it appears somewhat paradoxical that a scholar whose philosophy of history was so rooted in dedication to understanding the past on its own terms was so comfortable with the transformation of language in ways that could significantly affect present-day understanding. When partnered with Howard, who as translator 'likened himself to an impressionist painter', Paret produced a version of *On War* that spoke clearly to contemporary mores precisely because of the manner in which it was translated.[93] The Clausewitz that the pair presented was not Liddell Hart's 'Mahdi of Mass', but rather a Clausewitz that responded to Cold War anxieties—a 'liberal' advocate of limited war and of civilian control of the military.[94] As a number of critics have subsequently made clear, such an interpretation rested on particular English-language word choices, which ironed out the more unsettling inconsistencies and tensions that existed in the German-language text.[95]

As Strachan notes, readers of Howard and Paret's translation of *On War* responded to 'Earle's injunction that strategy was an activity to be pursued in peace as well as war' by focusing on the first chapter of the first book, 'the only book which Howard and Paret deemed to be fully finished and the one which they argued contained the most developed discussion of the relationship between war and policy'.[96] In this manner, there was at least an indirect connection between Earle's grand or national strategy and Paret's scholarship. Moreover, by producing what remains the standard translation of *On War* in the English

---

[91] C. von Clausewitz (ed. and trans. P. Paret and D. Moran), *Historical and Political Writings* (Princeton, NJ: Princeton University Press, 1992), xii.

[92] P. Paret, 'Translation, Literal or Accurate', *The Journal of Military History*, Vol. 78, No. 3 (July 2014), pp. 1078–9.

[93] Strachan, 'Michael Howard and Clausewitz', p. 146.

[94] For the 'Mahdi of Mass' argument see B. Liddell Hart, *The Ghost of Napoleon* (London: Faber & Faber, 1933), pp. 118–29.

[95] See J. W. Honig, 'Clausewitz's *On War*: Problems of Text and Translation', in Strachan and Herberg-Rothe, *Clausewitz in the Twenty-First Century*, pp. 57–73. M. Melvin, 'Revisiting the Translators and Translations of Clausewitz's *On War*', *British Journal of Military History*, Vol. 8, No. 2 (September 2022), pp. 77–102. Strachan, 'Michael Howard and Clausewitz', pp. 143–60. Strachan, *The Direction of War*, pp. 34–5, 51–6.

[96] Strachan, *The Direction of War*, pp. 34–5.

THE RECEPTION OF PARET'S *MAKERS* AND ITS LEGACY 197

language, Paret and Howard accelerated the ascendency of Clausewitz in the post-Second World War period. Paret's chapter on Clausewitz for his *Makers*, meanwhile, constituted a secondary effort towards the same goal, but one which was more explicitly rooted in his historical approach, and consistent with his thinking about war. In this respect, a key difference between Paret's piece and Hans Rothfels's 1943 effort is instructive. While both men were keen to present Clausewitz in the context of his own life and times, Rothfels's most significant contribution lay in his stress on 'the connection between war and politics' in *On War*, which elevated focus away from the tactical and reframed the strategic purview of Clausewitz's work for an English-speaking audience.[97] Paret, on the other hand, was not interested in making points about strategy. Rather, his contribution dwelled upon what he presented as Clausewitz's primary goals: 'one, to penetrate by means of logical analysis to the essence of absolute war, "ideal" war in the language of the philosophy of the time; the other, to understand war in the various forms it actually takes, as a social and political phenomenon, and in its strategic, operational, and tactical aspects'.[98] Paret's overriding concern was to show how Clausewitz illuminated the phenomenon of war itself, within which strategy was a subset of activity. Thus he concluded that 'Clausewitz ranges far beyond the parameters of success and failure in which strategic thought moves to explore the ultimate nature and dynamic of war'.[99]

In his reflections on the state of strategy in 1980, Ropp mused on the manner in which the focus of military thought followed success and power. 'The language and methods of military thought are often those of the most recent exemplar,' he wrote. 'The Napoleonic upheaval left the language of strategy French. Its exemplar was Napoleon [...] After the "lesser" crises of 1854–1871, the language of strategy was German or French, its exemplar Moltkean.'[100] If the transcendence of Clausewitz in the twentieth century did not fit this pattern, there were other respects in which the *Makers* books did follow something of this logic. Indeed, when set against each other the transformations are quite apparent.

In seeking to explain the development of warfare and strategy in a European framework, with a particular focus on the nineteenth and twentieth centuries, the original *Makers* cleaved rather closely to the pattern identified by Ropp. Whilst it did not entirely exclude consideration of other national experiences—whether that of the Italian city states through the lens of Machiavelli, or of the Soviet Union through the eyes of Lenin, Trotsky, and Stalin—the core of the book lay on a Franco-German axis. As well as its treatments of Jomini and Clausewitz—both, in Earle's words, 'interpreters of Napoleon'—the book included essays on Vauban, Frederick the Great, Moltke and Schlieffen, du Picq and Foch, the colonial

---

[97] See H. Rothfels, 'Clausewitz', in Earle, *Makers*, pp. 103–6.
[98] P. Paret, 'Clausewitz', in Paret, *Makers*, p. 198.   [99] Ibid., p. 213.
[100] DSP. Ropp, 'The Present State of Strategy', p. 11.

198   MAKING MAKERS

experiences of Bugeaud, Gallieni, and Lyautey, Delbrück, Ludendorff, Maginot, and the predominantly French focus of Ropp's 'continental doctrines of sea power'. With the addition of the concerns of the Second World War, expressed most forcefully in Earle's introduction and his concluding piece, 'Hitler: The Nazi Concept of War', this amounted to over half of the book.

By the 1980s it was clear that *Makers* could not remain a preparatory text for American ascendency, but needed instead to acknowledge the rise of the USA to superpower status. Thus Paret was explicit in acknowledging that his *Makers* had 'far more to say about American strategy than did its predecessor'.[101] Because of the expansion in the size of the book, this new emphasis did not need to come at the expense of pre-existing chapter headings. Indeed, given the centrality of the Second World War to America's rise, the significance of the fight against Germany, and the importance of German military theorists, treatment of Germany was revised but not diminished.[102] The most significant consequence of the shift in focus was the effect that it had on consideration of late nineteenth-century French military thinking, with Etienne Mantoux and Stefan Possony's chapter on du Picq and Foch excised for the 1986 edition. Instead, treatment of both individuals was reduced and subsumed within Michael Howard's broader examination of 'the doctrine of the offensive' prior to 1914. Coverage of French experiences would have been further diminished had Paret followed through on his initial desire to drop the chapter on French colonial warfare, on the grounds that it 'scarcely deserves a separate essay'.[103]

The emphasis on German and French, then German and American experiences, across both published versions of *Makers* had an additional and yet more significant consequence: it left consideration of the British experience in a curious position. The relative neglect of British strategic thinkers had not gone unnoticed in reactions to Earle's edition. As well as being a matter of comment amongst reviewers, it was an issue that Earle had recognized and sought to remedy as he turned his attention to revisions for a second edition. Since the revised edition did not materialize, and because Paret, Craig, and Gilbert felt no particular need to augment the focus on the British as part of their planning, the successor edition largely carried the stance of the original through to the 1980s.

The chief point of continuity between the two volumes was a focus on the thinking of Liddell Hart. In planning for the successor edition, Paret thought Arpad Kovacs's pseudonymous effort for Earle 'probably the weakest piece in the volume', and that 'an essay on land strategy in the 20s and 30s, which concludes

---

[101] Paret, 'Introduction', in Paret, *Makers*, p. 6. McInnes thought the emphasis on the USA 'one of the more important and interesting changes in the book as a whole', but one that brought the risk that 'a lack of balance appears in the work'. McInnes, 'Strategic Doctrine and Political Practice', p. 155.

[102] Although Paret removed Hans Speier's chapter on Ludendorff, the additional pieces by Rothenberg and Geyer strengthened coverage of Germany.

[103] MLP, PUP, Box 344, Folder 3 (CO728), Paret to Bailey, 19 May 1982.

THE RECEPTION OF PARET'S *MAKERS* AND ITS LEGACY   199

with an analysis of blitzkrieg doctrines' represented the best replacement.[104] In the event, the 1986 edition retained the emphasis on Liddell Hart's ideas on limited liability coupled with a new focus on the military thought of Charles de Gaulle, their thinking on mechanized warfare providing the link between the two.[105] The choice elicited comment. As Strachan observed, by framing Liddell Hart's contribution only with reference to inter-war military policy the editors spurned the opportunity to consider the entirety of his ideas 'as a body of thought in themselves'.[106] Brian Holden Reid, meanwhile, noted that the chapter 'compounds the staggering omission of J. F. C. Fuller from the 1943 edition, all the more remarkable because his brooding and iconoclastic spirit pervades several of the essays in both editions'.[107]

In fact, Earle had at least recognized the potential for a dedicated chapter on Fuller, in combination with de Gaulle, as one of the potential inclusions for a revised *Makers*, although no substantive work was undertaken for the chapter, and no one was designated to write it. Although there was nothing to suggest that a separate chapter on Fuller was ever considered for the Paret edition, he was not entirely absent from its pages. Fuller's ideas were mentioned not only in Bond's and Alexander's inter-war chapter, but also in Shy's piece on Jomini, Weigley's on American strategy, McIsaac's on air power, and Carver's chapter on conventional war. Equally, Kovacs included some discussion of Fuller alongside his treatment of Liddell Hart in the 1943 edition, since it was almost impossible to discuss the ideas of the pair in isolation. Nevertheless, the preference for Liddell Hart across the two editions, albeit in a limited guise, was marked, and it is hard to avoid concluding that in this respect, personal connections played a role. Liddell Hart was the man with whom Earle had pre- and post-war relations, not Fuller, and, as we have seen, the Englishman was keen to have his say over the chapter that bore his name. Whilst Earle was no pushover—indeed, he was highly critical of Liddell Hart's wartime stance—the effect of the latter episode was to keep Liddell Hart in the frame for a future edition, even if he might have become a focus of greater criticism. Fuller, meanwhile, had suffered a decline in reputation in the years preceding the Second World War, and his membership of the British Union of Fascists likely rendered him an unacceptable presence in the initial considerations for *Makers*.[108]

---

[104] MLP, PUP, Box 344, Folder 3 (CO728), Paret to Bailey, 19 May 1982.

[105] The essay was written by Brian Bond and Martin Alexander, who were responsible for the British and French portions respectively. In 1977 Brian Bond had published *Liddell Hart: A Study of his Military Thought*. Although not a sanctioned biography, it presented the only book-length account of Liddell Hart's intellectual development in print at that time. For the circumstances of publication, see Bond, *Military Historian*, pp. 110–11. Martin Alexander would go on to publish *The Republic in Danger: General Maurice Gamelin and the Politics of French Defence* in 1993.

[106] Strachan, review of *Makers*, p. 160.   [107] Holden Reid, review of *Makers*, p. 90.

[108] On Fuller and Fascism, see A. J. Trythall, *'Boney' Fuller: The Intellectual General 1878–1966* (London: Cassell, 1977), pp. 180–212. B. Holden Reid, *J. F. C. Fuller: Military Thinker* (London, Macmillan, 1987), pp. 175–96. Gat, *A History of Military Thought*, pp. 551–8.

200 MAKING MAKERS

For the 1986 volume, personal connections continued to bind the contributors to Liddell Hart, including Paret, who had developed a relationship with Liddell Hart in the late 1950s and 1960s. Although Howard observed that 'Peter and Basil were strongminded men with ideas of their own who did not get on at all well', when he encountered them together in the USA in 1965, Paret held Liddell Hart in sufficient esteem to arrange for him to become Visiting Professor at UC Davis that year, and they continued to correspond after Liddell Hart's return to the United Kingdom.[109] Aside from Paret, both Brian Bond and Michael Howard—in common with many other young military historians in the post-Second World War period—also encountered Liddell Hart at formative periods in their intellectual development and benefitted from the mentorship that the 'Captain who teaches Generals' was keen to provide.[110] Like Earle, they were not inclined to accept Liddell Hart's oeuvre without reservation: both developed a critical stance on their erstwhile mentor in the scholarship they produced after his death in 1970.[111] Yet neither man was inclined to minimize his significance as a historic strategic thinker as a result.

If the persistence of human connections played a role in shaping *Makers* by reinforcing the prominence of Liddell Hart, an absence of British advocates played its role in another respect. The lack of attention paid to British imperial military thinking relative to the French experience was a feature of Paret's *Makers* noted by more than one reviewer.[112] The essay on this subject which appeared in the 1986 edition, 'Bugeaud, Galliéni, Lyautey', was one of the few that retained the title of the same piece from the 1943 edition but handed authorship to a different individual.[113] In this case, Douglas Porch used the opportunity this presented to engage in a thoroughly revisionist assessment that underscored the deficiencies of Jean Gottmann's original.[114] Nevertheless, the essay itself was only included because of Paret's unexplained decision to move forward with it despite his initial strong reservations. The most likely justification was that a chapter on warfare in the age of high imperialism provided balance and continuity for the later essay on

---

[109] Howard, *Captain Professor*, pp. 180–1. Danchev, *Alchemist of War*, p. 240. For the UC Davis sojourn, see the correspondence between the two in the Liddell Hart Centre for Military Archives, holding LH 1/566.

[110] Danchev, *Alchemist of War*, pp. 249–52. For Howard's relationship with Liddell Hart, see Howard, *Captain Professor*, pp. 154–5. Howard, *The Causes of Wars*, 2nd edn. (Cambridge, MA: Harvard University Press, 1984), pp. 198–208. B. Holden Reid, 'The Legacy of Liddell Hart: The Contrasting Responses of Michael Howard and André Beaufre', *British Journal for Military History*, Vol 1. No. 1 (2014), pp. 66–80. For Bond's relationship with Liddell Hart, see Bond, *Military Historian*, pp. 20–4, 110–11.

[111] See Bond, *Liddell Hart*, and Howard, *The Causes of Wars*, pp. 169–87.

[112] See Strachan, review of *Makers*, and Holden Reid, review of *Makers*.

[113] The other examples were Paret on Clausewitz and Shy on Jomini. Philip Crowl's essay on Mahan used the subtitle 'The Naval Historian' rather than Margaret Tuttle Sprout's 'Evangelist of Seapower'.

[114] For a comparison between the two pieces see Finch, *A Progressive Occupation?*, pp. 34–47.

THE RECEPTION OF PARET'S *MAKERS* AND ITS LEGACY   201

revolutionary war. Shy and Collier's essay, however, situated its subject in a broader revolutionary and colonial context in its own right.

The same chapter also provided the only references in the book to the work of Charles Callwell, aside from an admission by Porch in his bibliographical notes that 'no equivalent of C. E. Callwell's *Small Wars* [...] exists for France'.[115] As the foremost British thinker on colonial war at the turn of the twentieth century, whose credentials were bolstered by a more substantial published treatment of colonial war than those produced by Bugeaud, Gallieni, and Lyautey, Callwell offered the most viable alternative to the French thinkers. By choosing not to pivot towards such a figure, Paret perpetuated the tendencies of Earle's group. Reflecting the American and French backgrounds and interest of those involved in devising the project, at no point did British figures play an explicit role in considerations for the chapter. Even during planning in the 1940s it was first listed as 'Colonial and Frontier Warfare: Washington, Lyautey and Others', before assuming its final form. The consequences of this are hard to assess with absolute certainty. Amongst military historians at least, Callwell was not an unknown figure in the post-Second World War era.[116] Yet it is clear that the resurgence of interest in his work on colonial warfare—he wrote about much else besides—was due to developments independent of the *Makers* project, beginning with the reissue of *Small Wars* in the 1990s, bolstered by the search for historical precedents for contemporary counterinsurgency that began in the 2000s, and culminating most recently in Daniel Whittingham's intellectual biography.[117] Incorporating him into *Makers* in 1986 might have accelerated this process.

Of all the ways in which *Makers* related to British strategic thought, however, the absence of British naval strategic thinkers from its pages was both the most significant and the most consequential. Earle, of course, had recognized the broader deficiency in the treatment of naval matters in 1944. Ostensibly, it was a curious oversight, since he had developed ideas on grand strategy and national security which, by their nature, incorporated the maritime aspect of national power. Likewise, the work of his seminar included much discussion of naval affairs expressed in this manner. At the same time, it can be understood as a reflection of the limits of intersection between seminar and book, and of the preoccupations of those who were most involved in assembling the latter. In this respect, it should be underlined that *Makers* was shaped not only by the national

---

[115] J. Shy and T. Collier, 'Revolutionary War', in Paret, *Makers*, pp. 830–1. 'Bibliographical Notes', in Paret, *Makers*, p. 901.

[116] For example, *Small Wars* formed the major source for the chapter 'Colonial Warfare, and Its Contribution to the Art of War in Europe' in Strachan, *European Armies and the Conduct of War*, pp. 76–89.

[117] *Small Wars* was reissued both by Greenhill publishers in 1990 and by the University of Nebraska Press in 1966, with an introduction by Douglas Porch. For the contemporary rise in scholarly interest in Callwell, see D. Whittingham, *Charles E. Callwell and the British Way in Warfare* (Cambridge: Cambridge University Press, 2020), pp. 4–12.

202 MAKING MAKERS

proclivities of those who contributed to it, but also by a preference for strategy as a product of, and in relation to, the land domain. The Earle edition was even organized in a manner that presented 'sea and air war' as a small, specific, section, in contrast to the implicit land-centrism of much of the rest of the book.

Although arranged on different lines, the Paret edition replicated the essence of this orientation. Admittedly it brought a greater emphasis on US naval power in practice, particularly in relation to the conduct of the Second World War, which was aligned to the focus of the book and its augmentation.[118] At the same time Paret elected not to reuse Ropp's chapter on 'Continental Doctrines of Sea Power' on the grounds that it was 'not an essential contribution', thereby diminishing its coverage of European—and particularly French—naval thinking.[119] In this respect, the proclivities of the editorial group continued to exert a marked influence on the shape of the book. In short, Paret, Craig, and Gilbert were more assured in their understanding of land warfare than war at sea. Indeed, it is telling that in considering whether Sprout's chapter on Mahan was fit to be reprinted, Paret and Craig had to admit that 'we have insufficient knowledge to judge this piece'.[120] The next most important figure in influencing the composition of Paret's *Makers*, Michael Howard, was equally drawn towards land warfare and showed far less concern for naval affairs.[121] It thus becomes less surprising that, across both volumes, treatment of naval strategy was uneven, with Mahan the only constant presence.

Things might have been different. Had Herbert Rosinski brought his expertise to bear in his chapter on 'The National Factor in Military Thought' instead of disregarding Earle's instructions, the 1943 edition might have produced a more extensive discussion of national strategy incorporating its maritime dimension. Moreover, had Bernard Brodie remained at the IAS beyond 1941, his then-close relations with Earle would undoubtedly have resulted in significant involvement in the preparation of the book at a time when his focus on maritime matters was absolute. Indeed, it was Brodie who offered the most thorough critique of the limitations of the naval aspects of Earle's *Makers*, particularly with reference to the British. As far as a remedy was concerned, one of the challenges was the apparent lack of a theorist around whom the whole British experience could coalesce. Rather, British naval strategy presented as a tradition partly associated with a number of important individuals, many of whom offered examples of practice over print, and so worked against the 'great thinker' framework of the original edition.

Nevertheless, Brodie was clear that one British strategist deserved a dedicated treatment: Julian Corbett. Given their respective backgrounds, it is unsurprising

---

[118] See chapters by Maurice Matloff and D. Clayton James.
[119] MLP, PUP, Box 344, Folder 3 (CO728), Paret to Bailey, 19 May 1982.
[120] MLP, PUP, Box 344, Folder 3 (CO728), Paret to Bailey, 19 May 1982.
[121] Strachan, 'Michael Howard and Clausewitz', p. 147.

THE RECEPTION OF PARET'S *MAKERS* AND ITS LEGACY   203

that Ropp and Schurman shared this view. Schurman had already cast scholarly attention on Corbett, whilst Ropp provided the only references to him in his chapter for the 1943 edition.[122] It is clear, moreover, that *Makers Revisited* would have given considerable attention to maritime strategy with a specific focus on Corbett's contribution. This was an area in which Ropp and Schurman's project was rather more insightful than Paret's: the 1986 edition contained no references to Corbett whatsoever. The near-complete absence of Corbett from the pages of *Makers* was a consequence of human and institutional developments as much as intellectual persuasion. As we have seen, Corbett's legacy was not well captured within academic institutions, and his death in 1922 limited his personal influence in the inter-war period. If this obscured him from the view of those engaged in preparing the book at the IAS, Earle did develop a proxy link to Corbett once the book was published. This came via his interactions with Herbert Richmond, 'his most important intellectual follower'.[123] At this stage, however, Richmond was too worn out and too overcommitted to put the case for Corbett in writing. Thereafter, Corbett's reputation tended to suffer from scholarly assessments that diminished his 'pre-war consequence and wartime impact, mistaking modest irony for a confession of irrelevance', such that it was only after the Cold War ended that his revival began.[124]

Just as for Callwell, then, it is possible to imagine that Corbett's inclusion amongst the makers of strategy assembled by Earle and Paret might have led to his achieving more widespread recognition at an earlier stage, and beyond naval specialists. This would likely have brought with it significant consequences. Scrutiny of Corbett's *Some Principles of Maritime Strategy*, alongside his other works, might have illuminated his role in establishing the idea of a British way of war, and perhaps made clearer the unattributed debt that Liddell Hart owed him for his less nuanced articulation, so leading to a more cautious embrace of the latter in the first edition.[125] In conjunction with this, Corbett's development of a theory which embraced both the land and maritime dimensions of strategy— written in the era before the advent of air power—would have provided a welcome multi-domain approach in a volume that often, in the detail, treated strategy in single dimensions. Equally, his use of Clausewitz's *On War* as a key source in

---

[122] See Ropp, 'Continental Doctrines of Sea Power', in Earle, *Makers*, pp. 453–4.

[123] Lambert, *The British Way of War*, p. 8.

[124] Ibid., pp. 2–7. The proceedings of the Naval War College conference in 1993 marked a key stage in this process, see J. Goldrick and J. Hattendorf (eds.), *Mahan Is Not Enough: The Proceedings of a Conference on the Works of Sir Julian Corbett and Admiral Sir Herbert Richmond* (Newport, RI: Naval War College Press, 1993).

[125] A. Gat, *A History of Military Thought: From the Enlightenment to the Cold War* (Oxford: Oxford University Press, 2001), pp. 675–81. Lambert, *The British Way of War*. See also A. Gat, 'The Hidden Sources of Liddell Hart's Strategic Ideas', *War in History*, Vol. 3, No. 3 (July 1996), pp. 293–308. It is worth noting in this respect that Daniel Whittingham has also advanced the argument that Callwell's role in advocating a 'British way of war' should be acknowledged. See Whittingham, *Charles E. Callwell and the British Way in Warfare*, pp. 2–4, 240–8.

204   MAKING MAKERS

developing his own theory would have raised questions about the applicability of the Prussian's thought beyond the land domain.[126] Furthermore, his development of 'major' and 'minor' strategy might have provided thoughtful fuel for Earle as he contemplated the parameters of his own concept of strategy.[127] Corbett's work would have provided substance to the vision of 'grand' or 'national' strategy espoused by Earle, but insufficiently elaborated in the pages of his book, and treated in narrower terms by Paret. On this last point, similar inspiration might also have been drawn from explicit consideration of the work of Fuller, whose notion of grand strategy as 'the transmission of power in all its forms, in order to maintain policy', the applicability of which extended to peacetime, presaged much of Earle's formulation.[128]

Makers and the Ancients

As the title indicated, *Makers of Modern Strategy* was concerned with modern, rather than ancient, strategy. In the 1940s the parameters of what was considered 'modern' seem to have been implicitly accepted rather than discussed, moulded in good part by the insights that the core contributors could best supply. Equally, there was no consideration of whether the boundaries might be extended to incorporate great thinkers of the ancient world. Paret, Gilbert, and Craig saw no need to revise this stance in the 1980s. To criticize either edition for failing to include an ancient dimension would therefore be unjust. At the same, part of the legacy of the *Makers* project lay the role it played in opening up avenues for the exploration of the makers of strategy of an earlier age. The roots of this can be seen with Earle's *Makers* itself. Gilbert's chapter on Machiavelli, in particular, through discussion of his *Art of War*, highlighted the inspiration that the Roman military system supplied to the Florentine, thus emphasizing the unavoidable link between ancient and modern thinking through the Renaissance.[129] It was hardly surprising that Ropp—so committed to thinking about the origins of Earle's *Makers* and what Earle's group had considered 'makers', 'modern', and 'strategy' to

---

[126] For the influence of Clausewitz on Corbett see Gat, *A History of Military Thought*, pp. 480–93, and D. M. Schurman, *The Education of a Navy: The Development of British Naval Strategic Thought, 1867–1914* (London: Cassell, 1965), pp. 163–7, 174–7.

[127] For a précis of Corbett's contribution to strategic thought see Strachan, *The Direction of War*, pp. 136–50. D. Morgan-Owen, 'History and the Perils of Grand Strategy', *The Journal of Modern History*, Vol. 92, No. 2 (June 2020), pp. 361–4. Milevski, *The Evolution of Modern Grand Strategic Thought*, pp. 36–42.

[128] See J. F. C. Fuller, *The Reformation of War* (London: Hutchinson & Co., 1923), pp. 211–28. Also Milevski, *The Evolution of Modern Grand Strategic Thought*, pp. 47–51.

[129] See F. Gilbert, 'Machiavelli: The Renaissance of the Art of War', in Earle, *Makers*, pp. 16–19, and F. Gilbert, 'Machiavelli: The Renaissance of the Art of War', in Paret, *Makers*, pp. 21–3. Henry Guerlac's chapter on Vauban also emphasized the inspiration provided by the ancients. See also Gat, *A History of Military Thought*, pp. 3–11.

THE RECEPTION OF PARET'S *MAKERS* AND ITS LEGACY 205

be—took matters one step further. Moved by a sense of historical completeness he extended the purview of his companion work to encompass 'classical strategists'. Here again was an instance in which, however eccentric his approach, Ropp's *Makers Revisited* looked to move in directions that neither Earle nor Paret countenanced, and which he ensured included consideration of the maritime as well as the land dimensions.

Despite the demise of Ropp's project, and Paret's disinterest in such matters, a more tangible legacy in ancient strategy began to develop shortly after the publication of the 1986 edition. In the first instance this came indirectly through *The Making of Strategy*. In seeking to 'offer its readers an introduction to the wide variety of factors that influence the formulation and outcome of national strategy' in what they thought to be more substantive terms than *Makers*, Murray, Knox, and Bernstein adopted a longer chronology.[130] Thus, the first two chapters of their book dealt with Athenian strategy against Sparta and Roman strategy against Carthage respectively.[131]

A more substantial and direct link to the *Makers* books came with the publication of Victor Davis Hanson's edited collection *Makers of Ancient Strategy* in 2010. Unlike Murray et al., who positioned their work as a partial reaction to Paret's *Makers*, Hanson aligned his work with the previous editions, describing it as both 'a prequel' and 'the third work on the makers of strategy'.[132] Insofar as it was the third *Makers* title published by Princeton University Press, the latter claim was accurate. It was not, however, the third book to claim the *Makers* mantle, since an earlier publication by John Baylis and John Garnett on the *Makers of Nuclear Strategy* had looked to capitalize on the end of the Cold War to assess the legacy of nuclear thinkers, and had done so with explicit reference to Earle's work.[133]

Nevertheless, in conjunction with this stance, Hanson made explicit reference to the historical contexts in which the first two books were created and to the circumstances in which his own volume was compiled, setting the essential continuity of the experience of war and the wisdom of strategic thinkers against contemporary transformations in the character of war. If the Second World War and the Cold War were 'unavoidable presences in the background' of Earle's and

---

[130] W. Murray and M. Grimsley, 'Introduction: On Strategy', in Murray, Knox, and Bernstein (eds.), *The Making of Strategy*, p. 6.

[131] D. Kagan, 'Athenian Strategy in the Peloponnesian War' and A. Bernstein, 'The Strategy of a Warrior-State: Rome and the Wars against Carthage, 264–201 B.C.', in Murray, Knox, and Bernstein (eds.), *The Making of Strategy*, pp. 24–55 and 56–84.

[132] V. Davis Hanson, 'Introduction: Makers of Ancient Strategy. From the Persian Wars to the Fall of Rome', in V. Davis Hanson (ed.), *Makers of Ancient Strategy: From the Persian Wars to the Fall of Rome* (Princeton, NJ: Princeton University Press, 2010), p. 2.

[133] Its editors mused, 'Arguably, we are still close to the nuclear age to reflect objectively on its thinkers, but it did seem appropriate to make a tentative assessment and to gather their thoughts in a single book.' Its nine chapters on individual thinkers included one on Bernard Brodie, and its authors included Michael Howard and Lawrence Freedman. J. Baylis and J. Garnett (eds.), *Makers of Nuclear Strategy* (London: Pinter Publishers, 1991), p. 4.

206 MAKING MAKERS

Paret's books, Hanson emphasized that his book was produced 'during so-called fourth-generational warfare'.[134] Yet just as the older books 'cautioned against assuming that the radical changes in war making of their respective ages were signs that the nature of conflict had also changed', so did his. 'The theme of all three volumes remains constant,' he argued: 'the study of history, not recent understanding of technological innovation, remains the better guide to the nature of contemporary warfare'.[135] Unchanging human nature offered the grounds for this assertion, opening a through-line to worlds and people who might otherwise appear remote from present-day concerns. Hanson went so far as to argue that ancient thinkers exhibited 'an honesty of thought and a clarity of expression not always found in military discussions', even if the absence of abstract theory from the classical sources meant that their strategy was often more implied than explicit.[136]

In this way, Hanson presented the relationship between past and present in a manner that was closer to Earle's stance than Paret's. Similarly, his organizational principle overtly mirrored Earle's emphasis on particular individuals, considering the contributions of such figures as Pericles, Epaminondas, Alexander the Great, Julius Caesar, and even the slave rebellion leader Spartacus, across ten chapters spanning a thousand years, beginning with the Greco-Persian Wars and ending with the collapse of the Roman Empire. In practice, however, the focus on individuals formed a guiding principle rather than a fixed rule, with some of the contributions offering appraisals of broader phenomena during the period: the importance of fortifications, urban warfare, ancient counter-insurgency, and the defence of frontiers.[137] Ultimately, the ancient makers proved no more malleable than the modern makers.

In bringing together a group of classicists and historians to address the ancient dimensions of strategy Hanson's project also reflected the persistence of the division between ancient historians and their modern counterparts, which made the inclusion of ancient strategists in Earle's and Paret's volumes unfeasible. In the twentieth century, *Makers* in its published guises was a project led and shaped by modern historians, none of whom was inclined to straddle the ancient and modern worlds. A few exceptions of an earlier age, such as Hans Delbrück, may have sought to encompass both, but with the growth of research specialization and the resultant development of deep empirical study of specific periods this became increasingly uncommon. Equally, it should be underlined that the absence of ancient figures who have become part of the canon of strategic thinkers from the pages of *Makers* can also be explained by the centrality of those figures to

---

[134] On fourth-generation warfare see T. X. Hammes, *The Sling and the Stone: On War in the 21st Century* (St Paul, MN: Zenith Press, 2006).
[135] Hanson, 'Introduction', in *Makers of Ancient Strategy*, pp. 1–2.   [136] Ibid., pp. 4–5, 9–10.
[137] Ibid., see chapters 3, 6, 7, and 10.

THE RECEPTION OF PARET'S *MAKERS* AND ITS LEGACY   207

disciplines outside of historical study. This is particularly so in the case of Thucydides, who assumed a mantle as 'the father of realism' in the decades after 1945. As the Cold War developed Thucydides's *History of the Peloponnesian War* offered an attractive framework for understanding the confrontation between an Athens-like USA and a Sparta-esque Soviet Union, with its author portrayed as 'the first to realize the inevitability of power politics in an anarchic international system'.[138] If this process began after Earle's *Makers* was published, it is worth noting that the esteem afforded to Thucydides gathered much of its momentum only in the late 1970s and 1980s: that is to say, it ran parallel to the period in which Paret and his co-editors undertook their project.[139] Meanwhile, Thucydides's centrality to professional military education, the other great source of interest in his thinking in the post-war United States, took root only from 1972 with the introduction of his work as the central text in the strategy and policy pillar of the new Naval War College curriculum introduced as part of the 'Turner Revolution'.[140] Much of the appeal of Thucydides at that time stemmed from the military soul-searching caused by the Vietnam War, which could be conceptualized as the USA's Sicilian expedition.[141] While the USA did not experience a defeat by the Soviet Union akin to Athens's humbling by Sparta, the end of the Cold War did little to stem rising interest in applying Thucydides's history to the contemporary international system.[142] In this manner, Thucydides's thinking has continued to be represented through a contemporary lens that emphasizes power distribution, the causes of wars, and the grand strategic considerations of prolonged conflict. As Williamson Murray has stressed, however, 'this Greek historian's interests ranged from the highest levels of grand strategy to that of the battlefield, where men engage in the merciless processes of killing each other'.[143] Such range, of course, aligns him comfortably with Earle's parameters of strategy.

Much the same reasoning accounts for the absence from the published versions of *Makers* of another great strategic thinker whose reputation in the English-speaking world has seen a dramatic increase since 1945: Sun Tzu. Sun Tzu's *The Art of War* was not unknown in Western countries prior to the Second World War. In 1772 a French Jesuit missionary, Jean Amiot, produced the first European language translation, which Adam Parr has recently demonstrated

---

[138] E. Keene, 'The Reception of Thucydides in the History of International Relations', in C. Lee and N. Morley (eds.), *A Handbook to the Reception of Thucydides* (London: Wiley, 2015), p. 363.

[139] Ibid., pp. 360–6. See also L. M. Johnson Bagby, 'The Use and Abuse of Thucydides in International Relations', *International Organization*, Vol. 48, No. 1 (winter 1994), pp. 131–53.

[140] A. Stradis, 'Thucydides in the Staff College', in *A Handbook to the Reception of Thucydides*, pp. 425–45. The 'revolution' was named after Rear Admiral Stansfield Turner (1923–2018), then president of the Naval War College.

[141] Ibid., pp. 433–8.

[142] See, for example, G. Allison, *Destined for War: Can America and China Escape Thucydides' Trap?* (Boston, MA: Houghton Mifflin Harcourt, 2017).

[143] W. Murray, 'Thucydides: Theorist of War', *Naval War College Review*, Vol. 66, No. 4 (autumn 2013), pp. 32–3.

208 MAKING MAKERS

played a significant role in influencing Joly de Maizeroy's articulation of the concept of strategy in the late eighteenth century.[144] At the beginning of the twentieth century, the first English translations were produced by the soldier Everard Calthrop (1905) and the sinologist Lionel Giles (1910). It was only with the publication of Samuel B. Griffith's translation in 1963 that Sun Tzu became the object of a dramatic increase in popularity.[145] According to Tian Luo, the overall citation rate for English-language translations of *The Art of War* has been rising since 1945, with a notable increase in frequency since the end of the Cold War. Within this trend, Griffith's book constitutes the single most-cited translation of Sun Tzu's work.[146]

Griffith, a decorated United States Marine Corps veteran who had served several stints in China during his career and had learned Mandarin, undertook his translation as part of a doctoral study that he began at the University of Oxford after his retirement in 1956. His translation found a broader audience than previous efforts in part because it resonated during the early growth of strategic studies, offered ostensibly 'timeless' strategic precepts, and spoke to contemporary rather than historical concerns. As Peter Lorge has shown, Griffith, who had earlier translated Mao Tse Tung's writings on guerrilla warfare, was motivated to bring his work swiftly to publication so that soldiers and policy makers in the United States in particular might benefit from Sun Tzu's insights in contending with the challenges of revolutionary and irregular war. Moreover, just as had been the case with *Makers*, the presence of Liddell Hart loomed over the endeavour—indeed loomed larger still. Liddell Hart, who wrote the foreword to the 1963 publication, had cultivated the roles of mentor and unofficial advisor to Griffith during the latter's doctoral studies, which included reading and commenting on the drafts of his chapters. Through this engagement, the foreword, and Griffith's own study of Liddell Hart's work, the links between Liddell Hart, Sun Tzu, and the notion of 'indirect' strategy were strengthened in the final years of Liddell Hart's life.[147] Consequently, as Lorge concludes, 'the modern, Western reading, or perhaps Anglo-American reading of Sunzi put forth in 1963 has far more to do with B. H. Liddell Hart's thinking than with Master Sun's'.[148]

---

[144] A. Parr, *The Mandate of Heaven: Strategy, Revolution, and the First European Translation of Sunzi's Art of War (1772)* (Leiden & Boston: Brill, 2019), pp. 216–20.

[145] Sun Tzu (trans. S. Griffiths), *The Art of War* (Oxford: Clarendon Press, 1963), pp. 179–83. Griffiths offers a summary of earlier translations into other languages including German and Russian. For later English-language translations see T. Luo, *Translation, Reception and Canonization of the Art of War: Reviving Ancient Chinese Strategic Culture* (London: Routledge, 2022), pp. 6–8.

[146] Luo, *Translation, Reception and Canonization of the Art of War*, pp. 101–4. See also A. Corneli, 'Sun Tzu and the Indirect Strategy', *Rivista di Studi Politici Internazionali*, Vol. 54, No. 3 (July–September 1987), pp. 419–45. Corneli identifies two 'waves' of interest in Sun Tzu, the first in the 1960s, which he associates with the Griffith translation and interest in Maoist revolutionary war, and the second in the 1980s, which related rather to Sun Tzu's insights on intelligence and deception.

[147] See Lorge, *Sun Tzu in the West*, especially pp. 136–75.   [148] Ibid., p. 215.

THE RECEPTION OF PARET'S *MAKERS* AND ITS LEGACY   209

Whilst it is clear, then, that Sun Tzu's popularity grew dramatically after the publication of Earle's *Makers*, the total absence of reference to him in that book can still be considered somewhat curious. The earlier translation by Giles was available in the United States during the Second World War, and formed part of a miscellany entitled *Roots of Strategy*, published in 1944. Moreover, as Griffith himself pointed out, the lack of reference to Sun Tzu was particularly strange given that *Makers* was published at a time when 'United States forces were engaging the Japanese, who for centuries had been his most devoted disciples'.[149] If part of the answer to that question was that *Makers* focused on Japanese naval rather than military conduct, it still sits uneasily with Kiralfy's argument that the Japanese navy was 'the floating wing of a powerful army'.

Paret, meanwhile, although certainly acquainted with Griffith as early as the 1950s, when both men were studying for doctoral degrees in England, showed no interest in Sun Tzu in relation to his book.[150] Nevertheless, Paret's *Makers* did not neglect Sun Tzu entirely, with references to his thinking in both Carver's chapter on conventional war after 1945 and Shy and Collier's chapter on revolutionary war. Carver emphasized that during the Sino-Indian War of 1962 the Chinese had 'followed the tenets of Sun Tzu [...] that one should seek victory in the shortest possible time, with the least possible effort, and at the least cost in casualties to one's enemy, remembering that one had to continue to live next door to him when the fighting was over'.[151] Shy and Collier, on the other hand, went against the prevailing consensus by casting doubt on the relevance of the ancient thinker as a source of modern approaches, arguing that 'what remains unclear is how important Sun Tzu and the "mandate of heaven" have been in any continuing non-Western approach to the problem of revolutionary warfare' and suggesting that the 'Westernization' of such thought was more apparent.[152] They did, however, give ample attention to Mao Tse-tung, as well as Ho Chi Minh and Vo Nguyen Giap. Only Ropp's *Makers Revisited*, with its explicit incorporation of ancient and modern Chinese military thinking, incorporated both Sun Tzu and Mao.

Conclusion

Paret's book cemented the legacy of *Makers* in a manner that was not only intellectual but financial too. Ever since it first appeared on the market in the 1940s, *Makers* had enjoyed healthy sales. The rapid disappearance of the first run of ten thousand copies in just a few months after the publication of Earle's edition

---

[149] Sun Tzu (trans. S. Griffiths), *The Art of War*, p. 183.
[150] Lorge, *Sun Tzu in the West*, p. 144.
[151] M. Carver, 'Conventional Warfare in the Nuclear Age', in Paret, *Makers*, p. 800. There is a similar reference on p. 814.
[152] Shy and Collier, 'Revolutionary War', in Paret, *Makers*, p. 823.

210 MAKING MAKERS

foreshadowed the consistency with which the book would be bought in subsequent years. In the decades after 1945 *Makers* sold tens of thousands of copies, and its very marketability made it a candidate for updating. That much had been clear to Bailey as early as the 1960s, and it was no less so in the 1980s as sales continued at an impressive rate. Even before the release date in March 1986, the press had reason to feel confident that the new edition would usher in a new wave of interest in the book.[153] In January 1986, Elizabeth Gretz reported much interest and numerous pre-orders from attendees at the AHA conference the previous month.[154] In a draft letter to contributors, meanwhile, Loren Hoekzema noted that Oxford University Press would publish a British edition, that an arrangement had been made for 3,500 hardback copies to be sent to the Book of the Month Club, and that the press expected to sell around one thousand copies annually to the US Air Force Academy, to be followed by orders from other military educational institutions.[155] The pre-orders were matched by post-publication sales. Just two weeks after the book was released over 2,500 paperback and 345 hardback copies had been sold.[156] By June over 300 paperbacks were being sold weekly, with a new run of 10,000 copies scheduled for the following month.[157] These impressive figures continued throughout the rest of the decade. In February 1989 the press reprints manager described the book as 'one of the perennial stars of our list', noting that 1,060 hardback and 30,810 paperback copies had been sold by that date.[158]

When the successor appeared, reviewers noted that the original had been 'widely assigned in courses on military affairs and international relations', with the assumption that the new volume would occupy the same position.[159] Nevertheless, as Hoekzema's reference to ongoing US Air Force Academy orders indicated, the biggest single market for the book lay in military education. This, too, held a mirror to the Earle edition, which had benefitted from military institutions' expansion of educational provision to meet the demands of mobilization at scale. By the 1980s, however, PUP staff knew that military colleges and service academies were increasingly inclined to compile their own in-house readers, for which they would seek permission to reprint chapters from Earle's volume which

[153] Data from Google's Ngram Viewer suggests that references to the term 'Makers of Modern Strategy', already increasing into the 1980s, continued their upward trend after 1986, reaching a peak in 1991, which then gave way to a more sustained level of references throughout the 1990s, 2000s, and 2010s than had been the case in the thirty years prior. https://books.google.com/ngrams/graph?content= Makers+of+Modern+Strategy&year_start=1943&year_end=2019&corpus=26&smoothing=3.

[154] MLP, PUP, Box 350, Folder 2 (CO728), Elizabeth Gretz to Paret, 15 January 1986.

[155] MLP, PUP, Box 344, Folder 1 (CO728), Hoekzema. Draft letter to contributors. No date.

[156] MLP, PUP, Box 350, Folder 3 (CO728), Hoekzema to Paret, 14 April 1986.

[157] MLP, PUP, Box 350, Folder 3 (CO728), Hoekzema to Stephen Van Evera, 11 June 1986.

[158] MLP, PUP, Box 344, Folder 2 (CO728), Deborah Tegarden to Martin Alexander, 10 February 1989.

[159] Headrick, review of Paret, *Makers*, p. 139.

THE RECEPTION OF PARET'S *MAKERS* AND ITS LEGACY   211

they considered to have continuing utility.[160] The publication of Paret's *Makers* made such practices redundant whilst also creating a lucrative new revenue stream.

Such developments would suggest that *Makers* was more of a textbook than Paret cared to admit, and that it had been the same for the Earle edition. There is certainly an element of truth to this. Paret's *Makers* remains a widely cited work. Google Scholar, itself an incomplete record, lists some 1,435 citations for the overall work alone, as well as hundreds of additional citations for various chapters.[161] Yet whilst the volume has long provided a reference point for those seeking to build knowledge of war and strategy, it is equally clear that many of its chapters reflected scholarship already achieved, rather than the creation of new knowledge. On one level, this is an unsurprising deduction. After all, an established reputation in a particular field with corresponding publications formed the essential criteria by which potential contributors were judged. Yet this tendency was more pronounced in the case of the Paret edition than it had been for Earle's *Makers*, for which, it will be recalled, a number of authors were tasked to write to specific subjects in order to meet a need. Moreover, as the reaction to Michael Geyer's chapter in the Paret volume demonstrated, departure from this practice drew comment. Geyer's piece was praised by a number of reviewers partly because it was an outlier that exhibited the promise of future scholarship.

If this suggested that *Makers* was not, in itself, an innovative work of scholarship, it was still the case that the contributions of both published editions towards the establishment of a modern canon of strategic thinkers were significant. This did not mean, however, that the canon *Makers* presented was complete. As this chapter has shown, the books omitted consideration of certain figures whose reputations as strategic thinkers were either established or grew considerably in the post-world war era. In some cases—especially where such figures were bolstered by disciplinary currents external to the history of war—the reasons for this were understandable. In other cases, such omissions were a reflection of the intellectual interests, even limitations, of the editorial teams involved, in which case Ropp's *Makers Revisited* often provided an alternative vision. The same logic applied to the consideration of 'strategy' itself. In this respect, as we have seen, the difference between Earle and Paret was most pronounced. While Earle's paramount interest lay in strategy, which he used as the prism for an examination of

---

[160] MLP, PUP, Box 350, Folder 3 (CO728), Memorandum, Loren H to Joan Palatine cc: Herb, Mary Mellow, Eliz G., 10 December 1985. Memorandum, Loren H to Mary Mellow/Joan Palatine cc: Herb, Eliz Gretz, 18 December 1985.

[161] See https://scholar.google.com/scholar?hl=en&as_sdt=0%2C5&q=makers+of+modern+strat egy&btnG=.

212 MAKING MAKERS

war, Paret's interest always lay more in war than it did in strategy. For this reason, he offered far less in terms of the conceptualization of strategy than his predecessor. It is perhaps unsurprising, then, that those who look to Paret's *Makers* for an engagement with strategy ahead of war have sometimes found it a lesser offering.

Making Makers: The Past, the Present, and the Study of War. Michael P. M. Finch, Oxford University Press.
© Michael P. M. Finch 2024. DOI: 10.1093/9780191959257.003.0006

Conclusion

Historians of War and the Lineage of *Makers*

'Military history is now too important to be left to the military historians.'

—Sir Michael Howard, 2014[1]

Through an exploration of the projects led by Earle, Ropp, and Paret, this study has illuminated the ways in which *Makers of Modern Strategy* was conceived, created, and reconceived anew. In so doing it has sought to consider the twentieth-century *Makers* project in terms of both contexts and contingency. The contexts from which *Makers* emerged, which included the early twentieth-century growth of the notion that 'what touches all is the business of all' as much as the Second World War and the Cold War era, were important in setting the agendas followed within the pages of the published books, as well as Ropp's never-published companion. They formed as significant a part of the intellectual contours of the works as the individuals and events examined in the chapters of which they were comprised. Yet it seems equally apt to emphasize the roles of chance and the individual in the processes that made the books. This book, after all, has focused predominantly on a different set of 'makers': not practitioners or theorists as such—perhaps with the partial exception of Earle—but those scholars who made it their goal to corral contributors and played a significant role in curating the canon of strategic thinkers for the post-world war era. Theirs are not stories of the inevitable triumph of superior ideas. Success or failure was conditioned by choices, fortunes, and connections alongside talent, and the constellations that emerged from the groups to which those individuals belonged. Scholarship is subject to its own forms of friction, from which it cannot be separated any more than war itself.

In charting developments over the course of the twentieth century, this study has also underscored the centrality of history and historians to the *Makers* project. From Earle's original in the 1940s to Paret's successor in the 1980s, by way of

---

[1] Howard was endorsing the newly established *British Journal for Military History*. The full endorsement can be found here: https://bjmh.gold.ac.uk/about. See also M. Ford, 'Between Academe and the Armed Forces: Professional Boundary Disputes and the Future of Military History', *Ares & Athena*, Occasional Papers of the Centre for Historical Analysis and Conflict Research, No. 14 (February 2019), p. 30.

214   MAKING MAKERS

the unfulfilled 'revisit' led by Ropp, the concerns of such editor-historians consistently shaped the way in which *Makers* was made. Likewise, the roster of contributors enlisted by the editors heavily favoured historians. No matter that contemporary concerns ran through it—especially in its original form—*Makers* was made by historians. Indeed, it was no less historical for its contemporary dimensions. The lenses of past and present always play a role in the historian's understanding of their craft, even if the configuration of one and the other changes with time and in accordance with individual understanding.

This point bears emphasis less for reasons of proprietary amongst disciplines— although it is true that Earle, in particular, was cast in a variety of different academic guises in the decades after his death—and more for the place that *Makers* has come to assume in the foundations of strategic and security studies. In this regard, understanding *Makers* as a historical enterprise, the parameters and purview of which changed with the passage of decades, helps explain both the appeal of Earle's book and the sense amongst some that Paret's successor was a lesser publication. Indeed, it is somewhat paradoxical that the project as a whole can be understood to have become less interdisciplinary over time, not more. Of all *Makers*'s editors Earle was the most comfortable with a somewhat fluid disciplinary identity, the most prepared to speak and write not only as a historian but more broadly as a social scientist. If this was as much the consequence of a more general fluidity between disciplines which existed in the first decades of the twentieth century, by the time Paret took the reins of the successor volume disciplinary identities had become more sharply defined. It was hardly surprising, then, that his limited engagement with the concept of strategy, or the ways in which his mass of historian contributors tackled their subjects, might appear unsatisfactory to the non-historian.

If *Makers* was a historical project, however, it is equally important to note that it incorporated a number of different kinds of historian, all of whom brought distinct outlooks to bear on their work. This is true of the contributors, amongst whose ranks could be found historians of countries such as Germany, France, and Russia, alongside others. It is even more apparent in the case of the books' editors and would-be editors. As far as the original volume was concerned, John Keegan was quite right in surmising that 'there is a strong feel about the first edition of minds being wrenched out of their accustomed paths to confront subjects both unfamiliar and inimical to them.'[2] Earle, along with Craig, Gilbert, and many of those who wrote for the book, came to the subject of war from a different specialization. Earle's successor, Paret, although more overtly grounded in the history of war, was equally invested in the history of art and culture, and was careful to ensure that he struck a balance between the two areas of research across his

---

[2] J. Keegan, 'Grand Illusions', *The New York Review of Books*, 17 July 1986.

career. Ropp's collaborator, Don Schurman, was an imperial and maritime historian who also made a significant contribution to British political history through his work on the Disraeli project. What bound them together was their status as historians of war. Only Ropp, it seems, thought of himself as a military historian without reservation.

Ropp understood the transformative effect of the first edition, considering it a direct and powerful episode in his becoming a military historian. Yet he also believed—erroneously—that the shortcomings of Earle's volume could be partly explained by the same fact: had the contributors been military historians, with a better understanding of what that entailed, then the book that they produced would have been stronger for it. In fact, the diverse scholarly backgrounds of those involved with the project, rather than being a source of weakness, were a source of strength. The larger history of the *Makers* project suggests that success was more likely where the approach taken was widely conceived within the parameters of historical study, inclusive of some non-historians' perspectives, and not hamstrung by the more constrained connotations that were already well established in relation to military history by the 1940s. Military history was treated with a degree of circumspection by Earle, who understood it in terms of battles and operations and so as a smaller component within the larger study of war, although he thought the subject important enough to include as a specific chapter in his book. Paret tended to think along similar lines.

Yet Ropp's approach to military history was not constrained to the battlefield. He thought in terms which encompassed political, social, and economic factors. In this sense, the difference between his understanding of military history and Paret's understanding of the history of war was slight. It reflects a tension which existed in the historical study of war throughout the twentieth century and persists to the present day. Robert Citino, for example, has positioned military history in the twenty-first century as a 'big tent' incorporating 'war and society', 'traditional operational historians', and newer trends such as the history of memory and cultural approaches, such that military historians 'continue to pursue a research agenda that in its breadth and sophistication takes a back seat to no other area of historical inquiry'.[3] Such an interpretation, however, is highly reliant on the willingness of individuals to buy into it. There is no abiding consensus. The history of the *Makers* project offers a reflection of those concerns, underlining the importance that such distinctions held for many of those involved with it. As Paret stressed in 1986—keen to establish the intellectual lineage of *Makers* from Earle's concerns through to his own—the book had 'provided two generations of readers with a rich fund of knowledge and insight; for some, very likely, it has been their only encounter with the sophisticated study of war, as opposed to its

---

[3] Robert M. Citino, 'Military Histories Old and New: A Reintroduction', *The American Historical Review*, Vol. 112, No. 4 (October 2007), pp. 1070–1.

216 MAKING MAKERS

drum-and-bugle variety'.[4] This was not simply an exercise in petty semantics. Rather, it was a crucial component of scholarly identity, integral to defining approaches to the book and to the wider study of war.

At the same time the *Makers* project shows that, from Earle, through Ropp, to Paret, there existed a persistent desire to apply breadth to the historical study of war which belies the oft-presented narrative that positions the emergence of a 'new' military history in the 1960s in opposition to an older, purely operational, and therefore narrower approach. The editors of *Makers* in the post-Second World War era were alive to this fact. Thus Paret pointed out the inaccuracy of the word 'new' in describing such a historical approach, when in many respects it represented the continuation of something established much earlier in the century, rather than an abrupt rupture.[5] In a similar vein, Ropp's tendency to cast himself as a 'Delbrückian' scholar was highly significant in pointing to the deeper roots of the broad understanding of war. Taken as a whole, then, the makers of *Makers* appear as exemplars of a constituency of historians who dedicated themselves to understanding war in its fullest terms, incorporating the application of force, events far from the battlefield, and the link between the two, and who were often critical of those who wholly neglected either of those elements. The significance of this point should not be limited to the manner in which historians reflect on their appreciation of military history or the history of war, however it is termed. It also speaks to the role of history in strategic studies. As Hew Strachan has written, here there is 'the need for a much more creative engagement with the past, to recognise that the function of history in strategic studies is to encourage understanding, not to stress continuity or to show that history repeats itself (which it does not)'.[6] History provides foundations for the understanding of war and strategy, of course, but it is not limited to this. It seeks understanding in its own right.

None of this is to suggest that the historians under scrutiny here embraced all new developments in the field of history without reservation throughout their careers. On the contrary, they were marked by a scepticism towards the newest trends in historical scholarship and an often pessimistic attitude towards the future of the discipline as they reached retirement.[7] In the late 1970s Ropp

---

[4] P. Paret, 'Introduction', in P. Paret, *Makers of Modern Strategy: From Machiavelli to the Nuclear Age* (Princeton, NJ: Princeton University Press, 1986), p. 5.

[5] P. Paret, 'The New Military History', *Parameters*, Vol. 21 (autumn 1991), pp. 11, 15.

[6] H. Strachan, 'The Future of Strategic Studies: Lessons from the Last "Golden Age"', in R. Glenn (ed.), *New Directions in Strategic Thinking 2.0* (Canberra, ANU Press: 2018), pp. 164–5.

[7] Such views appeared to be relatively common amongst their peers. William Palmer concluded that in their retirement 'the members of this generation look uneasily at what their profession has become. Among the Americans, most are dismayed at the fragmentation of the profession, which they attribute primarily to the seeming obsession with race, gender, and ethnicity'. See W. Palmer, *Engagement with the Past: The Lives and Works of the World War II Generation of Historians* (Lexington, KY: University of Kentucky Press, 2001), p. 304.

HISTORIANS OF WAR AND THE LINEAGE OF *MAKERS*   217

expressed reservation towards a younger generation of historians 'giving their students an understructured [sic], overspecialized education, so that they can emote about their chosen few social problems'.[8] His attitude bore similarities to Craig, who was concerned for what he perceived as the fragmentation of the discipline, particularly as he approached his tenure as president of the American Historical Association. Returning from the 1981 AHA conference, Craig recorded that the programme had been 'too heavily slanted toward new subjects (women, alcohol, poverty, quantification, etc.)' to be interesting to him: 'I find that gap between the real world and the world that the new breed of historians inhabits troubling,' he wrote, 'and I wonder whether I should not attempt to deal with the problems this poses in my presidential address.'[9] The following year Craig delivered his lecture under the title 'The Historian and the Study of International Relations', which built on earlier thoughts he had entertained 'urging a return to diplomatic and military history after years of neglect'.[10] Likewise Paret sometimes lamented the apparent direction of academic history. In 1985, for example, reporting his experience of a conference to Gilbert, he bemoaned the audience's inability to grasp substantive issues and their preoccupation with less important details. 'I came away from the meeting,' he wrote 'with the feeling that communication between historians was almost impossible.'[11]

Much of this concern related back to anxieties over the status of war amongst the areas that historians were prepared to study. What Earle had enunciated in a more general sense—that scholars should not cede ground on account of their abhorrence of the subject, not least because they had something worthwhile to bring to the study of the phenomenon—was echoed by Ropp in his argument that historians should not turn away from it simply because they did not 'like it, or believe in it, or because it is very difficult for us to understand'. Paret, too, carried this sentiment through to his *Makers*, writing that 'the history of war should also be studied in order to understand the past itself. Historians have sometimes been reluctant to acknowledge this necessity [...] war is so tragic and intellectually and emotionally so disturbing that they have tended to sidestep it in their research.'[12] As this study has shown, these entreaties reflected, in turn, a widely held idea of

---

[8] DSP, Theodore Ropp, 'Clio and her Daughters. History 352.' [n.d.], 5.
[9] Craig Diaries, Tagebuch Vol. 36, Journal, September 1981–July 1982. 30 December 1981, pp. 137–8.
[10] Craig Diaries, Tagebuch Vol. 36, Journal, September 1981–July 1982. 28 October 1981, pp. 63–4. The address was subsequently published in the American Historical Review. As the title suggests, Craig's emphasis was placed more firmly on the history of international relations, diplomatic and political history, rather than military history. G. Craig, 'The Historian and the Study of International Relations', *The American Historical Review*, Vol. 88, No. 1 (February 1983), pp. 1–11. The address did not provoke quite the storm he had anticipated. Rather, Craig noted that such comments as he received 'were positive enough to encourage me to believe that its argument was not unpopular'. Craig Diaries, Tagebuch Vol. 37, Journal, July 1982–April 1983. 30 December 1982, p. 202.
[11] Paret to Gilbert, 28 June 1985. Gilbert Papers, Box 14/P, Paret. HI.
[12] Paret, 'Introduction', in Paret, *Makers of Modern Strategy*, p. 8.

218 MAKING MAKERS

the liberal aversion to the study of war, which was articulated in tandem with the very emergence of academic military history itself, and which persisted throughout the Cold War era to the present day. It is not difficult to find contemporary equivalents to Michael Howard's 1960s portrayal of 'a certain fear in academic circles, where military history is liable to be regarded as a handmaid of militarism, that its chief use may be propagandist and "myth making"'.[13]

Yet it is equally possible to draw from the history of the *Makers* project a quite contrary conclusion: that historians devoted themselves rather consistently to the study of war throughout the twentieth century, even if they did not do so in numbers that would have satisfied the most ardent advocates.[14] In his study of the 'World War II generation' of historians, William Palmer notes that whilst he had approached his research with the notion that 'the Depression was the single most powerful influence on this generation', responses from such figures as Lawrence Stone, William McNeill, Hugh Trevor-Roper, and Gordon Craig all indicated 'the importance of their military experience on their historical work'. Of their war

[13] M. Howard, 'The Use and Abuse of Military History', *Royal United Services Institution Journal* (1962), p. 4. See, for example, Jeremy Black's observation of the 'penchant for historians in other, allegedly more relevant, fields to dismiss much military history as irrelevant both to courses dealing with the broader development of Western or World civilization, and to their particular fields of expertise', or John Lynn's notion that opponents of the specialization believe 'that military historians must like, or at least approve of, war and its horrendous costs'. J. Black, *Rethinking Military History* (London: Routledge, 2004), p. 27. J. A. Lynn II, 'Breaching the Walls of Academe: The Purposes, Problems, and Prospects of Military History', *Academic Questions*, Vol. 21 (2008), p. 32.

[14] It may be objected that such a reading sits uneasily with the idea of the marginalization and dwindling numbers of self-described military historians in US universities. Yet military historians are far from the only group within the profession to perceive themselves as uniquely beleaguered, and are perhaps not even justified in lamenting a downward trend. For example, a 2015 study of historical specialization over a forty-year period from 1975, compiled using the American Historical Association's *Directory of History Departments, Historical Organizations and Historians*, demonstrated that military history was one of eleven topical fields which experienced growth over the entire period. By contrast, social, intellectual, and diplomatic history experienced sustained decline. Admittedly, the growth that military history experienced during the period at hand was gentle—the 2.6 per cent share of faculty registered in 2015 stood only slightly higher than it did in 1975—and the final figure came after a five-year period of relative contraction. Nevertheless, such figures reflect the reality that military history has long been a minority preserve within US universities, whilst also raising the question of what proportion of historical studies military history should occupy. See R. B. Townsend, 'The Rise and Decline of History Specializations over the Past 40 Years', *Perspectives on History: The Newsmagazine of the American Historical Association*, December 2015, https://www.historians.org/publications-and-directories/perspectives-on-history/december-2015/the-rise-and-decline-of-history-specializations-over-the-past-40-years. On the comparative travails of diplomatic history, see T. W. Zeller, 'The Diplomatic History Bandwagon: A State of the Field', *The Journal of American History*, Vol. 95, No. 4 (March 2009), pp. 1053–73, M. Trachtenberg, 'The State of International History', *E-International Relations*, 9 March 2013: https://www.e-ir.info/2013/03/09/the-state-of-international-history/, H. Brands, 'The Triumph and Tragedy of Diplomatic History', *Texas National Security Review*, Vol. 1, No. 1 (December 2017), pp. 132–43. Moreover, as the authors of a recent study on the place of the military in US civic education have shown, academics' perceptions of the health of the field are wedded to their definitions of military history. Self-described 'new military historians' felt far more positive about the present and the future than those 'traditional' military historians who saw their more battle-oriented colleagues retire without like-for-like replacements. D. Downs and I. Murtazashvili, *Arms and the University: Military Presence and the Civic Education of Non-Military Students* (Cambridge: Cambridge University Press, 2012), p. 284.

HISTORIANS OF WAR AND THE LINEAGE OF *MAKERS*   219

involvement he concluded: 'they fought, they analyzed, they taught, they wrote, and they volunteered on behalf of the crusade against fascism. [...] More subtly, many of them also developed further insights about their discipline from the crucible of military service.'[15] The persistence of *Makers* in the decades after the end of the Second World War ended attests to the long shadow cast by that experience. Moreover, those invested in the project, while often deeply sensitive to the idea of aversion to the study of war and fearful that the lack of military experience in subsequent generations would exacerbate this, were rather less cognizant of an alternate and enduring trend. The experience of war—whether direct or indirect—engendered opposition in some but sparked interest in others, and this applied both to teacher-scholars and their students.[16] There has long been a non-bellicose appetite for the study of war, and there will likely continue to be for as long as war exists.

Soon after the publication of the original edition, *Makers* began to acquire a reputation as a classic work on strategy and war. Certainly, by the 1960s such a judgement had become well set. It did not matter that parts of the book were outdated. They could be updated, or revisited, or remade. In the event, such goals proved more challenging than anticipated by those who wished to achieve them. Even so, it seemed to do more good than harm to the status of the original that a book written to meet the contemporary needs of the early 1940s was still being used in the late stages of the Cold War. Such longevity did little to diminish its 'classic' status, and by the time the successor finally arrived it inculcated a sense of legacy in those who appraised it. The academic lineage of the volumes only added to this notion. Almost all those concerned with sustaining the project after the Second World War had been directly involved in the first edition or were connected to it one step removed. Ropp the contributor attempted to become Ropp the editor. Paret was a close colleague of the associate editors who had benefited from their patronage, and had studied with Howard, whose approach to war studies had been influenced by the book. Gilbert and Craig, meanwhile, provided continuity from the original to the successor by maintaining their associate editor status, even if this obscured the true nature of their roles.

After the publication of Paret's *Makers* the personal connections that linked the old to the new began to fade away. At the same time, new developments strengthened the legacy of the book. Murray, Knox, and Bernstein's *The Making of Strategy* underlined the significance of Earle's and Paret's efforts, even as its editors

---

[15] Palmer, *Engagement with the Past*, pp. xiii, 87–8. Also pp. 72–88.

[16] Mac Coffman, it will be recalled, noted the boom in enrolments he experienced during the height of the Vietnam era protests. Similarly, after *Makers* Paret reflected that it was during the professional nadir of the 1960s 'that almost imperceptibly a change set in which now has gone far to raise interest in the historical interpretation of war and its attendant elements and placed it on a firmer, less contentious footing in American colleges and universities'. P. Paret, *Understanding War: Essays on Clausewitz and the History of Military Power* (Princeton, NJ: Princeton University Press, 1992), p. 220.

220   MAKING MAKERS

positioned their work as a partial reaction against them. Hanson, by contrast, presented his *Makers of Ancient Strategy* as a descendent, although it could be more accurately described as counterpart to publications that never sought to cast their consideration of strategy back into the classical world.

In the time that this book was written the legacy and lineage of *Makers* in the twenty-first century was cemented with the completion of a direct successor, Hal Brands's *The New Makers of Modern Strategy: From the Ancient World to the Digital Age*. As a scholar who embraces the study of history for the benefit of the present, it should come as little surprise that Brands positions his *Makers* with due regard for both the context of his predecessors and the circumstances under which his own was created.[17] His book represents a 'third generation' that 'comes as the shadows cast by competition and conflict are growing longer and it often seems that authoritarian darkness is drawing near'.[18] His injunction that 'serious people can no longer believe, as was sometimes argued a generation ago, that war—and perhaps strategy itself—have become passé in an era of post-Cold War peace' carries forward his predecessors' insistence on the importance of the 'serious' or 'sophisticated' study of war.[19] Yet his faith in the power of historical understanding to ameliorate a future course—'the better we understand the history of strategy, the more likely we are, in the exacting future that awaits us, to get it right'—as much as his presentation of strategy as existing beyond war and encompassing '*all* forms of power to prosper in an unruly world' mark him as an inheritor of Earle rather than Paret.[20] If, in this sense, *The New Makers* represents a return to the tone and vision of the original, in another respect it marks a departure. By embracing a scope that runs from antiquity to the twenty-first century, it is able to encompass both Thucydides and Sun Tzu, amongst other figures quite unknown to Earle's and Paret's books, in a manner that only Ropp's *Makers Revisited* came close to emulating. In this way it resolves an intellectual bifurcation, bringing these crucial figures in the post-Second World War canon of strategic thinkers together with those long championed by historians of war under a single cover. *Makers* evolves.

Making Makers: The Past, the Present, and the Study of War. Michael P. M. Finch, Oxford University Press.
© Michael P. M. Finch 2024. DOI: 10.1093/9780191959257.003.0007

---

[17] For Brands's approach to history and contemporary challenges see C. Edel and H. Brands, *The Lessons of Tragedy: Statecraft and World Order* (New Haven, CT: Yale University Press, 2019), H. Brands, *The Twilight Struggle: What the Cold War Teaches Us about Great-Power Rivalry Today* (New Haven, CT: Yale University Press, 2022).

[18] H. Brands, 'Introduction. The Indispensable Art: Three Generations of *Makers of Modern Strategy*', in H. Brands (ed.), *The New Makers of Modern Strategy: From the Ancient World to the Digital Age* (Princeton, NJ: Princeton University Press, 2023), p. 13.

[19] Ibid., p. 2.   [20] Ibid., pp. 1, 13.

APPENDIX

Contributors and Collaborators in the *Makers* Project, 1943–86

This appendix contains an alphabetized collection of biographical sketches of individuals associated with the Earle and Paret editions of *Makers of Modern Strategy*, as well as Ropp's *Makers of Modern Strategy Revisited*. It includes all those who wrote for those projects, members of Earle's seminar at the Institute for Advanced Study, and a number of other figures who did not fit into either category but who played a significant role with regard to one or more of the books. Although in most cases I have been able to collate information to form rounded summaries of an individual's career and scholarly works, information on some of the more obscure figures has been harder to source, and I have refrained from including certain elements—such as dates of birth or death—unless I had a high degree of certainty that the information was correct. The preponderance of historians, or the historically trained, is a notable feature of this list, although equally noteworthy is the range of historical specialisms in evidence.

Albion, Robert G. (1896–1983): member of Earle's seminar 1941–2. Studied at Bowdoin College then served in the US Army during the First World War, before undertaking a PhD in history at Harvard University, which he completed in 1924. Joined Princeton University in 1922, becoming professor and assistant dean of the Faculty of History, 1929–43. He was Assistant Director of Naval History and Historian of Naval Administration for the Department of the Navy, 1943–50. Returned to Harvard in 1948 as Gardiner Professor of Oceanic History and Affairs, retiring as emeritus professor in 1963. His works included *Forests and Sea Power: The Timber Problem of the Royal Navy* (1926), *Sea Lanes in Wartime: The American Experience* (1942, with Jennie Barnes Pope), and *Makers of Naval Policy, 1798–1947* (1980, edited by Rowena Reed).

Alexander, Martin (b. 1955): contributor to Paret's *Makers*. Studied for a DPhil in history at the University of Oxford, completed in 1983. He was lecturer in French and British History at Southampton University, 1982–93, Professor of Contemporary History and Politics, University of Salford, 1993–2001, then Professor of International Relations, Aberystwyth University until his retirement, then becoming emeritus professor. His works include *The Republic in Danger: General Maurice Gamelin and the Politics of French Defence, 1933–1939* (1993), *France and the Algerian War, 1954–1962: Strategy, Operations and Diplomacy* (2002, co-edited with John F. V. Keiger), and *Anglo-French Defence Relations between the Wars* (2002, co-edited with William Philpott).

Ayedelotte, Frank (1880–1956): second director of the Institute for Advanced Study, 1939–47. Studied at Indiana University, then taught in Louisville, Kentucky, where he met and was tutored by Abraham Flexner, prior to winning a Rhodes Scholarship to Oxford (1905–7). Taught at Indiana University, then in 1915 became a professor of English at the Massachusetts Institute of Technology. From 1921 to 1939 he was president of Swarthmore College, Pennsylvania. Guided the IAS out of its early period of financial instability, supported Earle in his endeavours, and encouraged IAS faculty and members to support the Allied war effort.

222 MAKING MAKERS

Bailey, Herbert S. (1921–2011): director of the Princeton University Press. Joined the US Navy after graduation from Princeton University in 1942. Instructed officers in the use of radar at Harvard and Princeton and wrote a radar manual for instructors. At age thirty-two, succeeded Datus Smith as director of the Princeton University Press, where he worked from 1946 until his retirement in 1986. His longstanding interest in *Makers of Modern Strategy* was a crucial factor in the development and publication of the Paret edition.

Bailey, Thomas A. (1902–83): member of Earle's seminar, 1939–40. Obtained his undergraduate and postgraduate qualifications from Stanford University, completing a PhD in history in 1927. Taught at the University of Hawaii, 1927–30, then returned to Stanford, where he became Margaret Byrne Professor of American History, retiring in 1968. He was a member of the IAS, 1939–40. A political and diplomatic historian of the United States, he was the author of numerous works including *Theodore Roosevelt and the Japanese-American Crisis* (1934), *Woodrow Wilson and the Lost Peace* (1944), *Woodrow Wilson and the Great Betrayal* (1945), *The Man in the Street* (1948), and the high school textbook *The American Pageant* (1956).

Bond, Brian (b. 1936): contributor to Paret's *Makers*. Studied Modern History at the University of Oxford 1956–9, then for an MA at King's College London, awarded in 1962. His thesis was supervised by Sir Michael Howard. Lecturer at the University of Exeter in 1962, he then spent four years as a lecturer at the University of Liverpool, before joining the Department of War Studies at King's in 1966. He remained at King's for the rest of his career, becoming professor in 1986 and emeritus professor in 2001. In 1996 he was made a fellow of King's College London. A specialist in British military history, his publications include *The Victorian Army and the Staff College* (1972) and *The Unquiet Western Front* (2002). As a young man, he forged a close relationship with Sir Basil Liddell Hart. After the latter's death he published *Liddell Hart: A Study of His Military Thought* (1977).

Brodie, Bernard (1910–78): member of Earle's seminar, 1940–1. Studied at the University of Chicago, obtaining a PhD in 1940, then taught at Dartmouth College, 1941–3. In 1943 he joined the US Naval Reserve and then served in the Office of the Chief of Naval Operations. In 1945 he became an associate professor of International Relations at Yale University. In 1951 he left Yale to become a senior staff member at the RAND corporation, before finally moving to UCLA in 1966 as professor of Political Science, where he remained until retirement in 1977. A pioneering figure in strategic studies, he began his career as a specialist in naval strategy, then directed his focus on nuclear strategy. His works include *Sea Power in the Machine Age* (1941), *A Layman's Guide to Naval Strategy* (1942), *The Absolute Weapon* (ed. 1946), and *Strategy in the Missile Age* (1959).

Brinton, Crane (1898–1968): contributor to Earle's *Makers*. After undergraduate studies at Harvard University, won a Rhodes Scholarship to the University of Oxford, where he studied for a PhD, which he received in 1923. He then returned to Harvard, where he taught throughout his career, becoming McLean Professor of Ancient and Modern History from 1946 until his death. Principally known as a historian of France, his research interests also incorporated British and American history. His works include *The Jacobins* (1930), *The Lives of Talleyrand* (1936), *The Anatomy of Revolution* (1938), and *Ideas and Men: The Story of Western Thought* (1950).

Carver, Michael (Field Marshal Lord) (1915–2001): contributor to Paret's *Makers*. Joined the British Army after leaving school, passing out from Sandhurst at the top of his class in 1934 and commissioning into the Royal Tank Corps. During the Second World War he was a staff officer in the Western Desert campaign, then commanded armour at the regimental and then brigade level during the Italian campaign, the Normandy campaign, and the advance into Germany. After the war he held a variety of staff and command posts, rising to become Chief of the General Staff, 1971–3, and then Chief of the Defence Staff

CONTRIBUTORS AND COLLABORATORS, 1943–86   223

until his retirement in 1976. He was made a life peer, Baron Carver, in 1977. He wrote numerous books on twentieth-century military history, including *El Alamein* (1962), *Tobruk* (1964), and *War since 1945* (1980).

Chew, Ernest (b. 1942): contributor to Ropp's *Makers Revisited* and member of Ropp's Singapore seminar. A graduate of the University of Singapore, he studied for a PhD in History at the University of Cambridge, completed in 1970. Joined the University of Singapore in 1970, succeeding Wong Lin Ken as head of the Department of History, 1983–92, and then serving as dean of the Faculty of Arts and Social Sciences, 1991–7. Editor, with Edwin Lee, of *A History of Singapore* (1991).

Chinard, Gilbert (1881–1972): member of Earle's seminar 1939–40. Studied at the universities of Poitiers and Bordeaux, then emigrated to the USA in 1908, where he taught at the City College of New York, then at Brown University, 1908–12, and the University of California, Berkeley, 1912–19. At Johns Hopkins University, 1919–36, he was professor of French and comparative literature, and then Pyne Professor of French at Princeton University, 1937–50. On retirement he was made emeritus professor, and was a member of the IAS for Fall term 1950. A literary historian, his works include *L'exotisme américain dans l'oeuvre de Chateaubriand* (1918), *Thomas Jefferson, the Apostle of Americanism* (1929), and *Honest John Adams* (1933).

Chung, Ong Chit (1949–2008): contributor to Ropp's *Makers Revisited* and member of Ropp's Singapore seminar. Studied at the University of Singapore, then for an MA in Military History at Duke University, and finally for a PhD in International History at the London School of Economics, 1981–5. Lecturer and then senior lecturer in History at the National University of Singapore, 1978–93, he became a Member of the Parliament of Singapore in 1988, holding a seat for almost all of the following twenty years. Author of *The Landward Defence of Singapore* (1988) and *Operation Matador: Britain's War Plans against the Japanese, 1918–1941* (1997). After his death the Department of History, National University of Singapore established a memorial scholarship in his name.

Collier, Thomas W. (1927–2022): contributor to Paret's *Makers*. Enlisted with the USMC in 1944, attended West Point, 1948–52, and served three tours in Vietnam between 1962 and 1967. Taught at West Point then retired as a lieutenant-colonel in 1972. Worked as a civilian historian for the United States European Command Headquarters in Stuttgart, Germany, 1972–8. Studied for, but did not complete, a PhD in History at the University of Michigan. Taught at the University of Michigan and the University of Eastern Michigan.

Cot, Pierre (1895–1977): member of Earle's seminar, spring 1941. French radical politician and a leading figure in the French Popular Front of the 1930s. Deputy for Savoy in the National Assembly, he was Minister for Air under the Daladier ministry, 1933–4, and again under the first Blum ministry, 1936–7. He was Minister for Commerce under the second Blum ministry, 1938. With the fall of France, he went first to the United Kingdom, then to the USA, where he taught at Yale. In the USA he had contacts with Soviet intelligence and has been accused of being a Soviet spy. In 1943 he was made a member of the French Committee of National Liberation and in 1944 he was sent by de Gaulle on a mission to the USSR. In 1945 he once again became a member of the National Assembly, losing his seat in 1958. He was re-elected a final time in 1967–8.

Craig, Gordon (1913–2005): editorial assistant on Earle's *Makers* and later Paret's *Makers*. Completed a PhD in History at Princeton University in 1941, then taught at Yale and Princeton until 1942, when he took a job as an analyst in the Office of the Coordination of Information at the OSS, then worked for the State Department. Returned to teaching at Princeton in early 1943 at which point he became involved in the *Makers* project. Joined the United States Marine Corps in 1944, becoming an intelligence officer, but postings kept him in the USA until August 1945. In 1946 became an associate professor of History at

224   MAKING MAKERS

Princeton, then in 1961 he moved to Stanford University where he became J. E. Wallace Sterling Professor of History in 1969. He was made emeritus professor in 1979. Trained as a diplomatic historian, he became a specialist in Germany history. His numerous works include *The Politics of the Prussian Army 1640–1945* (1955), *The Germans* (1981), and *The Triumph of Liberalism: Zürich in the Golden Age, 1830–1869* (1988). His involvement with Paret's *Makers* was more prolonged and influential than with Earle's book.

Crowl, Phillip A. (1914–91): contributor to Paret's *Makers*. Studied at Swarthmore College, Yale University, and the University of Iowa, then obtained a PhD from Johns Hopkins University in 1942. During the Second World War served as a naval officer in the Pacific theatre. After the war taught at Princeton University, was a historian in the Office of the Chief of Military History, Department of the Army, and an intelligence officer in the Department of State. He was professor of History at the University of Nebraska, 1967–73. In 1973 he joined the US Naval War College, becoming Ernest J. King Professor of Maritime History, before retiring in 1980 as emeritus professor. His works include *Maryland during and after the Revolution* (1943), *The Campaign in the Marianas* (1960), *The U.S. Marines and Amphibious War* (1951, with Jeter A. Isely), and *Seizure of the Gilberts and Marianas* (1955, with E. G. Love).

Dennery, Etienne (1903–79): member of Earle's seminar, 1940–1. Studied history and geography at the École Normale Supérieure, 1923–6. Taught at the École libre des sciences politiques, the École des hautes études commerciales, and the Institut des hautes études internationales. Co-founder and secretary-general of the Centre d'études de politique étrangère, 1935–40. Member of the IAS, 1940–1. Member of de Gaulle's France Libre. After the war, worked for the French Ministry of Foreign Affairs, served as ambassador to Poland, 1950–4, Switzerland, 1954–61, and Japan, 1961–4, finally becoming head of the Bibliothèque Nationale, 1964–75. Author of *Asia's Teeming Millions and Its Problems for the West* (1931).

DeWeerd, Harvey (1902–79): contributor to Earle's *Makers*. Member of Earle's seminar, 1941–2. A graduate of Hope College in 1924, he completed a master's degree at the University of Michigan in 1925. He taught at Colorado Agricultural College and Michigan State University, before joining Denison University in 1929 as an assistant professor of History. At Denison, he studied for a PhD at the University of Michigan, which was awarded in 1937. In 1942 he was commissioned in the US Army and assigned as an associate editor of *Infantry Journal*, 1942–5. In 1946 he joined the University of Missouri as professor of History, leaving in 1952 for a position as a senior staff member with the RAND corporation, where he remained until his retirement in 1967. His works include *Great Soldiers of the Two World Wars* (1941), *Great Soldiers of World War II* (1944), and *President Wilson Fights His War* (1968).

Earle, Edward Mead (1894–1954): editor of *Makers of Modern Strategy: Military Thought from Machiavelli to Hitler* (1943). Joined the US Army in 1917 after finishing undergraduate study at Columbia University, but did not fight in Europe. Briefly worked in banking before returning to graduate study at Columbia and completing a PhD in History in 1923. Became professor of history at Columbia, but was compelled to resign due to ill health. Returned to teaching in the 1930s at Barnard College. Hired by Abraham Flexner as one of the first professors in the newly constituted School of Economics and Politics at the IAS, where he remained until his death. Established seminar group on the 'military and foreign policies of the United States' in 1939, which ran throughout the Second World War under various monikers. Served the US war effort in various capacities, working with the Office of Strategic Services and the USAAF on strategic bombing. His work with the latter took him to the United Kingdom in 1944 and Germany in 1945. At the conclusion of the war he was invited to undertake a multi-volume operational history of the USAAF in Europe. Awarded the US Presidential Medal for Merit and the French Legion d'Honneur

CONTRIBUTORS AND COLLABORATORS, 1943–86   225

for his wartime activities. Although he wrote a number of essays, articles, and pamphlets, his only research monograph was the book of his dissertation, *Turkey, the Great Powers, and the Bagdad Railway* (1924). Aside from *Makers*, he also edited *Modern France: Problems of the Third and Fourth Republics* (1951).

Flexner, Abraham (1866–1959): founding director of the Institute for Advanced Study, 1930–9. Studied at Johns Hopkins University and began his career as a teacher, founding an experimental school in his hometown of Louisville, Kentucky in the 1890s. He worked for the Carnegie Foundation, publishing an influential report on the state of medical education in the USA and Canada, then between 1912 and 1928 he worked for the Rockefeller Foundation. During the 1930s he worked with benefactors Louis Bamburger and Caroline Bamburger Fuld to establish the Institute for Advanced Study, Princeton. Here he was responsible for hiring Earle, although the two developed a somewhat fractious relationship thereafter. Forced out of the IAS in 1939, in his retirement he remained active as a writer and consultant.

Fox, William T. R. (1912–88): member of Earle's seminar, 1941–2. Studied at Haverford College, then at the University of Chicago, obtaining a PhD in 1940. Worked as a research assistant to Quincy Wright at Chicago, taught at Princeton University, 1941–3, then Yale University, 1943–50. In 1950 he joined Columbia University, becoming the inaugural director of the Institute of War and Peace Studies in 1951 and, in 1968, James T. Shotwell Professor of International Relations. He remained at Columbia until his retirement in 1980, becoming emeritus professor. A scholar of international relations, his works include *The Super-Powers: The United States, Britain, and the Soviet Union—Their Responsibility for Peace* (1944), *The American Study of International Relations* (1967), and *A Continent Apart: The United States and Canada* (1985). He was also a contributor to Bernard Brodie's *The Absolute Weapon* (1946).

Freedman, Sir Lawrence (b. 1948): contributor to Paret's *Makers*. Studied at the universities of Manchester and York before completing a DPhil at the University of Oxford in 1975, working under the supervision of Sir Michael Howard. He joined King's College London as professor and head of the Department of War Studies, 1982–97, later serving as head of the School of Social Science and Public Policy, 2000–3, and finally university vice principal, 2003–13. On retirement in 2014 he was made professor emeritus, and in 1992 was made a fellow of King's College London. Began his career as a specialist in nuclear strategy, publishing *The Evolution of Nuclear Strategy* (1981), later wrote the *Official History of the Falklands Campaign* (2 vols., 2005), and *Strategy: A History* (2013). Between 2009 and 2016 he was a member of the committee of the Chilcot Inquiry into the Iraq War.

Geyer, Michael (b. 1947): contributor to Paret's *Makers*. Earned a PhD from Albert Ludwigs University, Freiburg, 1976. From there went to St Anthony's College, University of Oxford, as a postdoctoral researcher, then taught at the University of Michigan in Ann Arbor. Joined the University of Chicago in 1986, becoming Samuel N. Harper Professor of German and European History. A senior fellow of the American Academy in Berlin, he is now professor emeritus. His works include *A Shattered Past: Reconstructing German Histories* (2002, with Konrad Jarausch), *War and Terror in Contemporary and Historical Perspective* (2003, ed.), and *Beyond Totalitarianism: Stalinism and Nazism Compared* (2009, edited with Sheila Fitzpatrick).

Gilbert, Felix (1905–91): editorial assistant on Earle's *Makers* and later Paret's *Makers*. Member of Earle's seminar, 1939–42. Studied under Friedrich Meinecke at the University of Berlin, completing a doctoral study on Johann Gustav Droysen in 1931. Thereafter became a specialist in the history of the Italian Renaissance, whose notable works include *Machiavelli and Guicciardini: Politics and History in Sixteenth Century Florence* (1965) and *The Pope, His Banker and Venice* (1980). He left Germany for the United Kingdom in 1933

226   MAKING MAKERS

but was unable to secure an academic post and moved on to the United States in 1936. There he taught at Scripps College, California, before going to the IAS in 1939. Worked for the Central European Section of the Research and Analysis Branch at the OSS, 1943–5, which sent him to London and Paris in 1944. In 1945 work with the State Department took him to Germany to observe reconstruction work. Joined Bryn Mawr College in 1946 and remained there until 1962, when he returned to the IAS as a professor, remaining there for the rest of his life. He played an influential role in the early shaping of the book project that would become *Makers* and provided the bulk of editorial assistance to Earle, handing the role over to Craig in its closing stages. His influence and interest in Paret's *Makers* project was less pronounced.

Gottmann, Jean (1915–94): contributor to Earle's *Makers*, and member of Earle's seminar, 1942. Born in Kharkiv, Ukraine to parents killed during the Russian revolution, he was raised by an aunt who took him to Paris. Studied history and geography at the Sorbonne, where he was appointed a research assistant in human geography in 1937. Fled Paris after the Battle of France, on account of his Jewish heritage, arriving in the USA in December 1941. After a year at the IAS he taught at Johns Hopkins University from 1943 to 1948. A member of the Free French organization, in 1945 he returned to France to work for the minister of national economy. Taught at the Institut d'Etudes Politique at the University of Paris from 1948 to 1956, then became research director of the Twentieth Century Fund at New York from 1956 to 1961. Became professor of Geography at the Ecole des Hautes Etudes between 1960 and 1984, and professor of Geography and a fellow of Hertford College, University of Oxford, from 1968 to 1983. Best known for his book *Megalopolis: The Urbanized Northeastern Seaboard of the United States* (1961).

Guerlac, Henry (1910–85): contributor to Earle's *Makers* whose essay was reprinted in Paret's *Makers*. Historian of science who studied at Cornell University and gained a doctorate from Harvard University in 1941. Taught at Harvard and the University of Wisconsin, and was historian at the Radiation Laboratory of MIT. In 1946 returned to Cornell, where he was made Goldwin Smith Professor of the History of Science in 1964. The son of French emigrant who had also been a professor at Cornell, much of his work focused on France, notably his book *Lavoisier: The Crucial Year*, which won the Pfizer Prize in 1959. He retired in 1975 and was award the Chevalier de la Légion d'Honneur by the French government in 1982. His doctoral student and teaching assistant Harry S. Woolf went on to become the fifth director of the IAS.

Herz, John H. (1908–2005): member of Earle's seminar, 1939–40. Studied at the universities of Freiburg, Heidelberg, and Berlin, then obtained a PhD in public law from the University of Cologne, 1931. Worked as a clerk in Dusseldorf, 1931–3. Migrated to Switzerland in 1935 to escape Nazi oppression, then in 1938 moved to the USA where he was a member of the IAS. During the Second World War he was a political analyst in the Central European Section of the Office of Strategic Services, and after the war worked for the Intelligence and Research Office of the Department of State. Taught at Howard University, 1941–52, then joined the City College of New York, retiring in 1977 as emeritus professor. A scholar of international relations, his works include *Political Realism and Political Idealism* (1951), *Major Foreign Powers* (1952, edited with Gwendolen Carter), and 'Idealist Internationalism and the Security Dilemma' in *World Politics,* Vol. 2, No. 2.

Holborn, Hajo (1902–69): contributor to Earle's *Makers*. A specialist in the history of modern Germany, he gained a doctorate in history from the University of Berlin in 1924 for a study on Bismarck and Turkey (1878–1890) supervised by Friedrich Meinecke, and his habilitation from the University of Heidelberg in 1926. Lecturer at the University of Heidelberg, 1926–31, and then at the University of Berlin, 1931–3, in the latter period he was also Carnegie Professor of History and International Relations at the Deutsche

CONTRIBUTORS AND COLLABORATORS, 1943–86   227

Hochschule für Politik. His departure from Germany in 1933 was heavily influenced by consideration of his Jewish wife, Annemarie. Arriving in the USA in 1934 he joined Yale University, where he worked for the next thirty-five years, becoming Randolph Townsend Professor of History in 1946 and then Sterling Professor of History from 1959 until his death. Between 1943 and 1945 worked for the Research and Analysis Branch of the Office of Strategic Services.

Howard, Sir Michael (1922–2019): contributor to Paret's *Makers*. Served with the Coldstream Guards in the Second World War and was awarded the Military Cross for actions at Monte Cassino. Returned to Oxford in 1945 to complete his undergraduate degree, then took a position as an assistant lecturer in History (later full lecturer) at King's College London. In 1953 became lecturer in Military Studies (later War Studies) and worked to found the Department of War Studies, which was established in 1961. He was made professor in 1964, then joined the University of Oxford in 1968, appointed first as fellow in Higher Defence Studies, then Chichele Professor of the History of War in 1977, and finally Regius Professor of Modern History in 1980. From 1989 to 1993 he was Robert A. Lovett Professor of Military and Naval History at Yale University. He was a founder of the Institute for Strategic Studies (later the International Institute for Strategic Studies) in 1958. Howard's scholarship ranged across the fields of military history and strategic studies. His book *The Franco-Prussian War* (1961) is considered a pioneering work of post-Second World War 'war and society' scholarship. Doctoral supervisor to Peter Paret during the late 1950s, he later worked with his former student on a new translation of Carl von Clausewitz's *On War* (1976). During the preparation of Paret's *Makers* he was an important consultative figure, who suggested a number of the chapter authors.

Hubbard, Deborah A. (1916–2011): member of Earle's seminar, 1941–2. Graduated from Bryn Mawr College, 1938. Member of staff of the American Council, Institute of Pacific Relations, 1939–40. Attended the Havana Conference in 1940. Worked as a research assistant in the School of Economics and Politics at the IAS, 1940–2. Her duties included contributing to the preparation of the *War and National Policy* (1942) syllabus edited by Grayson Kirk and Richard Poate Stebbins. Married in July 1942, and described in her New York Times wedding announcement of 25 June 1942 as 'a student and writer on international affairs and economics'.

James, Doris Clayton (1931–2004): contributor to Paret's *Makers*. Graduated from Southwestern at Memphis (now Rhodes College) in 1953, he completed a PhD at the University of Texas at Austin in 1964. He taught at Louisiana State University of Alexandria, then in 1964 he was appointed assistant professor at Mankato State College, Minnesota (now Minnesota State University, Mankato). In 1965 he went to Mississippi State University, becoming distinguished professor in 1978, before moving to the Virginia Military Institute in 1988, where he was John Biggs Chair in Military History until his retirement in 1996. His works include *Antebellum Natchez* (1968), *The Years of MacArthur* (3 vols., 1970–85), and *Refighting the Last War: Command and Crisis in Korea, 1950–1953* (with Anne Sharp Wells, 1992).

Kahn, Robert A.: member of Earle's seminar, 1941–2. Obtained a Doctor of Law from the University of Vienna in 1930, and later graduated from the Columbia University School of Library Service in 1940. He wrote essays on public law and was listed by Earle as a 'bibliographical and research assistant' in a wartime report to the IAS director.

Ken, Wong Lin (1931–83): studied at the University of Malaya, then undertook a PhD in History, which he completed in 1959, thereafter becoming a lecturer at the University of Singapore. He was Singapore's first ambassador to the United States, 1967–8. Elected to the Parliament of Singapore, 1968–76, he served as Minister for Home Affairs, 1970–2. In 1973 he became head of the Department of History at the National University of Singapore,

228 MAKING MAKERS

holding the position until his death in 1983. Author of *The Trade of Singapore, 1819–69* (1961) and *The Malayan Tin Industry to 1914* (1965). Helped facilitate Ropp and Schurman's stay in Singapore and their seminar series at the university.

Kiralfy, Alexander (1899–1981): contributor to Earle's *Makers*. Son of the impresario Bolossy Kiralfy, he joined Paramount Pictures International in the 1920s and worked in the Statistical Unit of the Accounts and Statistical Department until his retirement in 1967. Alongside this work he maintained an interest in military and naval affairs, particularly in relation to the Pacific, researching and writing articles and serving as military analyst for *Asia* magazine during the Second World War. He was the author of *Victory in the Pacific: How We Must Defeat Japan* (1942).

Kovacs, Arpad: contributor to Earle's *Makers* who wrote under the pseudonym Irving M. Gibson. Born in 1898, he served in the Austro-Hungarian army during the First World War. He obtained a PhD in History from the University of Chicago in 1934 for a dissertation entitled 'Nation in Arms and Balance of Power: The Interaction of German Military Legislation and European Politics, 1866–1914'. He became professor of History at St John's University, Brooklyn. A specialist in European and particularly French military affairs, he also published *The Twentieth Century: An Abstract of the Main Events Which Have Shaped Our Times* (1960), *Let Freedom Ring* (1961), and *Saint Vincent de Paul* (1961).

Lauterbach, Albert T. (1904–86): member of Earle's seminar, 1940–1. Earned a PhD from the University of Vienna, 1925, and was a member of the IAS, 1940–1. Professor of Economics at Sarah Lawrence College, he was made professor emeritus in 1972. His works include *Economics in Uniform: Military Economy and Social Structure* (1943), *Economic Security and Individual Freedom: Can We Have Both?* (1948), *Enterprise in Latin America: Business Attitudes in a Developing Economy* (1966), and *Psychological Challenges to Modernization* (1972).

Lockwood, William W. (1906–78): member of Earle's seminar, 1940–1. Graduated from DePauw University in 1927, he went on to study Economics at Harvard, earning an MA in 1929. He taught at Bowdoin College, 1929–30. He then worked for the Institute of Pacific Relations, first as research secretary, 1935–40, then executive secretary, 1941–3. He was a member of the IAS, 1939–41. During the Second World War he served with the US Army, overseeing research and analysis for the Office of Strategic Services unit attached to Chennault's 14th Air Force in Kunming, China. In 1946 he joined Princeton University, rising to become professor of Politics and International Affairs by 1955—having completed his interrupted Harvard University PhD in 1950—and retiring in 1971. A specialist in Asian economics and politics, he was the author of *The Economic Development of Japan* (1954).

Mantoux, Etienne (1913–45): contributor to Earle's *Makers*, and member of Earle's seminar, 1941–2. French economist and air force officer who fought in the Battle of France. Travelled to the USA in summer 1941 under a Rockefeller Fellowship to the IAS. Joined the Free French forces in early 1943 and fought in the Western European campaign. Died in Germany on 29 April 1945. His book, *The Carthaginian Peace, or The Economic Consequences of Mr Keynes* was published posthumously in 1946.

Matloff, Maurice (1915–93): contributor to Paret's *Makers*. Graduated from Columbia University in 1936 and taught at Brooklyn College, before enrolling in the US Army during the Second World War. After the war he joined the US Army Center of Military History as a civilian and completed his PhD at Harvard University in 1956. From 1970 until his retirement in 1981 he was chief historian at the Center of Military History. After retirement he taught at Georgetown University until 1992. He was sole author of *Strategic Planning for Coalition Warfare, 1943–1944* (1959) and co-author of *Strategic Planning for Coalition Warfare, 1941–1942* (1953).

CONTRIBUTORS AND COLLABORATORS, 1943–86   229

McIsaac, David (1935–2014): contributor to Ropp's *Makers Revisited* and to Paret's *Makers*. Studied history at Trinity College and graduated from its Air Force ROTC programme in 1957, then went on to postgraduate study at Yale University in 1958, before undertaking a PhD in history at Duke University, completed in 1970. Served in Vietnam in 1971, then joined the History Department at the Air Force Academy. He was chief of military history at the Air War College, 1979–81, then joined the Air Power Research Institute, Air University, 1982–91. He retired as a lieutenant colonel. Author of *Strategic Bombing in World War Two: The Story of the United States Strategic Bombing Survey* (1976).

Menderhausen, Horst (1911–2003): member of Earle's seminar, autumn 1940. Studied at the universities of Freiburg, Berlin, and Heidelberg, before undertaking a PhD at the University of Geneva, completed in 1937. He then held a Rockefeller Fellowship, which allowed him to study in Norway and the United States, 1937–8. He was Cowles Commission Research Fellow and then instructor in Economics at Colorado College, 1938–41, professor of Political Economy at Bennington College, Vermont, from 1941 to 1948, and economist and assistant chief of Price Control for the US Military Government for Germany, 1946–8. He joined the RAND corporation in 1956 as a senior social scientist, remaining in that post for twenty years, until becoming a consultant in 1976. His works include *The Economics of War* (1941), *Terms of Trade between the Soviet Union and the Smaller Communist Countries, 1955 to 1957* (1959), *The Terms of Soviet-Satellite Trade: A Broadened Analysis* (1959), and *Coping with the Oil Crisis: French and German Experiences* (1976).

Neumann, Sigmund (1904–62): contributor to Earle's *Makers*. Studied at the University of Heidelberg and the University of Grenoble, and then for a PhD at the University of Leipzig, completed in 1927. Taught at Leipzig, then in 1928 joined the Deutsche Hochschule für Politik, where he became professor of Political Sociology and Modern History. Emigrated to the United Kingdom in 1933, where he was a Rockefeller Research Fellow at the Royal Institute of International Affairs and the London School of Economics. Arriving in the USA in 1934 he joined Wesleyan University, where he remained for the rest of his life, becoming Andrus Professor of Government and Social Science in 1944 and the first director of the Center for Advanced Studies, 1959–62. Served as consultant for the Office of Strategic Services, 1944–5. After the war, worked towards the reconstruction of the social sciences in German universities. Author of *Permanent Revolution: The Total State in a World at War* (1942), *The Future in Perspective* (1946).

Palmer, Robert Roswell (1909–2002): contributor to Earle's *Makers* whose essay was reprinted in Paret's *Makers*. Studied at the University of Chicago, then for a PhD at Cornell University, which he completed in 1934. Appointed a lecturer at Princeton University in 1936, during the Second World War he worked for the Historical Section of the War Department. In 1952 he was made Dodge Professor of History at Princeton. In 1963 he became dean of faculty at Washington University in St Louis, and in 1967 was made dean of faculty at Princeton. In 1968 he became professor at Yale University, retiring in 1977. In retirement he was a visiting professor at the University of Michigan, and then the IAS. A renowned historian of the French revolution, his major works include *Twelve Who Ruled: The Committee of Public Safety during the Terror* (1941), *The Age of Democratic Revolution: A Political History of Europe and America, 1760–1800* (2 vols., 1959–64), and *The Improvement of Humanity: Education and the French Revolution* (1985).

Paret, Peter (1924–2020): editor of *Makers of Modern Strategy: From Machiavelli to the Nuclear Age*. Born in Germany, he migrated to Austria in 1933, France in 1934, and then to the USA in 1937. His undergraduate study at the University of California, Berkeley was interrupted by service with the US Army during the Second World War. After the war he completed his degree in 1949, then moved to Europe and worked as a journalist for six

230   MAKING MAKERS

years, before undertaking a PhD at King's College London under the supervision of Sir Michael Howard. He was a research associate at the Center of International Studies at Princeton University, 1960–2, joined the University of California Davis in 1962, and then Stanford University in 1969, where he was appointed Raymond A. Spruance Professor of International History in 1977. In 1986, shortly after the publication of his *Makers*, he joined the IAS, where he remained for the rest of his career, becoming emeritus professor in 1997. Although he was equally interested in the history of art and culture, he is best known for his works on German history and Clausewitz, particularly *Yorke and the Era of Prussian Reform* (1966), *Clausewitz and the State* (1976), and the translation of *On War* (1976), which he edited with Howard.

Pintner, Walter (1931–2015): contributor to Paret's *Makers*. Studied Liberal Arts at the University of Chicago, then for a PhD in History at Harvard University, which he completed in 1962. Between 1956 and 1958 he worked at the intelligence division of the US State Department. Taught at Princeton University and then Cornell University, where he would remain for the rest of his career. A specialist in Imperial Russian history, his major publications include *Russian Economic Policy under Nicholas I* (1967) and *Russian Officialdom: The Bureaucratization of Russian Society from the Seventeenth to the Twentieth Century* (1980). He wrote a number of research articles on Russian military history.

Poole, DeWitt Clinton (1885–1952): member of Earle's seminar, autumn 1941. Studied French at the University of Wisconsin, graduating in 1906, and for a master's degree at George Washington University, completed in 1910. He joined the American Foreign Service, and served as vice-consul in Berlin, 1911–14, and then Paris, 1914–15. In 1917 he was made vice consul in Moscow, and consul general the following year. From here he oversaw US intelligence activity during Bolshevik rule until his departure in September 1918. He left the foreign service in 1930 and became director of the School of Public and International Affairs, Princeton University until 1939. During the Second World War he was head of the Foreign Nationalities Branch of the Office of Strategic Services. After the war's end he was president of the National Committee for a Free Europe, then head of the Free Europe University in Exile. An edited version of his oral 'reminiscences' was published as *An American Diplomat in Bolshevik Russia* (edited by Lorraine M. Lees and William S. Rodner, 2014).

Porch, Douglas (b. 1944): contributor to Paret's *Makers*. Studied at Sewanee: The University of the South, then at the University of Cambridge, completing a PhD in 1972. He taught at Aberystwyth University, was professor of Strategy at the US Naval War College, Mark Clark Professor of History at the Citadel, and Professor of National Security Affairs and chair of the Department of National Security Affairs at the Naval Postgraduate School, where he remained until retiring as professor emeritus. A specialist in French military history, his works include *Army and Revolution: France 1815–1848* (1974), *The March to the Marne* (1981), *The French Foreign Legion* (1991), and *Counterinsurgency: Exposing the Myths of the New Way of War* (2013).

Possony, Stefan (1913–95): contributor to Earle's *Makers* and a member of Earle's seminar, 1941–2. Born in Vienna, he migrated to France in 1938 where he worked for the Foreign Ministry and the Air Force. Emigrated to the USA in 1940 and became a Carnegie Fellow at the IAS. Joined the Psychological Warfare Branch of the Office of Naval Intelligence in 1942, broadcasting into Austria, and contributed to the formal demand for surrender issued by the US government to the emperor of Japan. After 1945 became an intelligence specialist for the USAF, taught international politics at Georgetown University. In 1955 moved to the University of Pennsylvania to teach on war, politics, and strategy. Joined the Hoover Institution in 1961. With J. E. Pournelle, authored *The Strategy of*

CONTRIBUTORS AND COLLABORATORS, 1943–86   231

Technology: Winning the Decisive War (1970), which provided inspiration for the Reagan Administration's 'Star Wars' Strategic Defence Initiative, on which he later worked.

Rice, Condoleezza (b. 1954): contributor to Paret's *Makers*. Studied at the University of Denver and then University of Notre Dame, before returning to the University of Denver to study for a PhD in Political Science, completed in 1981. Joined Stanford University in 1981, where she became provost, 1993–9. Advisor to the Joint Chiefs of Staff, 1987, and director of Soviet and East European Affairs on the National Security Council, 1989–91, during the presidency of George W. Bush she served as National Security Advisor, 2001–5, then Secretary of State, 2005–9. Author of *The Soviet Union and the Czechoslovak Army* (1985).

Ropp, Theodore (1911–2000): contributor to Earle's *Makers*, and prospective editor of *Makers of Modern Strategy Revisited*. Completed his PhD in history at Harvard University in 1937 under the supervision of diplomatic historian William L. Langer. Joined Duke University in 1938 and remained there for the rest of his career, offering the university's first courses in naval and military history. With I. B. Holley, supervised almost fifty PhD students in military history over a thirty-five-year period. A founder of the Duke University of North Carolina National Security Policy Seminar, which later became the Triangle Institute for Security Studies. Author of *War in the Modern World* (1959). His dissertation was published as *The Development of a Modern Navy: French Naval Policy, 1871–1904* in 1987.

Rosinski, Herbert (1903–62): member of Earle's seminar, 1940–1. Obtained a PhD in 1930 from the University of Berlin for a study of autarky in Japan, but developed expertise that also spanned naval affairs and the German army. In 1936 he left Germany for the United Kingdom, having lost his ability to work on account of having a Jewish grandfather. In 1939 he was interned as an enemy alien, then in 1940 travelled to the USA. Here he did not secure a permanent academic post, although after the IAS he lectured at the Fletcher School at Tufts and was a military analyst for the Voice of America. After the war he continued to lecture at such institutions as the Naval War College, the National War College, the Industrial College of the Armed Forces, and the Canadian Institute of International Affairs. During the 1950s he was affiliated with the Council on Foreign Relations. Although he was an active scholar, much of his work was not published. His best-known work was *The German Army* (1939), a revised edition of which appeared in 1944.

Rothenberg, Gunther (1923–2004): contributor to Paret's *Makers*. Born in Berlin, his family left Germany to escape persecution as Jews, travelling first to the Netherlands and then to Palestine, where he joined the Haganah. Served with the British Army Service and Intelligence Corps from 1941, in Egypt, Italy, and Austria, and was awarded the Distinguished Conduct Medal and the Medal of Merit. Worked for US intelligence in Austria, 1948, and returned to Palestine to rejoin Haganah and the Israeli Defence Force in the War of Independence. Migrated to the USA in 1949 and served in the US Air Force Intelligence Branch, including in Korea, whilst also studying for a PhD at the University of Illinois. Subsequently worked at the University of New Mexico for ten years, then joined Purdue University in 1973. Retiring from Purdue in 1999, he moved to Australia, where he was a visiting fellow at Monash University, 1995–2001. He was a noted historian of Austrian and Napoleonic military history, whose many publications included *The Art of Warfare in the Age of Napoleon* (1978) and *The Army of Francis Joseph* (1976).

Rothfels, Hans (1891–1976): contributor to Earle's *Makers*. A student under Friedrich Meinecke at the University of Freiburg and later the University of Berlin, he served as a reserve second lieutenant in the First World War until he lost a leg in a riding accident in late 1914. Thereafter studied for his doctorate at Heidelberg University under Hermann

232 MAKING MAKERS

Oncken, which was awarded in 1918 for a thesis on Carl von Clausewitz. Employed by the German Imperial Archive from 1920, received his habilitation in 1924 from the University of Berlin for a study on Bismarck and was then awarded a chair at the University of Königsberg in 1926. Dismissed from his post in 1934 on account of his Jewish heritage, he nevertheless remained in Germany until 1939. He joined St John's College, Oxford as a research fellow and was subsequently interned on the Isle of Man in 1940. He then emigrated to the USA, teaching first at Brown University from 1940 and then the University of Chicago, where he was professor of Modern History from 1946 to 1956. In 1951 he took a position as professor of Modern History at the University of Tübingen and returned to Germany. He was made professor emeritus at the same institution from 1959 until his death. As well as his studies of Clausewitz and Bismarck, he researched on East Central Europe and in 1948 published *The German Opposition to Hitler*.

Rumney, Jay (1905–57): member of Earle's seminar, 1939–40. Obtained a PhD from the University of London in 1933, then served as Assistant Director of the Institute of Social Research, London, 1934–8. Emigrated to the USA in 1938, where he was a member of the IAS, 1938–40, working as a research assistant to Professor David Mitrany. Joined Rutgers University in 1940 as professor of Sociology and later chair of the Department of Sociology, remaining there until his death. An expert in sociology and penology, his works include *Herbert Spencer's Sociology: A Study in the History of Social Theory* (1934), *Probation and Social Adjustment* (1952, with Joseph P. Murphy), and *Sociology: The Science of Society* (1953, with Joseph Maier).

Schurman, Donald MacKenzie (1924–2013): collaborator with Theodore Ropp on *Makers Revisited*, co-organizer of Ropp's Singapore seminar, and author of several prospective chapters for the book. Served with the Royal Canadian Air Force in the Second World War. After the war studied at Acadia University, then for a doctorate in History at the University of Cambridge, which he completed in 1955. Taught at the Royal Military College of Canada, then became professor of History at Queens University Ontario. A naval and imperial historian, known especially for his book *The Education of a Navy: The Development of British Naval Strategic Thought, 1867–1914* (1965), Schurman was also co-founder of the Disraeli Project in 1972, dedicated to the location, collation, and publication of the papers of Benjamin Disraeli.

Shy, John (1931–2022): contributor to Paret's *Makers*. Graduated from West Point in 1952, served in Japan until 1955, then left the army and studied at the University of Vermont and then Princeton University, obtaining a PhD in 1961. Taught at Princeton until 1968, then joined the University of Michigan, retiring as professor emeritus in 1996. He was the author of *Toward Lexington: The Role of the British Army in the Coming of Revolution* (1966), *A People Numerous and Armed: Reflections on the Military Struggle for American Independence* (1976), and—with Peter Paret—*Guerrillas in the 1960s* (1962).

Smith, Datus C. (1907–99): graduated from Princeton University in 1929, edited the *Princeton Alumni Weekly*, then joined the Princeton University Press in 1940, becoming editor in 1942. Left the press in 1953 and committed himself to Franklin Publications, of which he became director in 1952. Under Smith's direction Franklin Publications secured translation rights for *Makers of Modern Strategy* in multiple languages. President of the Association of American University Presses, 1947–9. After leaving Franklin, he was president of the US Committee for Unicef, member of the US National Commission for UNESCO, and trustee of the Asia Society.

Speier, Hans (1905–90): contributor to Earle's *Makers*. Studied at the University of Berlin, then undertook a PhD at the University of Heidelberg, completed in 1928. Between 1931 and 1933 he was a lecturer in Political Sociology at the Hochshule für Politik in Berlin and an assistant in the Department of Economics at the University of Berlin. In 1933 he

CONTRIBUTORS AND COLLABORATORS, 1943–86   233

emigrated to the USA to join the New School for Social Research, New York as professor of Sociology. From 1942 to 1946 his work in service of the US war effort included stints at the Foreign Broadcast Intelligence Service and the Office of War Information. In 1948 he became head of the new Social Science Division at the RAND corporation, where he was also a member of the research council, 1960–8. From 1969 to 1973 he was Robert M. MacIver Professor of Sociology and Government at the University of Massachusetts, Amherst. His numerous publications include *German Radio Propaganda* (with Ernst Kris, 1944) and *German White-Collar Workers and the Rise of Hitler* (1986).

Sprout, Harold (1901–80): member of Earle's seminar, 1939–42. Obtained an undergraduate degree from Oberlin College, 1924, then pursued graduate study at the University of Wisconsin, gaining a PhD in political science and law in 1929. He was an assistant professor at Miami University in Ohio, then an assistant professor at Stanford University, 1929–31. In 1931 he joined the faculty of politics at Princeton, where he would remain for the rest of his life, becoming Henry Grier Bryant Professor of Geography and International Relations in 1952 and McCosh Faculty Fellow in 1966. At retirement in 1969, he was made professor emeritus of International Relations and research associate in International Studies.

Sprout, Margaret Tuttle (1903–2004): contributor to Earle's *Makers*, and member of Earle's seminar, 1939–42. Obtained an undergraduate degree from Oberlin College, 1925, and a master's degree in Geography from the University of Wisconsin, 1929, she moved to Princeton in 1931 with her husband Harold. The couple worked in partnership on research projects until Harold's death in 1980, co-authoring *The Rise of American Naval Power* (1939), *Towards a New Order of Sea Power* (1940), *The Ecological Perspective in Human Affairs* (1965), and *The Context of Environmental Politics: Unfinished Business for America's Third Century* (1978). In 1972 the International Studies Association founded a prize in their name, to honour their pioneering work in the study of international environmental problems.

Stacey, Charles Perry (1906–89): member of Earle's seminar, 1939–40. Studied for an undergraduate degree at the University of Toronto, 1924, and a second degree at the University of Oxford, 1929, then for a PhD at Princeton University, completed in 1933. Between 1930 and 1940 he taught in the Department of History at Princeton. During the Second World War he was historical officer at Canadian Military Headquarters, London. In 1945 he became director of the Historical Section of the General Staff and oversaw the production of the official history of Canadian military operations during the war. In 1959 he moved to the University of Toronto, becoming Distinguished Professor of Military History, retiring in 1976. His works include *Canada and the British Army* (1936), *Quebec, 1759: The Siege and the Battle* (1959), and *A Very Double Life: The Private World of Mackenzie King* (1976).

Stebbins, Richard Poate (1913–2011): member of Earle's seminar, 1940–1. Son of the author Lucy Poate Stebbins, with whom he co-authored three books, studied English at Harvard as an undergraduate then for a PhD in History. In 1941, prepared *War and National Policy: A Syllabus* with Grayson Kirk, as part of the work undertaken by the Earle group at the IAS. Awarded a Guggenheim Fellowship in political science in 1945 and later affiliated to the Council on Foreign Relations, for which he edited the annual review *The United States in World Affairs*. A close friend of Herbert Rosinski, in 1949 Stebbins married Maria-Luise, who had divorced Rosinski the same year. The trio lived together in the Stebbins' New York home. In 1989 Stebbins published *The Career of Herbert Rosinski: An Intellectual Pilgrimage* in tribute to his late friend.

Vagts, Alfred (1892–1986): member of Earle's seminar, 1939–42. Served as a lieutenant in the German army during the First World War, afterwards resuming studies at the University of Munich, then undertaking a PhD in History at the University of Hamburg,

234 MAKING MAKERS

completed in 1927. Worked as a teaching assistant at the Institut für auswärtige Politik, Hamburg, 1923–32, and held a Rockefeller Fellowship in the USA, 1927–30. Emigrated to the USA in 1933, appointed a visiting professor at Harvard University, 1938–9, then member of the IAS, 1939–42. Worked for the Board of Economic Warfare, 1942–5. After the war and for the rest of his life, worked as an independent scholar. Best known for *A History of Militarism* (1939), he played a role in early discussions of the book that would become Earle's *Makers*, but did not write anything for it.

Von Brevern, Maxim (1888–1952): member of Earle's seminar, 1940–1. Studied for a PhD at the University of Washington, completed in 1937 with the submission of a thesis entitled 'The New Poland, the Polish Corridor, and the Free City of Danzig'. He remained at the University of Washington as a faculty member, serving as executive secretary of the Bureau of International Relations, and reaching the rank of associate professor in 1942. He was a member of the IAS in Fall term 1941.

Von Hagen, Mark (1954–2019): contributor to Paret's *Makers*. Obtained an undergraduate degree from Georgetown University in 1976, an MA from the University of Indiana in 1978, and a PhD from Stanford University in 1985. He taught at Columbia University, 1985–2007, where he was also director of the Harriman Institute for Russian, Eurasian and Eastern European Studies. In 2007 he moved to Arizona State University, where he remained until his death. In 2003 he was commissioned by the *New York Times* to investigate the 1931 reportage of their Pulitzer Prize-winning Moscow bureau chief Walter Duranty. A specialist in Russian and Ukrainian history, with a particular interest in war and military institutions, his works include *Proletarian Dictatorship: The Red Army and the Soviet Socialist State, 1917–1930* (1990) and *War in European Borderland: Occupations and Occupation Plans in Galicia and Ukraine, 1914–1918* (2007).

Warner, Edward Pearson (1894–1958): contributor to Earle's *Makers*. Completed an undergraduate degree at Harvard University, then studied mechanical and aeronautical engineering as a postgraduate at the Massachusetts Institute of Technology. He taught at MIT and became associate professor (1920–4), professor (1924–9), and non-resident professor (1929–36) of aeronautical engineering. Towards the end of the First World War he was appointed chief physicist of the National Advisory Committee for Aeronautics at Langley Field. Between 1926 and 1929 he was First Assistant Secretary of the Navy. Between 1938 and 1945 he worked for the Civil Aeronautics Authority and its successor, the Civil Aeronautics Board. He was president of the Council of the Provisional International Civil Aviation Organization and then of the International Civil Aviation Organization, 1945 to 1957. Author of *Airplane Design: Performance* (1927).

Weigley, Russell F. (1930–2004): contributor to Paret's *Makers*. Studied at Albright College, then pursued a PhD in History at the University of Pennsylvania, which he completed in 1956. Taught at Pennsylvania, 1956–8, then Drexel University, 1958–62, before joining Temple University, where he remained until he retired 1999 as distinguished university professor. A specialist in the military history of the United States, best known for his books *The American Way of War* (1972) and *Eisenhower's Lieutenants: The Campaign of France and Germany, 1944–45* (1981).

Weiller, Jean Sylvain (1905–2000): member of Earle's seminar, 1940–1. Awarded a DSc from the University of Paris in 1929, he worked in the economics division of the League of Nations. He was a member of the IAS between 1941 and 1943. After the Second World War he worked on the Havana Charter and was involved in negotiations towards the General Agreement on Tariffs and Trade. He taught at the University of Poitiers before moving to the University of Paris, where he taught from 1955 to 1971. He was a founding member of the *Revue Economique* and a contributor to Georges Gurvitch's *Traité de sociologie*.

CONTRIBUTORS AND COLLABORATORS, 1943–86   235

Weinberg, Albert Katz (1899–1973): member of Earle's seminar, 1939–41. Studied at Columbia University, Berlin University, and Göttingen University, then for a PhD at Johns Hopkins University, completed in 1931. Fellow of the Walter Hines Page School of International Relations, 1930–9, then Albert Shaw Lecturer in Diplomatic History, 1939–40, at Johns Hopkins University. After a year at the IAS, he was awarded a Guggenheim Fellowship, 1941–2. During the Second World War he was an analyst in the Civil Affairs Section of the Office of Strategic Services, chief of the Reports Division in the United Nations Relief and Rehabilitation Administration, senior editor and then chief of the Civil Affairs Section in the Office of the Chief of Military History. Author of *Manifest Destiny: A Study of Nationalist Expansionism in American History* (1935) and co-author (with Harry L. Coles) of *Civil Affairs: Soldiers Become Governors* (1964).

Wheeler, Everett: contributor to Ropp's *Makers Revisited*. Studied at Indiana University Bloomington, and for a PhD at Duke University, completed in 1977. He was a member of the IAS in spring term 1984, a research assistant at the IAS, 1984–5, and has held research awards from the Alexander von Humboldt Foundation and the Harry Frank Guggenheim Foundation. He is Scholar in Residence of Classical Studies at Duke University. A specialist in ancient military history, his works include *Stratagem and the Vocabulary of Military Trickery* (1988) and *The Armies of Classical Greece* (ed., 2007). His 1994 article 'Methodological Limits and the Mirages of Roman Strategy' was awarded a Moncado Prize by the Society for Military History.

Whittlesey, Derwent (1890–1956): contributor to Earle's *Makers*. Studied at the University of Chicago, then briefly taught history at Denison University, 1915–16, before serving in the First World War. On his return, studied for a PhD in history and geography at the University of Chicago, completed in 1920. Instructor and then associate professor in the Department of Geography, University of Chicago, 1920–8. He joined Harvard University in 1928 and remained there until his death, becoming professor in 1943. Author of *The Earth and the State: A Study of Political Geography* (1939), *German Strategy of World Conquest* (1942), and *Environmental Foundations of European History* (1949).

Woolf, Harry S. (1923–2003): fifth director of the Institute for Advanced Study, 1976–87. Studied Mathematics at the University of Chicago, then for a PhD in the History of Science at Cornell University, which he completed in 1955, working under the supervision of Henry Guerlac. Worked at the University of Washington, 1955–61, then Johns Hopkins University, 1961–76, where he was made Willis K. Shepard Professor of the History of Science, and served as provost, 1972–6. After serving as IAS director, was made professor-at-large, 1987–94, then professor-at-large emeritus, 1994–2003. Author of *The Transits of Venus: A Study of Eighteenth-Century Science* (1959).

Bibliography

Archival Sources

Liddell Hart Centre for Military Archives, King's College London, London
    Liddell Hart Papers
Seeley G. Mudd Manuscript Library, Princeton University, Princeton, NJ
    Edward Mead Earle Papers
    Princeton University Press Archives
Shelby White and Leon Levy Archives Center, Institute for Advanced Study, Princeton, NJ
    Faculty Files—Earle
    Stern Vertical Files
    Members—Mantoux, Etienne
    Members—Possony, Stefan Thomas
Hoover Institution Library and Archives, Stanford, CA
    Felix Gilbert Papers
Stanford University Archives, Stanford, CA
    Gordon Craig Papers
Division of Rare and Manuscript Collections, Cornell University Library, Ithaca, NY
    Henry Guerlac Papers
Sterling Memorial Library, Yale University, New Haven, CT
    Walter Lippmann Papers
Bibliothèque Nationale de France, Paris
    Gottmann Papers
Archives of the Institute for Historical Research, London
Donald MacKenzie Schurman Papers, in the care of Prof. Greg Kennedy, Defence Studies Department, King's College London

Secondary Works

Allison, Graham, *Destined for War: Can America and China Escape Thucydides' Trap?* (Boston, MA: Houghton Mifflin Harcourt, 2017)

Anon., 'Our Military History', *Infantry Journal*, Vol. 9, No. 3 (November–December 1912), pp. 376–82

Anon., 'X. Proceedings of the Conference on Military History', *Annual Report of the American Historical Association for the year 1912* (Washington, 1914), pp. 157–97

Ashworth, Lucian M., 'Did the Realist-Idealist Great Debate Really Happen? A Revisionist History of International Relations', *International Relations*, Vol. 16, No. 1 (April 2002), pp. 33–51

Ashworth, Lucian M., 'A Forgotten Environmental International Relations: Derwent Whittlesey's International Thought', *Global Studies Quarterly*, Vol. 1, No. 2 (June 2021), pp. 1–10

Aston, Sir George (ed.), *The Study of War for Statesmen and Citizens* (London: Longmans, Green and Co., 1933)

238 BIBLIOGRAPHY

Bacevich, Andrew J., 'Strategic Studies: In from the Cold', *SAIS Review*, Vol. 13, No. 2 (summer–fall 1993), pp. 11–23

Bailey, Herbert S., *The Art and Science of Book Publishing* (Athens, OH: Ohio University Press, 1990)

Baltzly, Alexander, 'Robert Matteson Johnston and the Study of Military History', *Military Affairs*, Vol. 21, No. 1 (spring 1957), pp. 26–30

Bassford, Christopher, *Clausewitz in English: The Reception of Clausewitz in Britain and America 1815–1945* (New York and Oxford: Oxford University Press, 1994)

Bauer, Richard H., 'Hans Delbrück', in B. Schmitt (ed.), *Some Historians of Modern Europe: Essays in Historiography by Former Students of the Department of History of the University of Chicago* (Chicago, IL: University of Chicago Press, 1942), pp. 100–129

Baylis, John and Garnett, John (eds.), *Makers of Nuclear Strategy* (London: Pinter Publishers, 1991)

B. D. H., 'Ten Important Books: Strategic Thought', *The Army Historian*, No. 3 (spring 1984), pp. 11–15

Beach, Jim, 'The British Army, the Royal Navy, and the "Big Work" of Sir George Aston, 1904–1914', *The Journal of Strategic Studies*, Vol. 29, No. 1 (February 2006), pp. 145–68

Bessner, Daniel, *Democracy in Exile: Hans Speier and the Rise of the Defence Intellectual* (Ithaca, NY and London: Cornell University Press, 2018)

Betts, Richard K., 'Should Strategic Studies Survive?', *World Politics*, Vol. 50, No. 1 (October 1997), pp. 7–33

Bientinesi, Fabrizio, 'An "Austrian" Point of View on Total War', in Fabrizio Bientinesi and Rosario Patalano, *Economists and War: A Heterodox Perspective* (London: Routledge, 2017), pp. 16–32

Black, Jeremy, *Rethinking Military History* (London: Routledge, 2004)

Blazich Jr, Frank A., 'Fifty Years of Interdisciplinary Scholarship: A Brief History of the Triangle Institute for Security Studies' (February 2009) http://tiss-nc.org/wp-content/uploads/2014/08/Final-TISS-Complete-History-24-February-2009.pdf.

Bond, Brian, *Liddell Hart: A Study of His Military Thought* (Aldershot: Gregg Revivals in association with Department of War Studies, King's College London, 1991)

Bond, Brian, *Military Historian: My Part in the Birth and Development of War Studies* (Solihull: Helion & Co., 2018)

Bonner, Thomas Neville, *Iconoclast: Abraham Flexner and a Life in Learning* (Baltimore, MD: The Johns Hopkins University Press, 2002)

Borowski, Harry (ed.), *The Harmon Memorial Lectures in Military History, 1959–1987* (Washington, D.C.: Office of Air Force History, United States Air Force, 1988)

Bowditch, John, 'War and the Historian', in Henry Stuart Hughes, Myron P. Gilmore, and Edwin C. Rozwenc (eds.), *Teachers of History: Essays in Honor of Laurence Bradford Packard*, (Ithaca, NY: Cornell University Press, 1954), pp. 320–40

Brands, Hal, 'The Promise and Pitfalls of Grand Strategy', US Army War College, Strategic Studies Institute Monograph (August 2012)

Brands, Hal, *What Good Is Grand Strategy? Power and Purpose in American Statecraft from Harry S. Truman to George W. Bush* (Ithaca, NY: Cornell University Press, 2014)

Brands, Hal, 'The Triumph and Tragedy of Diplomatic History', *Texas National Security Review*, Vol. 1, No. 1 (December 2017), pp. 132–43

Brands, Hal, *The Twilight Struggle: What the Cold War Teaches Us about Great-Power Rivalry Today* (New Haven, CT: Yale University Press, 2022)

Brands, Hal (ed.), *The New Makers of Modern Strategy: From the Ancient World to the Digital Age* (Princeton, NJ: Princeton University Press, 2023)

BIBLIOGRAPHY   239

Brodie, Bernard, *Sea Power in the Machine Age* (Princeton, NJ: Princeton University Press, 1941)

Brodie, Bernard, *A Guide to Naval Strategy*, 3rd edn. (Princeton, NJ: Princeton University Press, 1944)

Brodie, Bernard, 'Review of *Makers of Modern Strategy*', *The American Journal of International Law*, Vol. 38, No. 4 (October 1944), pp. 754–5

Brodie, Bernard, 'Trafalgar for Japan', *The Nation*, 11 November 1944

Brodie, Bernard (ed.), *The Absolute Weapon: Atomic Power and World Order* (Yale University: Institute of International Studies, 1946)

Brodie, Bernard, 'Strategy as a Science', *World Politics*, Vol. 1, No. 4 (July 1949), pp. 467–88

Bucholz, Arden, *Hans Delbrück and the German Military Establishment: War Images in Conflict* (Iowa City, IA: University of Iowa Press, 1985)

Bucholz, Arden, 'Hans Delbrück and Modern Military History', *The Historian*, Vol. 55, No. 3 (spring 1993), pp. 517–26

Buzan, Barry and Hansen, Lene, *The Evolution of International Security Studies* (Cambridge: Cambridge University Press, 2009)

Callaci, Emily, 'On Acknowledgments', *American Historical Review*, Vol. 125, No. 1 (February 2020) pp. 126–31

Campbell, John P. 'An Update on the Interpretation of the Ultra Documentation', *Archivaria* 26 (summer 1988), pp. 184–8

Carr, Edward Hallett, *What Is History?*, 2nd edn. (London: Penguin, 1987)

Carr, Edward Hallett, *The Twenty Years' Crisis, 1919–1939*, reissued with a new preface from Michael Cox (London: Palgrave Macmillan, 2016)

Carver, Michael, *Out of Step: The Memoirs of Field Marshal Lord Carver* (London: Hutchinson, 1989)

Chung, Ong Chit, *Operation Matador: Britain's War Plans against the Japanese, 1918–1941* (Singapore: Times Academic Press, 1997)

Citino, Robert M., 'Military Histories Old and New: A Reintroduction', *The American Historical Review*, Vol. 112, No. 4 (October 2007), pp. 1070–90

Clausewitz, Carl von (ed. and trans. P. Paret and D. Moran), *Historical and Political Writings* (Princeton, NJ: Princeton University Press, 1992)

Cochran, Jr., Alexander S., '"MAGIC," "ULTRA," and the Second World War: Literature, Sources, and Outlook', *Military Affairs*, Vol. 46, No. 2 (April 1982), pp. 88–92

Coffman, Edward M., 'The Course of Military History in the United States since World War II', *The Journal of Military History*, Vol. 61, No. 4 (October 1997), pp. 761–75

Cohen, Eliot, review of *Makers of Modern Strategy* in *Foreign Affairs*, Vol. 76, No. 5 (September–October 1997), p. 220

Corbett, Julian, 'The Revival of Naval History', *The Contemporary Review*, 1 July 1916, pp. 734–40

Corneli, Alessandro, 'Sun Tzu and the Indirect Strategy', *Rivista di Studi Politici Internazionali*, Vol. 54, No. 3 (July–September 1987), pp. 419–45

Craig, Gordon, *The Germans* (New York: G. P. Putnam's Sons, 1982)

Craig, Gordon, 'The Historian and the Study of International Relations', *The American Historical Review*, Vol. 88, No. 1 (February 1983), pp. 1–11

Craig, Gordon, 'Insight and Energy: Reflections on the Work of Felix Gilbert', in H. Lehmann (ed.), Felix Gilbert as Scholar and Teacher (German Historical Institute, Washington, D.C. Occasional Paper No. 6), pp. 17–28

Craig, Gordon and George, Alex (eds.), *Force and Statecraft: Diplomatic Problems of Our Time* (New York and Oxford: Oxford University Press, 1983)

240 BIBLIOGRAPHY

Craven, Wesley Frank, 'Why Military History?', in Harry R. Borowski (ed.), *The Harmon Memorial Lectures in Military History, 1959-1987* (Washington, D.C.: Office of Air Force History, United States Air Force, 1988), pp. 9-23

Curro Cary, Francine, *The Influence of War on Walter Lippmann 1914-1944* (Madison, WI: State Historical Society of Wisconsin for the Dept. of History, University of Wisconsin, 1967)

Danchev, Alex, *Alchemist of War: The Life of Basil Liddell Hart* (London: Weidenfeld and Nicolson, 1998)

Davis Biddle, Tami and Citino, Robert M., 'The Role of Military History in the Contemporary Academy', Society for Military History White Paper (November 2014), https://www.smh-hq.org/whitepaper.html

Deutsch, Harold C., 'The Historical Impact of Revealing the Ultra Secret', *Parameters*, Vol. 7, No. 3 (January 1977), pp. 16-32

Deutsch, Karl W., 'Quincy Wright's Contribution to the Study of War: A Preface to the Second Edition', *Conflict Resolution*, Vol. 14, No. 4 (December 1970), pp. 473-8

Dighton, Adam, 'Army Officers, Historians and Journalists: The Emergence, Expansion and Diversification of British Military History, 1854-1914' (PhD thesis, University of Salford, 2016)

Downs, Donald, and Murtazashvili, Ilia, *Arms and the University: Military Presence and the Civic Education of Non-Military Students* (Cambridge: Cambridge University Press, 2012)

Delbrück, Hans, *Numbers in History* (London: University of London Press, 1913)

Delbrück, Hans (ed. and trans. A. Bucholz), *Delbrück's Modern Military History* (Lincoln, NE: University of Nebraska Press, 1997)

Earle, Edward Mead, *Turkey, the Great Powers, and the Baghdad Railway* (New York: Macmillan, 1923)

Earle, Edward Mead, 'The Outlook for American Imperialism', *Annals of the American Academy of Political and Social Science*, Vol. 108 (July 1923), pp. 104-7

Earle, Edward Mead, 'Problems of Eastern and Southeastern Europe', *Proceedings of the Academy of Political Science in the City of New York*, Vol. 12, No. 1 (July 1926), pp. 265-8

Earle, Edward Mead, *American Military Policy and National Security* (New York: Academic of Political Science, 1938)

Earle, Edward Mead, 'National Defense and Political Science', *Political Science Quarterly*, Vol. 55, No. 4 (December 1940), pp. 481-95

Earle, Edward Mead, 'National Defense: A Program of Studies', *The Journal of the American Military Institute*, Vol. 4, No. 4 (winter 1940), pp. 199-208

Earle, Edward Mead, 'Political and Military Strategy for the United States', *Proceedings of the Academy of Political Science*, Vol. 19, No. 2 (January 1941), pp. 2-9

Earle, Edward Mead, *Against This Torrent* (Princeton, NJ: Princeton University Press, 1941)

Earle, Edward Mead, 'The Princeton Program of Military Studies', *Military Affairs*, Vol. 6, No. 1 (spring 1942), pp. 21-6

Earle, Edward Mead, *Makers of Modern Strategy: From Machiavelli to Hitler* (Princeton, NJ: Princeton University Press, 1943)

Earle, Edward Mead, 'Power Politics and American World Policy', *Political Science Quarterly*, Vol. 58, No. 1 (March 1943), pp. 94-106

Earle, Edward Mead, 'The Influence of Air Power upon History', *Yale Review*, Vol. 35, No. 4 (June 1946), pp. 577-93

Earle, Edward Mead, 'A Half-Century of American Foreign Policy: Our Stake in Europe, 1898-1948', *Political Science Quarterly*, Vol. 64, No. 2 (June 1949), pp. 168-88

Earle, Edward Mead, 'Notes on the Term Strategy', *Naval War College Information Service for Officers*, Vol. 2, No. 4 (December 1949), pp. 1-20

BIBLIOGRAPHY   241

Earle, Edward Mead, *Nationalism and Internationalism: Essays Inscribed to Carlton J. H. Hayes* (New York: Colombia University Press, 1950)

Earle, Edward Mead, *Modern France: Problems of the Third and Fourth Republics* (Princeton, NJ: Princeton University Press, 1951)

Earle, Edward Mead, 'The American Stake in Europe: Retrospect and Prospect', *International Affairs*, Vol. 27, No. 4 (October 1951), pp. 423–33

Eckel, Jan, 'Hans Rothfels: An Intellectual Biography in the Age of Extremes', *Journal of Contemporary History*, Vol. 42, No. 3 (July 2007), pp. 421–46

Edel, Charles, and Brands, Hal, *The Lessons of Tragedy: Statecraft and World Order* (New Haven, CT: Yale University Press, 2019)

Ekbladh, David, 'Present at the Creation: Edward Mead Earle and the Depression-Era Origins of Security Studies', *International Security*, Vol. 36, No. 3 (winter 2011/12), pp. 107–41

Ekbladh, David, 'The Interwar Foundations of Security Studies: Edward Mead Earle, the Carnegie Corporation and the Depression-Era Origins of a Field', *Global Society*, Vol. 28, No. 1 (2014), pp. 40–53

Farrell Brodie, Janet, 'Learning Secrecy in the Early Cold War: The RAND Corporation', *Diplomatic History*, Vol. 35, No. 4 (September 2011), pp. 643–70

Fergie, Dexter, 'Geopolitics Turned Inwards: The Princeton Military Studies Group and the National Security Imagination', *Diplomatic History*, Vol. 43, No. 4 (September 2019), pp. 644–70

Finch, Eleanor H., 'Quincy Wright, 1890–1970', *The American Journal of International Law*, Vol. 65, No. 1 (January 1971), pp. 130–1

Finch, Michael P. M., *A Progressive Occupation? The Gallieni-Lyautey Method and Colonial Pacification in Tonkin and Madagascar, 1885–1900* (Oxford: Oxford University Press, 2013)

Finch, Michael P. M., 'Edward Mead Earle and the Unfinished *Makers of Modern Strategy*', *The Journal of Military History*, Vol. 80, No. 3 (July 2016), pp. 781–814

Finch, Michael P. M., 'Theodore Ropp's *Makers of Modern Strategy Revisited* and the Course of Military History', *The Journal of Military History*, Vol. 82, No. 4 (October 2018), pp. 1231–57

Flexner, Abraham, 'A Modern University', *Atlantic Monthly*, Vol. 136 (October 1925), pp. 530–41

Flexner, Abraham, 'The Usefulness of Useless Knowledge', *Harper's Magazine*, No. 179 (June/November 1939), pp. 544–52

Fordham, Elizabeth, 'Universities', in J. M. Winter and J.-L. Robert (eds.), *Capital Cities at War: Paris, London, Berlin 1914–1919*, Vol. 2: *A Cultural History* (Cambridge: Cambridge University Press, 2007), pp. 235–79

Fox, William T. R., '"The Truth Shall Make You Free": One Student's Appreciation of Quincy Wright', *Conflict Resolution*, Vol. 14, No. 4 (December 1970), pp. 449–52

Freedman, Lawrence, 'The Meaning of Strategy: Part I: The Origin Story', *Texas National Security Review*, Vol. 1, No. 1 (December 2017), pp. 90–105

Freedman, Lawrence, 'The Meaning of Strategy: Part II: The Objectives', *Texas National Security Review*, Vol. 1, No. 2 (March 2018), pp. 34–56

Fuller, John Frederick Charles, *The Reformation of War* (London: Hutchinson & Co., 1923)

Fuller, Jr., William C., review of *Makers of Modern Strategy* in *The Journal of Modern History*, Vol. 61, No. 1 (March 1989), pp. 133–5

Gat, Azar, 'The Hidden Sources of Liddell Hart's Strategic Ideas', *War in History*, Vol. 3, No. 3 (July 1996), pp. 293–308

242 BIBLIOGRAPHY

Gat, Azar, *A History of Military Thought: From the Enlightenment to the Cold War* (Oxford: Oxford University Press, 2001)

Gilbert, Felix, 'From Clausewitz to Delbruck and Hintze: Achievements and Failures of Military History', *Journal of Strategic Studies*, Vol. 3, No. 3 (1980), pp. 11–20

Gilbert, Felix, *A European Past: Memoirs, 1905–1945* (New York and London: Norton, 1988)

Goldrick, James, and Hattendorf, John (eds.), *Mahan Is Not Enough: The Proceedings of a Conference on the Works of Sir Julian Corbett and Admiral Sir Herbert Richmond* (Newport, RI: Naval War College Press, 1993)

Gooch, John, 'The Maurice Debate 1918', *Journal of Contemporary History*, Vol. 3, No. 4 (October 1968), pp. 211–28

Gooch, John, 'The Men in the Size 10 Helmets', *The New York Times*, 17 July 1986

Gray, Colin, 'National Style in Strategy: The American Example', *International Security*, Vol. 6, No. 2 (autumn 1981), pp. 21–47

Gray, Colin, 'Nicholas John Spykman, the Balance of Power, and International Order', *Journal of Strategic Studies*, Vol. 38, No. 6 (2015), pp. 873–97

Gropman, Alan, 'Landmarks in Defense Literature', *Defense Analysis*, Vol. 7, No. 1 (1991), pp. 111–16

Gross, David, 'The "New History": A Note of Reappraisal', *History and Theory*, Vol. 13, No. 1 (February 1974), pp. 53–8

Hammes, T. X., *The Sling and the Stone: On War in the 21st century* (St Paul, MN: Zenith Press, 2006)

Handel, Michael, *Masters of War: Sun Tzu, Clausewitz and Jomini* (London: Frank Cass, 1992)

Hanson, Victor Davis (ed.), *Makers of Ancient Strategy: From the Persian Wars to the Fall of Rome* (Princeton, NJ: Princeton University Press, 2010)

Hattendorf, John, 'The Study of War History at Oxford, 1862–1990', in J. Hattendorf and M. Murfett, *The Limitations of Military Power: Essays Presented to Professor Norman Gibbs on His Eightieth Birthday* (Basingstoke: Macmillan, 1990), pp. 3–61

Headrick, Daniel, review of Paret *Makers* in *Technology and Culture*, Vol. 29, No. 1 (January 1988), pp. 139–41

Hearnshaw, F. J. C. *The Centenary History of King's College London, 1828–1928* (London: G. G. Harrap & Co., 1929)

Herring, George C., 'A SHAFR Retrospective', *Diplomatic History*, Vol. 31, No. 3 (June 2007), pp. 397–400

Herubel, Jean-Pierre V. M. and Goedeken, Edward A., 'Trends in Historical Scholarship as Evidenced in the *The American Historical Review*: 1896–1990', *Serials Review*, Vol. 19, No. 2 (summer 1993), pp. 79–83

Higham, John, *History: Professional Scholarship in America* (Baltimore, MD: Johns Hopkins University Press, 1983)

Holden Reid, Brian, *J. F. C. Fuller: Military Thinker* (London, Macmillan, 1987)

Holden Reid, Brian, review of *Makers of Modern Strategy* in *History*, Vol. 73, No. 237 (February 1988), pp. 89–90

Holden Reid, Brian, 'The Legacy of Liddell Hart: The Contrasting Responses of Michael Howard and André Beaufre', *British Journal for Military History*, Vol. 1, No. 1 (2014), pp. 66–80

Honig, Jan Willem, 'Clausewitz's *On War*: Problems of Text and Translation', in H. Strachan and A. Herberg-Rothe (eds.), *Clausewitz in the Twenty-First Century* (Oxford: Oxford University Press, 2007), pp. 57–73

BIBLIOGRAPHY 243

Howard, Michael, 'The Use and Abuse of Military History', *Royal United Services Institution Journal*, Vol. 107, No. 625 (1962), pp. 4–10

Howard, Michael, 'Can the West Win the Next World War?', *The Sunday Times*, 16 July 1978

Howard, Michael, *The Causes of Wars*, 2nd edn. (Cambridge, MA: Harvard University Press, 1984)

Howard, Michael, 'Men against Fire: Expectations of War in 1914', *International Security*, Vol. 9, No. 1 (summer 1984), pp. 41–57

Howard, Michael, 'Grand Strategy in the Twentieth Century', *Defence Studies*, Vol. 1, No. 1 (spring 2001), pp. 1–10

Howard, Michael, *Captain Professor* (London: Bloomsbury, 2006)

Howard, Michael, 'Clausewitz *On War*: A History of the Howard–Paret Translation', in H. Strachan and A. Herberg-Rothe (eds.), *Clausewitz in the Twenty-First Century* (Oxford: Oxford University Press, 2007), pp. v–viii

Howard, Michael and Sparrow, John, *The Coldstream Guards, 1920–1946* (London: Oxford University Press, 1951)

Huard, Paul, 'The Battle over U.S. Military History', *War Is Boring*, 28 April 2016, https://medium.com/war-is-boring/the-battle-over-u-s-military-history-94dc2c82c3d6

Hunt, Barry, *Sailor-Scholar: Admiral Sir Herbert Richmond, 1871–1946* (Waterloo, Ontario: Wilfrid Laurier Press, 1982)

Hyam, Ronald, *Understanding the British Empire* (Cambridge: Cambridge University Press, 2010)

Institute for Advanced Study and Arntzenius, Linda G. (eds.), *Institute for Advanced Study: An Introduction*, 2nd edn. (Princeton, NJ: Institute for Advanced Study, 2009)

Irish, Tomas, *The University at War, 1914–25* (Basingstoke: Palgrave Macmillan, 2015)

Irish, Tomas, 'From International to Inter-Allied: Transatlantic University Relations in the Era of the First World War, 1905–1920', *Journal of Transatlantic Studies*, Vol. 13, No. 4 (2015), pp. 311–25

Irish, Tomas, 'Scholarly Identities in War and Peace: The Paris Peace Conference and the Mobilization of Intellect', *Journal of Global History*, Vol. 11, No. 3 (November 2016), pp. 365–86

Johnston, Robert M., *Napoleon: A Short Biography* (New York: Henry Holt & Co., 1904)

Johnston, Robert M., *Leading American Soldiers* (New York: Henry Holt & Co., 1907)

Johnston, Robert M., *The French Revolution: A Short History* ((New York: Henry Holt & Co., 1909)

Johnston, Robert M., 'What Can Be Done for Our Military History', *Infantry Journal*, Vol. 9 (September–October 1912), pp. 236–9

Johnston, Robert M., *Arms and the Race: The Foundations of Army Reform* (New York: The Century Co., 1915)

Johnston, Robert M., *General Foch, the Man of the Hour* (New York: A. L. Burt Co., 1918)

Jones, Spencer, *From Boer War to World War: Tactical Reform of the British Army, 1902–1914* (Norman, OK: University of Oklahoma Press, 2012)

Kaplan, Fred, *The Wizards of Armageddon* (Stanford, CA: Stanford University Press, 1991)

Karsten, Peter, 'Demilitarizing Military History: Servants of Power or Agents of Understanding?', *Military Affairs*, Vol. 36, No. 3 (October 1972), pp. 88–92

Keegan, John, 'Grand Illusions', *The New York Review of Books*, 17 July 1986

Keene, Edward, 'The Reception of Thucydides in the History of International Relations', in C. Lee and N. Morley (eds.), *A Handbook to the Reception of Thucydides* (London: Wiley, 2015), pp. 355–372

244 BIBLIOGRAPHY

Kennedy, Greg and Neilson, Keith (eds.), *Far Flung Lines: Studies in Imperial Defence in Honour of Donald Mackenzie Schurman* (London: Frank Cass, 1996)

Kennedy, Paul, 'Grand Strategy in War and Peace: Toward a Broader Definition', in P. Kennedy (ed.), *Grand Strategies in War and Peace* (New Haven, CT: Yale University Press, 1991), pp. 1–7

Kennedy, Paul, 'The Fall and Rise of Military History', *Military History Quarterly*, Vol. 3, No. 2 (1991) pp. 9–12

Kiralfy, Alexander, 'Why Japan's Fleet Avoids Action', *Foreign Affairs*, Vol. 22, No. 1 (October 1943), pp. 45–58

Kirk, Grayson and Stebbins, Richard Poate (eds.), *War and National Policy: A Syllabus* (New York: Farrar & Rinehart, Inc., 1942)

Kovacs, Arpad, 'French Military Institutions before the Franco-Prussian War', *The American Historical Review*, Vol. 51, No. 2 (January 1946), pp. 217–35

Kovacs, Arpad, 'French Military Legislation in the Third Republic 1871–1940', *Military Affairs*, Vol. 13, No. 1 (spring 1949), pp. 1–13

Krieger, Leonard and Stern, Fritz (eds.), *The Responsibility of Power: Historical Essays in Honor of Hajo Holborn* (London: Macmillan, 1968)

Lambert, Andrew, *The Foundations of Naval History: John Knox Laughton, the Royal Navy and the Historical Profession* (London: Chatham Publishing, 1998)

Lambert, Andrew, *The British Way of War: Julian Corbett and the Battle for a National Strategy* (New Haven, CT: Yale University Press, 2021)

Lambert, Andrew, 'Laughton's Legacy: Naval History at King's College London', *Historical Research*, Vol. 77, No. 196 (May 2004), pp. 274–288

Laugeson, Amanda, *Taking Books to the World: American Publishers and the Cultural Cold War* (Boston, MA: University of Massachusetts Press, 2017)

Lehmann, Hartmut (ed.), *Felix Gilbert as Scholar and Teacher* (German Historical Institute, Washington, D.C., Occasional Paper No .6)

Lehmann, Hartmut and Sheehan, James (eds.), *An Interrupted Past: German Speaking Refugee Historians in the United States after 1933* (Washington, D.C. and Cambridge: German Historical Institute and Cambridge University Press, 1991)

Liddell Hart, Basil, *The Ghost of Napoleon* (London: Faber & Faber, 1933)

Lippmann, Walter, 'The Serious Study of War', *The Washington Post*, 30 October 1943

Little, Ann M., 'Here We Go Again: Military Historian Complains That No One Teaches or Writes about Military Any More, Part Eleventybillion', *Historiann*, 19 March 2016, https://web.archive.org/web/20160805212953/https://historiann.com/2016/03/19/here-we-go-again-military-historian-complains-that-no-one-teaches-or-writes-about-military-history-any-more-part-eleventybillion/

Lorge, Peter, *Sun Tzu in the West: The Anglo-American Art of War* (Cambridge: Cambridge University Press, 2022)

Luo, Tian, *Translation, Reception and Canonization of the Art of War: Reviving Ancient Chinese Strategic Culture* (London: Routledge, 2022)

Luvaas, Jay, *The Education of an Army: British Military Thought, 1815–1940* (Chicago, IL: University of Chicago Press, 1964)

Lynn, John A., 'The Embattled Future of Academic Military History', *The Journal of Military History*, Vol. 61, No. 4 (October 1997), pp. 777–89

Lynn, John A., 'Breaching the Walls of Academe: The Purposes, Problems, and Prospects of Military History', *Academic Questions*, Vol. 21 (2008), pp. 18–36

Lyons, Gene M. and Morton, Louis, *Schools for Strategy: Education and Research in National Security Affairs* (New York: Praegar, 1965)

BIBLIOGRAPHY 245

Mahan, Alfred Thayer, 'Subordination in Historical Treatment', in *Annual Report of the American Historical Association for the Year 1902* (Washington, 1903), pp. 47–64

Mantoux, Etienne, *The Carthaginian Peace, or The Economic Consequences of Mr Keynes* (London: Oxford University Press, 1946)

Matloff, Maurice, 'The Nature and Scope of Military History', in R. Weigley (ed.), *New Dimensions in Military History* (San Rafael, CA: Presidio Press, 1975), pp. 387–410

McInnes, Colin, 'Strategic Doctrine and Political Practice', *Review of International Studies*, Vol. 14, No. 2 (April 1988), pp. 153–60

Mearscheimer, John, *Liddell Hart and the Weight of History* (London: Brassey's Defence, 1988)

Melvin, Mungo, 'Revisiting the Translators and Translations of Clausewitz's *On War*', *British Journal of Military History*, Vol. 8, No. 2 (September 2022), pp. 77–102

Michaels, Jeffrey, 'Revisiting General Sir John Hackett's *The Third World War*', *British Journal for Military History*, Vol. 3, No. 1 (November 2016), pp. 88–104

Michaels, Jeffrey and Ford, Matthew, 'Grand Strategy or Grant Strategy? Philanthropic Foundations, Strategic Studies and the American Academy', *Journal of Strategic Studies*, Vol. 46, No. 4 (2023), pp. 764–86

Milevski Lukas, *The Evolution of Modern Grand Strategic Thought* (Oxford: Oxford University Press, 2016)

Miller Lane, B., 'Felix Gilbert at Bryn Mawr College', in Harmut Lehmann (ed.), *Felix Gilbert as Scholar and Teacher* (German Historical Institute, Washington, D.C., Occasional Paper No. 6), pp. 11–16

Millis, Walter, *Military History* (Washington, D.C.: Service Center for Teachers of History, Publication Number 39, 1961)

Mitchell, Wesley C. et al., 'Discussion: The Bases of an American Defense Policy: Armed Forces', *Proceedings of the Academy of Political Science*, Vol. 19, No. 2 (January 1941), pp. 49–57

Molloy, Sean, *The Hidden History of Realism: A Genealogy of Power Politics* (London: Palgrave Macmillan, 2006)

Morgan-Owen, David, 'History and the Perils of Grand Strategy', *The Journal of Modern History*, Vol. 92, No. 2 (June 2020), pp. 351–85

Morgan-Owen, David and Finch, Michael, 'The Unrepentant Historian: Sir Michael Howard and the Birth of War Studies', *The British Journal of Military History*, Vol. 8, No. 2 (September 2022), pp. 55–76

Morillo, Stephen, with Pavkovic, Michael F., *What Is Military History?*, 2nd edn. (Cambridge: Polity, 2013)

Morton, Louis, 'The Historian and the Study of War', *The Mississippi Valley Historical Review*, Vol. 48, No. 4 (March 1962), pp. 599–613

Murray, Williamson, 'Thoughts on Grand Strategy', in W. Murray, R. H. Sinnreich, and J. Lacey (eds.), *The Shaping of Grand Strategy* (Cambridge: Cambridge University Press, 2011), pp. 1–33

Murray, Williamson, 'Thucydides: Theorist of War', *Naval War College Review*, Vol. 66, No. 4 (autumn 2013), pp. 1–17

Murray, Williamson, Knox, MacGregor, and Bernstein, Alvin (eds.), *The Making of Strategy: Rulers, States, and War* (Cambridge: Cambridge University Press, 1994)

Neale, J. E., 'Albert Frederick Pollard', *The English Historical Review*, Vol. 64, No. 251 (April 1949), pp. 198–205

Neer, Robert, 'The U.S. Military Is Everywhere, Except in History Books', *Aeon*, 16 March 2016, https://web.archive.org/web/20160711223312/https://aeon.co/ideas/the-us-military-is-everywhere-except-history-books

246 BIBLIOGRAPHY

Novick, Peter, *That Noble Dream: The 'Objectivity Question' and the American Historical Profession* (Cambridge: Cambridge University Press, 1988)

Oman, Charles, *On the Writing of History* (London: Routledge, 1939)

O'Neill, Robert, 'From Childhood to Maturity: The SDSC, 1972–82', in D. Ball and A. Carr (eds.), *A National Asset: 50 Years of the Strategic and Defence Studies Centre* (Acton ACT: ANU Press, 2016), pp. 49–71

O'Neill, Robert and Horner, David M. (eds.), *New Directions in Strategic Thinking* (London: Allen and Unwin, 1981)

O'Shanahan, William, 'The Literature on War', *The Review of Politics*, Vol. 4, No. 2 (April 1942), pp. 206–22

O'Shanahan, William, 'The Literature on War: Part II', *The Review of Politics*, Vol. 4, No. 3 (July 1942), pp. 327–46

Palmer, William, *Engagement with the Past: The Lives and Works of the World War II Generation of Historians* (Lexington, KY: University of Kentucky Press, 2001)

Paret, Peter, 'The French Army and la Guerre Révolutionnaire', *Journal of the Royal United Services Institution*, Vol. 104 (February 1959), pp. 59–69

Paret, Peter, 'A Total Weapon of Limited War', *Journal of the Royal United Services Institution*, Vol. 105 (February 1960), pp. 62–9

Paret, Peter, *Internal War and Pacification: The Vendée, 1789–1796*, Research Monograph No.12, Center of International Studies (Princeton, NJ: Princeton University, 1961)

Paret, Peter, *Guerrillas in the 1960s*, Center of International Studies (Princeton, NJ: Princeton University, 1962)

Paret, Peter, 'Hans Delbruck on Military Critics and Military Historians', *Military Affairs*, Vol. 30, No. 3 (November 1966), pp. 148–52

Paret, Peter, *Yorck and the Era of Prussian Reform 1807–1815* (Princeton, NJ: Princeton University Press, 1966)

Paret, Peter, 'The History of War', *Daedalus*, Vol. 100, No. 2 (spring 1971), pp. 376–96

Paret, Peter, *Clausewitz and the State* (Oxford: Clarendon Press, 1976)

Paret, Peter, *Makers of Modern Strategy: From Machiavelli to the Nuclear Age* (Princeton, NJ: Princeton University Press, 1986)

Paret, Peter, 'The New Military History', *Parameters*, Vol. 21 (autumn 1991), pp. 10–18

Paret, Peter, *Understanding War: Essays on Clausewitz and the History of Military Power* (Princeton, NJ: Princeton University Press, 1992)

Paret, Peter, 'Crossing Borders', *Historically Speaking*, Vol. 4, No. 2 (November 2002), pp. 8–10

Paret, Peter, 'Translation, Literal or Accurate', *The Journal of Military History*, Vol. 78, No. 3 (July 2014), pp. 1077–80

Parr, Adam, *The Mandate of Heaven: Strategy, Revolution, and the First European Translation of Sunzi's Art of War (1772)* (Leiden and Boston: Brill, 2019)

Plfanze, Otto, 'The Americanization of Hajo Holborn', in H. Lehmann and J. Sheehan (eds.), *An Interrupted Past: German Speaking Refugee Historians in the United States after 1933* (Washington, D.C. and Cambridge: German Historical Institute and Cambridge University Press, 1991), pp. 170–79

Poe II, Bryce, 'British Army Reforms, 1902–1914', *Military Affairs*, Vol. 31, No. 3 (autumn 1967), pp. 131–8

Pogge von Strandmann, Harmut, 'The Role of British and German Historians in Mobilizing Public Opinion in 1914', in B. Stuchtey and P. Wende (eds.), *British and German Historiography, 1750–1950: Traditions, Perceptions, and Transfers* (Oxford: Oxford University Press, 2000), pp. 335–72

Possony, Stefan, 'Japanese Naval Strategy', *United States Naval Institute Proceedings*, Vol. 70, No. 5 (May 1944), pp. 515–24

Porter, Patrick, *Military Orientalism: Eastern War through Western Eyes* (London: Hurst, 2009)

Porter, Patrick, 'Beyond the American Century: Walter Lippmann and American Grand Strategy, 1943–1950', *Diplomacy & Statecraft*, Vol. 22, No. 4 (2011), pp. 557–77

Preston, Andrew, 'National Security as Grand Strategy: Edward Mead Earle and the Burdens of World Power', in E. Borgwardt, C. McKnight Nichols, and A. Preston (eds.), *Rethinking American Grand Strategy* (Oxford: Oxford University Press, 2021), pp. 238–53

Rabinbach, Anson, 'The Making of *Makers of Modern Strategy*: German Refugee Historians Go to War', *The Princeton Library Chronicle*, Vol. 75, No. 1 (autumn 2013), pp. 97–108

Ramsey, Paul Michael, 'Professor Spenser Wilkinson, Admiral William Sims and the Teaching of Strategy and Sea Power at the University of Oxford and the United States Naval War College, 1909–1927', in N. Rodger, J. Dancy, B. Darnell, and E. Wilson (eds.), *Strategy and the Sea: Essays in Honour of John B. Hattendorf* (Rochester, NY: Boydell Press, 2016), pp. 213–25

Ritter, Gerhard, *German Refugee Historians and Friedrich Meinecke: Letters and Documents, 1910–1977*, trans. A. Skinner (Leiden: Brill, 2010)

Robertson, Sir William, *Soldiers and Statesmen, 1914–1918*, 2 vols. (London: Cassell, 1926)

Robinson, James Harvey, *The New History: Essays Illustrating the Modern Historical Outlook* (New York: Macmillan, 1932. First published 1912)

Ropp, Theodore, 'The Teaching of Military History', *Military Affairs*, Vol. 13, No. 1 (spring 1949), pp. 14–19

Ropp, Theodore, *War in the Modern World* (Durham, NC: Duke University Press, 1959)

Ropp, Theodore, 'Duke University: University of North Carolina National Security Policy Seminar', *Military Affairs*, Vol. 27, No. 1 (spring 1963), pp. 8–15

Ropp, Theodore, 'Military History and the Social Sciences', *Military Affairs*, Vol. 30, No. 1 (spring 1966), pp. 8–13

Ropp, Theodore, 'Forty Years of the American Military Institute', *Military Affairs*, Vol. 35, No. 3 (October 1971), pp. 89–91

Ropp, Theodore, 'Military Historical Scholarship since 1937', *Military Affairs*, Vol. 41, No. 42 (April 1977), pp. 68–74

Ropp, Theodore, 'Strategic Thinking since 1945', in R. O'Neill and D. M. Horner (eds.), *New Directions in Strategic Thinking* (London: Allen and Unwin, 1981), pp. 1–13

Ropp, Theodore (ed. S. Roberts), *The Development of a Modern Navy: French Naval Policy, 1871–1904* (Annapolis, MD: Naval Institute Press, 1987)

Schmidt, Brian (ed.), *International Relations and the First Great Debate* (London and New York: Routledge, 2012)

Schroeder, Paul, 'Historical Reality vs. Neo-Realist Theory', *International Security*, Vol. 19, No. 1 (summer 1994), pp. 108–48

Schroeder, Paul, 'History and International Relations Theory: Not Use or Abuse, but Fit or Misfit', *International Security*, Vol. 22, No. 1 (summer 1997), pp. 64–74

Schurman, Donald M., *The Education of a Navy: The Development of British Naval Strategic Thought, 1867–1914* (London: Cassell, 1965)

Seipp, Adam R., '"Visionary Battle Scenes": Reading Sir John Hackett's *The Third World War, 1977–85*', *The Journal of Military History*, Vol. 83, No. 4 (October 2019), pp. 1235–57

Sheehan, James, 'Gordon Alexander Craig (1913–2005)', *Central European History*, Vol. 40, No. 1 (March 2007), pp. 134–5

248 BIBLIOGRAPHY

Shore, Elliot, 'Carrie Bamberger Frank Fuld', *Jewish Women: A Comprehensive Historical Encyclopedia*, 27 February 2009, Jewish Women's Archive, https://jwa.org/encyclopedia/article/fuld-carrie-bamberger-frank, accessed 27 July 2020

Showalter, Dennis, 'A Modest Plea for Drums and Trumpets', *Military Affairs*, Vol. 39, no. 2 (April 1975), pp. 71–4

Showalter, Dennis, review of *Makers of Modern Strategy* in *Military Affairs*, Vol. 51, No. 2 (April 1987), p. 100

Silove Nina, 'Beyond the Buzzword: The Three Meanings of "Grand Strategy"', *Security Studies*, Vol. 27, No. 1 (2018), pp. 27–57

Sinnreich, Richard Hart, 'Awkward Partners: Military History and American Military Education', in W. Murray and R. Hart Sinnreich (eds.), *The Past as Prologue: The Importance of History to the Military Profession* (Cambridge: Cambridge University Press, 2006), pp. 55–77

Skinner, Quentin, 'Meaning and Understanding in the History of Ideas', *History and Theory*, Vol. 8, No. 1 (January 1969), pp. 3–53

Skinner, Quentin, *Visions of Politics*, Vol. 1: *Regarding Method* (Cambridge: Cambridge University Press, 2002)

Smith, Jr., Datus C., 'Ten Years of Franklin Publications', *ALA Bulletin*, Vol. 57, No. 6 (June 1963), pp. 507–12

Snyder, Jack, *The Soviet Strategic Culture: Implications for Limited Nuclear Operations* (Santa Monica, CA: RAND Corporation, 1977)

Soffer, Reba, 'Duty, Character and Confidence: History at Oxford, 1850–1914', *The Historical Journal*, Vol. 30, No. 1 (March 1987), pp. 77–104

Spenser Wilkinson, Henry, *The University and the Study of War* (Oxford: Clarendon Press, 1909)

Spenser Wilkinson, Henry, *Thirty-Five Years, 1874–1909* (London: Constable and Company, 1933)

Spiller, Roger, 'Military History and Its Fictions', *The Journal of Military History*, Vol. 70, No. 4 (October 2006), pp. 1081–97

Spykman, Nicholas, *America's Strategy in World Politics: The United States and the Balance of Power* (New Haven, CT: Yale University, Institute of International Studies, 1942)

Stebbins, Richard Poate, *The Career of Herbert Rosinski: An Intellectual Pilgrimage* (New York: P. Lang, 1989)

Steiner, Barry, *Bernard Brodie and the Foundations of American Nuclear Strategy* (Lawrence, KA: University Press of Kansas, 1991)

Stern, Beatrice, 'A History of the Institute of Advanced Study' (unpublished ms, 1964)

Stevenson, David, 'Learning from the Past: The Relevance of International History', *International Affairs*, Vol. 90, No. 1 (2014), pp. 5–22

Stone, John, 'George Orwell on Politics and War', *Review of International Studies*, Vol. 43, part 2 (2016), pp. 221–39

Strachan, Hew, *European Armies and the Conduct of War* (London: Allen & Unwin, 1983)

Strachan, Hew, review of *Makers of Modern Strategy* in *The English Historical Review*, Vol. 103, No. 406 (January 1988), pp. 158–60

Strachan, Hew, 'The Lost Meaning of Strategy', *Survival*, Vol. 47 No. 3 (autumn 2005), pp. 33–54

Strachan, Hew, 'How Is War Directed? The Problem of Strategy', Humanitas lecture for CRASSH, University of Cambridge, delivered 3 February 2011, https://www.youtube.com/watch?v=FHWyffZn5-c

Strachan, Hew, 'Clausewitz and the First World War', *The Journal of Military History*, Vol. 75, No. 2 (April 2011), pp. 367–91

Strachan, Hew, *The Direction of War: Contemporary Strategy in Historical Perspective* (Cambridge: Cambridge University Press, 2013)

Strachan, Hew, 'The Study of War at Oxford 1909–2009', in C. Hood, D. King, and G. Peele (eds.), *Forging a Discipline: A Critical Assessment of Oxford's Development of the Study of Politics and International Relations in Comparative Perspective* (Oxford: Oxford University Press, 2014), pp. 204–21

Strachan, Hew, 'The Future of Strategic Studies: Lessons from the Last "Golden Age"', in R. Glenn (ed.), *New Directions in Strategic Thinking 2.0* (Canberra: ANU Press, 2018), pp. 149–66

Strachan, Hew, 'Michael Howard and Clausewitz', *Journal of Strategic Studies*, Vol. 45, No. 1 (February 2022), pp. 143–60

Stradis, Andreas, 'Thucydides in the Staff College', in C. Lee and N. Morley (eds.), *A Handbook to the Reception of Thucydides* (London: Wiley, 2015), pp. 425–45

Stevenson, David, 'Learning from the Past: The Relevance of International History', *International Affairs*, Vol. 90, No. 1 (2014), pp. 5–22

Stewart, Andrew, *Royal College of Defence Studies 1927–2017: Ninety Years of Preparing Strategic Leaders* (London: Royal College of Defence Studies, 2017)

Sumida, Jon Tetsuro, *Inventing Grand Strategy and Teaching Command: The Classic Works of Alfred Thayer Mahan Reconsidered* (Baltimore, MD: The Johns Hopkins University Press, 1997)

Sumida, Jon Tetsuro, 'Alfred Thayer Mahan, Geopolitician', *The Journal of Strategic Studies*, Vol. 22, Nos. 2–3 (1999), pp. 39–62

Summers, Jr., Harry, 'Bookshelf: New Lessons from Old Wars', *Wall Street Journal*, 9 May 1986

Sun Tzu (trans. S. Griffiths), *The Art of War* (Oxford: Clarendon Press, 1963)

Swinton, Ernest, *Over My Shoulder* (Oxford: George Ronald, 1951)

Taylor, A. J. P., 'Accident Prone, or What Happened Next', *The Journal of Modern History*, Vol. 49, No.1 (March 1977), pp. 1–18

Thatcher, Sandford G., 'Herbert S. Bailey, Jr. 12 July 1921–28 June 2011', *Proceedings of the American Philosophical Society*, Vol. 161, No. 1 (March 2017), pp. 69–83

Thursfield, Henry George, 'Richmond, Sir Herbert William (1871–1946)', rev. Marc Brodie, *Oxford Dictionary of National Biography*, Oxford University Press, 2004, http://www.oxforddnb.com/view/article/35743, accessed 5 September 2012

Townsend, Robert B., *History's Babel: Scholarship, Professionalization, and the Historical Enterprise in the United States, 1880–1940* (Chicago, IL: University of Chicago Press, 2012)

Townsend, Robert B., 'The Rise and Decline of History Specializations over the Past 40 Years', *Perspectives on History: The Newsmagazine of the American Historical Association*, December 2015, https://www.historians.org/publications-and-directories/perspectives-on-history/december-2015/the-rise-and-decline-of-history-specializations-over-the-past-40-years

Trachtenberg, Marc, 'The State of International History', *E-International Relations*, 9 March 2013, https://www.e-ir.info/2013/03/09/the-state-of-international-history/

Trythall, Anthony John, *'Boney' Fuller: The Intellectual General 1878–1966* (London: Cassell, 1977)

Van Riper, Paul, 'The Relevance of History to the Military Profession: An American Marine's View', in W. Murray and R. H. Sinnreich (eds.), *The Past as Prologue: The Importance of History to the Military Profession* (Cambridge: Cambridge University Press, 2006), pp. 34–54

Walt, Stephen, 'The Search for a Science of Strategy: A Review Essay', *International Security*, Vol. 12, No. 1 (summer 1987), pp. 140–65

250 BIBLIOGRAPHY

Walt, Stephen, 'The Renaissance of Security Studies', *International Studies Quarterly*, Vol. 35, No. 2 (June 1991), pp. 211–39

Weigley, Russell, *The American Way of War: A History of the United States Military Strategy and Policy* (Bloomington, IL: Indiana University Press, 1973)

Weigley, Russell, 'Review: Walter Millis and the Conscience of the Military Historian', *Reviews in American History*, Vol. 16, No. 3 (September 1988), pp. 500–5

Wheeler, Ted, 'Teacher, Scholar, Historian Adds Life to Academics', *The Stanford Daily*, 16 April 1982

Whiting, Allen S., 'In Memoriam: Quincy Wright, 1890–1970: A Symposium', *Conflict Resolution*, Vol. 14, No. 4 (December 1970), pp. 443–8

Whittingham, Daniel, *Charles E. Callwell and the British Way in Warfare* (Cambridge: Cambridge University Press, 2020)

Wilson, Peter, 'The Myth of the "First Great Debate"', *Review of International Studies*, Vol. 24, No. 5 (December 1998), pp. 1–16

Wilson Lyon, E., 'John Holland Rose', in B. Schmitt (ed.), *Some Historians of Modern Europe: Essays in Historiography by Former Students of the Department of History of the University of Chicago* (Chicago, IL: University of Chicago Press, 1942), pp. 367–91

Winter, Jay M., 'Oxford and the First World War', in B. Harrison (ed.), *The History of the University of Oxford*, Vol. 8: *The Twentieth Century* (Oxford: Oxford University Press, 1994), pp. 2–25

Wiseman, Geoffrey, review of *Makers of Modern Strategy* in *International Affairs*, Vol. 63, No. 3 (summer 1987), pp. 503–4

Wolters, Timothy S., 'Harvey DeWeerd and the Dawn of Academic Military History in the United States', *The Journal of Military History*, Vol. 85, No. 1 (January 2021), pp. 95–133

Wright, Quincy, *A Study of War*, 2 vols. (Chicago, IL: University of Chicago Press, 1942)

Yost, David, review of Paret *Makers* in *The Wilson Quarterly*, Vol. 10, No. 4 (autumn 1986), pp. 142–4

Zellen, Barry Scott, *State of Doom: Bernard Brodie, the Bomb, and the Birth of the Bipolar World* (London and New York: Continuum, 2012)

Zeller, Thomas W., 'The Diplomatic History Bandwagon: A State of the Field', *The Journal of American History*, Vol. 95, No. 4 (March 2009), pp. 1053–73

Index

Because the index has been created to work across multiple formats, indexed terms for which a page range is given (e.g., 52–53, 66–70, etc.) may occasionally appear only on some, but not all, of the pages within the range.

Albion, Robert G. 68, 221
Alexander, Martin 160, 199
American Historical Association 15–18
Anson, Sir William 24–5
Aston, Sir George 39–40
Aydelotte, Frank
  biography 221
  Earle's seminars and 64, 67–8
  letter to Charles Oman 72–6
  on the proposed *Makers* volume 66–7
  as a visiting/refugee scholar at IAS 79–81

Bacevich, Andrew J. 3
Bailey, Herbert S.
  biography 222
  as director of Franklin Publications 102
  interest in a revised *Makers* (1960s) 102–3, 143, 147
  interest in a revised *Makers* (Paret) 99, 134–5, 142–3, 154, 171
  interest in *Makers* 1, 99, 142–4
  at Princeton University Press 1, 143–4
  Ropp's *Makers Revisited* and 129–30
  on the seminar origin story 6
Bailey, Thomas A. 68, 222
Bamburger, Louis 52–3
Bamburger Fuld, Caroline 52–3
Bassford, Christopher 83, 194
Baylis, John 205
Beard, Charles A. 55
Bernstein, Alvin 9–10, 176–7, 185–6, 205, 219–20
Betts, Richard 192–3
Bohme, K. R. 125–6
Bond, Brian 160, 199–200, 222
Bowditch, John 114–15
Brands, Hal 3–4, 220
Brevern, Maxim von 68, 234
Brinton, Crane 74–5, 103, 157–8, 222
Brodie, Bernard
  biography 222
  critique of Kiralfy 90–2

at Earle's IAS seminar 42, 68, 76–7
Guide to Naval Strategy 91
as a possible contributor to *Makers* 76–7, 90, 95, 100, 105
at the RAND corporation 105
relationship with Earle 105–6
review of *Makers* 87–90
on sea power coverage in
  Makers 89–90, 202–3
'Strategy as Science' article 189–90
Bucholz, Arden 20–1
Burrows, Montagu 23–4

Callwell, Charles 25, 177, 201, 203–4
Carr, E. H. 40
Carver, Michael 159, 169–70, 199, 209, 222–3
Chew, Ernest C.T. 122–3, 126–7, 223
Chinard, Gilbert 68, 223
Chung Ong Chit 122–3, 223
Citino, Robert 215–16
Clausewitz, Carl von 77–8, 83, 138–9, 177, 180–1, 186–7, 194–7
Coffman, Edward 110–11
Cohen, Eliot 3
Collier, Thomas W. 157–8, 180–1, 200–1, 209, 223
Conger, Captain Arthur 15–16, 18–21
Corbett, Julian
  'Julian Corbett Prize' in naval history 36–7
  on Laughton 33
  legacy of 202–3
  in *Makers* 89–90, 117, 177, 202–4
  as a naval historian 30, 33–5
Cot, Pierre 68, 223
Cox, Michael 54–5
Craig, Gordon
  academic career 11, 103, 163–4, 216–17
  as associate editor on *Makers II* 10–11, 134–5, 145–6, 156–7, 163–4, 174–5, 192
  Bailey and an updated *Makers* 102–3, 143, 147
  biography 223–4

252   INDEX

Craig, Gordon (*cont.*)
  co-authored final chapter in *Makers II* 166–8, 177–8, 192–3
  contribution to *Makers* 78–9
  on the discipline of history 216–17
  at Earle's IAS seminar 68
  on Earle's terminology 122, 131
  as editorial assistant on *Makers* 10–11, 69–71
  on Geyer's chapter 182–3
  Makers Revisited (Ropp) and 119, 148–9
  portrait 164
  on the Reagan administration's lack of strategic thinking 163–6
  relationship with Paret 138–9, 145
  reviews of *Makers II* 177–8
  revised essay in *Makers II* 157
  the seminar origin story 6
Craven, Wesley Frank 108
Crowl, Philip 161, 224
Cunliffe, Sir Foster 24–5

Delbrück, Hans
  in *Makers* 44–5, 76, 78–9
  in *Makers II* 157
  Paret as a Delbrückian 142
  relationship with Meinecke 82
  Ropp as a Delbrückian 132–3
  the study of military history 14, 19–22, 27–8, 35–6
Dennery, Etienne 68, 224
Deutsch, Karl 41–2
DeWeerd, Harvey
  academic career 104–5
  biography 224
  contribution to *Makers* 68, 73–5, 78–9, 104–5
  at Earle's IAS seminar 68
  on Liddell Hart's critique 94–5
  omission from *Makers II* 157
  the proposal for *Makers* and 67, 82, 97
  at the RAND corporation 104–5
Dighton, Adam 22–3

Earle, Edward Mead see also *Makers of Modern Strategy* (Earle)
  academic career 11, 48–9, 54–5, 96–7, 137
  biography 224–5
  civilian understanding and engagement with war 13–14, 58–61, 105–6, 114–15
  contribution to *Makers* 73, 79, 87–8, 95
  death 7, 95
  engagement with Clausewitz 194
  engagement with strategy 176–7
  enlargement of war 57–8

Fox's involvement with 42
general operational history of the USAAF 87–8, 95
grand/national strategy concept 3–6, 11, 48, 62–3, 188–91, 196–7, 203–4
as a historian 7, 49, 55, 61
ill health 51, 54–5, 57, 95–6
at the Institute for Advanced Study 51, 54–5
legacy of *Makers* 95–8
Presidential Medal for Merit award 59
relationship with Brodie 105–6
relationship with Liddell Hart 92–3, 199
relationship with Oman 44–5
research career 96–7
research remit at IAS 55–8, 61–3, 69, 97
role of history in the study of war 11
security studies, foundation of 48–50
seminars at IAS 63–8, 79–80, 95
totalitarianism's challenges 48–9, 57–8
transatlantic influences on 44–5
Turkey, the Great Powers, and the Baghdad Railway 54–5, 61, 97
war-peace boundaries 48–9, 57–8, 187–91, 196–7
war service during the Second World War 68–9, 87–8
Ekbladh, David 3, 48–9, 61–2

Falls, Cyril 1–2
Fergie, Dexter 48–9
Flexner, Abraham
  biography 225
  forced resignation of 56–7
  foundation of the Institute for Advanced Study 48–9, 51–4, 79–80
  the modern university system and 51–3
  portrait 51
Fordham, Elizabeth 38
Fox, William T. R. 41–2, 68, 225
Franklin Publications 99–101, 143–4 *see also* Princeton University Press
Freedman, Lawrence 158, 225
Fuller, J. F. C. 177, 198–9
Fuller, William 180–2

Garnett, John 205
Gat, Azar 21–2
Germany
  Delbrück's pioneering scientific approach to military history 19–22
  power of the German army 21–2
Geyer, Michael 161, 169–70, 181–3, 225
Gilbert, Felix
  academic career 11, 103

as associate editor on *Makers II* 10–11, 134–5, 145–8, 174–5, 192
Bailey and an updated *Makers* 102–3, 143, 147
Bailey and an updated *Makers II* 143–4
biography 225–6
co-authored final chapter in *Makers II* 166–8, 177–8, 192–3
connections with IAS 146–7
contribution to *Makers* 76–9, 82
contribution to *Makers II* 157
on Delbrück 82
at Earle's IAS seminar 68
on Earle's terminology 122, 131
as editorial assistant on *Makers* 10–11, 69
on francophone and germanophone scholar's contributions 80
friendship with Paret 138–9, 145
Makers Revisited (Ropp) and 119, 148–9
portrait 70
the proposal for *Makers* and 67, 69, 82, 97
relationship with Guerlac 71–2
the seminar origin story of *Makers* 6, 67
as a visiting/refugee scholar at IAS 81–2
Gooch, John 158–9, 178–82
Gottmann, Jean
biography 226
contribution to *Makers* 68, 73–5, 78–9, 200–1
at Earle's IAS seminar 68
in *Makers II* 151, 200–1
as a visiting/refugee scholar at IAS 80–1
Great Britain (GB)
British strategic thinkers in *Makers* 198–9
British strategic thinkers in *Makers II* 177, 198–202
Laughton's naval history 28–30
officer education in military history 22–3
scholarly engagement with military history 22–5
Gretz, Elizabeth 171–2, 209–10
Griffith, Samuel B. 207–9
Gropman, Alan 2–3
Guerlac, Henry
academic career 103, 148
biography 226
contribution to *Makers* 71–2
in *Makers II* 180
omission from *Makers II* 151–3, 160
on the seminar origin story 71–2
on the success of *Makers* 83–4

Hackett, Sir John 159
Hagen, Mark von 161–2, 234
Hanson, Victor Davis 9–10, 177, 205, 219–20
Headrick, Daniel 179

Herz, John H. 68, 226
Higham, John 61–2
history
the 'new history' 61–2
the specialization and professionalization of 4–5, 49–50, 61–2
World War II generation of historians 218–19
Hoekzema, Loren 143–5, 148–50, 158, 160–2, 169–70, 209–11
Holborn, Hajo
academic career 103
biography 226–7
contribution to *Makers* 73–5, 81–2
revised essay in *Makers II* 157, 182–3
Holden Reid, Brian 180–2, 184, 198–9
Howard, Sir Michael
biography 227
conception of the history of war 141
contribution to *Makers II* 10–11, 135, 158–9, 170, 198
involvement with *Makers* 1–2, 5–6
military history in British universities 39–40
as a possible co-editor for *Makers II* 150, 158
relationship with Liddell Hart 200
relationship with Paret 10–11, 136–7
on the role of the historian 217–18
translation of *On War* (Clausewitz) 138–9, 177, 194–7
work on the 'Intelligence Histories' series 179
Hubbard, Deborah A. 68, 227
Hyam, Ronald 34–5

Institute for Advanced Study (IAS)
acknowledgement in *Makers II* 46–8, 147–8
agreement to a new *Makers II* 146–8
Carnegie Corporation funding for Earle's research 51–2, 62–4
connection with *Makers* 134–5
Earle's employment by 51, 54–7
Earle's research remit 55–8, 61–3, 69
Earle's seminars at 63–8, 79–80, 95
foundation of 48–9, 51–4
Gilbert's fellowship at 146–7
Paret's time at 138–9, 173–4
as rights holder to *Makers* 101–2
School of Economics and Politics 54, 56
School of Mathematics 53–4
seminar origin story for *Makers* 6, 42, 46–8, 66–7, 71–2, 134–5
visiting scholars 79–80

James, Doris Clayton 160, 227
Johansson, Bertil 125–6
Johnston, Robert Matteson 15–20

254 INDEX

Kann, Robert A. 68, 227
Kaplan, Fred 40–2
Keegan, John 159, 177–8, 180–3, 186–7, 214–15
Kennedy, Paul 110–11
Ken Wong Lin 128, 227–8
Kiralfy, Alexander 90–2, 100, 228
Knorr, Klaus 137–8
Knox, MacGregor 9–10, 176–7, 185–6, 205, 219–20
Kovacs, Arpad (Irving Gibson)
  biography 228
  contribution to *Makers* 83–4, 160, 198–9
  Liddell Hart's critique of 92–5

Lambert, Andrew 29, 33
Laughton, John Knox 14, 28–9, 33–7
Lauterbach, Albert T. 68, 228
Liddell Hart, Basil
  critique of Kovac's chapter 92–5
  The Ghost of Napoleon 131–2
  on the importance of war studies 108
  limited liability doctrine 94–5
  in *Makers* 177, 198–201
  in *Makers II* 160, 198–201
  relationship with Earle 92–3, 199
  relationship with Paret 137–8, 140, 200
  reputation 94–5
  review of *Makers* 46, 92–3
  Sun Tzu and indirect strategy 208
Lippmann, Walter 1–2, 84–5
Lockwood, William W. 68, 228
Luce, Admiral Stephen B. 29–30

MacIsaac, David 125–6, 180–1, 199, 229
Mahan, Alfred Thayer 15–16, 27–30, 76–7, 89, 117
Makers of Ancient Strategy (Hanson) 9–10, 177, 205–6, 219–20
Makers of Modern Strategy (Earle)
  air power coverage 87–8, 100, 102
  analysis of strategy in 187–91
  ancient strategy in 204–9
  British strategic thinkers in 198–9
  Brodie's critique of the Kiralfy chapter 90–2
  canon of strategic thought 4, 177, 194–204, 211–12
  Cold-War era translations 99–102, 143–4
  contributors 48, 67–8, 71–80, 184, 214–15
  contributor's royalty payments 146–7
  creation 48, 97–8
  critical reception/reviews 46–8, 83–90, 92–3, 186–7
  early outline for 72–6
  Franco-German focus of 82, 197–8

francophone and germanophone contributors 79–83, 97
grand/national strategy concept 3–6, 11, 48, 62–3, 188–91, 196–7, 203–4
initial proposal for 66–7
legacy of 1–6, 97–9, 103, 114, 220
Liddell Hart's thought in 177, 198–201
Makers II contrasted with 134–5, 162–3, 183–5
military history and 1–2, 5–6, 11, 114, 213–19
naval history coverage 88–90, 107, 201–4
outdated chapters (post-war decades) 100, 102
Princeton University Press and 46–8
professional military education and 2–3, 5
publication of 13
purpose of the book 5–6, 13–14, 49–51, 66–7, 80, 183–4
revised edition proposals 83–99
sales numbers 102, 144, 209–10
security studies, foundation of 3, 11, 48–50
seminar member-contributors 67–8, 72–80
seminar origin story 6, 42, 46–8, 66–7, 71–2, 134–5
strategic studies, foundation of 3, 5, 48–50, 219
Sun Tzu's absence from 209
as a textbook 210–11
title 66–7
war studies and 1–2, 5
World War II generation of historians 218–19
Makers of Modern Strategy: From Machiavelli to the Nuclear Age (*Makers II*, Paret)
  acknowledgement of IAS involvement in the original 46–8, 147–8
  air power coverage 151–3
  American strategic thought in 134, 150–1, 198
  analysis of strategy in 184, 186–7, 190–4
  ancient strategy in 204–9
  appraisal of and updates to Earle's *Makers* 144–5, 150–4, 160
  Bailey's involvement with 134–5, 142–3, 154
  British strategic thinkers in 177, 198–202
  canon of strategic thought 4, 177, 194–204, 211–12
  challenges 134–5
  contrasted with Earle's *Makers* 134–5, 162–3, 183–5, 209–10, 215–16
  contributors 134–5, 156–62, 184
  contributor's royalty payments 147–8
  cover design 171–3
  Craig's focus on contemporary concerns in 163–6

critical reception/reviews 3–5, 176–83,
  192–3, 210–11
disciplinary identities 214
editorial processes 168–71
form and presentation 170–1
Gilbert and Craig as associate editors 10–11,
  145–6, 174–5, 192
Gilbert and Craig's final chapter 166–8,
  177–8, 192–3
Howard as a possible co-editor 158
Howard's contributions to 158–60, 170
IAS agreement to 146–8
Liddell Hart's thought in 160, 198–201
marketing of 172–3
naval history coverage 201–4
nuclear power in 150–3, 158, 167
origins of 134, 142–6
Paret as editor 145–6, 154, 174–5
Paret's introduction 166–7, 186–7, 190–2
production process 134–5, 156–7
publication of 173–4
purpose of the book 5–6, 135, 184–5
role of Institute for Advanced Study 46–8
sales numbers 209–10
scoping the project 150–6
as a single volume 145
as a 'successor' to Earle's *Makers* 5, 134, 148,
  154–6, 172–3
table of contents 151–5, 160
as a textbook 210–11
title 171–2, 185–6
Makers of Modern Strategy Revisited (Ropp)
air power coverage 125
analysis of strategy in 192
Asian powers and strategy coverage 122–3,
  126–7, 133
authors 119–23
classical strategists in 204–5
Earle's terminology and editorial selection
  process 121–3, 131
failure of 130–3
Howard as a possible co-editor 150
middle powers in 125–6, 133
as a military history book 128, 131–3
naval history coverage 123–4, 177, 202–3
new chapters 119–27
and Paret's planned revised *Makers* 129–30,
  148–50
purpose of the book 118–21, 127, 130
Ropp's efforts to revise 48
Ropp's Singapore fellowship and 99–100,
  115–16, 118–21, 130–1
Ropp's vision for 6, 99–100
schedule 120

Schurman as co-editor 99–100, 118, 128–9
Schurman's contributions to 123–4
Makers of Nuclear Strategy 205
Making of Strategy, The (Murray *et al*) 9–10,
  176–7, 185–6, 205, 219–20
Malcolm, Angus 194–5
Mantoux, Etienne
  biography 228
  at Earle's IAS seminar 68
  omission from *Makers II* 151, 198
  as a seminar member-contributor 68,
    73–5, 78–9
  as a visiting/refugee scholar at IAS 80–1
Mantoux, Paul 80–1
Martin, Alexander 221
Masland, John 90
Matloff, Maurice 18–19, 109–10, 228
Maurice, Sir Frederick 14, 37–9
McInnes, Colin 180–5
Meinecke, Friedrich 82
Mendershausen, Horst 68, 229
Military Historian and Economist, The 18–19
military history *see also* war studies
  American academic engagement with 14–19
  in American universities 14–19, 40–3,
    108–11
  in British universities 22–7, 30–3, 36–40
  decline in the academic status of 111–12
  Delbrück's pioneering approach to 14, 19–22,
    27–8, 35–6
  in Europe during the First World War 30–6
  focus on military operations 2, 16–17
  in German universities 19–22, 35–6
  interdisciplinarity 111–13
  Makers and 1–2, 5–6, 11, 213–19
  new military history 142
  Paret's broader conception of the history of
    war 11, 139–42, 156, 174–5, 191–2, 214–15
  post-First World War opportunities for 36–43
  Ropp's influence in 107–9
  within the scientific study of
    history 17–22, 43–4
  in the twenty-first century 215–16
  war and society approach 2, 16–17
  war studies and 26–7
military institutions
  the German army 21–2, 35–6
  historical sections 19–22
  military history in Europe 19–20
  power of the German army 21–2
Millis, Walter 111–12, 114
Moran, Daniel 195–6
Murray, Williamson 3–4, 9–10, 176–7, 185–6,
  205, 219–20

256 INDEX

naval history *see also* Corbett, Julian
  Laughton's naval history 28–30, 33
  of Mahan in the US 27–30
  in *Makers* 88–90, 107, 201–4
  in *Makers II* 201–4
  in *Makers Revisited* 123–4, 177, 202–3
  Schurman's study of 116–18, 123–4
  study of in British universities 33–5
Neumann, Sigmund 74–6, 81–2, 229
*New Makers of Modern Strategy: From the
  Ancient World to the Digital Age, The*
  (Brands) 220

Oman, Sir Charles
  Earle's letters to 49–50
  in *Makers* 76
  as a military historian 23–4
  as a potential contributor to
    Makers 72–6, 78–9
  on the study of war 43–4
O'Neill, Robert 125–6
Oppenheimer, Robert 48–9, 64, 96, 102–3

Palmer, Robert Roswell 71–2, 86–7, 103,
  180, 229
Palmer, William 218–19
Paret, Peter see also *Makers of Modern Strategy:
  From Machiavelli to the Nuclear Age*
  (*Makers II*, Paret)
  academic career 11, 136–41
  biography 229–30
  broad conception of the history of war 11,
    139–42, 156, 174–5, 191–2, 214–15
  the canon of strategic thought 4, 177
  Clausewitz scholarship 138–9, 177, 180–1,
    186–7, 194–7
  as a Delbrückian 142
  on the discipline of history 216–18
  Earle's *Makers* and 142–3, 176
  engagement with strategy 176–7
  *French Revolutionary Warfare from Indochina
    to Algeria* 137
  as a military historian 139–41
  on New Military History 142
  portrait 140
  relationship with Howard 10–11, 136–7
  relationship with Liddell Hart 137–8,
    140, 200
  role of history in the study of war 11, 137–9
  Ropp's *Makers Revisited* and 129–30, 148–50
  on Ropp's status as a military historian
    107–8
  the School of Historical Studies at the
    IAS 173–4

  at Stanford University 139–40
  translation of *On War* (Clausewitz) 138–9,
    177, 194–7
  war service 135–7
peace studies 41–2
Pintner, Walter 161–2, 230
Pollard, Albert Frederick 36–7
Poole, DeWitt Clinton 68, 230
Porch, Douglas 158–60, 200–1, 230
Possony, Stefan
  biography 230–1
  contribution to *Makers* 68, 73–5, 78–9
  at Earle's IAS seminar 68
  omission from *Makers II* 151, 198
  on revisions to *Makers* 83–4
  as a visiting/refugee scholar at IAS 80–1
Princeton University Press
  ad for *Makers of Modern Strategy* 47
  Bailey's interest in *Makers* 99, 142–4
  publication of *Makers II* 129, 134–5,
    147, 173–4
  seminar origin story of *Makers* 46–8

Rabinbach, Anson 82
RAND corporation 104–5
Reid, Brian Holden 4–5
Rice, Condoleezza 161–2, 180–1, 231
Richmond, Sir Herbert 34–5, 89–90, 202–3
Riper, Lieutenant-General Paul Van 2–3
Robertson, Sir William 36
Robinson, James Harvey 61–2
Ropp, Theodore see also *Makers of Modern
  Strategy Revisited* (Ropp)
  on American military history in the
    1930s 18–19
  biography 231
  collaboration with Schurman 99–100
  contribution to *Makers* 6, 8–11, 88–9,
    99–100, 106–7, 114–15
  Corbett's significance 202–3
  as a Delbrückian 132–3
  on the discipline of history 216–18
  fascination with Earle's
    terminology 121–2, 131
  on the importance of war studies 108
  interdisciplinarity and military history
    111–13
  on the language of strategy 197
  lifelong relationship with *Makers* 10–11,
    106, 114–15
  as a military historian 106–9, 113–15,
    131–3, 214–16
  portrait 116
  on the role of the historian 99

teaching career 11, 107–14, 118
Visiting Fellowship in Canberra 125–6,
   128–9
visiting fellowship at Singapore
   University 99–100, 115–16
War in the Modern World 107, 114–15
Rose, John Holland 34
Rosinski, Herbert
   biography 231
   contribution to *Makers* 83, 202
   at Earle's IAS seminar 68
   review of *Makers* 87–9
   as a visiting/refugee scholar at IAS
   77–8, 80–1
Rothenberg, Gunther 161, 169–70, 182–3, 231
Rothfels, Hans
   biography 231–2
   Clausewitz scholarship 83
   contribution to *Makers* 73, 75, 81–2,
   157, 196–7
   as a student of Meinecke 82
Rumney, Jay 68, 232

Schroeder, Paul 192–3
Schurman, Donald
   biography 232
   as co-editor on *Makers Revisited*
   (Ropp) 99–100, 118, 128–9
   Corbett's significance 202–3
   The Education of a Navy 27–8, 30, 117
   as a historian of war 214–15
   as a naval historian 116–18, 123–4
   visiting fellowship at Singapore
   University 115–16, 118
security studies 3, 11, 48–50
Seversky, Alexander de 72–6
Showalter, Dennis 4–6, 142
Shy, John
   biography 232
   contribution to *Makers II* 157–8, 180–2,
   199–201, 209
   relationship with Paret 137–8, 157–8, 194–5
Smith Jr, Datus C. 99–101, 143–4, 232
Speier, Hans
   biography 232–3
   contribution to *Makers* 73–5, 81–2
   at the RAND corporation 104–5
   as a visiting/refugee scholar at IAS 104
Sprout, Harold 68, 233
Sprout, Margaret Tuttle 68, 76–9, 88–9,
   161–2, 233
Spykman, Nicholas 42–3
Stacey, Charles P. 68, 233
Stebbins, Richard P. 68, 233

Stern, Beatrice 55–6
Strachan, Sir Hew
   on Howard and Paret's translation of *On
   War* 196–7
   on *Makers* 3–4, 179
   on *Makers II* 4–5, 180–3, 198–9
   on the study of war within modern history
   32–3
   on Wilkinson and the study of war 26–7
strategic studies
   analysis of strategy in *Makers
   Revisited* 192, 197
   the canon of strategic thought 4, 177,
   194–204, 211–12
   grand strategy concept in *Makers* 3–6, 11, 48,
   62–3, 188–91, 196–7, 203–4
   the language of strategy 197
   Makers and the emergence of 3, 5, 48–50, 219
   post-war trajectory 105–6
   strategy analysis in *Makers* 187–8, 191–2
   strategy analysis in *Makers II* 184, 186–7, 190–4
Sumida, Jon 27–8
Summers, Harry G. 178–9
Sun Tzu 122–3, 127, 177, 207–9

Tashjean, Jean 148–50
Terraine, John 158–9
Thatcher, Sandford 131, 149–50
Thucydides 177, 206–7
Tunstall, Brian 116–17

United States of America (USA)
   Flexner and the modern university
   system 51–3
   Mahan's naval history 27–30
   military history in American
   universities 14–19, 40–3, 108–11
   study of the 'problem' of war 40–1
   turn towards grand strategy during
   WW II 62–3
   war-peace boundaries and the US
   position 58–60
University of Singapore 99–100, 115–17

Vagts, Alfred
   biography 233–4
   critique of in Earle's seminars 64
   on Earle's appointment to IAS 55
   at Earle's IAS seminar 68
   as a potential seminar member-
   contributor 68, 73, 76–7
   the proposal for *Makers* and 67, 82, 97
   as a visiting/refugee scholar at IAS 81–2
Veblen, Oswald 53–4, 56

258 INDEX

Walt, Stephen 181–2, 192–4
Warner, Edward Pearson 125, 234
war studies *see also* military history
   academic engagement with 14–15, 59–61
   civilian understanding and engagement
      with war 13–14, 37–8, 44, 49–50, 58–61,
      105–6, 114–15
   international contexts 14–15
   Makers and the emergence of 2
   military history and 26–7
   the 'problem' of war 40

Weigley, Russell 157–8, 180–1, 199, 234
Weiller, Jean Sylvain 68, 234
Weinberg, Albert K. 68, 235
Wheeler, Everett L. 122–4, 126–7, 235
Whittlesey, Derwent 86–7, 151, 235
Wilkinson, Henry Spenser 14, 20–1, 24–5,
      31–2, 37
Woolf, Harry S. 134–5, 147–8, 235
Wright, Quincy 40–1, 43

Yost, David 179, 183